STOIC ROMANTICISM AND THE ETHICS OF EMOTION

Stoic Romanticism and the Ethics of Emotion

Jacob Risinger

PRINCETON UNIVERSITY PRESS
PRINCETON & OXFORD

Copyright © 2021 by Princeton University Press

Princeton University Press is committed to the protection of copyright and the intellectual property our authors entrust to us. Copyright promotes the progress and integrity of knowledge. Thank you for supporting free speech and the global exchange of ideas by purchasing an authorized edition of this book. If you wish to reproduce or distribute any part of it in any form, please obtain permission.

Requests for permission to reproduce material from this work should be sent to permissions@press.princeton.edu

Published by Princeton University Press
41 William Street, Princeton, New Jersey 08540
6 Oxford Street, Woodstock, Oxfordshire OX20 1TR

press.princeton.edu

All Rights Reserved

ISBN 978-0-691-22312-4
ISBN (pbk.) 978-0-691-20343-0
ISBN (e-book) 978-0-691-22311-7

British Library Cataloging-in-Publication Data is available

Editorial: Anne Savarese and James Collier
Production Editorial: Jenny Wolkowicki
Cover design: Pamela L. Schnitter
Production: Brigid Ackerman
Publicity: Alyssa Sanford and Amy Stewart
Copyeditor: Maia Vaswani

Cover art: Francis Towne (1739–1816), *A Sepulchre by the Road between Rome and the Ponte Nomentano*, 1780. Watercolor with pen and ink, 327 × 378 mm © The Trustees of the British Museum.

This book has been composed in Miller

10 9 8 7 6 5 4 3 2 1

For Memory, on whom nothing is lost

CONTENTS

Acknowledgments · ix
List of Abbreviations · xiii

Introduction · 1

CHAPTER 1 Stoic Moral Sentimentalism from Shaftesbury to Wollstonecraft · 24

CHAPTER 2 Wordsworth and Godwin in "Frozen Regions" · 59

CHAPTER 3 Coleridge, Lyric Askesis, and Living Form · 89

CHAPTER 4 The True Social Art: Byron and the Character of Stoicism · 124

CHAPTER 5 Stoic Futurity in Sarah Scott and Mary Shelley · 160

CHAPTER 6 Emerson, Stoic Cosmopolitanism, and the Conduct of Life · 186

Notes · 217
Bibliography · 239
Index · 261

ACKNOWLEDGMENTS

A LINE FROM EMERSON'S "Experience" has always struck a chord. "All our days are so unprofitable while they pass, that 'tis wonderful where or when we ever got anything of this which we call wisdom, poetry, virtue. We never got it on any dated calendar day" (*EW* 3:24). Looking back, I myself sometimes wonder where or when all of the words and ideas I have assembled here made it onto the page. But I am quite sure that the fact they emerged at all owes more to the people I've been talking, thinking, and living with over a long interval than I could ever adequately convey. But it's worth a shot.

It is long past time to acknowledge the teachers who are often in mind when I am sitting down to write or getting ready to teach. I owe a great debt to Jana Haffley at Brebeuf Jesuit, who more than anyone else taught me how to write about literature and made that kind of writing seem like an odyssey all of its own. At Middlebury College, Stephen Donadio, John Elder, Bob Hill, Jay Parini, and Marion Wells showed me how to think about literature, but also about how it moves and lives. Formative, genial conversations with Stephen Gill and Duncan Wu at Oxford University first set me off down the path that led to this book.

At Harvard University, I was inexplicably fortunate to find kind, sensible, and intellectually generous advisors who helped me turn a strange intuition into a project that has rewarded my thought for almost a decade. My Cambridge sojourn would have been unimaginable without Jim Engell's wise counsel, deep curiosity, and expansive commitments. His inspiration was vital at the beginning, and his interest in this book has helped keep it going over the years. Larry Buell gamely agreed to follow me back into Romantic terrain, and his acuity and good sense have made this a better project, early and late. Helen Vendler asked the right questions and responded to my answers with extraordinary care. Her attention to the craft of writing remains an example to this day. Anyone who can read and decipher what follows with a modicum of pleasure also owes a debt to Helen. Andrew Warren encouraged me to lean into the complexity and taught me how to get it done. It is difficult to quantify the ridiculously large impact that friends at Harvard had on my thinking. The same goes for all the fun I had spending those years with Alison Chapman, Maggie Doherty, Maggie Gram, Kathryn Roberts, Stephen Tardif, Dave Weimer, Daniel Williams, and many others. Matt Ocheltree is a comrade-in-arms, inspired conversationalist, and trusted friend. His brainchild, "*the* Colloquium," enlivened my thinking in innumerable ways. Tim Michael, Jacob Sider Jost, and Julia Tejblum were friendly interlocutors in that forum, too. Owen Boynton's conversation and frequent trips to Cambridge were invaluable, and Tom Dingman, Will Cooper, and Catherine Shapiro made Harvard Yard feel like home. Gwen Urdang-Brown was always around to help keep the ship afloat.

I will never get over my good luck in the colleagues I found at Ohio State, who welcomed me back to the Midwest and gave me a perch in the universe from which I get to teach and think. So many friends and colleagues in Denney Hall have supported and encouraged me at every turn that it would stretch credulity to list them all. For their help and advice with the manuscript, I am particularly grateful to David Brewer, Molly Farrell, Angus Fletcher, Jill Galvan, Aman Garcha, Beth Hewitt, Drew Jones, Leslie Lockett, Sandra Macpherson, Sean O'Sullivan, Jim Phelan, Elizabeth Renker, David Riede, David Ruderman, Jen Schnabel, Jesse Schotter, Clare Simmons, Robyn Warhol, Roxann Wheeler, and Susan Williams. Jamison Kantor's arrival in Columbus and consequent friendship has been another lucky break. Michelle Herman was quick to make Columbus feel like home for my entire family. Wayne Lovely's administrative support has been vital all along.

Thinking alongside my students at Ohio State has shaped my thought and kept me on my toes at each and every stage. Extended dialogues with Abraham Dávila Corujo, Emma Fernandez, Joey Kim, and Jack Rooney have made more than a passing impression on this book.

Thanks to everyone in the wider world of Romantic and literary studies whose support, advice, questions, and provocations—not to mention their general friendliness and receptivity—have made me a happier scholar and this a better book: Sam Baker, Terry Castle, David Collings, Mary Favret, Anne-Lise François, Tim Fulford, William Galperin, Michael Gamer, Marilyn Gaull, Denise Gigante, Kevin Gilmartin, Bruce Graver, Richard Gravil, Sonia Hofkosh, Richard Lansdown, Charles Mahoney, Peter Manning, Tom Mole, Jonathan Mulrooney, Anahid Nersessian, Adam Potkay, Nicholas Roe, Meg Russett, Jonathan Sachs, Kenneth Sacks, Blakey Vermeule, and Nancy Yousef.

An early version of chapter 2 appeared in *ELH*.* I am grateful to Johns Hopkins University Press for permission to reprint that material here.

---

*Copyright © 2016 The Johns Hopkins University Press. The article first appeared in *ELH*, volume 83, issue 4, December 2016, pages 1043–73.

This book was helped along in substantial ways by a Jacob K. Javits Fellowship, and later by a Carl H. Pforzheimer Jr. Research Grant from the Keats-Shelley Association of America.

Anne Savarese at Princeton University Press took an interest in the project at an early stage, and I am deeply sensible of what this book owes to her care and diligence, as well as her patience. I am also grateful to Jenny Wolkowicki, Maia Vaswani, Virginia Ling, and everyone else at Princeton University Press who has helped usher this book through the press. At the top of that list are the anonymous press readers for this project, both of whose generous and incisive reports made me want to jump back into the manuscript all over again.

It is hard to imagine anything like this life or book of mine apart from the love and support of my parents, Amy and Jeff Risinger. Setting me off on my own path, they have never been far behind. By their example I know that "under the rocks are the words," and surely some of my words here are also theirs. My brothers Seth and Will and their families have always been there when it is time to close the books. Michael Risinger has long been an influential example of the pleasure of a life lived between pages. Lyla and Woody Peebles have always made me feel at home. Their inimitable hospitality has been a powerful example, and some of these pages were even started on their porch. I have learned more than I could say—and with much joy—from Mary Jo and Jack Risinger, Anne and Byron Barth, and Lyla and Blake McMullen over the years. Norman has been there from the beginning, and still would rather walk than write.

And then there are my daughters, Willa and Alice Risinger. While I have been slowly working away on this book, they have learned to walk, to revel in language, and to ride a bicycle, even to spread cream cheese on their own bagels. None of this would be possible without my wife Memory, whose resplendent mind and daily friendship have filled my life with happiness. From a snowy night in the North End to a long quarantine in Ohio, all of these pages have come into being in her company, the most extravagant gift of all. This book has always been for her.

ABBREVIATIONS

     A   Shaftesbury, *Askêmata*.

  BLJ   Byron, *Letters and Journals*.

     C   Shaftesbury, *Characteristics*.

   CW   Byron, *Complete Poetical Works*.

    DJ   Byron, *Don Juan*, vol. 5 of *Complete Poetical Works* (1986).

     E   Wordsworth, *Excursion*.

   EW   Emerson, *Collected Works*.

  JMN   Emerson, *Journals and Miscellaneous Notebooks*.

     L   M. Shelley, *Lodore*.

   MH   S. Scott, *Millenium Hall*.

    PJ   Godwin, *Enquiry Concerning Political Justice*, vol. 3 of *Political and Philosophical Writings*.

P Lects   Coleridge, *Lectures 1818–1819*.

  PPW   Godwin, *Political and Philosophical Writings*.

Prelude   Wordsworth, *Thirteen Book Prelude*.

   PW   Coleridge, *Poetical Works*.

  TMS   A. Smith, *Theory of Moral Sentiments*.

STOIC ROMANTICISM AND THE
ETHICS OF EMOTION

Introduction

THE CAMP FIRE that swept through the foothills of Northern California in November 2018 inverted an idyll, turning *Paradiso* into an *Inferno*. Burning for seventeen straight days, this fast-moving fire destroyed almost the entire town of Paradise, killing eighty-five people and consuming more than eighteen thousand structures. In his account in the *New York Times Magazine*, Jon Mooallem suggests that as Paradise was engulfed by fire it became "a zone at the limits of the American imagination—and a preview of the American future."[1] Katy Grannan's accompanying photographs depict what this unimaginable but unignorable future might look like: burnt skeletons of homes and automobiles cover a mountain landscape suffused in evening light. This Turneresque aura cannot soften the devastation that time has hardly touched, nor the ruined future it prefigures. The article ends with a refusal of easy optimism: "How did it end? It hasn't. It won't."[2]

Mooallem sketches out one possible response to such a catastrophic future in his vivid portrait of Joe Kennedy, a Cal Fire heavy-equipment operator with the "affect of a granite wall." Set down amid an unfathomable fire, Kennedy maneuvers through Paradise in a bulldozer, hacking away at any feature of the landscape that might facilitate the spread of the flames. As Mooallem puts it, "He worked quickly, brutally, unhindered by any remorse over the collateral damage he was causing." Pushing flaming cars out of the way, Kennedy clears an exit path for stranded evacuees. Tearing down hillsides, pushing through fire, confronting death up close, he keeps ever on the move. He was "a stoic figure somewhere inside the smoke, single-mindedly grinding through neighborhoods in his bulldozer, music blaring, chasing after flames as they stampeded uphill."[3]

In our ordinary language and collective discourse, Stoicism is troubled by a subtle equivocation. In one register, it implies acquiescence, unfeeling capitulation to a set of circumstances beyond one's control. Stoicism in this sense is simply quiet submission to a predetermined course. It involves no questioning, no swerves. This convergence of placidity and passivity lurks behind the recent vogue for the publicity poster designed by Britain's Ministry of Information at the start of the Second World War: "Keep Calm and Carry On." In the pages that follow, however, I will suggest that the possibility of Stoicism in modernity is also fostered by an alternative history, one in which its detachment was filtered through an age of Romanticism and revolution, aligning its power with a radical rejection of things as they are. In this sense, being a Stoic entails something other than passive surrender to an inevitable course of events. Stepping outside of the immediate sway of emotion leads not to apathy but to a strenuous concern for others, even strangers. It is less a retreat than a form of commitment. The Stoic doesn't stand by as the fire burns; he chases after it, cool and collected, ready to put it out.

What unlikely links make it possible to suggest that a firefighter in twenty-first century California might have been living out a distinctly Romantic inheritance? At the broadest level, *Stoic Romanticism and the Ethics of Emotion* represents my attempt to unearth a central moment in the shift of understanding that reconciled Stoicism—so often dismissed as solipsistic, unfeeling, or indifferent—with the affective crosscurrents of modern "expressive individualism."[4] What resonance could Stoic philosophy and its infamous apatheia hold for individuals in modernity whose very identities and ethical aspirations were increasingly tied to emotional intelligence and expression? Or, more simply, what made Stoicism a posture of commitment rather than an unfeeling form of renunciation? These might seem perilously open-ended questions, investigations best left to philosophers or historians of philosophy, but my argument in this book is a literary historical one by design. In *Philosophic Pride: Stoicism and Political Thought from Lipsius to Rousseau*, Christopher Brooke tracks the sinuous evolution of Stoicism through seventeenth- and eighteenth-century political philosophy, ending fittingly but rather abruptly with Mary Wollstonecraft and "the Revolutionary decade in France."[5] While Stoicism continued to resonate in political philosophy and many other fields of knowledge, I argue that its uptake in modernity was focalized by a range of imaginative writers from Wollstonecraft to Emerson who integrated its moral psychology into their own innovative poiesis, even as they approached its ethical aspiration in decisively revolutionary terms.

Borne along by literature's emergent interest in the "daily lives of ordinary people," Stoicism was often stripped of its severity, its tenets made newly apprehensible in a range of everyday postures and practices.[6] More than just an object of literature's attention, many of these self-reflexive practices worked to reshape its operative logic. As I will argue in what follows, Stoic ideas informed new accounts of lyric subjectivity, perceptions of literary character, and the mediating perspectives made possible by topographical verse. They disrupted an easy, autonomous notion of sympathy by calling for a more elaborate and expansive discipline of attention. Stoicism was often implicit in the fault lines that separated gender and genre, and it facilitated powerful new conceptions of irony and paradox. Putting all of this in broader terms, I argue that Stoicism nurtured literary transformation at precisely the same moment in which its irrelevance might have seemed assured. But this was hardly a one-sided exchange, for the subtle interleaving of literature and Stoicism in the late eighteenth century gave an antiquated philosophy a striking new zone of inhabitation: implicated in a new poetics that took "its origin from emotion recollected in tranquility," Stoicism had never seemed so imaginative, so visionary.[7]

An argument like this is bound to elicit misgivings, for conventional wisdom tends to depict Romanticism as an aesthetic and philosophical movement more preoccupied with "emotion" than "tranquility." Notorious for its ability to wriggle past attempts at definition and delineation, Romanticism contains multitudes, and yet it is almost always thought to involve a special or renewed valuation of feeling.[8] Given this widely shared presumption, making a sustained case for the formative impact of Stoicism on Romanticism might seem like a fool's errand from the outset. As the Scottish philosopher R. M. Wenley once put it, "if Romanticism be the retreat of reason before feeling and imagination, we should not expect Stoic moods."[9] In each of the following chapters, I show just how big an *if* adheres in Wenley's observation. But setting this conditional and its attempt at definition aside, Stoic Romanticism might just as easily seem a hybrid position rendered irrelevant by the slow decline of Stoicism earlier in the eighteenth century.

As a number of studies have argued, the most notable quality of Stoicism in eighteenth-century literary culture is its evanescence. In *Tropicopolitans*, Srinivas Aravamudan suggests that Joseph Addison's *Cato* (1712) "represents the last gasp of the earlier, more comprehensive Renaissance interest in Stoicism"—an important "coda," but just that: an endpoint.[10] Similarly attuned to its limited shelf life, Howard Weinbrot has argued that Stoicism's intermittent reappearance throughout the century tended to be almost immediately qualified by its repudiation: in his dramatic terms, Stoicism constantly "raises its hydra head only to be decapitated."[11] Robert Adams, a founding editor of the *Norton Anthology*, described Samuel Johnson's "The Vanity of Human Wishes" (1749) as nothing less than Stoicism's "swan song": "When we look through the nineteenth century for another work informed with stoicism, defined by stoicism, we look in vain. What happened to stoicism? Without undergoing refutation or criticism, without being so much as remarked in its stealthy departure, stoicism faded away and became obsolete."[12]

In a limited sense, all of these critics are right: after the spectacle of Addison's *Cato*, Stoicism too often seems to slip beneath the century's critical radar. In an age defined by sensibility and sentimentality, its greatest moments of visibility in literary culture are those ironic ones in which it is unmasked as stupid, hypocritical, egotistical, and unnatural. But if the rumors surrounding the demise of Stoicism are understandable, they remain—like so much of the dogma crystallized by literary periodization—greatly exaggerated. As impoverished as they are misleading, accounts of Stoic evanescence work in tandem with a teleology that looks forward to authentic emotional expression as both the breakthrough and bedrock of modern, expressivist aesthetics. But as I hope to make clear, this sense of Stoicism's superannuation obscures as much as it clarifies, especially when it comes to the philosophical commitments of Romanticism itself. In the chapters that follow, the course I chart through the Romantic century starts to look something like a map of collective misreading—a wide-ranging survey of familiar territory, but one designed to highlight what has been overlooked or misunderstood as the slow onset of powerful feeling is thought to signal Stoicism's obsolescence.

Stoic Resistance and the Resistance to Stoicism

At first glance, Romanticism can seem like a hotbed of resistance to the kind of Stoicism that pervaded Renaissance and Enlightenment culture. Take, for example, one of the devil's assertions in Blake's *Marriage of Heaven and Hell* (1790): "Those who restrain desire, do so because theirs is weak enough to be restrained."[13] Tackling prudential rationality head-on, Blake evokes an early vision of Romanticism in which "strong poets" pursue expression as the natural terminus of emotion.[14] But this succinct critique also focalizes a commonly held perspective on Stoicism, one in which its austerity is thought to reflect mere submission. By this logic, the ability to suppress an emotion or desire only illuminates its paucity in the first place. Restraint becomes a kind of disempowerment that one enacts upon oneself—a lazy contentment, or a kind of disenchantment that sidesteps action. The idea that Stoic reserve represents a counterproductive way of being in the world has attracted powerful adherents. In a post-Freudian age equipped with a vocabulary for identifying repression and other defense mechanisms, Stoicism is often consigned to the margins of modernity as an unhealthy or antiquated philosophy. Though Philip Rieff and others have posited "an indirect but genuine affinity between psychoanalysis and the psychological theories of Stoicism," Freud's own account of traumatic repression renders emotional detachment suspect, the sign of a dangerously illusory freedom.[15] While writers in the eighteenth century often took pains to foreground the "disingenuousness" of Stoicism, critics who took aim at the Stoics after (or even amid) Romanticism tended to describe it as a kind of "emotional impoverishment."[16] No less a figure than Hegel endorsed this sense of its delimited possibility in *The Phenomenology of Spirit* (1807). For Hegel, Stoicism was the product of a "time of universal fear and bondage," a "slave ideology" (to use Alexandre Kojève's term) that mistakes detachment as a form of freedom. Retreating into the realm of thought and "solid singleness," Hegel's Stoic justifies inaction and cultivates a "stolid lifeless unconcern which persistently withdraws from the movement of existence."[17]

Often employed to depict political apostasy as part of a more pervasive unconcern, the easy alignment of Stoicism and acquiescence has vastly misconstrued its force in the period. For many of the writers I take up in this book, Stoicism was a decisively radical term in a revolutionary age. Its impress on the literature of the period was heightened by its dramatic deployment over the course of the French Revolution. Long associated with Roman republicanism and its virtuous defenders, Stoicism also served as a "deep source" for an emergent discourse of natural and human rights that resulted in the *Déclaration des droits de l'homme et du citoyen* (1789).[18] This radical vein of Stoicism emerged in multiple forms on both sides of the Channel. It was a recurrent feature of the republican pageantry and ethos deployed by Maximilien Robespierre and other Jacobins, just as it was a theatrical resource for British radicals forced to endure William Pitt's "Reign of Alarm."[19] In France, Louis de Saint-Just described Stoic self-control as the healthy alternative to a reign of terror: "Stoicism, which is the virtue of the spirit and the soul, alone can prevent the corruption of a commercial republic which lacks manners. A republican government must have virtue for its principle: if not, there is only Terror."[20] In Britain, Stoic philosophy was a prominent catalyst for William Godwin's *Enquiry Concerning Political Justice* (1793), a text similarly committed to the idea that Stoic self-government would take the place of revolution and its worst excesses. Later, Wordsworth landed on Stoicism as a chief point of contention in his retrospective disenchantment with Godwin in *The Prelude* (1805).

I will dwell at more length on the revolutionary contours of Stoicism in chapter 2, but even this quick sketch speaks to its contested character in the Revolutionary controversy that rocked Britain in the 1790s. The character of Stoicism could shift with ideological perspective; it might appear to be the promising source of a new cosmopolitan reign of reason, but it struck other commentators as a hypocritical and notably unfeeling form of savagery. Either way, its alignment with the French Revolution was unsurprisingly equivocal, for the spectacular collapse of that revolution qualified an easy optimism in abstract morality across the board. The stock that figures like Godwin put into Stoic perfectionism plummeted along with their faith in the revolution's own perfectionist working possibilities.

It seems useful to foreground at the outset two implications of the whiplash wrought by this Stoic revolution and its quick implosion. Looking back at the French Revolution and its reversals, William Hazlitt described it as the ultimate face-off between experience and philosophy: "The French revolution was the only match that ever took place between philosophy and experience: and waking from the trance of theory to the sense of reality, we hear the words, *truth, reason, virtue, liberty*, with the same indifference or contempt, that the cynic who has married a jilt or a termagant, listens to the rhapsodies of lovers."[21] For Hazlitt, the blunt reality of the revolution laid waste to philosophical idealizations and abstractions; the siren song of philosophy would never sound quite so seductive again. At the same time, Stoicism was especially vulnerable to the bright light of reality. It had, almost from its origins, been maligned as a paradoxical philosophy that flew in the face of human nature. In this sense, the French Revolution became epic confirmation not just that fears about Stoic dissimulation were amply warranted, but that its vision of perfect dispassion was, as Pierre Hadot has put it, "more an inaccessible ideal than a concrete reality."[22] The reputation of Stoicism would not quickly recover from the horrifying aftermath of the revolution that often invoked its power. All the same, I want to suggest that the abrupt shuttering of Stoicism's revolutionary career gave it new life as an imperfect, diminished thing. One legacy of the revolution was a sustained mistrust of Stoicism in all its rigorous austerity. But stripped of its rigid perfectionism, Stoicism was reclaimed—sometimes hesitantly, often quietly—as an imperfect aspiration rather than an inflexible ideal, one whose emergence alongside a life of feeling made it particularly compatible with literature itself.

Once a catalyst for revolution, the Stoicism made imperfectly available in genres like the lyric survived to facilitate new ways of imagining or living out a lapsed revolutionary ideal. In spite of this productive repossession, however, the reputation of Stoicism within Romanticism was irrevocably hobbled by the lingering aura of its radicalism. What Robespierre called "the sublime sect of the Stoics" was so fully identified with the revolution in France—in both its aspirations and its fatal overextensions—that many writers resisted public acknowledgment of their own fascination with Stoicism.[23] This strategic silence meant that it often dropped out of the main current of literary history in the period, emerging if at all in what Simon Swift has described as "submerged and coded" form.[24]

The Low Road: An Exercise in Critical Semantics

Stretching from politics to poetics, Stoicism pervaded writing from the Romantic period. But what did Stoicism entail in the late eighteenth century, and what exactly do I mean by the term in this book? In Cicero's *De finibus*, Cato praises "the marvellously systematic way in which Stoic philosophy sets out its doctrines," asking hyperbolically, "Can you imagine any other system where the removal of a single letter, like an interlocking piece, would cause the whole edifice to come tumbling down?"[25] While an apt portrayal of an aspiration, this sense of Stoicism's necessary systematicity was unceremoniously refuted by its reception in modernity. In its earliest articulations, Stoicism was a threefold philosophy, a systematic view of the universe in which ethics, physics, and logic intertwined to make the individual a relatively insignificant part of a large cosmological whole. Though writers like Coleridge and Emerson never tired of pondering this comprehensive world view, Stoicism had—over many centuries—become more of a piecemeal affair, a philosophy that could exist alongside an increasingly individualistic ethos. Most Romantic readers approached Stoicism by way of its ethics. Attributable in part to reading habits, this shift reflected a transformation that had been afoot since Roman times. Zeno of Citium, the founder of the Stoic sect who first articulated its philosophy beneath the Stoa Poikile in Athens, wrote at least two dozen books. His successor Chrysippus was rumored to have authored no fewer than seven hundred texts, but save for a few fragments, all of these early works were lost. Much as today, readers in the long eighteenth century absorbed Stoicism from Roman practitioners like Epictetus, Seneca, and Marcus Aurelius, not to mention the recapitulation of Stoic teachings prominently available in Cicero's influential commentary.

Several centuries stood between these Roman Stoics and the school's Athenian origin at the turn of the third century BCE. The chronological distance separating Epictetus and his *Discourses* from the school's founding was comparable to the wide interval that stood between *Lyrical Ballads* and *The Canterbury Tales*. Over such a broad stretch of time, rigid tenets advanced by the early Stoics had been moderated and reinterpreted in new contexts. For these later Stoics, the ideal of a sage defined by ironclad emotional imperturbability was often approached as an impossibility. Seneca, for example, recognized what many eighteenth-century critics of Stoicism did not. The virtue of the sage was dependent upon his humanity and sensibility, not his insensibility:

> There are other things that strike the wise person even if they do not overthrow him, such as physical pain, loss of a limb, loss of friends and children, and during wartime the calamity of his fatherland in flames. I do not deny that the wise person feels these, for we do not endow him with the hardness of stone or of iron. To endure without feeling what you endure is not virtue at all.[26]

As Seneca's account of a sensitive but forbearing sage makes clear, the elimination of emotion was ultimately less important than its evaluation. In fact, Stoic invulnerability struck many commentators as impossible but also undesirable. Robert Burton quipped in *The Anatomy of Melancholy* that no mortal man could be free of "perturbations or if he be so, sure he is either a god or a block."[27] Traces of this more moderate vision of Stoic ethical practice were scattered throughout the eighteenth and nineteenth centuries. In the third installment of his *Imaginary Conversations* (1828), Walter Savage Landor imagined an apocryphal conversation between Epictetus and Seneca, one in which the unvarnished moral austerity of the former illuminates the perilously stylized philosophy of the latter:

> EPICTETUS: I should have remarked that, if thou foundest ingenuity
>   in my writings, thou must have discovered in them some deviation
>   from the plain, homely truths of Zeno and Cleanthes.
> SENECA: We all swerve a little from them.
> EPICTETUS: In practice too?
> SENECA: Yes, even in practice, I am afraid.[28]

For Landor, the philosophers have distinctly divergent personalities, and yet both acknowledge that the evolving relevance of Stoicism was dependent upon a certain amount of "deviation," a "swerve."

Suffice it to say, Stoicism as it streams through these pages is often a messy term. On the one hand, it was a formal philosophy with its own textual corpus. Served up to schoolboys year after year, it was also widely available in translation. One could, like Shelley, write to one's London publisher from the far corner of Wales and ask to have (among other texts) the "cheapest possible editions" of Seneca and Marcus Aurelius dispatched "very soon."[29] But more often than not, Stoicism spilled past these narrow channels to lend the aura of its moral psychology to a vast array of moods, moments, and discourses. There was, as Ralph Waldo Emerson put it, "a stoicism not of the schools, but of the blood" (*EW* 2:147). Emerson was hardly the only one to notice the easy slippage between disposition and doctrine. The *Oxford English Dictionary* makes it clear that the adjectival forms of Stoicism had been marking a similar transit from the early sixteenth century forward. To describe a temperament as "stoical" could imply philosophical alignment, or at least a strict attention to "the precepts of the Stoic philosophy." But the same word could just as easily activate a mere sense of temperamental resemblance: "Resembling a Stoic in austerity, indifference to pleasure and pain, repression of all feeling, and the like."[30] To borrow one of Alexander Nehamas's formulations, Stoicism was one of those abstract philosophical ideas "capable of living independently of their original manifestations."[31]

In this book, I have opted to approach Stoicism in the broadest possible terms, preferring the murkier challenge of tracing a philosophy that is never just precisely that. All of the authors I consider were familiar with Stoic texts, many of them intimately. But I have been struck by the suggestive complications that emerge out of the often-clumsy way in which they wield the term. Adventures in Stoic reception often involve such a wide-angled approach. In *Stoicism: Traditions and Transformations*, Steven Strange and Jack Zupko note that tracking Stoic influence often involves a choice between taking "the high road or the low road." The high road entails a dogged search for the exact provenance of Stoic ideas, an attempt to establish clear "proximity to the genuine article." By contrast, following the low road entails giving up clear "criteria for what counts as Stoic" in favor of "a looser, somewhat more impressionistic reading of Stoicism and what it means to be a Stoic."[32] In the pages that follow, I often keep to the low road out of a sense that the only way to accurately convey the real heft of Stoicism within Romantic discourse is to think carefully about its diffuse and often hazy manifestations. While I take pains to identify specific vectors of Stoic reception in what follows, I recognize that it was not just a system of ethics but an ethos, an aspect of character that was just as liable to end in caricature. In this sense, Stoicism fits a broader pattern of classical reception in the period, one in which ancient thought and culture were—in Jennifer Wallace's terms—"actively recreated or imagined, rather than passively inherited."[33] The Stoicism that emerges in the following pages takes many shapes, all of them foregrounding in their own way the prodigious and variable impress of ancient philosophy on an unfolding modernity. Stoicism can reflect a need for insulation from uncertainty or calamity, but it can also speak to a desire for the tranquility that might facilitate the creation of art. Depending upon the author, Stoicism can appear to be a kind of Christian consolation or a form of secular critique. Either way, its austerity often informs seemingly unphilosophical manifestations of fortitude and perseverance. For some writers it becomes a prompt for broad justice and cosmopolitan thinking; for others, it signals only the ascent of apathy or indifference. Sometimes it looks more like a style, a temperament, or even an affectation rather than bona fide philosophy itself. These shadowy instantiations might seem to suggest a gradual narrowing of Stoicism and its significance, but in fact they reflect the broad coordinates of an ancient philosophy that, in Charles Taylor's words, has been "transposed into a thoroughly modern position."[34]

Situating Stoic Romanticism

In its multifarious forms, the Stoicism I explore in the following pages looks more like a discipline of attention than a disavowal of affective capacity. In belaboring what Epictetus called making the correct "Use of the Appearances of Things," Stoics attend to the emotions and impressions that make up their own mental life, but they also lavish attentive judgment on the world that gives rise to those impressions.[35] This gap between reductive caricature and nuanced reality aligns Stoicism with resignation, humility, and other unpopular or pathologized "modes of self-limitation," which Steven Connor has thoughtfully explored in *Giving Way: Thoughts on Unappreciated Dispositions*. For Connor, a sense of the complex ethical positioning inherent in such "minorizing modes" has simply been lost as the long quest for more obvious forms of agency and empowerment drove them out of fashion. Connor's reparative account works toward a new understanding of the many ways in which "the mitigation of assertion and the attenuation of agency are indeed often powerfully affirmative and require skilled and attentive application."[36] I have conceived *Stoic Romanticism and the Ethics of Emotion* with a similarly reparative agenda, one that tries to think generatively about an impulse toward detachment that has, for several decades now, been viewed skeptically by critiques of Enlightenment rationality.

Thinking carefully about the competing and often radical overtones of Stoicism in the late eighteenth century seems especially consequential, however, for the tendency to equate Stoicism with repression has had a prominent afterlife in literary discourse. In a vein of especially influential historicist scholarship, Stoic detachment tends to be flagged as a form of false consciousness, part of a quest for self-coherence that works by occlusion, as if in denial. In this sense, the volitional power of Stoicism is easily confused for a mechanism of displacement or blockage. In *Romantic Moods*, for example, Thomas Pfau argues that "the seemingly stoic 'composure' and 'tranquility' of lyric or pastoral writing reveals itself as a phantasmagoria painstakingly elaborated so as to shelter its speakers from the impinging knowledge of their complicity in a historical world so entropic and volatile as to preclude its timely comprehension."[37] A similar kind of denial adheres in Ian Baucom's account of an "actuarializing discourse of stoic disinterestedness" that represses or denies the melancholy facts of history.[38] For Pfau and Baucom, Stoic composure points toward the historical harm that cannot or will not be comprehended. By contrast, many of the writers I consider draw on the Stoics in an effort—albeit often an imperfect one—to see the world and its harms more clearly, even justly. At many points in the book, I foreground the convergence of Stoicism and cosmopolitanism, an affiliation that was especially central to the Romantic reception of Stoicism, early and late.

As a correlative of this larger reappraisal, I try to think more generatively about various states of dispassion within Romanticism by resisting a tendency to equate a noticeable lack of emotion with trauma itself. Though trauma often results in what Pfau describes as "the nearly total absence of any affective or emotive disturbance," the same lack of feeling could also signal a number of other volitional possibilities.[39] The unfolding of Romanticism against a backdrop of what Mary Favret has called "everyday war" offers a convenient way of drawing out this distinction.[40] Jeffrey Cox's rehearsal of the seemingly endless parade of military entanglements of the period suggests how much trauma must have accompanied war and its "ongoing background state of terror."[41] For many of those in uniform, the atrocities encountered on the fields of Europe must have eluded timely comprehension, narration, and assimilation.[42] But other soldiers worked to cultivate the "Character of the Happy Warrior," a temperament on Wordsworth's mind after the proximate deaths of Lord Nelson and his own seafaring brother. Drawing on Stoicism to manage the pain, fear, and bloodshed that accompanied life in war could help a soldier turn all of the trials of an "exposed" existence to "glorious gain":

> In the face of these [he] doth exercise a power
> Which is our human-nature's highest dower;
> Controls them and subdues, transmutes, bereaves
> Of their bad influence, and their good receives;
> By objects, which might force the soul to abate
> Her feeling, render'd more compassionate;
> Is placable because occasions rise
> So often that demand such sacrifice;
> More skilful in self-knowledge, even more pure,
> As tempted more; more able to endure,
> As more expos'd to suffering and distress;
> Then, also, more alive to tenderness.[43]

For Wordsworth, Stoic management of feeling works against the always looming possibility of trauma and its affective abatement. Far from a denial of experience, it elicits "self-knowledge" and tends toward eudaimonia, not to mention "tenderness" itself. Nor, as Neil Ramsey demonstrates, did Stoic self-culture serve merely individualistic ends: the "stoical endurance" of wartime suffering fed into national narratives of identity and defense.[44] The happy warrior's Stoic balancing act might not stack up against various contemporary yardsticks for measuring emotional knowledge and well-being, but this anachronistic dissatisfaction need not obscure its influential and often radical force in the period.

In exploring some of the avenues opened up by volitional, nontraumatic, and always imperfect abstentions from the realm of affect, I have been galvanized by work in Romantic studies attuned to the ethical possibilities that emerge only when transcendence, self-expression, endless *Bildung*, and other forms of conventional Romantic egoism are set aside. In *Open Secrets: The Literature of Uncounted Experience*, Anne-Lise François suggests that her account of "minimal contentment" and "recessive action" is different in kind from "the tranquility of stoic self-sufficiency."[45] All the same, her patient evocation of "a readiness to go without" as something other than sublimation informs my sense of the subtle, fleeting power of apatheia in Romantic writing. But unlike many of the figures in *Open Secrets*, the writers I analyze here are rarely content to rest empty-handed. In my book, Stoic self-culture is less a form of abandonment than a radical commitment, an impulse toward world making—at once ethical, poetical, and political—in which justice is predicated on affective restraint. Many of the writers in these pages would happily take on the work of adjustment and the "habits of self-denial" that Anahid Nersessian has described as integral to Romanticism and its "pedagogy of utopian limitation."[46]

This dual sense of Stoicism as at once an aspirational ideal and an ordinary, nontraumatic habit speaks to its particular legibility in a literary and cultural field broadly attentive to the centrality of affect, a diffuse realm of felt intensities pithily glossed by Kate Singer as the "physiological, material, and figural movements through and beyond a variety of human and nonhuman bodies."[47] Though it might seem counterintuitive, I want to suggest that Romantic Stoicism is a corollary to the period's "gravitational pull toward feeling" rather than a blinkered rejection of that force.[48] To put it simply, a newly awakened sense of the transiency of affect drew renewed attention to an ancient but familiar philosophy for managing it.[49] Stoicism as a form of self-culture or a discipline of attention was particularly relevant in a world still assimilating Hume's destabilizing assertion that passions were "contagious" and passed "with the greatest facility from one person to another."[50] As a text like Coleridge's incomplete treatise "On the Passions" (1828) starts to make clear, the possibilities opened up by an "infinitely connectable, impersonal, and contagious" realm of affect were liberating but also destabilizing.[51] Methods for navigating feeling were eagerly sought.[52] Many of the writers I study in this book looked to Stoicism as an unwieldy array of practices and ideas that might, in Joel Faflak and Richard Sha's terms, preside over the emotional "matrix through which the world is brought to our sensoria."[53] In this role, Stoicism could be as unremarkably quotidian as affect itself, just another way of negotiating the in-between spaces of everyday life. Indeed, the literary case studies I have assembled here speak to how Stoicism underwrites the diverse "styles of composure" and "norms of self-management" that Lauren Berlant has described as emerging out of the affective impasse of history itself.[54]

All the same, it would be foolish to minimize a central distinction between Stoic moral psychology and much of the work associated with the study of affect in literary and cultural studies. For many theorists of affect, its power as an analytic category grows out of embodied intensities that remain "unassimilable" to cognition, while also opening up what Eve Sedgwick has described as a conceptual realm not shaped by "the commonsensical dualities of subject versus object."[55] For Brian Massumi, affect is "autonomous" by nature of its "singular openness."[56] The Stoics, by contrast, ascribed to a cognitive-evaluative model of emotion, one in which impressions emanating from the body and the world were not autonomous but ancillary to the perspective-shaping judgments of the mind itself. In A. A. Long's words, Stoicism's "rationalistic analysis of emotions and evaluations implies that they themselves, and the judgements on which they depend, are completely in our power, up to us, within the control of our will."[57] If affect theory prioritizes the power of the body, Stoicism makes a case for the power of the mind itself. And for all of the ways in which affect circulates in and among bodies and beings, the Stoics suggest that processing such circulation ultimately falls to individual subjects and their autonomous minds. To be sure, the story I tell about Stoicism in the Romantic period hardly validates these tidy distinctions. As we will see, more than a few writers approached Stoicism as a worthy ideal undercut by embodied existence and material reality more generally. Others saw it as inherently rhetorical and performative, a philosophy more suited to surface-level social interactions than intensely subjective self-culture. That said, Stoic moral psychology resonates with Romantic moral psychology for the same reason that Gerard Cohen-Vrignaud suggests contemporary affect theory has had a "negligible impact" on how scholars analyze various forms of feeling in the period. As he puts it, the intricacies of Romantic interiority are often out of step with the "interpersonal extensions" of affect itself.[58]

In exploring the vexed possibilities of Stoicism in the period, I try to foreground the complexities of a moment in which two different ways of "touching feeling" collide.[59] Amid this generative complexity, I want to emphasize two brief points at the outset. My first point turns on the possibility of a broad frame of reference toward which both modes of feeling aspired. One of the generative possibilities of a noncognitive account of affect lies in its power to overleap the isolating subjectivity of the buffered self, opening up a new atmosphere of intersubjectivity in the process. Set against this expansive potentiality, Stoicism might seem an inherently rearguard affair, a nervous shoring up of the citadel of the rational self. In stark contrast, however, one of the consistent transits I trace in this book runs from the Stoic evaluation of emotion toward the cosmopolitan ethics to which it was often thought to aspire. For a generation of writers shaped by the Enlightenment and the French Revolution, the Stoic regulation of affect was commonly affixed to a Stoic cosmopolitan ideal. This consanguinity seems essential: the regulation of affect as well as its profusion held out the promise that the links connecting an individual to the world could be reimagined or redrawn.

My second point is a simple historical one, a move to affirm a background consensus easily occluded by powerful methodological innovation at any moment. Coming to terms with the status and significance of feeling in the long eighteenth century entailed as fraught and unending a conversation as it seems likely to elicit in ours. Eve Sedgwick's appealingly ambivalent assertion that affect is "thoroughly embodied, as well as more or less intensively interwoven with cognitive processes" could just as well reflect a Romantic position.[60] Within this realm of clarifying indistinction, my hope in this book is to think searchingly about the role of Stoicism within the history and science of Romantic feeling, for as Bruce Graver notes, "Romantic theories of emotion begin with the Stoics, and thus are fundamentally, and paradoxically, classical."[61]

In thinking about how Stoicism defines a literary period often thought to mark its abeyance, I have drawn on scholars attentive to the history of emotions as well as the history of those practices and forms through which they cohere. In method and scope, my account of Romantic Stoicism resembles (though in different ways) Chris Jones's work on "radical sensibility," Adela Pinch's account of "epistemologies of emotion," Andrew Stauffer's history of Romantic anger, and James Chandler's "archaeology" of sympathy.[62] But amid the profusion of work on the historicity of emotion, my book speaks most directly to scholars who have paid particular attention to a countervailing interest in the regulation of that emotion. On this front I would single out Julie Ellison's *Cato's Tears and the Making of Anglo-American Emotion* as an especial catalyst. Weighing the competing claims of Stoicism and sensibility in a transatlantic context, Ellison's sense of Stoicism as a lived philosophy played out in a world of racial and gender inequality informs my own account of its radical and cosmopolitan capacities. But while Ellison's focus on eighteenth-century literary culture allows her to do little more than scratch the surface of Romanticism, I demonstrate that the destabilizing power of Stoicism was just as vital a feature of the next century's self-culture and global imaginings. In making this case, I have benefited from foundational work on Stoicism in the period, a great deal of which coheres around the well-documented Stoic proclivities of William Wordsworth, a philosophical persuasion explored most recently and compellingly by Graver and Adam Potkay.[63] Another prominent vein of Stoic inquiry focuses on Anna Barbauld, Mary Wollstonecraft, and other women writers who move—in Claudia Johnson's terms—to take up "the once-masculine virtues of stoic rationalism and self-control."[64] But even these important accounts of the persistence of Stoicism within Romanticism do not do full justice to its radical and poetic significance. Before I lay out the course of my argument through the chapters that follow, I want to bring that significance into range by showing how Stoicism and its "philosophic mental tranquillity" stand, forcefully and almost surreptitiously, at the center of familiar Romantic terrain.[65]

"The Torturing and Conflicting Throngs Within"

When Percy Shelley first caught sight of Mont Blanc, it seemed less a "soulless image" than a living presence, an entity as notable for its Stoicism as its sublimity (*Prelude* 6:454). In a letter to Thomas Love Peacock, Shelley called up personification in an attempt to evoke its power: "One would think that Mont Blanc, like the god of the Stoics, was a vast animal, and that the frozen blood for ever circulated through his stony veins."[66] This was the kind of image that would fuel William Butler Yeats in his mystical Shelleyan devotion, a premonition of that "rough beast" bound for Bethlehem to wreak havoc after twenty centuries of "stony sleep."[67] In "Mont Blanc" (1816), Shelley falls into apostrophe to make it clear that the mountain itself was teeming with such revolutionary possibility: "Thou hast a voice, great Mountain, to repeal / Large codes of fraud and woe."[68] Shelley's figural alignment of mountain and Stoic deity might simply reflect an attempt to embody a power made almost inscrutable by its vacancy, and yet I am struck by the possibility that the voice of the mountain might be a Stoic one. The channeling of "frozen blood" through "stony veins" mimics the slow crawl of its glaciers as they "creep / Like snakes" to overwhelm the living earth.[69] But this strange evocation of Stoicism amid one of European Romanticism's primal scenes results in an especially chilly view of fraud's evanescence. Early British advocates of the French Revolution had imagined it as an enkindling blaze that might lay despotism in ashes while illuminating Europe. Shelley's Stoic mountain god almost seems to mock that living power with an absence of heat, its "frozen blood" forever circulating yet unthawed all the same.

Three years later, the Stoics were again on Shelley's mind in "A Ravine of Icy Rocks in the Indian Caucasus."[70] It is easy enough to look past the short epigraph to *Prometheus Unbound* (1820), a stray line salvaged from Aeschylus's own lost version of the play that Shelley found in Cicero's *Tusculan Disputations*: "Audisne haec, Amphiarae sub terram abdite?"[71] Making sense of its significance requires a bit of patience. In reading the *Tusculan Disputations*, Shelley was working through one of the most significant accounts of Stoic moral psychology, a series of disquisitions that Cicero wrote shortly after the devastating loss of his daughter Tullia. Shelley borrows his epigraph from a point in the text in which Cicero treats self-mastery as the one thing necessary to "bear pain quietly and calmly."[72] Cicero pauses over the negative example of a figure sometimes described as Dionysius the Turncoat, an early student of the Stoic founder Zeno who recanted all of his Stoic training after an excruciating bout of kidney pain. Cicero assigns the line in question to the Stoic philosopher Cleanthes, who stomps his foot on the ground and calls out to the shade of Zeno in incredulity: "Audisne haec, Amphiarae sub terram abdite? [Do you hear this, Amphiaraus, in your home beneath the earth?]."[73] Stuck in an irresolute present, Cleanthes looks back with longing to the almost mythological self-mastery of an evanescent past.

As Earl Wasserman and others have noted, the epigraph works in at least two ways.[74] On the one hand, Shelley announces in no uncertain terms an interpretive rift in the Prometheus story. He scribbled the lines into his notebook under the heading "To the Ghost of Aeschylus," suggesting his own contempt for the Greek playwright's willingness to reconcile "the Champion with the Oppressor of mankind."[75] In Shelley's version of the play, Prometheus will not submit to Jupiter's tyranny. On the other hand, Cicero supplies more than a fragment ripe for ironic reversal. His exploration of self-mastery and the nature of grief reflects Prometheus's own austere resistance. In his preface to the "lyrical drama," Shelley makes it clear that Prometheus is as sage-like as they come; he is, "as it were, the type of the highest perfection of moral and intellectual nature."[76] Unsurprisingly, perhaps, the "ministers of pain and fear" dispatched by Jove to torture Prometheus elicit a response that would have made Zeno and Cleanthes proud. Threatening to overwhelm Prometheus with new forms of dread and desire, the Furies deploy the language of the crowd, comparing their affective (and noticeably embodied) tortures to "a vain loud multitude / Vexing the self-content of wisest men." Alert like any Stoic to the misapprehensions that emotion can allow, Prometheus shrugs off their attempt to shake his self-possession:

> Why, ye are thus now;
> Yet I am king over myself, and rule
> The torturing and conflicting throngs within,
> As Jove rules you when Hell grows mutinous.[77]

Crowd control is reimagined as a personal regimen, and given the chronological proximity of the Peterloo Massacre, the very fact of that reimagination might seem to entail a stark internalization of violence. Yet what looks like tyranny on one level turns out to be the secret of its elimination on the other. Prometheus's rule over himself becomes the model for overturning a world in which slavery in the broadest sense is made multitudinous by "fear and self-contempt and barren hope."[78]

While *Prometheus Unbound* validates the importance of enduring pain and remaining ever firm, Shelley's Stoic agenda extends beyond mere forbearance. Viewing new blasts of dread and desire against the reality of his own "calm power," Prometheus also denounces the false belief lurking in the grief that once gave rise to his awful curse: "Grief for awhile is blind, and so was mine."[79] As Cicero puts it, grief is "far remote from the wise man" because "it does not originate in nature but in an act of judgment, of belief."[80]

While chained to the mountain, Prometheus discovers a Stoicism capable of ushering in regime change, but its revolutionary power remains rooted in retrospection. In this sense, at least, *Prometheus Unbound* follows *Laon and Cythna* (1817) in imagining the proper conditions for a new revolution, one that will not be hobbled by the "dupes and slaves" who were "incapable of conducting themselves with the wisdom and tranquillity of freemen so soon as some of their fetters were partially loosened."[81] Taken as a whole, Shelley seems to suggest that the French Revolution—ultimately undone by its own "torturing and conflicting throngs"—was not quite Stoic enough. Emotional self-mastery might be arduous in its cultivation, but such private autonomy was the source of collective freedom. Another way of putting this would be to say that in *Prometheus Unbound*, Shelley portrays "Self-empire" as the necessary supplement to "the all-sustaining air," which is nothing less than "the majesty of love."[82] There is a distinct Stoic dimension to his ultimate envisioning of utopia:

> The loathsome mask has fallen, the Man remains,—
> Sceptreless, free, uncircumscribed,—but man:
> Equal, unclassed, tribeless and nationless,
> Exempt from awe, worship, degree, the King
> Over himself; just, gentle, wise,—but man:
> Passionless? no: yet free from guilt or pain,
> Which were, for his will made, or suffered them,
> Nor yet exempt, tho' ruling them like slaves,
> The clogs of that which else might oversoar
> The loftiest star of unascended heaven,
> Pinnacled dim in the intense inane.[83]

Like "the much admired *Republic* of Zeno," Shelley's utopian world is not divided up by tribe, class, or nation: there is rather "one way of life and order, like that of a herd grazing together and nurtured by a common law."[84] Integral to the cosmopolitanism that often went hand-in-hand with Stoicism, the self-mastery exhibited by Prometheus is effectively democratized. It becomes a common inheritance, a foundation for just and gentle dealings. Tyranny is replaced by self-rule, but all of this justice and wisdom does not result in the cold transcendence of human nature. There is no ultimate exit from the realm of passion, nor is earthly existence set aside for some dim region in the "intense inane."

Such a utopian prospect might seem like the utmost Stoicism could possibly offer, even for a poet always ready to rend the next veil. But in the same summer in which Shelley finished *Prometheus Unbound*, Thomas Love Peacock intimated—albeit in a backhanded kind of way—that Stoic detachment was a vital fixture of not just political power but poetical power as well. Designed to elicit Shelley's response, "The Four Ages of Poetry" (1820) traces the gradual rise and decline of modern British poetry. The essay is unstinting in its condemnation of poets like Coleridge, Scott, and Byron who do little more than produce "gewgaws and rattles for the grown babies of the age." Peacock's account of poetic decline is highly satirical; what looks like a condemnation of poetry in modernity actually encodes a vision of its most exalted possibility. This is especially the case when it comes to his account of the respective roles that feeling and "philosophic mental tranquillity" might play in poetry itself:

> The philosophic mental tranquillity which looks round with an equal eye on all external things, collects a store of ideas, discriminates their relative value, assigns to all their proper place, and from the materials of useful knowledge thus collected, appreciated, and arranged, forms new combinations that impress the stamp of their power and utility on the real business of life, is diametrically the reverse of that frame of mind which poetry inspires, or from which poetry can emanate. The highest inspirations of poetry are resolvable into three ingredients: the rant of unregulated passion, the whining of exaggerated feeling, and the cant of factitious sentiment: and can therefore serve only to ripen a splendid lunatic like Alexander, a puling driveller like Werter, or a morbid dreamer like Wordsworth. It can never make a philosopher, nor a statesman, nor in any class of life an useful or rational man.[85]

It is easy enough to catch Peacock playing the devil's advocate. After all, poetry must be doing something right if its ingredients are ultimately "resolvable" into Shakespeare's own triumvirate, the lunatic, lover, and poet in imagination "all compact." Peacock's exaggerated portrayal of poetry and philosophical rationality as polar opposites points to their inevitable inversion: poetry and "cool reason" were hardly antithetical. In his own terms, the "philosophic mental tranquillity which looks around with an equal eye on all external things" is precisely the state of mind from which Peacock thinks poetry emanates, especially if you aspire to be an unacknowledged legislator of the world. Barring that productive tranquility, poetry risks its own partiality, receding from "the real business of life" to rest in its own empty and exaggerated feeling. In "The Defense of Poetry," Shelley would uphold the inversion that Peacock only implied. Retaining all of its power of sympathy, Shelley collapsed the boundary between poetry and philosophy in heralding its ability to enlarge "the circumference of the imagination" by purifying the affections. In his suggestive Stoic terms, the most celebrated modern poets wield an "influence which is moved not, but moves."[86]

The Road Ahead

Ernst Cassirer once noted that Stoic philosophy was pivotal to the "formation of the modern mind and the modern world."[87] In chapter 1, I explore one facet of this emergence by examining how powerfully the Stoic substratum of eighteenth-century moral sentimentalism shaped Romantic notions of mind and world. After surveying the often-militant repudiation of Stoicism in eighteenth-century literary culture, I pause over an overlooked but consequential fracture in the moral philosophy of Shaftesbury and Adam Smith, one that Mary Wollstonecraft took up in her own feminist critique of sensibility. Though working in different ways, all three thinkers approached Stoicism as a necessary supplement to sympathetic connection, one that was crucial to life in an increasingly cosmopolitan and interconnected world. Following the crosscurrents of sympathy and Stoicism in their private and public works, I argue that Shaftesbury and Smith landed on an ethical impasse, one that would pit Burke against Wollstonecraft in the 1790s, igniting in the process a broad Romantic attempt to square ethics and aesthetics in a new way.

Chapter 2 takes up the legacy of the radical 1790s more directly by positing a subterranean connection between the Stoic radicalism that rocked Britain and France in the 1790s and Wordsworth's "mature" and much-maligned indifference. Thinking in these defamiliarizing terms seems useful, for Wordsworth's evolving response to Godwin's *Enquiry Concerning Political Justice* perfectly encapsulates the paradigmatic story about the Romantic generation's pivot from revolutionary fervor to political apostasy. It goes something like this: At the height of the French Revolution, Wordsworth was an ardent proponent of Godwin's *Political Justice*, a radical philosophy that promised "to abstract the hopes of man / Out of his feelings" (*Prelude* 10:807-8). But in the wake of that revolution's breakdown, Wordsworth took a bleaker view of systems of morality that fail "to melt into our affections."[88] My contention in this chapter is that the vast power of Stoic radicalism was not so easily put to rest. I tell a different story about Wordsworth's philosophical commitments and the trajectory of Romantic radicalism by exploring an overlooked affinity between Godwin's "Stoical Morality" and Wordsworth's moderated Stoicism in *The Excursion* (1814), a poem often censured—then and now—for its flat-footed conservatism.[89] While Godwin qualified his early Stoic convictions and embraced the empire of feeling, Wordsworth channeled his recalcitrant interest in Stoic radicalism through the figure of the stone, separating a philosophical attitude from its customary rhetoric and political extremity.

Taking these radical and cosmopolitan connotations of Stoicism for granted, the next two chapters consider its complex relation to two central literary categories: lyric and character. Chapter 3 is perhaps best glossed with a line from Thomas De Quincey, who once confessed that while he could occasionally "agree with the gentlemen in the cotton-trade at Manchester in affecting the Stoic philosophy," he remained on the "look out for some courteous and considerate sect that will condescend more to the infirm condition of an opium-eater."[90] In this chapter, I turn not to De Quincey but Coleridge in exploring a consequential disconnect between Stoic philosophy and corporeal reality. Coleridge occupies a strange position in a study of Romantic Stoicism: what he described as his own "utter impotence of the *Volition*" thwarted his attempts at emotional regulation, but he spent more time contemplating the history and efficacy of Stoicism than almost any other writer of the period.[91] While drawn to Kant's and Spinoza's modern renditions of Stoic ethics, Coleridge was deeply skeptical about what he described as the most "peccant part of Stoicism," the discrepancy between its moral psychology and the fact of embodied selfhood. I argue that this interest was borne out most substantively, if a bit surprisingly, in the realm of lyric.[92] In reading "Ode to Tranquillity" in relation to his better known conversation poems, I argue that Coleridge approached the lyric as not just a genre or an artistic artifact but an askesis or practice, a technology of the self by which emotion, opinion, and mental impressions might be evaluated, attenuated, or affirmed.

In chapter 4, I argue that while the pageant of his bleeding heart might have made him infamous, Byron was deeply attuned to the intricate permutations of emotional detachment. Galvanized by the Horatian *nil admirari* and other Stoic commonplaces, Byron investigated Stoicism at the level of character, a nebulous concept that straddled the ethical, the social, and the literary. In *Don Juan* and other narratives, Stoicism transcends culture and class even as it is approached as a surface-level, exteriorized phenomenon. The unlikely consonance of Byron's own performative detachment and the Stoic postures of marginalized figures was significant and destabilizing. Byron intuited—and, indeed, interrogated—the way in which a Stoic ethos blurred social distinctions by forging lines of affinity between elite citizens of the world and the wretched of the earth. In their attempts "to steel / The heart against itself," Byron's Stoic characters capture the spirit of a critical age, one in which cosmopolitan detachment could also lead to irony and other modern forms of alienation (*CW* 2:117).

In very different ways, the final two chapters of this book explore Stoic Romanticism as a vanguard movement, the shape of a future in the works but still to come. In chapter 5, I turn from poetry to the novel to consider two texts at opposite ends of the Romantic timeline, both of which attempt to unlock the reorienting, feminist possibilities inherent in Stoicism by bringing it in line with a precarious propriety. In *Millenium Hall* (1762), Sarah Scott imagines a world in which virtuous retirement and the regulation of feeling could result in paradoxically extensive benevolence. I trace the reappearance of this radical potentiality in Mary Shelley's *Lodore* (1835), a late, transatlantic novel whose tidy conclusion is undone by Fanny Derham, a "quixotic" character with a penchant for reading Cicero's *Tusculan Disputations*. A haunting rendition of Mary Wollstonecraft, Fanny Derham is also an outsized figure of the future, a woman whose transformative Stoic vision demands not "a few tame lines" but "the gift of prophecy" itself (*L* 448).

Finally, I look across the Atlantic in chapter 6 to suggest that Emerson's gnomic essays reflect, theorize, and call for a bold American extension of the Stoic Romanticism I have been tracking throughout the book. In a late journal, Emerson claimed that the doctrines of "Zeno & the Stoic sect" could be reduced to one thought: "self-reliance" (*JMN* 13:463). While his Stoicism is often described as a late and disenchanted formation, I argue that his idealism was Stoic from the outset. In a range of essays, Emerson mercilessly investigated an intuition that troubled Smith and his Romantic inheritors: however pleasurable, sympathy was incommensurate with ethical action. Like the Stoics, Emerson deployed paradoxical rhetoric to make a case for the broad justice of Stoic cosmopolitanism in a sentimental age. In owning up to his own Stoic tendencies, Emerson, like the other writers in this book, articulated a complex and challenging vision of how ethical self-culture might lead to widespread social reform.

As even this quick delineation of my argument suggests, the vision of Stoicism that emerges over the course of the book entails a demanding sense of how individuals—even in the midst of their ordinary lives—might reimagine their perception of and relation to a vast world. But Stoicism did not always emerge in such grandiose terms. A letter from November 1822 finds John Keats trying to articulate an unfamiliar and seemingly barren sense of self: "I sometimes feel not the influence of a Passion or Affection during a whole week—and so long [as] this sometimes continues I begin to suspect myself and the genuineness of my feelings at other times."[93] There is a hesitancy to this acknowledgment, as if Keats worried that a deeply engrained, almost inexplicable Stoicism might render him cold and unpoetical. But the contrary reality seems equally compelling: arriving at a place beyond the influence of passion foregrounds its power in the first place. Calling affect into question is the sign of its ultimate affirmation. T. S. Eliot was thinking along similar lines in "Tradition and the Individual Talent" when he suggested that Wordsworth's account of powerful feeling recollected in tranquility was "not quite the whole story." In notably Stoic terms, Eliot suggests that poetry "is not a turning loose of emotion, but an escape from emotion; it is not the expression of personality, but an escape from personality." His next sentence—offered without explanation or elaboration—strikes me as particularly resonant: "But, of course, only those who have personality and emotions know what it means to want to escape from these things."[94] Eliot's understated "of course" is a wonderfully overworked prepositional phrase, for in unweaving literary historical distinctions, it makes a counterintuitive perspective on the Romantic project seem almost too obvious to be stated. Hardly oppositional, emotion and Stoic tranquility were inherently correlative.

CHAPTER ONE

Stoic Moral Sentimentalism from Shaftesbury to Wollstonecraft

THE UNLIKELY EMERGENCE of sympathy out of an age of reason has been exhaustively surveyed in studies that crisscross the humanities and social sciences. Starting in the eighteenth century, human beings were, in Jon Mee's terms, "increasingly defined as sympathetic creatures across a whole range of discourses and practices."[1] This broad propensity underwrites the outsized significance of the sympathetic imagination in British Romanticism, becoming in many quarters an ethical raison d'être for literature itself. As journalists, cognitive scientists, and defenders of the humanities frequently remind us, literature conducts readers out of their familiar perspectives and worlds. It becomes a training ground for the formation of sympathy and emotional intelligence.[2]

There is nothing new about sympathy's privileged place in discourse. For Lord Kames, sympathy was "the great cement of human society."[3] In *Elements of Moral Science* (1790), James Beattie made it the sine qua non of humanity itself: "Sympathy with distress is thought so essential to human nature, that the want of it has been called *inhumanity*."[4] As one manifestation of what Steven Goldsmith has called a "built-in mechanism of self-supersession," sympathy points to the way in which affective response tends to be perceived as a prerequisite for ethical awareness: "Through emotion, we are told, consciousness redistributes attention to objects and aspects of experience outside the subject's current horizon of awareness, thereby allowing the subject to unsettle, estrange, and even surpass its ruling assumptions."[5] Yet for all its moral efficacy, accounts of sympathy's value often sidestep the fact of its limitations and blind spots. Charles Lamb had comic intentions in his essay "Imperfect Sympathies" (1821), but his skeptical take was hardly an isolated one: "I can feel for all indifferently, but I cannot feel towards all equally."[6] Alert to this difficulty, early expositors of sympathy linked its power to a countervailing Stoic imperative. Shaftesbury and Adam Smith were influential expounders of the moral force of passion and sympathy, and yet, as I argue below, each of these thinkers prominently engaged the Stoics in the course of shaping a new rhetoric of sentiment. Writing at the end of the century, Mary Wollstonecraft took that same Stoicism for granted, radicalizing its cosmopolitan possibility for a new generation of writers.

Anthony Pagden has argued that in the "heady mix" of Enlightenment philosophy Stoicism was the "element that provided the basis of the understanding of human society, and it was Stoicism that led first to the creation of the science of man and thence to the birth of cosmopolitanism."[7] In spite of this centrality, interest in sympathy's Stoic substratum has failed to keep pace with the vast amount of attention that sentimentalism elicits, greatly impoverishing our sense of the Enlightenment's bequest to Romanticism and, by extension, to modernity. This chapter attempts to rectify the balance by tracing a split impulse in Romantic ethics—an ambivalence about the ethical status of emotion, represented most distinctly by the disparity between Kant and his sentimental precursors—back to the overlapping exposition of Stoicism and sympathy in eighteenth-century moral sentimentalism.[8] Most accounts of Romanticism and its infamous moral imagination overlook the implications of this convergence: in its affinity with sympathy, Stoic detachment could make a surprising claim on art itself. And yet exploring this possibility entails disregarding much Stoic skepticism, then as now.

Monstrous Virtue and Common Life

At first glance, Stoicism seems antithetical to the kind of moral reflection that the cult of feeling would sustain. It would not be hard to assemble a sizable commonplace book of passages in which eighteenth-century writers take Stoicism to task for its hypocrisy, its inhumanity, or its impracticality. In one of the century's defining set pieces, Alexander Pope explodes overly simplistic accounts of an "Age of Reason." Anticipating Hume's famous formulation in the *Treatise*, Pope contends that when sailing on "life's vast ocean," passion is the empowering gale that makes the determinations of reason possible. But in the lines that precede this assertion, Pope makes his case for passion by castigating the Stoics:

> In lazy Apathy let Stoics boast
> Their Virtue fix'd; 'tis fix'd as in a frost,
> Contracted all, retiring to the breast;
> But strength of mind is Exercise, not Rest.[9]

Unwilling to chip away at that frozen internal sea, Pope's shiftless Stoic turns his back on the affective labor that sympathy demands. He aims for constancy, but with a contracting and "retiring" virtue, he never gets past insensibility. Such a retiring virtue stands at odds with the cognitive balancing act that a new science of man seemed to demand. Pope was hardly alone in depicting Stoic apathy as a kind of self-inflicted folly. David Hume described the Stoics as "Pretenders to Wisdom," and he argued that their efforts to eliminate passion and prejudice resulted only in the disabling elimination of "the most enduring Sentiments of the Heart, and all the most useful Byasses and Instincts, which can govern a human Creature."[10] In another essay, Hume casts the aspiring Stoic as a disproportionate moralist, a man whose attempts to moderate passion are inefficacious and out of touch with common life:

> A man may as well pretend to cure himself of love, by viewing his mistress through the *artificial* medium of a microscope or prospect, and beholding there the coarseness of her skin, and monstrous disproportion of her features, as hope to excite or moderate any passion by the *artificial* arguments of a SENECA or an EPICTETUS. The remembrance of the natural aspect and situation of the object, will, in both cases, still recur upon him. The reflections of philosophy are too subtle and distant to take place in common life, or eradicate any affection. The air is too fine to breathe in, where it is above the winds and clouds of the atmosphere.[11]

For Hume, the philosophy of Seneca and Epictetus operates like a medium. It could shift one's perspective as handily as any microscope, but its purchase on reality was both temporary and illusory. By contrast, the natural proportions of passions and objects were intractable, and could not easily be rescaled. Half a century later, Coleridge would describe a similarly contrived attempt to eliminate passion. In "Dejection: An Ode" (1802), he bemoans his own abstruse attempt "to steal / From my own nature all the natural Man."[12] In both cases, the corrective—a perspective at once "too subtle and distant"—only reaffirms the naturalness of the affections in common life.

For Hume, the modulating viewpoint afforded by prospect and microscope grants the Stoic little more than an illusory clarity, a disproportionate and fantastical perspective that seems to glance back at *Gulliver's Travels* (1726) and its own perspectival play. While never mentioning the Stoics outright, Swift's scathing account of the Houyhnhnms amounts to one of the most prominent Stoic takedowns of the century. As a race of sage, even Stoic, horses whose pursuit of dispassionate reason displaces sympathy, pity, and natural affection, the Houyhnhnms lead Gulliver "to view the Actions and Passions of Man in a very different Light."[13] The final act of Swift's unsettling satire tends to be seen as a general onslaught against the tyranny of reason, but Swift has his sagacious equines take up several of the scandalous positions that set Stoic doctrine so fiercely at odds with common life. Aping Stoic cosmopolitanism and its disinterested transcendence of partial passion, the Houyhnhnms' pursuit of universal benevolence noticeably outweighs the pull of ordinary domestic attachments: "FRIENDSHIP and *Benevolence* are the two principal Virtues among the *Houyhnhnms*, and these are not confined to particular Objects, but universal to the whole Race. For a Stranger from the remotest Part is equally treated with the nearest Neighbour, and wherever he goes, looks upon himself at home."[14] Aligned with the idea of being at home in the universe, this disinterested bid for justice might seem uncontroversial in theory; after all, friendship seems a distinctly human and humanizing virtue. But in delineating the practical applications of this abstract position, Swift cuts closer to home. The Houyhnhnms, for example, elevate universal virtue over particular attachments, even when it comes to the settlement and "Regulation of Children": "As for Instance, if a *Houyhnhm* hath two Males, he changeth one of them with another that hath two Females: And when a Child hath been lost by any Casualty, where the Mother is past Breeding, it is determined what Family in the District shall breed another to supply the Loss."[15] Swapping their children back and forth with no trace of an emotional bond, the Houyhnhnms—in a clear caricature of the Stoics—undervalue what thinkers as diverse as Hobbes and Smith describe as the natural affection of a parent for a child. (Though, as I make clear in what follows, this scandalous example of Stoic severity is not as straightforward as it seems, and there is much debate in the eighteenth century about what the "natural affections" truly entail.)

A similar detachment typifies the Houyhnhm attitude toward death and grief. When Houyhnhnms die, their friends and relations express "neither Joy nor Grief at their Departure; nor does the dying Person discover the least Regret that he is leaving the World." Gulliver recounts the story of a Houyhnhnm who lost her husband in the morning, only to stop by a house party later in the day where she behaved "as cheerfully as the rest."[16] While Gulliver greets this self-control with admiration, the satirical effect depends upon its complete mismatch with conventional, sentimental morality. Inhumanity and insensibility become the wages of perfection. In another context, Swift himself made his own thoughts on the Stoical Houyhnhnm world view abundantly clear: "THE Stoical Scheme of supplying our Wants, by lopping off our Desires; is like cutting off our Feet when we want Shoes."[17]

The warped domesticity of the Houyhnhnms, the mistress under the microscope, the drastic response to a lack of shoes: each example portrays Stoicism as dangerously incompatible with sentimentalism and, by extension, common life. Such a critical mass of contrarian perspective might seem to undercut from the outset my argument about the centrality of Stoicism in the period. But in lining up these knee-jerk reactions, I want to evoke the way in which a perennial critique that portrayed Stoicism as an extreme and dogmatic position—a case of what Johnson called "wild enthusiastick virtue"—obscured its nuanced role in the sociable and philosophical fabric of eighteenth-century life.[18] The variety of Stoicism I attend to in this chapter (not to mention the book as a whole) never attains the ironclad perfection of the Houyhnhnms, nor does it set as its goal the outright elimination of passion. For Smith, Shaftesbury, and Wollstonecraft it becomes instead a complement to the work of sympathy, a prompt for judgment that moderates rather than overrides the claims of sentiment. In this sense, I follow Adam Potkay in emphasizing the centrality of a modest and "moderated Stoicism" in the eighteenth century, a Stoicism "made compatible with a just and rational sympathy."[19] Samuel Johnson evoked this softer, more moderate stance in—of all places—an essay on the weather: "It was the boast of Stoick philosophy, to make man unshaken by calamity, and unelated by success, incorruptible by pleasure, and invulnerable by pain; these are heights of wisdom which none ever attained, and to which few can aspire; but there are lower degrees of constancy necessary to common virtue."[20] While Stoicism had long been beset by hyped-up diatribes against its lofty vanity and impractical morality, these blanket dismissals intensified at the same moment that moral philosophers like Smith and Shaftesbury characterized a "lower degree" of Stoicism as a necessary ethical resource in a commercial and conversable world.[21]

All of this can be said in another way: Stoicism partakes of a broader paradigm shift, one that, in Addison and Steele's terms, "brought Philosophy out of Closets and Libraries, Schools and Colleges, to dwell in Clubs and Assemblies, at Tea-Tables, and in Coffee-Houses."[22] Though tied to a set of ideas emerging out of a comprehensive world view in ancient Greece, Stoicism had—over time—become less of an extreme position and more of a piecemeal affair. The eighteenth century was a crucial interval in this evolution, for in this period Stoicism was less frequently approached as the special privilege of an apparitional sage. Reimagined as a temperament or even a tactic, Stoicism was a widely (if imperfectly) inhabitable philosophy, an attitude suitable for encountering the duties of common life. In this sense, Stoicism could persist even in the absence of all its formal and philosophical underpinnings. For Johnson, the learned Stoicism of Lipsius found its echo in "the common voice of the multitude uninstructed by precept, and unprejudiced by authority."[23] Hume struck a similar chord in his essays on the four philosophers. On the one hand, he acknowledged that Stoicism was an ancient "philosophical sect" with its own doctrine. But in broader terms, he recognized that it was one of the "sentiments of sects, that naturally form themselves in the world, and entertain different ideas of human life and happiness."[24]

The point I want to make about Stoicism as a commonplace possibility is in many ways an inversion of Lynn Festa's account of sensibility and its unimpeded circulation. For Festa, sensibility "is not restricted by social prerequisites." Its structure and significance remain "accessible even to those lacking a classical education or knowledge of social decorum."[25] The Stoic's stiff upper lip could be just as ubiquitous and philosophically resonant as sympathetic tears. To be sure, Stoicism fulfills this egalitarian mandate less persuasively than its sentimental counterpart: transmitted by a classically educated elite, its uptake was often allied with masculine propriety and good breeding. For Ellison, Shaftesbury's Stoicism is part of an elite Whiggish ethos, one that was "performed for appreciative insiders" in what amounted to a skeptical dismissal of "the enthusiasm of other social orders."[26] Similarly classed, Smith's gendered account of conscience was anything but impartial, and the heroic register of what Martha Nussbaum has called his "macho Stoicism" was hardly all-encompassing.[27] But despite the exclusivity of their articulations, Smith and Shaftesbury sketch out the possibility of a yet wider diffusion of Stoicism in "social Behaviour," one unmoored from the printed page of formal philosophy.[28] Smith, for example, suggests that the "profoundest philosophy" was anticipated—however imperfectly—in "the ordinary commerce of the world," a realm of experience that he dubbed "the great school of self-command" (*TMS* 139, 145). Wollstonecraft would illuminate the contradictions inherent in Smith's attempt to stretch out the boundaries of an ancient school of philosophy, but the ambition resonated in other quarters. A year before the publication of Smith's *Theory*, Elizabeth Carter—bluestocking exemplar and preeminent translator of Epictetus—argued that from the right perspective the abstruse philosophy of the Stoics could speak to "the Generality of Mankind": "Even now, their Compositions may be read with great Advantage, as containing excellent Rules of Self-government, and of social Behaviour."[29] But as her friend Catherine Talbot noted, Carter's translation also made Epictetus available to the generality of "womankind."[30] Three years later, Sarah Pennington included Epictetus, Seneca, and Cicero on a list of books of the "instructive Kind" in *An Unfortunate Mother's Advice to Her Absent Daughters* (1761).[31] In her *Letters on Education* (1790), Catherine Macaulay averred that sixteen-year-old boys and girls were ready for Seneca, Epictetus, and Cicero's *De Officiis*.[32]

In spite of their own delimited perspectives, I take Shaftesbury and Smith as influential prime movers in a broader attempt to redefine and expand Stoicism's potentiality in a sentimental and sociable world. In this sense, Chris Jones rightfully contends that while Shaftesbury argued for equality only among a cultured elite, "his formulations were taken out of this context to become the basis of a radical, even revolutionary, ideology."[33] Wollstonecraft was a vital figure in this radicalization, even if her own egalitarian impulses were themselves imperfect. I will have more to say about Stoicism's redeployment within common life in what follows, for, as we will see, this transposition underlies a broad Romantic tendency to ally its ethos more forcefully with slaves, soldiers, vagrants, and pedlars than philosophers. From Thomas De Quincey forward, admiration for such silent endurance has struck many critics as inherently suspect, a naturalization of suffering and a disavowal of responsibility.[34] But in another sense, the slow mobilization of Stoicism in common life reflected a new interest in an old ideal of natural equality. Amid the French Revolution, and after the *Déclaration des droits de l'homme et du citoyen* (1789), the Stoic cosmopolitan possibilities lurking in Shaftesbury's and Smith's moral philosophy could be seen in a new light. If Stoicism could prop up the old social order, it could also cross-examine its smooth operation, giving rise to the possibility of extraordinary justice in the process.

Shaftesbury: Between Stoicism and Sentiment

Dreams. Dreams . . . a Dark Night. dead Sleep. Starts. disturbing Visions. faint Endeavours to awake . . . a sick Reason. Labrynth. Wood. Sea . . . Waves tossing. Billows. Surge. the driving of ye Wreck . . . Giddy Whirlwinds. Eddyes, and ye over-whelming Gulph.

How emerge? When gain ye Port, ye Station, Promontory? . . . ἡ δὲ ἕστηκε, καὶ περὶ αὐτὴν κοιμίζεται τὰ φλεγμήναντα τοῦ ὕδατος [which yet stands firm and sees the boiling waters round it fall to rest].

Awake. rouze. shake off the Fetters of ye Enchanteress. begin. (A 216)

In this fragmentary passage from his private notebooks, Shaftesbury almost seems to reach across the century and write himself into the Romantic sublime. Lines like these would seem unremarkable in any of Coleridge's *Notebooks*. Here, they epitomize Burke's account of sublime terror a half-century before its articulation: "No passion so effectually robs the mind of all its powers of acting and reason as fear."[35] In Shaftesbury's stark vision, a flurry of motion taunts the "faint Endeavours" of agency. The alliterative trifecta of dreams, death, and darkness bears down on a besieged reason, and the confined stasis of a forest labyrinth inexplicably becomes the vertiginous exposure of a bark tossed about by the sea. Like Stephen Dedalus, Shaftesbury is caught up in a nightmare from which he is trying to awake, but the nightmare he evokes in the notebook turns out to represent nothing other than life in the polite world itself. In the private space of the notebooks, a staunch advocate of civility brushes up against the specter of its discontent. Unceremoniously trivialized, the sociable existence celebrated by Shaftesbury at other moments becomes, here, "this Sink, these Dreggs, this Guise of a World" (A 216).

As an enthusiastic advocate of nature, reverie, and the natural affections, Shaftesbury is often flagged as a distant progenitor of Romantic aesthetics, so perhaps it is unsurprising to find him suffering from a bout of their weltschmerz. But the complexity of Shaftesbury's affective legacy becomes evident in the quick recalibration of his ruminations. Weaving a metaphorical landscape from Marcus Aurelius into his own self-interrogation, Shaftesbury invokes a vision of Stoic fixity as a kind of ballast, a force that might redress the disorientation wrought by life in the polite world: "Stand firm like a promontory, upon which the waves are always breaking. It not only keeps its place, but stills the fury of the waves."[36] The simple image belies an elaborate philosophical position. While on one level encoding no more than a desire for fortitude and perspective, a topography set apart from an encircling chaos, Shaftesbury's bid for solid ground also marks the central place of the Stoics in his own account of sympathetic sociability. Under the sign of Marcus Aurelius, he works to counteract the inertia of life in society while also reclaiming for the mind its native "powers of acting and reason."[37] In these efforts, sensibility and natural affection—the dynamos that power so much of Shaftesbury's public philosophy—are reinscribed as a crippling encumbrance, a ball and chain, an "Enchanteress." Eight paragraphs later, in an equally fragmentary line of thought, he forces himself to acknowledge again their flawed existence: "Remember therefore how falln . . . Compassion. Sympathy. Relation. Family. Publick" (*A* 218).

Shaftesbury's invocation of Marcus Aurelius was hardly an aberration. He modeled his unpublished exercises—described by successive editors as his "regimen" or "*askêmata*"—on the Stoic emperor's own unpublished *Meditations*, and he emblazoned this particularly striking example of Stoic imagery on the title page of *Characteristics* (1711). This Stoic preoccupation has struck most of the Third Earl's modern commentators as a remarkable facet of his intellectual formation. Robert Voitle has even proposed that Shaftesbury's notebooks contain "the finest examples of purely Stoic thought since Marcus Aurelius wrote down his own meditations."[38] Nevertheless, Shaftesbury's enthusiasm for Epictetus and Marcus Aurelius can seem a sideshow to his more fundamental moral sentimentalist innovation, a nostalgic back-formation set against a world in which passion was—in Albert Hirschman's words—gradually "rehabilitated as the essence of life."[39] For Shaftesbury, however, Stoicism was a central mechanism of that rehabilitation, a private or even covert form of self-practice that was integral to the sentimental work of civic transformation.

My interest in foregrounding that practice here is largely anachronistic, born out of a sense that Shaftesbury's pioneering account of sympathy is rife from the outset with an ambivalence that many Romantic writers intuit in its operation. Figures like Wordsworth and Shelley who were drawn to Shaftesbury's harmonious, organic, and imitable order of nature were indirectly in tune with the Third Earl's Stoic vision of the cosmos.[40] But I want to suggest that they were also inheritors of a related instability in his moral philosophical speculation. As we will see, Wordsworth, writing in 1815, had good reason to describe Shaftesbury as an author "at present unjustly depreciated."[41] Shaftesbury's Stoicism prompted a deep skepticism about the limited scale and mechanical nature of sympathy, even as it fostered questions about the representational character and moral ends of fellow feeling. From this equivocal origin, it is hardly surprising that Romantic writers often grapple with the difficult asymmetries of a recalcitrant sympathy. David Simpson, for example, has made much of the way in which Wordsworth's poetry "shows not only the aspiration to common feeling but also the sheer difficulty of imagining or experiencing it."[42] Nor is it a coincidence that Shaftesbury figures prominently in Nancy Yousef's account of the way in which a nonreciprocal intimacy fostered by proximity becomes the "special province" of a Romantic poetics "that at once assimilates and forsakes the affective confidence of sentimentalism."[43] Indeed, Shaftesbury's unpublished Stoic reflections only bolster Yousef's contention that what Shaftesbury calls "natural affection" can be an individualized formation "troublingly dissociated from the perception of others."[44] At the same time, I want to suggest that Shaftesbury's reflections transpose natural affection from the proximately interpersonal to the cosmopolitan realm, a crucial Stoic move that prefigures one radical Romantic attempt to look past the limitations of sympathetic feeling.

I want to pause over the ambiguity of this inheritance, for it draws attention to the seemingly paradoxical fact that one of the eighteenth century's most vociferous Stoics also happened to be the instigator of a broad realignment in ethics, one that placed moral evaluation squarely within the realm of the emotions. In hindsight, however, this sense of contradiction—reinforced by all of the caricatures of dogmatic Stoicism detailed above—starts to look more apparent than real.

Affect and Opinion

Published just sixty years after Hobbes's *Leviathan* (1651), Shaftesbury's *Characteristics of Men, Manners, Opinions, Times* was a wide-ranging and wildly variegated overture to a century of sentimental moral philosophy. Running through ten editions before the onset of the French Revolution, *Characteristics* set the terms for a broad pivot in moral philosophy, a turn away from the lingering shadow of Hobbesian self-interest and the stark portrayal of human existence it sponsored. For Hobbes, life in the state of nature was infamously "solitary, poor, nasty, brutish, and short," a *bellum omnium contra omnes* (war of all against all) that grew out of the "natural passions of men, when there is no visible power to keep them in awe."[45] Shaftesbury started with an antithetically optimistic account of human affectivity, one that culminated in a defense of man's inherent and rational sociability. There was no need to conjure a hypothetical, presocial "rough draft" of human nature; "social intercourse and community" were themselves man's "natural state" (*C* 285, 283).

Shaftesbury imagined his sociable repudiation of Hobbes as the manifestation of a broad fault line in philosophy, a rough divide that separated his own Stoic outlook from the Epicureanism he ascribed to Hobbes and Locke. Shaftesbury's aversion to modern outgrowths of Epicureanism was as vehement as Coleridge's would be a century later. While ancient and modern manifestations of Epicureanism culminated in "inaction and retreat," Shaftesbury placed himself at the cutting edge of the Stoic line, a position that he saw as culminating in "action, concernment in civil affairs, [and] religion."[46] His Stoic rejoinder to Hobbes entailed a bold reconceptualization of emotion and innate sociability, one that would reorient British moral philosophy for the rest of the century. This was Shaftesbury's paradigm-shifting move, a position that gave rise to a century of admirers and innovation in moral philosophy, even as it provoked the ridicule of figures like Mandeville, who rated Shaftesbury's "calm virtue" as good for little more than to "breed drones" or "qualify a man for the stupid enjoyments of a monastic life."[47]

In *An Inquiry Concerning Virtue and Merit*, a treatise later collected in *Characteristics*, Shaftesbury describes this sociable propensity as a self-evident proposition. Nothing, he notes, is "more apparent than that there is naturally in every man such a degree of social affection as inclines him to seek the familiarity and friendship of his fellows" (*C* 215). John Locke presided over Shaftesbury's early education and might even have assisted at his birth, but for Shaftesbury this natural desire for social affection represented a clear ethical refutation of his one-time tutor's campaign against innate ideas. Nonplussed by Locke's "super-speculative philosophy" and its epistemological hand-wringing, he remained committed to the idea that natural affection is "inwardly joined to us and implanted in our natures" (*C* 131, 216). At other moments, he even suggested that "implanted natural affection" was as natural to human beings as digestion was to the stomach, or breathing was to the lungs (192). In *The Moralists*, a "Philosophical Rhapsody" lodged at the heart of *Characteristics*, the sage-like Theocles describes this implanted propensity as a kind of "instinct," a correlative to taste that could provide unfiltered access to the affections: "No sooner are actions viewed, no sooner the human affections and passions discerned (and they are most of them as soon discerned as felt) than straight an inward eye distinguishes and sees the fair and shapely, the amiable and admirable, apart from the deformed, the foul, the odious or the despicable" (*C* 325–26). Normalized over time, this involuntary ability to detect and decipher "human affections and passions" would lead Shaftesbury's inheritors to talk about a "moral sense," a formulation implying a mode of apprehension that could bypass reason and cognition. Though Shaftesbury rarely invoked the term, his spirited endorsement of such an innate faculty led Andrew Kippis—William Godwin's tutor at Hoxton Academy—to describe him as "the Head of the School of the sentimental Philosophy."[48]

While Shaftesbury instigated a broad realignment in ethics, the persistence of terms like "instinct" and "sensation" have made it easy to streamline his sense of sympathy's operation, making it seem like a desirably inevitable and autonomic process. Later in the century, David Hume would describe sympathy as a free and easy faculty that makes passions "pass with the greatest facility from one person to another, and produce correspondent movements in all human breasts."[49] For Shaftesbury, however, this ease of transmission was as much a danger as a source of ethical potentiality. To direct sympathy toward a meaningful end, shared feelings had to be subject to evaluation. It is in this sense that Shaftesbury latches onto a Stoic account of the emotions as integral to the work of sympathy itself.

While much of Shaftesbury's Stoic reputation rests on private material that remained unpublished until the twentieth century, the first edition of *Characteristics* announced its centrality to his thought with an elusive visual paratext. In a self-designed frontispiece that abuts the title page, Shaftesbury alludes to two pivotal quotations, one from Epictetus and one from Marcus Aurelius (see figure 1). At first glance, the engraving seems inconspicuous, even insignificant. A noonday sun casts its rays over a tranquil bay where several ships rest safely at harbor. In the foreground, an urn filled with water stands upon a pedestal. Unruffled by wind, the surface of the water quietly absorbs a ray of the sun's light. A motto derived from the *Meditations* of Marcus Aurelius hovers beneath the circular line that bounds the sky: "Πάντα Ὑπόληψις," "All is opinion." However enigmatically, Shaftesbury's Stoicism stands at the threshold of his work, "the fringe of the printed text, which, in reality, controls the whole reading."[50] But if Shaftesbury sets up an abstruse Stoicism as an interpretive key to the philosophical miscellany that follows, he does so with the split agenda of one who speaks in parable, concealing as much as he gives away. Later editions of *Characteristics* introduced the innovation of a caption to the frontispiece, one that directed readers to an obscure footnote in the text's third volume where both quotations were printed in Greek. But this desire to throw a line to readers was balanced by an investment in their mystification. Shaftesbury's instructions to his engraver concede as much: "None

FIGURE 1. Frontispiece to Shaftesbury's *Characteristicks of Men, Manners, Opinions, Times* (London, 1727). (Courtesy of the Rare Books and Manuscripts Library of the Ohio State University Libraries)

will be the wiser for this reference, except those who deserve it, and ought to have what light can be given 'em on such terms as these."⁵¹

So how, then, are we to make sense of the split path through *Characteristics*, where only a fit audience emboldened by "finer and truer wit" (*C* 8) has ready access to the Stoic moral psychology that Shaftesbury adopts as the groundwork for his defense of the natural affections? At a crucial point in *The Moralists*, Theocles reflects that everyone must, "in some manner or other, either skillfully or unskillfully philosophize" (*C* 336). The tendency to distinguish between multiple levels of the same phenomenon becomes a recurring feature of Shaftesbury's project; he draws a line between being "sociable" and "truly sociable," just as at other moments he differentiates between two kinds of laughter or two kinds of joy. In each case, a common conception or norm is distinguished from a rarefied manifestation, a testament to Shaftesbury's concerted investment in "good breeding" and aristocratic cultivation (*C* 407).[52] His influential perspective on the ethics of emotion manifests a comparable split: if a natural, instinctual sympathy is a universal bequest that works against the illusory egoism of Hobbes, there remains the further and more difficult question of what knowledge or belief such sympathetic emotions actually encode. From this rarefied perspective sympathy looks more like a form of judgment than an instinctual response.

The strikingly cognitive tenor of Shaftesbury's sympathy is immediately evident in the touchstone passage from Marcus Aurelius that Shaftesbury's frontispiece depicts: "All depends on your opinions: These are in your power. Remove, therefore, when you incline, your opinion; and then, as when one has turned the promontory, and got into a bay, all is calm; so, all shall become stable to you, and a still harbor."[53] Following Marcus, Shaftesbury approaches emotions as representations of things in the world. While often coincident with felt sensations or bodily traces, they were, at heart, judgments that reflected the way in which the *hêgemonikon*, or "ruling faculty," assigned value to one's experience of the world.[54] Marcus's suggestion that everything "depends on your opinions" is not an appeal to relativism. It is, instead, an acknowledgement that emotions are prompted not by things in themselves, but by one's estimation or opinion of those things. As Samuel Johnson put it in *The Rambler*, emotions like fear are judgments that can simply be "eradicated like other false opinions."[55] Nor were the passions as such the only mental phenomenon that weighed on an aspiring Stoic's attention. As Lawrence Klein has noted, Shaftesbury followed the lead of Epictetus, who saw attentiveness to emotion as just one facet of a larger ethical task: "making correct use of mental impressions."[56] In *Characteristics*, Shaftesbury takes the fear of death as an example. Until the last moment of life, death itself can hardly be said to disturb us. It is, rather, the "opinion or apprehension of evil and calamity" implicit in our fearful imaginings of death that result in "disappointment and disturbance" (*C* 422). For a Stoic like Marcus Aurelius, this mismatch between the world and one's affective representations of it necessitated paying attention to "all arising imaginations" in the mind so that "none may insinuate themselves, till you thoroughly comprehend them."[57] For Shaftesbury and his Stoic precursors, the introspective work of rectifying the opinions inherent in emotion necessitated an internalized discourse, a dialogue in which one is—in David Marshall's terms—"turned into one's own witness."[58] For Pierre Hadot, this dialogic practice was "the central node of the whole of Stoicism."[59] An important feature of Shaftesbury's philosophy, this markedly Stoic dialogism would figure prominently in Smith's *Theory of Moral Sentiments* and become a resonant subtext for Coleridge's conversation poems. Rooted in this dialogism, Stoic moral psychology was not antithetical to sympathy but crucial to its allocation. Shaftesbury would adopt this insight as the oblique epitome of his sociable project.[60]

False Humanity and a Sympathizing of the Whole

Drawing on the military metaphors that pervade Roman Stoicism, Shaftesbury sketched out his self-regulatory method in imaginative terms, urging his reader to "set afoot the powerfullest faculties of his mind" and the "best forces of his wit and judgment in order to make a formal descent on the territories of the heart" (*C* 158). The heart's affections were central to Shaftesbury's ethics and aesthetics, but only to the extent that they bore the impress of "wit and judgment." As the heart becomes occupied territory, even what J. B. Schneewind has described as Shaftesbury's "generous passions" start to seem less immediate or intuitive, prone rather to their own representations and misrepresentations.[61]

The prominence of this destabilizing affective ambiguity is writ large in one of Shaftesbury's preferred metaphors. In *Characteristics*, he is quick to claim "these very natural affections" as an integral facet of human nature, no less than the "mainsprings of this machine" itself (*C* 54). But at other moments, the mechanical metaphor threatens to collapse upon itself, turning an innate capacity into a passive, autonomic force. In his *Askêmata*, Shaftesbury warns himself against a tendency "to receive impressions from every thing, & Machine-like to be mov'd & wrought upon, wound up, & govern'd exteriourly, as if there were nothing that rul'd within, or had ye least controul" (*A* 188). Without Stoicism and its mediating self-practice, even beneficent passions could seem external and anarchic. Mechanical impressions bypassed the mind's power to give and withhold assent. More pressingly, even minor affective aberrations could result in drastic shifts. Reflecting on his own "impetuouse, furiouse, impotent Temper," Shaftesbury reminded himself that his mind was like "certain Machines y^t are fast'ned by many Wedges." If one wedge was even casually dislodged, the shaking frame might push the whole machine out of joint. In the private, allusive space of his exercises, a reference to Epictetus immediately follows these reflections on mechanical passion: "take care not to harm your own ruling faculty," your *hêgemonikon* (*A* 189n). Entertaining the false opinions inherent in unexamined passion could disrupt one's entire mental economy. In the social world, it was necessary to come "on ye Stage as an Actor, not as a Machine" (*A* 216).

Shaftesbury's mistrust of the mechanical moves in a different direction than its Romantic sequel, for he laments a responsiveness to external shaping that Coleridge would, in fact, celebrate. In these examples,

Shaftesbury's mistrust of machinelike receptivity grows not out of a disparagement of the affections per se, but out of a sense that—improperly regulated—they might pervert or render passive a more active capacity for benevolence. But later in the *Askêmata*, moral sentimentalism itself is subjected to a withering critique. The sympathy and fellow feeling that loom so large in studies of Shaftesbury are suddenly described as routinized, mechanical processes, mere habits of a mind when it is acting "like a Machine in ye common way of Life." Only at this extreme does it become clear how fully Shaftesbury's Stoic practice destabilizes the standard account of his sentimentalism, even if it ultimately signals the possibility of its reformation:

> To *com-passionate*. i.e.: to joyn with in Passion, or be passionate with ... This in one Order of Life is right & good. nothing more harmoniouse. and to be without this, or not to feel this, is unnatural, horrid, immane. How else wou'd ye Machine perform? for this is meant still of ye Machine, or what is all one, the Mind, Nature, or Temper, as it is when [acting] like a Machine in ye common way of Life, in Animals & Men-Animals; where there is no better Rule than ye Speciousness of ye Object; nor no other Force to act by, but the Force of the Πάθη [passions] rais'd from thence; where ye only Energy is from Pain & Pleasure Sorrow & Transport; and where Men being light & heavy, airy & clouded, allways under ye power of Passion, allways passionate, allways miserable, in their own Cases, & about their own affaires; it would be unequal, unjust, unsociable, & hard, not to be so, in ye affairs of others, & be Wretched too for Company. (*A* 254)

Shaftesbury's reflection starts out as one expects it might: compassion, an outgrowth of natural sociability, meets with approbation. A person devoid of its harmonizing virtue would be "immane," "inhumanely cruel or savage," more suited to the Hobbesian state of nature than an emerging public sphere.[62] But with a caustic rhetorical question, Shaftesbury seems to overturn his own moral philosophical innovation. Compassion—a faculty that he himself aligns with the better angels of our nature—suddenly becomes a commonplace mechanical contrivance, an animalistic impulse. Unmoored from attentive self-practice, it easily falls prey to false appearances. In a world of overpowering perturbations, "ye Speciousness of ye Object" becomes the rule as the smooth façade of sensibility papers over the just measure and extent of one's social relations. To use Mandeville's term, compassion run amok could turn a thoughtful philosopher into a good "drone," a moral agent who had lost sight of the fact that emotions were not just impulses but evaluations of the world.

Shaftesbury's critique of mechanical compassion was part of a broader campaign waged in his *Askêmata* against what he called "fals[e] Humanity" (*A* 257). In the private realm of his notebooks, he dismissed affections that lead to "Sociable Acts & Commerce wth Mankind" as "*Sickness*" of "a dangerouse kind" (*A* 212–13). Later, in an extraordinary passage, he warns against harboring any passion that reflects an overly high opinion of outward things, passions that can show up in "any form or speciouse Shape": "Friendlyness, Humanity, Amicable-Pleasures, social Joys, Sympathy, Naturall Affection, Endearment, Tenderness, Love" (*A* 252). Once again, Shaftesbury uses the word "speciouse" to mark the distance between false appearance and a justified opinion or belief. The "Amicable-Pleasures" of sympathy can easily misrepresent reality, losing their ethical significance in the process. This list of compassion and its cognates—a compendium of the virtues Shaftesbury is thought to value and embody—immediately precedes a stark imperative: "remember here is ye Poyson here the Corruption, the Dissolution of all" (*A* 252).

It is easy to take Shaftesbury's bleak account of "false humanity" as the sign of a great fissure in his philosophy, one that separated his somber private reflections from what Potkay has described as his public attempt to inaugurate "modern moral philosophy in terms of passion and sentiment."[63] After all, the mere extension or replication of feeling was no guarantee of its merit or justice. Sympathy could become its own kind of solipsism. Fostered by intimacy and social intercourse, its logic was all too easily tied to one's place in a "private system" rather than a "universal" or "general system" (*C* 169). Detached from the Stoic premise that "each particular has relation to all in general," compassion could actualize a delimited kind of harmony, buttressing the social order rather than upholding the ontological order of Shaftesbury's cosmos (*C* 275). At its worst, it could become a mere echo chamber for misapprehensions and false appraisals. Shaftesbury accounts for these vulnerabilities with a split verdict. In "one Order of Life," sympathy was part of "ye Order of things"—an illustration of the "fair . . . Side of Nature" (*A* 254). But considered in light of a higher order, it could seem "inconsistent with all true Affection & with that high & principal Natural Affection, wch in a Mind soundly rational is, as it were, in the Place of all" (*A* 254). In this sense, Shaftesbury's mistrust of sympathy was directed less at its aspiration than at its range. What was needed was "a sympathizing of the Whole," a validation of affections that expressed a justified opinion or belief about one's place in a broader universe (*A* 92). In this redefined sense, Shaftesbury set "enlarged affection" against localized sympathy as the proper ethical catalyst for a "citizen or commoner of the world" (*C* 255, 233).

The Perils of Natural Affection

Thomas Pfau has drawn attention to the broad and seemingly incoherent "semantic band-width" allotted to terms like "affection" in *Characteristics*, noting that this ambiguity was part of the point, an intentional alternative to reductive categories.[64] Yet Shaftesbury's account of natural affection surpasses this level of muddled significance. Deployed incongruously in public and private writings, it becomes an unstable, contradictory term. In the *Inquiry*, natural affection seems straightforward enough, a blanket term meant to encompass "parental kindness, zeal for posterity, [and] concern for the propagation and nurture of the young" (*C* 192). Almost a biological force, it grows out of kinship and proximity. The natural affection that exists "between the sexes" gives rise to an attachment for offspring and, eventually, to an ever-expanding network of "kindred and companions" (*C* 51). For Shaftesbury, natural affection is a "herding principle and associating inclination," one that starts with reproduction and child-rearing only to lead to other forms of public "correspondency and union" (*C* 51–52). Like breeding itself, it marks the convergence of nature and culture, as well as the way in which nature can be disciplined into culture. Nation, language, and the trappings of collective life point back to the origin of natural sociability, even as they speak to its limitations.

But like compassion, natural affection is subjected to rigorous interrogation in the *Askêmata*. Here, Shaftesbury admonishes himself "not to think any more of *Naturall affection* in ye imperfect & vulgar sence; but according to the just sense & meaning of the word, & what it imports" (*A* 79). In this redefined sense, he differentiates between the "NATURAL AFFECTION *of a rational creature*, capable of knowing Nature, and of considering the Good & Interest of the Whole" and the "lower" or "subordinate" affections, however natural they might seem:

> This is the Province of the truly Wise Man & who is consciouse of things humane & Divine; how to submit all his Affections to the Rule & Government of the Whole; how to accompany with his whole mind, that supream & perfect Mind & Reason of the Univers. This is *to live according to Nature; to follow Nature*, and *to own & obey Deity*. If I have Friends; I act the part of a Friend: if I am a Father, the part of a Father: if I have a City or Country, I studdy its Good & Interest; I cherish it as I ought; I hazzard my Self for it, & do all y^t in me lyes. (*A* 77–78)

In drawing a contrast between a heightened, Stoic sense of natural affection and its more conventional signification, Shaftesbury immediately qualifies this assertion by detailing what following "the rule and government of the whole" might actually entail:

> If I must no longer be a Father; if Children or Friends are taken from me; If He who gave me a Country & a Nation, take it back, and either by warr or any other means cause it to cease or perish; all is well: I am Free & unconcernd; So that I have done my part for my Country; so y^t I have not been wanting to my Friend; so that I have acted the part of a Father—But shall I not bemoan my Child? shall I be thus indifferent, & unconcern'd? shall I have no more Naturall Affection?—Wretch! consider what it is thou callst Naturall Affection. W^{ch} way canst thou have *Naturall* Affection, whilst this thou callst so, is still retaind? (*A* 78)

In a wrenching about-face, affection for a child or a country becomes not the foundation for "correspondency and union" but its antithesis. Emotions that seemed to correspond with justified belief become, suddenly and unequivocally, mere opinions—false representations that misconstrue "the Rule & Government of the Whole." For Shaftesbury, then, natural affection means two entirely different things, one of which is primal and instinctual, and one of which is decidedly Stoic and dispassionate. Taken up in complicated ways by the Romantics, this dichotomy never really goes away.

In advancing this austere account of natural affection, Shaftesbury seems to revel in his most Houyhnhnm-like guise. But he quickly folds Epictetus into his private reflections with a reminder that *"Of things y^t are; some are of our own power & Jurisdiction: some not"* (*A* 79). Opinions fall within the realm of one's power, and emotion is a principal manifestation of those opinions. However natural, grief at the loss of a child or a country reflects the false opinion that one's good was tied to a particular person or location. From a different angle, even compassion and other beneficent emotions lose their ethical cogency when they obscure the relationship between an individual and the whole. In its perfect form, natural affection was abstract and general, not concrete or particular. This line of thought was hardly confined to his private writings. In *Characteristics*, Shaftesbury describes such an encompassing frame of reference in these terms:

> But lest any should imagine that . . . a small tincture of social inclination should be thought sufficient to answer the end of pleasure in society and give us that enjoyment of participation and community which is so essential to our happiness, we may consider, first, that partial affection, or social love in part, without regard to a complete society or whole, is in itself an inconsistency and implies an absolute

contradiction. Whatever affection we have towards anything besides ourselves, if it be not of the natural sort towards the system or kind, it must be of all other affections the most dissociable and destructive of the enjoyments of society. (*C* 205)

For Shaftesbury, to feel a "small tincture" of sympathy or to experience "social love in part" was to fail to see the forest for the trees. Emotions like grief, parental love, and patriotism were all "partial affections." Focused on a small sliver of society, one's "kind," or perhaps even a single person, they were by necessity capricious, of uncertain duration, and insecure. Over the course of the century, poets and novelists would increasingly adopt these "primary duties and affections" as the basis of their art, but for Shaftesbury the limited sway of these affective commitments illuminated by contrast the austere necessity of a cosmopolitan view.[65]

In *The Moralists*, Theocles regales Philocles with the virtues inherent in such a Stoic perspective: "O Philocles! How little do you know the extent and power of good nature and to what an heroic pitch a soul may rise which knows the thorough force of it and, distributing it rightly, frames in itself an equal, just and universal friendship!" (*C* 256). Looking past the limitations of sympathy and compassion, Theocles, like Shaftesbury himself, redefines the nature of "good nature." Like natural affection in its most exalted form, this just and universal sympathy is predicated on the introspective mandate of Stoic moral psychology. Reconciliation with the universe and its order demands both "freedom from our passions" and a "harmony of the affections" (*C* 334). But for a skeptic like Philocles, such an "enlarged affection" seemed just beyond the bounds of possibility. While acknowledging that he could "compass" a "plain natural love," affection of "this complex, universal sort" seemed at once too abstract and incomprehensible (*C* 256). Later in the century, Lord Kames would pose a similar critique of Shaftesbury's universal benevolence. In his view, elevating the good of the "whole species" at the expense of "partial benevolence" was merely to "build castles in the air."[66] In the 1790s, however, this austere but aspirational castle building entailed a vocabulary that, in Chris Jones's words, "could provoke persecution and imprisonment."[67] Shaftesbury's incipient radicalism would become apparent only in time. Following the crosscurrents of sympathy and Stoicism in the privacy of his notebooks, Shaftesbury landed on an ethical impasse—a disjuncture between the local embeddedness of the affections and the sway of cosmopolitan reason—that would pit Burke against Wollstonecraft and Godwin in the consequential Revolutionary controversy that rocked Britain in the 1790s.

Adam Smith: Stoicism and the "Ordinary Commerce of the World"

Like Shaftesbury, Adam Smith kept looking back to the Stoics in his attempt to illuminate the nature of sympathy and sociability. When Smith assembled a small collection of ancient texts for the edification of the young Duke of Buccleuch, he insisted that his charge acquire two copies of Epictetus, a standard-sized version of the *Discourses* as well as a smaller pocket edition. I am tempted to take Smith's insistence on a second, smaller text as a sly nod to the intellectual portability of Stoicism, and yet it was also a clear affirmation of its suitability for worldly uptake. At once personal and practical, the teachings of Epictetus could come in handy while navigating the world. Smith had carried his own copy of Epictetus's *Enchiridion* around since his university days, and his lifelong interest in the Stoics made a substantial impact on the articulation and evolution of his moral philosophy.[68] In his final edition of the *Theory of Moral Sentiments*—published in the early days of the French Revolution, and just before his death, in July 1790—Smith goes so far as to assert that self-command, with all of its Stoic resonance, is the virtue from which "all the other virtues seem to derive their principal lustre" (*TMS* 241). But if Smith followed Shaftesbury in looking back to Epictetus in advancing a sentimental ethics of the future, he made it clear that his own Stoic formation diverged from the Third Earl's brooding self-reflection and tendency to withdrawal. In his *Lectures on Rhetoric and Belles Lettres*, Smith notes that Shaftesbury's writings suggest a man "of a very puny and weakly constitution," a writer whose "feebleness of body as well as mind" prevents him "from engaging in the pursuits which generally engross the common sort of men."[69] As Wollstonecraft and many later commentators would note, Smith's own *Theory* could hardly lay claim to the multiplicity of perspectives that made up a truly common life. Even so, his account of Stoicism's pivotal role within moral sentimentalism moves what Smith described as Shaftesbury's own interest in "maintaining a proper balance of the affections" in a decidedly public direction (*TMS* 293). Shaftesbury approached Stoicism as an inherently private self-practice that made public life possible. By contrast, Smith saw a flexible version of Stoic moral psychology as integral to the cognitive work of sympathy itself, an alignment that made Stoicism a residual facet of most social experience.

Smith starts by grounding the possibility of sympathy in a central limitation. Distrustful of Hume's account of the way in which "affections readily pass from one person to another," Smith foregrounds our lack of direct access to the feelings of others.[70] If my brother is tied up and tortured on the rack, my senses—and certainly any inchoate moral sense—will never replicate the experience of his suffering. Even so, fellow feeling is not undone by this epistemological skepticism. The incommunicability of the affections only ennobles the imagination, a projective faculty that allows us to inhabit the life situations of others so that we might "form some idea" of the feelings and sensations they produce (*TMS* 9). Though he saw the imagination as almost inevitably prone to overshoot or fall short of its mark, Smith set it at the very heart of our ongoing attempts to assess the sentiments of others as well as our own. The empirical cast of his moral spectatorship is untenable without an element of imaginative expressivity, a necessary condition that has led critics to approach Smithian sympathy as a kind of "virtual reality" in tune with the discursive practices of literature itself.[71] David Marshall, for example, has emphasized the "theatrical situation" of Smith's moral philosophy, while Ian Duncan and Rae Greiner have described Smith as one of the tributaries pouring into the rising tide of fictionality itself, a theorist (in Greiner's words) whose "protocols of sympathy" underwrite "some of realism's most familiar techniques."[72] Smith's proto-phenomenological account of the moral imagination has made him an equally vital touchstone in discussions of that other emergent genre of subjective interiority, the Romantic lyric.

While most attempts to think Smith's *Theory* in literary quarters note his Stoical tendencies in passing, he is most often cast as an expositor of sensibility and the "amiable" virtues of "indulgent humanity." Only rarely does his equally significant embrace of the "awful" virtues of "self-denial" and "self-government" come into focus (*TMS* 23). This is a consequential reorientation, for to use Percy Shelley's famous terms, Smith suggests that it is not just the sympathetic imagination but a Stoic-like regulation of that imagination that allows an individual to "put himself in the place of another and of many others," to experience the pains, pleasures, and feelings of his species as his own.[73] As I will suggest below, Smith parts ways with his Stoic antecedents when it comes to our ability to think meaningfully about beneficence at the scale of the species, those many invisible "others" who fall just outside our ken. At the same time, Stoic detachment was so powerfully embedded within Smith's mechanism of sympathy that it ultimately outstrips that mechanism, becoming for Godwin, Wollstonecraft, and many later writers an illustration of—as well as an answer to—sympathy's glaring insufficiency in a world newly attentive to the suffering wrought and "brought home" by its global systems (*TMS* 9).[74]

While literary studies of sentimentalism tend to shortchange Smith's multifarious Stoicism, it has been a topic of sustained inquiry and fierce debate for Smith's philosophical commentators. For the editors of the Glasgow Edition of Smith's works, Stoicism not only represented the chief influence on Smith's moral philosophical thought but it "permeated his reflection over the whole range of ethics and social science."[75] The significance of this prominence is altogether more controversial: commentators who make a case for Smith's real investment in Stoic ideas are more or less counterbalanced by those who see him as invoking the Stoics only to draw a distinction between an ancient philosophy and his own contrasting position. It is easy enough to see how Smith and the Stoics could seem to stand on two separate sides of an intractable divide.[76] Like other Scottish Enlightenment thinkers, Smith saw emotion, sentiment, and the social affections as central to a new science of man. The vast significance he ascribed to sentiment as the almost unavoidable medium of collective life suggests an obvious rejection of the austerity and "perfect apathy" of the Stoics. Smith himself could draw an unequivocal hard line. In early editions of *Theory*, he differentiated his own moral spectatorship from the emotional intolerance of the Stoics, who "*appear* to have regarded every passion as improper, which made any demand upon the sympathy of the spectator" (*TMS* 273n, emphasis mine). Later, in a moment of rare humor, he suggested that the "metaphysical sophisms" advanced by the ancient Stoics could "seldom serve any other purpose than to blow up the hard insensibility of a coxcomb to ten times its native impertinence" (*TMS* 143). As Emma Rothschild and Samuel Baker have suggested, Smith's take on the otherworldly perfectionism of the Stoics could veer toward irony, as if they could not take a joke.[77]

But Smith's "gentle mockery" of rigid Stoic doctrine went hand in hand with his own contribution to the old attempt to reimagine how Stoicism might be freed from its own native impertinence.[78] Like Seneca and Cicero, he retained an interest in the "imperfect, but attainable virtues" that made up the "practical morality of the Stoics" (*TMS* 291–92). His aggregate take on Stoicism across the *Theory of Moral Sentiments* is suggestively equivocal. Smith was deeply mistrustful of the "sublime doctrines" and "absurd" paradoxes of the Stoics (*TMS* 289, 291). He claims in no uncertain terms that the aloof wisdom of sage-like perfection represented "a miscarriage of every thing which Nature has prescribed to us as the proper business and occupation of our lives" (*TMS* 293). All the same, the tenacity of Smith's interest in the Stoics across several decades of revision suggests an equally significant unwillingness to relinquish their influential moral psychology.

Stripped of its rigid perfectionism, a shadow form of Stoicism manifested most prominently in its evaluative and therapeutic self-discipline was for Smith a fixture of "the business and occupation of our lives."

Smith's intuition about the resonance of Stoicism in public and private life owes as much to sociological description as it does to philosophical prescription. Living the sentimental hustle of everyday life simply involved frequent acts of cultivated insensibility—flattening the pitch of one's passion, or rapidly adopting a "degree of that coolness" toward fortune that often paved the way for composure (*TMS* 22). Passions were all too liable to "rush headlong" toward action and misrecognition, especially if their "violent agitations" were given free reign; even amiable feelings could be "extravagantly disproportioned to the value of their objects" (*TMS* 263, 33). This kind of affective turbulence had fueled Shaftesbury's anxiety that the give-and-take of sociable life could drastically undermine the autonomy of the self. For the Third Earl, the Stoic project of claiming power over these mental impressions—of restoring some sense of proportion between an emotion and its object—necessitated a regime of rigorous, self-reflexive bookkeeping. For Smith, however, Stoic self-examination becomes a part of sociable exchange rather than its quiet supplement. The everyday interactions that so often elicit passionate response also work to interrogate and shape that response.

The well-known mechanics of Smith's sentimental morality turn on an affective disjunction, a rift between the experience of two disparate individuals bridged by two different "efforts." Sympathy—the effort of any person to access via imagination the feelings of another—is predicated on self-command, the ability of that other person "to bring down his emotions to what the spectator can go along with" (*TMS* 23). The formulation is simple enough in theory, but for Smith, this prototypical exchange is almost always a fraught and incommensurate affair: a father who has lost his son, like the sailor who has lost his leg, must exhibit extraordinary feats of self-command to enjoy the merest sympathy from an uninjured spectator. Nor is there anything immediate or contagious about the exchange of sentiment here. In Mary Fairclough's resonant terms, Smith makes sympathy "a quasi-conscious evaluative principle."[79] Two affective capacities converge, and the reciprocal task of imagining the feelings of the other becomes the occasion for a reevaluation of one's own feelings. The most obvious manifestation of Stoic detachment falls on the suffering side of this exchange, with emotional regulation becoming both ticket and condition of entry to the consoling realm of sensibility.[80] And yet for both figures the self-alienating mechanism of sympathy results in a cognitive reappraisal of passion. Seen from a vantage point outside the self, the grieving father can temper his "clamorous grief" into a newly "restrained and corrected" emotion, just as the spectator can transpose an "indolent and passive fellow-feeling" into a more "vigorous and active sentiment" (*TMS* 24, 245, 70). The virtual reality of sympathy is its own kind of therapy, and it does not seem too far-fetched to see both sufferer and spectator as following the lead of Epictetus and Shaftesbury in their attempts to interrogate and exert control over mental impressions. Indeed, the social convergence of perspectives facilitated the kind of mental self-examination that Epictetus was always advocating. As he put it in his *Discourses*, "Socrates said, that we are not to lead an unexamined Life; so neither are we to admit an unexamined Appearance; but to say, 'Stop: let me see what you are, and whence you come.'"[81] Like Stoic discernment, Smith's model of sympathy necessitated "bestowing upon every object the precise degree of attention it deserved" (*TMS* 273).

In this sense, the ethical project of Smith's *Theory* lies not so much in the expansion of affect as in the evaluation of it. The crucial mechanism for this allotment of attention was Smith's impartial spectator, a catalyzing conceptual innovation that would take root across the Romantic generations, showing up in texts as discrepant in their visions of futurity as Godwin's *Political Justice*, Hazlitt's *Essay on the Principles of Human Action*, and Mary Shelley's *The Last Man*.[82] In turning monologic introspection into an imaginatively discursive exchange, Smith looked back to Shaftesbury and his "self-examining practice and method of inward colloquy" (*C* 146), a genre that Mikhail Bakhtin linked to Stoics like Epictetus and Marcus Aurelius who preferred "*an active dialogic approach to one's own self*" over and above "passive self-observation."[83] Intermittently invested with the authority of conscience and social propriety, Smith freighted his "supposed impartial spectator" with many names. Always figured as ubermasculine, the spectator is "the man" or even the "demigod" "within the breast" (*TMS* 130–31). Parrying egotistical self-absorption by imaginative acts of self-division, an individual in the Smithian moral universe constantly reevaluates the partiality of his motives and affections by becoming the spectator of those impressions, by putting himself in what Shaftesbury called "the Place of all" (*A* 254). As Smith puts it, "We can never survey our own sentiments and motives, we can never form any judgment concerning them; unless we remove ourselves, as it were, from our own natural station, and endeavor to view them as at a certain distance from us." It is only through "some secret reference" to the imagined judgment of another that the evaluation of our own sentiments becomes meaningfully available (*TMS* 110). Impartiality in this sociable model of spectatorship is not identical to insensibility, nor is its perspective merely an admonishment toward complete sage-like apatheia. As a heuristic toward self-examination, the impartial spectator's most substantial debt to the Stoics was a methodological one. In Martha Nussbaum's terms, Smith found in Stoicism "a good way of correcting for what is unbalanced and partial in our passions, through the device of the spectator."[84]

The implications of this debt echo throughout the chapters that make up my study, for if Smith's account holds weight, Stoicism stands at the very heart of the Romantic aggrandizement of sympathy. As a conduit of sympathy, the poet recollecting powerful feeling in tranquility is not so different from the Smithian agent who can "enter more coolly into the sentiments of the indifferent spectator" after a "paroxysm of emotion" has passed (*TMS* 157–58).[85] In both cases, the imaginative reconstruction of a feeling is unthinkable without its evaluation. Wordsworth once described Smith as "the worst critic, David Hume not excepted, that Scotland, a soil to which this sort of weed seems natural, has produced," and yet on the Stoical aspect of sympathy they were suggestively aligned.[86] But if Stoicism played a role in Smith's account of sympathy, it was also implicated in the Romantic exploration of that sympathy's asymmetries and inadequacies. On this front Smith's *Theory* is also revelatory.

Adam Smith's Earthquake Drill

Like the Stoics, Smith approached sentiments as propositions or beliefs, a constant stream of opinions and evaluations activated by life in the world. Smith's account of the spectator finds in the imagined, multiperspectival experience of society not only a method for evaluating one's "inward sentiments and feelings," but a recognition that such evaluation is impossible without detachment from the engrossing immediacy of affective experience (*TMS* 147). This vision of impartiality has—early and late—struck many critics as a precarious and illusory ideal, one liable to reflect social conventions rather than advance a true objectivity. Like so many forms of Enlightenment rationality, the liberatory possibilities of Smith's "view from nowhere" can seem little more than the idealized sensibility of a masculine ruling elite. Literary historians have been especially alert to the coercive implications of such a delimited but powerful notion. For David Palumbo-Liu, Smith's impartial spectator threatens to become little more than a "delivery system," a set of social conventions that advance social tranquility by converting "otherness to sameness."[87] In John Bender's influential analysis, Smith's impartial spectator is an almost perfect manifestation of the penitentiary ideal. By facilitating "a system of interlocking psychological representations of punishment," its work is tantalizingly omniscient but also "strenuously normative" and existentially isolating.[88] Thomas Pfau has argued that Smith's commitment to this kind of disciplinary logic can be seen in his "strategic" conversion of his Stoic antecedents. For Pfau, this strategic misreading of the Stoics is a tragically reductive one, a turn away from introspective self-mastery in favor of undue attentiveness to "the social currency of *behavior*" and the "smooth operation of social life."[89]

But if the impartial spectator was born out of the tacit hegemony of a genteel male ethos, it also emerges in Smith's *Theory* as the key imaginative mechanism for transcending that norm, a way of pushing past the localizing presuppositions of any delimited coterie. Stoicism occupies a strikingly hybrid position in Smith's thought. As a social yet introspective method linking self-command to self-evaluation, it is omnipresent in the affective assessments that make up ordinary moral life. But the clarifying power of affective detachment also becomes a fixation for Smith at those points where self-command intersects with sympathy around questions of justice. As a correlative of the impartial spectator, Stoic apatheia works like conscience itself to facilitate the "proper comparison between our own interests and those of other people" (*TMS* 134). Smith takes Stoic cosmopolitanism—and especially the doctrine of *oikeiosis*—as the ultimate impartial guide for transcending "narrow affective entanglements" in an expansive world.[90] At various points, Smith draws a clear analogy between the distancing impulse of the impartial spectator and Stoic ethics themselves:

> Man, according to the Stoics, ought to regard himself, not as something separated and detached, but as a citizen of the world, a member of the vast commonwealth of nature. To the interest of this great community, he ought at all times to be willing that his own little interest should be sacrificed. Whatever concerns himself, ought to affect him no more than whatever concerns any other equally important part of this immense system. We should view ourselves, not in the light in which our own selfish passions are apt to place us, but in the light in which any other citizen of the world would view us. (*TMS* 140–41)

What is Smith's impartial spectator, the cornerstone of his *Theory*, but a reimagination of the Stoic imperative to view ourselves "in the light in which any other citizen of the world would view us"? In both cases, a distanced assessment of personal passion is the requisite precondition for adequately extending our concern past "what particularly concerns ourselves" to the many distant others who make up "this immense system" (*TMS* 140). And yet in spite of the analogy, this ideal of dispassionate world citizenship is a noticeably unstable one in the *Theory of Moral Sentiments*. As a high-water mark for ethical attentiveness, Stoicism also designates a boundary for sympathy, the point at which its beneficent aspirations start to break down. Unlike Shaftesbury, Smith is noticeably skeptical about setting natural affection aside in favor of "a sympathizing of the whole" (*A* 92).

As a perspectival ideal—a clarifying view of our own sentiments from a global vantage point—Smith's use of Stoicism is suggestively contradictory. A moderated form of Stoicism is necessary to redirect what he calls the "natural inequality of our sentiments," the way in which our passive feelings and habitual sympathies bend the world out of proportion (*TMS* 136). But Smith also belabors a striking limit to that redirection, a point beyond which the expansive range of any individual's ethical attentiveness runs up against the "the weakness of his powers" and "the narrowness of his comprehension" (*TMS* 237). Smith confronts this conundrum with a vivid hypothetical scenario in the second edition of his *Theory*: "Let us suppose that the great empire of China, with all its myriads of inhabitants, was suddenly swallowed up by an earthquake, and let us consider how a man of humanity in Europe, who had no sort of connexion with that part of the world, would be affected upon receiving intelligence of this dreadful calamity" (*TMS* 136). Like so many other Enlightenment thinkers, Smith takes up the unsettling philosophical implications of the quake that rocked Lisbon on All Saints' Day in 1755. The Lisbon earthquake was the most forceful seismic event to hit Europe in recorded human history.[91] Displacing this catastrophe while substantially inflating its already unfathomable mortality prompts a stark, demystified reflection on the power of sensibility across vast distances. The "man of humanity in Europe"—an aggressively amiable figure, almost a caricature of Smithian sympathy—is exposed as a rhetorical, insular, and inefficacious being. An earthquake of this magnitude would provoke an outpouring of "melancholy reflections," "humane sentiments," and "fine philosophy." At the same time, it might leave the tranquility of most Europeans largely, even comfortably, intact. A "man of humanity in Europe" could still fall asleep with "the most profound security." The "most frivolous disaster," even the loss of his little finger, might affect him more substantially than the death of millions (*TMS* 136). In the face of this catastrophe, all of the standard outlets of affect are incommensurate with ethical response.

Smith's decision to stage his seismic calamity in China becomes a notable example of what Eric Hayot has described as a long-standing tendency to take China as a seemingly extraneous but in fact revelatory figure of relation for Western modernity. For Hayot, China exists in such examples as "a horizon neither of otherness nor of similarity, but rather of the very distinction between otherness and similarity," a horizon "that marks the limit of the universal as a transcendental field."[92] At this point of clarifying indistinction, the impartial spectator's disinterested spectatorship is especially indispensable, and yet Smith retreats from the equalizing power of its abstract vision. The earthquake scenario leads Smith to consider in turn two philosophical solutions to distant suffering: the sympathetic expansion of sensibility, a move to "feel for others as we naturally feel for ourselves," and the Stoic curtailment of that sensibility, a move to "feel for ourselves as we naturally feel for others" (*TMS* 139). The upshot of the comparison is striking: while Smith drastically qualifies the power of sympathy, he treats Stoicism as a noticeably effectual and yet strikingly unnatural way of mitigating the "natural misrepresentations of self-love" (*TMS* 137).

Though quick to note that more than the equanimity of a European spectator is at stake, Smith undercuts the illusory pretensions of "extreme sympathy," a stance that calls into question its adequacy in less drastic contexts. His point is not a subtle one: for Smith, the force of sympathy simply fades with distance. To interest ourselves in the misfortunes of those who are unknown and far away is "absurd and unreasonable." He describes such long-range sympathy as a kind of "artificial commiseration" that often ends in "affected and sentimental sadness." If we are to address "those miseries which we never saw," Stoic self-command must recalibrate the drift of our amiable but unreliable impulses. In critiquing the mechanism of sympathy he often celebrates, Smith sounds quite a bit like Shaftesbury in his *Askêmata*. The speculative demands of a "vast system" illuminate the paltry power of the moral sense: "It is not the soft power of humanity, it is not that feeble spark of benevolence which Nature has lighted up in the human heart, that is thus capable of counteracting the strongest impulses of self-love" (*TMS* 140, 139, 137). More fundamental to Smith's *Theory* than the "soft power" of sympathy is the ethical evaluation of emotion that precedes it: "it is only by consulting this judge within, that we can ever see what relates to ourselves in its proper shape and dimensions" (*TMS* 137, 134).

Smith's account of sympathy's imperfect operation across long distances owes much to the Stoic doctrine of *oikeiosis*, an influential idea that I will discuss at length in this book's final chapter on Emerson.[93]

Originally formulated by Hierocles but made familiar to figures like Smith by its prominent treatment in Cicero's *De Officiis*, *oikeiosis* resists exact translation. Arising from *oikos*, or household, it conveys a sense of "affinity" or "familiarization." Hierocles imagined human community as a series of concentric circles emanating out from a self to encompass one's family, one's country, and ultimately the entire human community. Connecting a responsibility to self with an imperative for justice, *oikeiosis* bears witness to the reality that human affection diminishes with distance.[94] For the Stoics, however, this intractable reality of existence demanded a different kind of moral effort, a diminishment of sensibility whereby one comes to see distant others and one's nearest neighbors, even one's own family, in an equal light. In blunt terms, scaling back our sympathy even to nothing—feeling less—was the precondition to expanding the range of our concern, to feeling for more. To borrow from Greiner's description of a different case of Smithian insensibility, cosmopolitan detachment "accomplishes more than a championing of Stoical self-control, for a generative open-endedness adheres in that insensible, empty 'nothing.'"[95]

In the wake of his hypothetical earthquake example, Smith reaffirms the link between Stoicism and his own model of impartial spectatorship. Notably suspending his customary skepticism, Smith emphasizes how effectual, proper, and even "natural" such a Stoic aspiration might be:

> How difficult soever it may be to attain this supreme degree of magnanimity and firmness, it is by no means either absurd or useless to attempt it. Though few men have the stoical idea of what this perfect propriety requires, yet all men endeavour in some measure to command themselves, and to bring down their selfish passions to something which their neighbor can go along with. But this can never be done so effectually as by viewing whatever befalls themselves in the light in which their neighbours are apt to view it. The stoical philosophy, in this respect, does little more than unfold our natural ideas of perfection. There is nothing absurd or improper, therefore, in aiming at this perfect self-command. Neither would the attainment of it be useless, but, on the contrary, the most advantageous of all things, as establishing our happiness upon the most solid and secure foundation, a firm confidence in that wisdom and justice which governs the world, and an intire resignation of ourselves, and of whatever relates to ourselves to the all-wise disposal of this ruling principle in nature. (*TMS* 141)[96]

Smith is quick to qualify this striking vision of Stoic possibility: it is, he notes, a model of perfection that is rarely attained. All the same, he characterizes the aspirational expansion of one's neighborhood to encompass the world as anything but absurd. In this pursuit, the impartial spectator effects a redefinition of the natural orientation of affection itself. The most natural affections are not the local, concrete ones that relate to ourselves but the abstract, impartial ones that mark our alignment with the "great community" or "immense system" (*TMS* 140). Productive of both happiness and justice, there is a utopian aspect to this cosmic vision—a reminder, perhaps, of the Stoic roots of Smith's infamous invisible hand.[97] And yet this vision of Stoic possibility would not last. Thirty years after writing this passage, Smith struck it for a less favorable account of Stoic detachment. In 1790, he reaffirms a conventional understanding of the natural affections, arguing that a man who "appears to feel nothing for his own children" would be brutish and detestable (*TMS* 143). In a new history of moral philosophy appended to that edition of the text, Smith suggests that the "sublime contemplation" of the Stoics was incompatible with "every thing which Nature has prescribed to us as the proper business and occupation of our lives" (*TMS* 293). Like Burke, Smith ends by ceding moral priority to our little platoon of friends and family, which was after all the "little department in which we ourselves have some little management and direction" (*TMS* 292).

In backpedaling from his tentative but utopian Stoic vision, Smith suggests that "poets and romance writers" like Richardson, Racine, and Voltaire are "much better instructors than Zeno, Chrysippus, or Epictetus" (*TMS* 143). The idea that poets and novelists might be better purveyors of "private and domestic affections" than Stoic philosophers seems relatively uncontroversial. Such a claim squares with all of the period-defining presumptions about literature at the end of the eighteenth century. Indeed, Smith's own willingness to downgrade philosophy in advancing the cultural capital of literature seems somewhat counterbalanced by the way in which his own moral psychology has become paradigmatic for interpreting that same literature. But this was not the end of the story, for the 1790s would give rise to a redefinition of poetry and romance, one I will suggest approaches these forms as adept at encompassing not just the domestic affections but the Stoic impulse that called those affections into question. Encountering Smith on the other side of revolutionary upheaval, Romantic writers could find in his *Theory* not just an account of sympathy but a theorization of the Stoic dialogism without which that sympathy would remain merely local and inherently limited.

Coda: Wollstonecraft and "Emotions which Reason Deepens"

Shortly after Smith published the *Theory of Moral Sentiments*, Edmund Burke sent him a fan letter, praising his "happy illustrations from common Life and manners" as well as his sublime style, making especial note of "that fine Picture of the Stoic Philosophy towards the end of your first part which is dressed out in all the grandeur and Pomp that becomes that magnificent delusion."[98] The equivocation on display in the phrase "magnificent delusion" is telling, for as I have argued throughout, Smith's tendency to revel and even build on the magnificent possibilities of Stoicism was only slightly less prominent than his acknowledgment of its misleading perfectionism. If Burke too cannot help but acknowledge the allure of the Stoic vision, his ambivalent rhetoric at least makes it clear that Smith did well to explode that vision once and for all. But as my next chapter makes clear, the French Revolution and its concrete pursuit of *liberté*, *égalité*, and *fraternité* made the largely unactuated cosmopolitanism lurking in Shaftesbury's and Smith's thought suddenly pressing. In fact, Burke's own polemical defense of the "the moral constitution of the heart" in *Reflections on the Revolution in France* would catapult the "magnificent delusion" of the Stoics into the center of political and literary discourse in the 1790s.[99]

In pivoting from eighteenth-century moral philosophy to Romanticism itself, I want to suggest that Mary Wollstonecraft's first, swift response to Burke and her subsequent *A Vindication of the Rights of Woman* (1792) draw down the full force of Stoicism within the moral sentimentalist tradition. At first glance this might not seem obvious, for in Wollstonecraft's writing the Stoics are everywhere and nowhere. She rarely mentions a particular Stoic philosopher, and her own reframing of moral sentimentalism resists Smith's urge to recapitulate the history of various systems of moral philosophy. But the impress of Stoicism is evident throughout her writing in several modes, stretching from *Original Stories from Real Life; With Conversations Calculated to Regulate the Affections* (1788) to her more familiar political works. Wollstonecraft was also alert to the way in which the radical potential of Stoicism was clouded by various prejudicial conceits. Reviewing Catherine Macaulay's *Letters on Education* (1790), she noted that "the doctrines of the Stoics are clearly stated by Mrs. M. and some unjust aspersions wiped off, which bigotry and ignorance have industriously propagated, to render doctrines ridiculous or odious, which deserve respect."[100] Like Shaftesbury and Smith, Wollstonecraft looked past misleading caricatures of "odious" Stoic perfectionism to delineate the cosmopolitan vision that a rational, evaluative model of emotion might foster in the fullness of time.

Wollstonecraft's excavation of Stoic moral sentimentalism also entailed a critique of its exclusions. Convinced that Smith's impartiality was a misleading ruse, she noted that any seemingly impartial bystander was captive to "his own prejudices, beside the prejudices of his age or country."[101] Even the pronouns in her critique illustrated the problem: Smith's moral sentimentalism was an inherently masculine affair. As Carol Kay has observed most pointedly, Wollstonecraft was alert to the gendered disparity by which Smith's account of amiable and awful virtues "seems to divide up the whole moral psychology by a suggested sex difference that is not acknowledged."[102] And yet her sense of the exclusions inherent in the "*macho* austerity" of the republican ideal—a vision at once aristocratic, masculine, and Stoical—did not result in its renunciation.[103] In fact, her recuperation of Stoic virtue suggests the expansive possibility of an austere but imperfect ideal, one poised to become more egalitarian and accessible to feminist appropriation. Wollstonecraft's strenuous redefinition lessened the gap between Stoicism and common life even while playing up its radicalism as a counterpoint to sympathy. What Richard Polwhele castigated as the "stern serenity" of Wollstonecraft and other "unsex'd females"—the pursuit of philosophy "midst the democratic storm"—was in many ways the first face of Romantic Stoicism.[104]

Following Shaftesbury, Wollstonecraft's Stoic reappraisal of sensibility had a distinctly cosmopolitan upshot. For Wollstonecraft, the fumes of Burke's blind and incoherent feeling resulted in the scuttling of rational cognition even as they suggested a sentimentalism run amok. In this sense, both *Vindications* represented a notable onslaught against the hollowness and "pampered sensibility" of the figure whose ineffectuality is so damning in Smith's earthquake example: "a man of humanity in Europe."[105] Wollstonecraft placed great stock in "the natural emotions of the heart" yet remained skeptical of any affective morality unconstrained by rationality.[106] Like Shaftesbury and Smith, she evokes an instinctual moral sense only to disavow it, rejecting the idea that there is some "mysterious instinct" in the soul that makes virtue the product of "blind impulse." For Wollstonecraft, all is lost if emotional apprehension is sundered from "the tedious labour of ratiocination."[107] But the question of any individual's navigation of feeling was connected both politically and ethically to a wider world. Countering Burke's sentimental localism, Wollstonecraft champions the Stoic side of sympathy, setting "rational affections" above "partial feelings," while castigating the impulse of a mind that "confines its benevolence" solely to a "narrow circle."[108] Wollstonecraft takes up the central impasse in moral sentimentalism I have been describing throughout the chapter and sets it at the heart of the nascent Revolutionary controversy: How might Stoic detachment facilitate the passage from partial affections to a larger whole?

In the opening salvo of the controversy, Richard Price had proclaimed that "a narrower interest ought always to give way to a more extensive interest."[109] Rather surreptitiously, Shaftesbury's model for privately managing and extending the affections is caught up in the enkindling blaze of a revolution that Price hoped might sweep through Europe. Though acknowledging that Price's reflections were as yet a utopian reverie, Wollstonecraft did not adulterate his "sublime system of morality." As she put it in *A Vindication of the Rights of Men*, "in my eye all feelings are false and spurious, that do not rest on justice as their foundation, and are not concentred by universal love."[110] For Wollstonecraft, the Stoic self-regulation that realigns the passions with reason results in their expansion.

But cued to the differential expectations wrought by gender, Wollstonecraft approached Stoic self-regulation as not just a method for amplifying altruism but one for obtaining agency in the process. Like Shaftesbury, she recognized that Stoicism could elicit a paradoxically expansive range of ethical concern, but in her political theory a similar vein of austere self-culture becomes nothing less than a catalyst for "a revolution in female manners," one in which women might "labour by reforming themselves to reform the world."[111] For Claudia Johnson, this revolutionary labor was a direct outgrowth of the scandal of Burke's effete sensibility, a dereliction of masculine duty that made the "tattered ill-fitting mantle of rational masculinity" newly available for feminist appropriation. After all, someone had to "shoulder the once-masculine virtues of stoic rationalism and self-control."[112] In Wollstonecraft's parsing, the marginalization of Stoic cosmopolitanism within moral sentimentalism was not just a political liability but an opportunity to redraw the gendered boundaries that restricted the moral purview of women by aligning them so indiscriminately with feeling.

In vociferously defending local sympathies and little platoons, Burke made a cultural ideal out of a compulsory narrowing of outlook, one that Wollstonecraft recognized as a hindrance to women everywhere. While observing that women are often thought to possess "more sensibility, and even humanity" than men, Wollstonecraft notes that this acute sensibility is narrowly channeled from the cradle so that women are caught up in "narrow affections, to which justice and humanity are often sacrificed."

In the present state of society, women "have their attention naturally drawn from the interest of the whole community to that of the minute parts." Looking specifically to Smith's *Theory* and coining a new word, Wollstonecraft suggests that women are all too often "*localized*" by their overstretched sensibilities.[113] Rooted in the natural equality of all human beings, Stoic rationality promised an alternative to this gendered provincialism, the possibility of becoming a citizen of the world. For, after all, "miserable indeed, must be that being whose cultivation of mind has only tended to inflame its passions! A distinction should be made between inflaming and strengthening them. The passions thus pampered, whilst the judgement is unformed, what can be expected to ensue?"[114] In the typecast annals of literary history, one answer might be the affective excess of Romanticism itself. But as I will suggest in what follows, Wollstonecraft's clarion call for a mitigated Stoicism that might result in new and expansive forms of autonomy would echo throughout the 1790s, putting Stoicism at the very heart of Romanticism itself.

CHAPTER TWO

Wordsworth and Godwin in "Frozen Regions"

> *Does not the stone rebuke me*
> *For being more stone than it?*
> —SHAKESPEARE, *THE WINTER'S TALE*

IN 1826, HENRY CRABB ROBINSON BROACHED the subject of Wordsworth's posthumous reputation in a letter fraught with prophetic anxiety:

> I assure you it gives me real pain when I think that some future commentator may possibly hereafter write: "This great poet survived to the fifth decennary of the nineteenth century, but he appears to have died in the year 1814, as far as life consisted in an active sympathy with the temporary welfare of his fellow-creatures. He has written heroically and divinely against the tyranny of Napoleon, but was quite indifferent to all the successive tyrannies which disgraced the succeeding times."[1]

In his *Diary*, Robinson had defined indifference as "a want of passion."[2] Here, he sets this unfeeling indifference beside the failure of sympathy as looming signs of a poetic death-in-life, anticipating many future commentators who approach *The Excursion* (1814) as the beginning of the end of Wordsworth's aesthetic and political promise. Accounts of this infamous decline—described by H. W. Garrod as "the most dismal anti-climax of which the history of literature holds record"—frequently posit a connection between Wordsworth's emotional calcification and poetic failure.[3] For Frances Ferguson, his decline was the inevitable result of "the asceticism of his poetics."[4] More dramatically, Michael Cooke described Stoicism as "the enemy of Wordsworth's muse," a philosophical disposition that

[59]

"posed a threat to romantic poetry, to the romantic spirit itself."[5] A further leap of associative logic tends to connect what Thomas McFarland called Wordsworth's "well-known stoicism" with his "well-known political conservatism."[6] In 1933, for example, Edith Batho defended Wordsworth from the many critics who dismissed him as "a reactionary and obscurantist in whom the springs of human pity and feeling had dried up."[7] For Mary Shelley, however, no defense could excuse Wordsworth's lack of feeling and the apostasy it sanctioned. After reading *The Excursion* in September 1814, she noted, quite coolly, "He is a slave."[8]

From Mary Shelley forward, critics have tended to approach *The Excursion* as a clear harbinger of Wordsworth's growing apathy, but critical desire to read the poem as a future-oriented index of change has obscured its retrospective orientation. At almost every turn, Wordsworth's various avatars in *The Excursion* pause to interrogate the moral significance of emotion, often entertaining a Stoic perspective that thwarts expectations about the inherently affective underpinnings of Romanticism. For Wordsworth, this was not a diminished perspective, but the late echo of a philosophical stance that had captured his attention in the radical 1790s. In this chapter, I argue that his sustained consideration of Stoicism in *The Excursion* involved a self-conscious reexamination of his early attraction to the radical philosophy of William Godwin. Though the product of a very different political context, Wordsworth's dialogic critique of passion in *The Excursion* resembles his response to an earlier and more revolutionary moment, to a time when he counted himself "amongst the dispassionate advocates of liberty and discussion."[9] In a broader philosophical context, Wordsworth's reassessment of Godwinian thought in *The Excursion* marks him as an inheritor of the impasse in eighteenth-century moral philosophy that I examined in the last chapter. For both Wordsworth and Godwin, the attempt to reconcile Stoicism with everyday life prompted a turn back to eighteenth-century moralists like Shaftesbury and Adam Smith, both of whom approached Stoicism as integral to sociability and broad justice. Far from replacing what Northrop Frye called a "reptilian Classicism" with a "mammalian Romanticism," writers like Wordsworth and Godwin inherited an ethics of sentiment already radically destabilized by its Stoic foundations.[10]

Though overshadowed by the rhetoric of passion and powerful feeling, Stoicism constituted a central but equivocal set of ideas in Romantic writing. In a series of important essays, Bruce Graver has argued that the ancient Stoics offered one of the most thorough and well-known accounts of affective experience available to Romantic writers. In his terms,

"Romantic theories of emotion begin with the Stoics, and thus are fundamentally, and paradoxically, classical."[11] For Graver and scholars attuned to the survival of Stoicism within Romanticism, Wordsworth has always been a crucial figure. The singular prominence of Wordsworth's Stoicism in the period owes much to Jane Worthington's mid-twentieth-century observation that his poetry was suffused by "a wealth of pure Stoic philosophy expressed in language frankly reminiscent of the Latin writers."[12] Building on Worthington's insight, many critics have been alert to what Lionel Trilling once described as "the Wordsworthian quality that is very close to Stoic *apatheia*, to not-feeling."[13]

Rather than make another case for Wordsworth's Stoic credentials, I argue in this chapter that his philosophical poetry reflects—and continues to be reflected by—a crucial facet of Stoicism's reception in Romanticism and, by extension, in modernity: the way in which its restraint was variably portrayed as revolutionary or acquiescent. This indeterminacy has uniquely shaped Wordsworth's critical fortunes.

Stoicism is often described as inherently conservative, an affirmation of detachment and determinism that sets aside any hope of altering the reality of a given world. Pope's famous line from the *Essay on Man*— "Whatever IS, is RIGHT"—reflects a trust in the providential order of the universe that resonates with a classic Stoic view of how the physical world operates.[14] In the face of such an intractable world, Stoic moral psychology can seem little more than "a technique for 'surviving' the world rather than reforming it."[15] Hegel endorses this sense of Stoicism's delimited possibilities in *The Phenomenology of Spirit* (1807), a Romantic-era text that has had an outsized impact on literary theory and modern thought. Critical accounts that link Wordsworth's apathy—from the Greek *apatheia*, "without feeling"—to his reactionary politics share broad commonalities with Hegel's discussion of Stoicism in the *Phenomenology*. For Hegel, Stoicism is the product of a "time of universal fear and bondage," a slave ideology that mistakes detachment as a form of freedom.[16] From this Hegelian perspective, the kind of poetical retreat embraced by Wordsworth and the Lake Poets resembles the self-defeating outlook of an unhappy consciousness, a precursor to egotistical sublimity and its solipsism. For Wordsworth, however, the distinctly radical deployment of Stoicism in the 1790s made it more than an abstract, acquiescent stage in the evolution of mind. Wordsworth first encountered Roman Stoicism via Seneca and Cicero at Hawkshead Grammar School, and both writers were well represented in his library at Rydal Mount.[17] But for Wordsworth, the specific contours of classical Stoicism were ultimately eclipsed by its outsized significance in the 1790s, a moment in which Stoicism and revolution went hand in hand. In this heightened context, the most influential Stoic thinker to cross Wordsworth's path was not Seneca or Epictetus, but Godwin.

Godwin's *Enquiry Concerning Political Justice* (1793) resists easy classification and tends to be allied with a kaleidoscopic array of philosophical positions, ranging from anarchism and utilitarianism to moral perfectionism. For Wordsworth, however, the antipathy to emotion and private affections on display in the first edition of *Political Justice* aligned it with the philosophy of the Stoics above all else. Wordsworth's most direct account of his fascination with Godwinian philosophy appears in *The Prelude*. Disregarding the complexity of Godwin's nine-hundred-page treatise, he underscores instead the dispassionate orientation of Godwin's philosophical attempt

> to abstract the hopes of man
> Out of his feelings to be fix'd thenceforth
> For ever in a purer element. (*Prelude* 10:807–9)

Neglecting questions of property, punishment, and gratitude, Wordsworth links both the appeal and the inadequacy of Godwin's system to the critique of passion that informs its politics. In describing Godwinian disinterestedness as a "tempting" scheme that makes space for the passions "to work / And never hear the sound of their own names," he portrays Godwin's rejection of emotion as deceptive and self-aggrandizing, an illusion in which enthusiasm is fueled by the semblance of its absence (*Prelude* 10:810, 812–13). But what looks like a dismissive oversimplification actually anticipates Godwin's own substantive critique. When Godwin drew up a list of the principal errors that undermined the first edition of *Political Justice*, all three of his objections fell in line with Stoicism, broadly conceived:

> The Enquiry concerning Political Justice I apprehend to be blemished principally by three errors. 1. Stoicism, or an inattention to the principle, that pleasure and pain are the only bases upon which morality can rest. 2. Sandemanianism, or an inattention to the principle, that feeling, and not judgement, is the cause of human actions. 3. the unqualified condemnation of the private affections.[18]

By the time Wordsworth and Coleridge published *Lyrical Ballads*, Godwin had twice revised *Political Justice*, with each successive version moderating his Stoic outlook by placing new emphasis on "private affections" and the role of feeling in "human actions." In attributing his dispassionate perspective to Sandemanianism—a particularly strict form of religious dissent—Godwin acknowledged the irrational roots of his own Enlightenment project, one in which the hyperrational perfectibility of *Political Justice* springs from a deep religiosity rather than a secular critique.[19] With its Christian substratum and flexible moral psychology, Godwin's revised conception of Stoicism bears more than a passing resemblance to Wordsworth's moderated Stoicism in *The Excursion*. Indeed, the conflation of piety and Stoic philosophy makes Godwin's radicalism surprisingly consonant with what Willard Spiegelman has described as Wordsworth's "mature, even preacherly stoicism."[20] In *The Prelude*, however, Wordsworth relies on a static, uncritical conception of Godwin, one that occludes revisions to *Political Justice* as well as the increasingly moderate position that both writers came to share. The centrality of *The Prelude* in the Romantic canon has only exacerbated this misprision, helping to make Godwin—in Mark Canuel's formulation—"one of the most misunderstood of all Romantic writers."[21] For Wordsworth and so many later Wordsworthians, it has been easy to follow Coleridge in dismissing Godwin's ethical thought as little more than a "Stoical Morality which disclaims all the duties of Gratitude and domestic Affection."[22]

At the same time, Wordsworth's skeptical critique of Godwinian Stoicism was a paradoxical product of his own desire. The formidable detachment that Godwin extolled held a sublime appeal that cut through Wordsworth's retrospective irony:

> what delight!
> How glorious! in self-knowledge and self-rule
> To look through all the frailties of the world
> And, with a resolute mastery shaking off
> The accidents of nature, time, and place
> That make up the weak being of the past,
> Build social freedom on its only basis,
> The freedom of the individual mind,
> Which, to the blind restraint of general laws
> Superior, magisterially adopts
> One guide, the light of circumstances, flash'd
> Upon an independent intellect. (*Prelude* 10:818–29)

In Wordsworth's brief rendering, Godwinian "self-rule" resembles what I described as the strikingly cognitive tenor of Shaftesbury's Stoicism in the last chapter. Since experience of the world results from one's perception of it—with all of the volition and judgment that perception implies—any individual has a power over circumstance and its affective resonance.

Shaftesbury's favorite passage from Marcus Aurelius noticeably falls in line with Wordsworth's account of Godwin's position: "ALL depends on your opinions: These are in your power" (*C* 423). At first glance, Wordsworth seems to summarize this position only in order to dismiss it, but Jonathan Wordsworth has drawn attention to his noticeable attempt to deflect the "obvious comparisons between Godwinian arrogance and Wordsworthian egotistical solitude."[23] Linking social and political freedom to a more integral mental freedom, Wordsworth discredits Godwinian philosophy by suggesting that its absurd faith in rationality makes it paradoxically irrational. But fractures in Wordsworth's satirical control point to a fascination that counterbalances his critique. Though changed by time and circumstance, the "indisturb'd delight" that Wordsworth attributed to Godwin's scheme reappears at the end of *The Prelude* in a rhapsodic celebration of the "genuine Liberty" of a mind that has "sovereignty within and peace at will" (*Prelude* 10:838, 13:122, 114).

Wordsworth's disenchantment with Godwin's unfeeling philosophy tends to be flagged as a central rupture in his poetic development, but only because Wordsworth himself forcefully set the precedent for this partition. In his abbreviated and unpublished "Essay on Morals" (1798), he claimed that "such books as Mr Godwyn's" fall short of "their intended good purposes" because they fail not only to "melt into our affections" but to incorporate themselves "with the blood & vital juices of our minds."[24] Put simply, Godwin's model of morality was too abstract for a poet attempting to write a new kind of poetry attentive to "the fluxes and refluxes of the mind when agitated by the great and simple affections of our nature."[25] In spite of these self-defensive assertions, the Stoic outlook that Wordsworth found in *Political Justice* outlasted his various political commitments and shaped his mature ethical sensibility. If this unexpected continuity belies Wordsworth's simplistic account of a swerve away from abstract philosophy toward passionate poetry, it also unsettles the privileged place that emotion and affect tend to occupy in Romantic ethics and aesthetics. In *The Spirit of the Age* (1825), William Hazlitt compared Godwin's extreme objectivity to William Parry's thwarted quest for an arctic transit from the Atlantic to the Pacific. The conceit allowed him to depict the Romantic valorization of passion as the happy by-product of an ethical fascination with a place beyond passion:

> Captain Parry would be thought to have rendered a service to navigation and his country, no less by proving that there is no North-West Passage, than if he had ascertained that there is one: so Mr. Godwin has rendered a service to moral science, by attempting (in vain) to pass

the Arctic Circle and Frozen Regions, where the understanding is no longer warmed by the affections, nor fanned by the breeze of fancy![26]

Much of Wordsworth's poetry celebrates the power and warmth of those affections, and yet *The Excursion* shows that Wordsworth, like Godwin, was prone to tarry in those "Frozen Regions" of the mind. In charting a philosophical continuity that transcends obvious shifts in ideology, my argument revisits James Chandler's insight that Wordsworth's "programmatic poetry," influenced by Edmund Burke, was "conservative from the start."[27] Chandler's exposition of Wordsworth's latent Burkeanism points to the possibility of an alternative coherence. If Burke's account of sentiment and prejudice colors even Wordsworth's radical years, then the Stoicism of Godwin's system—"the grandeur of its views, and the fortitude of its principles"—could easily inform a later text like *The Excursion*.[28] Burke's influence was, in Chandler's terms, "a touchy subject" that Wordsworth "preferred not to face."[29] The same could be said of Godwin's Stoicism: willfully overlooked but never abandoned, its insistent reappearance in *The Excursion* disrupts the complacency that lets generalizations about Wordsworth's politics eclipse his central ethical commitments.

The Perils of Revolutionary Stoicism

In 1799, Robert Southey confessed that at the height of the French Revolution he had "counteracted Rousseau by dieting upon Godwin and Epictetus."[30] Seven years later, he offered a more elaborate account of his revolutionary Stoicism: "I carried Epictetus in my pocket till my very heart was ingrained with it. . . . [T]he longer I live, & the more I learn, the more am I convinced that Stoicism, properly understood, is the best & noblest system of morals."[31] In the polemical debates surrounding the French Revolution, reason was often pitted against sentiment in the fraught attempt to isolate the true foundation of political justice. Burke's sensibility deviated from the dispassionate rationalism of figures like Godwin, who saw the progress of truth as indebted not to "the frenzy of enthusiasm, but [to] the calm, sagacious and deliberate effort of reason" (*PJ* 111). While Godwin himself was often depicted as a "caricature of the unfeeling rationalist, the coldest-blooded metaphysician of the age," Southey's emphatic recollection of his revolutionary interest in Epictetus points to a different story, one that attests to the significance and ideological complexity of Stoicism in a revolutionary age.[32] Indeed, the explicit, public, and insistent association of Stoicism and revolutionary culture makes Wordsworth's and

Godwin's self-proclaimed attraction to Stoic ethics representative of a much broader tendency.

Shuttled between various ideological persuasions, Stoic philosophy was a point of contention in both radical and reactionary responses to the French Revolution. In *Reflections on the Revolution in France*, Edmund Burke deployed Stoic caricature to ridicule French politicians who aped a "bold, hardy genius" in espousing paradoxical principles that ran contrary to nature:

> These paradoxes become with them serious grounds of action, upon which they proceed in regulating the most important concerns of the state. Cicero ludicrously describes Cato as endeavouring to act in the commonwealth upon the school paradoxes which exercised the wits of the junior students in the stoic philosophy. If this was true of Cato, these gentlemen copy after him in the manner of some persons who lived about his time—*pede nudo Catonem*.[33]

For Burke, the mark of a "true lawgiver" was a "heart full of sensibility." In falling prey to the prevalent idea that "an unfeeling heart, and an undoubting confidence, are the sole qualifications for a perfect legislator," members of the National Assembly substituted calculation and hubristic speculation for what Wordsworth would later call "the primary laws of our nature."[34] Impervious to the claims of real life, Stoicism became, for Burke, a tenuous school exercise.

Burke's critique of fashionable French Stoicism alludes to a fundamental question posed by Horace in his *Epistles*: "If Anyone imitates Cato, stern of face, barefooted and wearing mean clothes, does he also represent the morals and virtue of Cato?"[35] The stakes of the broad association between Stoicism and revolution in the 1790s rest on how one answers such a question, for as Dorinda Outram has argued, classical Stoicism served as a ready source of rhetoric and "role-playing models" for French politicians attempting to replace the values of an aristocratic culture with individual virtue and self-sovereignty. For Outram, such political theater balanced a modest philosophical pretext with an ambitious practical agenda.[36] For Robespierre, St. Just, and other Jacobins, much could be gained by approximating the detachment of a figure like Cato, who would embrace death over tyranny, or the severity of a figure like Brutus, who would sacrifice his sons to preserve the Republic. But in emulating the sublime detachment of a Brutus or a Cato, authority and symbolism outweighed the value of philosophical precision. The doctrinal particulars of revolutionary Stoicism were less important than its ubiquity.

Robespierre, for example, argued before the National Convention that while the "idle hypotheses of various philosophers" were more important to metaphysicians and "eternal wranglers" than practical legislators, the example of Stoicism could exert a powerful force in political life. After praising Cato's and Brutus's dedication to "the sublime sect of the Stoics" and its founder Zeno, he described the emulation of the Stoics as valuable in moments of political turmoil and transition:

> Cato never wavered between Epicurus and Zeno. Brutus and his illustrious colleagues, who shared his dangers and his glory, also belonged to the sublime sect of the Stoics, who entertained such exalted views of the dignity of man. Stoicism produced the noble emulation of Brutus and of Cato, in the fearful epochs that followed the fall of Roman liberty; that preserved the honour of human nature, degraded, not only by the vices of the descendants of Caesar, but by the criminal apathetic patience of the people.[37]

Disambiguated from an apathy that tolerates tyranny, Robespierre's Stoicism sets personal passion aside and endures sacrifice and hardship to preserve liberty. Surpassing mere emulation, Brutus's and Cato's inflexible love of liberty gave rise to a pervasive new iconography in revolutionary France: a bust of Brutus stood beside the orator's tribune at the National Convention, and Parisians could stroll down recently renamed streets like the Rue de Brutus or the Rue de Cato.[38]

Though eliding the philosophical complexity of Stoic ethics, such iconography and nomenclature spoke to the powerful resonance of Stoic detachment in both France and Britain. As French cathedrals were converted into Temples of Reason, Robespierre and the National Convention replaced Christianity with a "cult of the Supreme Being." This transformation called, among other things, for yearly festivals dedicated "to heroism," "to disinterestedness," and "to stoicism."[39] Nor was the British press blind to Robespierre's Stoic playacting: in 1794, the *Whitehall Evening Post* claimed that he was born "almost without any passion whatever, or rather endowed with the powerful art of hiding all those passions which might endanger his popularity and impair his success."[40] Similarly, a correspondent for the *Sun* observed that Robespierre, affecting the utmost simplicity, had "worn the same coat nearly these two years" and lodged "at a Carpenter's house, with all the plainness of a Stoic philosopher."[41] These critiques of Robespierre's disingenuousness point toward a skepticism that many British readers shared. In a parliamentary debate on the course of the war with France, Charles James Fox linked French Stoicism with "the brutality of savages" and warned that, if unchecked, it would spread across Europe and "overwhelm the World." The *Sun* reported his speech as follows:

> In common with every friend to Mankind, he must lament that the horrible massacres which were daily perpetrating in France, and the general misery in which the European World was involved, seemed unfortunately to have had the effect of hardening the hearts of men.... In parting with those sympathetic feelings which lead us to participate in the joys or sorrows of our fellow-creatures, we had relinquished the best attributes of our Nature, and the strongest safeguard of our Virtue.... Such cold and selfish Stoicism, so contrary to the beauty of the Christian System, and so subversive of the true dignity of Man, ought to be checked in its progress, lest Europe should once more become barbarous, and ignorance, cruelty and darkness once more overwhelm the World.[42]

Over the course of the 1790s, Burke's widely disseminated disenchantment with abstract rights prompted a broad reinvestment in the power of the public affections at the expense of Stoic philosophy. Indeed, after the execution of Robespierre, the distance separating the spectacle of revolutionary Stoicism from authentic dispassion became all too apparent.

But retrospective critique does not diminish the allure of Stoicism in the early 1790s. For Wordsworth, the experience of revolutionary Stoicism was channeled most pointedly through Godwin's philosophy. Like Robespierre, Godwin was a self-proclaimed emulator of Cato from an early age.[43] Later, in *Political Justice*, he translated Cato's iconographic Stoicism into a political principle, asserting that the "man, who is accustomed upon every occasion to consult his reason, will speedily find a habit of this nature growing upon him, till the just and dispassionate value of every incident that befals him will come at length spontaneously to suggest itself" (*PJ* 197–98). *Political Justice* boldly probed the efficacy of cool reason applied to "extreme cases," but primarily in the hope that Stoic detachment would become a facet of ordinary experience (*PJ* 198). For Godwin, crisis was the backdrop against which the "calm, sagacious, and deliberate effort of reason" emerged most forcefully (*PJ* 111). While Burke held crises like the mob attack on Versailles as "events" in which "passions instruct our reason," Godwin adopted a contrary stance.[44] In a notorious example of this dispassionate doctrine, he asks in *Political Justice* whether a man whose palace was in flames should save François Fénelon, the archbishop of Cambrai, or his own mother from a burning garret. Elevating the greater good over his own little platoon, Godwin claims that since

Fénelon will benefit the cause of justice much more than one's mother, he should be saved: after all, "What magic is there in the pronoun 'my,' to overturn the decisions of everlasting truth?" (*PJ* 50).

What Charles Lamb called Godwin's "famous fire case" was a more theoretical version of Brutus's willingness to sacrifice his sons for the greater good of the Republic. Both cases turned on a Stoic ethic that set "the benefit of the whole" above merely partial passions (*PJ* 49). As Peter Singer and others have noted, the varying responses to Godwin's notorious thought experiment mapped out the boundaries of a fierce debate over impartialism in ethics that continues to resonate.[45] Published just before the Reign of Terror, *Political Justice* catapulted Godwin into "the firmament of reputation"; as Hazlitt put it, "no one was more talked of, more looked up to, more sought after."[46] But the backlash was fierce, and many of Godwin's Romantic contemporaries would have taken solace in Bernard Williams's famous contention that searching for a justification to prioritize one's mother or one's wife when confronted with a disaster was simply to have "one thought too many."[47] At the same time, the extremity of the example crystallized, for Godwin, a virtue that could take milder forms in common life. For Wordsworth, Godwinian Stoicism ultimately takes root not in the realm of abstract political philosophy, but amid distinctly ordinary life.

Resolution, Independence, and Indifference

Wordsworth's lyrics are populated by figures whose quiet endurance and emotional vacuity testify to his deep interest in the efficacy of everyday Stoicism. Unaccountably placid and always passive, and hardly acting though acted-upon, figures like Michael, Margaret, the discharged soldier, and the Old Cumberland Beggar all explore emotional detachment as a virtue that emerges out of "incidents and situations from common life."[48] The leech-gatherer in "Resolution and Independence" stands as an especially central example of Wordsworth's post-Godwinian attempt to examine the value of detachment, fortitude, and emotional regulation. In the poem, Wordsworth invokes the fate of Chatterton and Burns to testify to an affective imbalance that had, at times, overshadowed his own existence. For Wordsworth, the problem was precisely that

> It sometimes chanceth, from the might
> Of joy in minds that can no farther go,
> As high as we have mounted in delight
> In our dejection do we sink as low.[49]

Countering this vacillation, the leech-gatherer emerges in this poem as a paradigm of tempered equipoise. Though hardly attempting to forge new social freedoms or overleap "the blind restraint of general laws," the leech-gatherer resembles a simplified rendition of Wordsworth's Godwinian fantasy in *The Prelude*: "shaking off / The accidents of nature, time, and place," he looks through the frailty of the world and becomes, for Wordsworth, an exemplar of wise forbearance (*Prelude* 10:826, 10:821–22). It is almost as if the title of the poem anticipates Wordsworth's Godwinian satire in *The Prelude*. With his own "*resolute* mastery" and "*independent* intellect," the leech-gatherer becomes an uncanny pastoral manifestation of virtues that Wordsworth associated with Godwin's philosophy (*Prelude* 10:821, 829, my emphases).

Wordsworth's initial figurative description of the leech-gatherer marks his fascination not with the old man's virtue or constancy but with his sublime insensibility:

> As a huge Stone is sometimes seen to lie
> Couch'd on the bald top of an eminence;
> Wonder to all who do the same espy
> By what means it could thither come, and whence;
> So that it seems a thing endued with sense:
> Like a Sea-beast crawl'd forth, which on a shelf
> Of rock or sand reposeth, there to sun itself.[50]

While the remarkable simile here is often thought to be the beastly one, Wordsworth's figurative equation of a man and a stone carries more philosophical weight. In imagining the leech-gatherer as a stone on top of an eminence, Wordsworth isolates a perspective from which profound autonomy appears incommensurate with any explicable means; as he put it in his *Guide to the Lakes*, such stones defy "conjecture as to the means by which they came thither."[51] But the obscurity of means to an end can hardly stand as proof of vigorous autonomy, for to aspire to the condition of a stone is to be both a product and a part of nature's process. Wordsworth's recumbent sea-beast points tacitly to Hobbes, whose chapter "Of the Liberty of Subjects" in *Leviathan* asserts that "when the impediment of motion is in the constitution of the thing itself, we use not to say it wants the liberty, but the power, to move, as when a stone lieth still or a man is fastened to his bed by sickness."[52] Devoid, as Wordsworth himself acknowledges, "of so much of the indications of life and motion," the stone marks a transposition of Godwin's inherently political Stoicism, a swerve away from a discourse of political liberty to a more essential kind of agency.[53] Hobbes had characterized the stone's immobility as an incapacity. In "Resolution and Independence," Wordsworth claims that the ability to remain unmoved is in fact its own kind of power.

Obdurate and unfazed by shifting fate and fortune, the figure of the stone exemplifies Wordsworth's latent attraction to a Stoicism that the leech-gatherer comes to represent. Paul Fry has emphasized the centrality of stoniness in Wordsworth's poetry, playfully riffing on "A slumber did my spirit seal" to observe that "'rocks and stones' make up two-thirds of the Wordsworthian cosmos."[54] Fry reads Wordsworth's "minerality" as a grayscale testament to "the ontic unity of all things," but this identification is predicated on the long-standing power of stone to signify what Fry calls "philosophical calm."[55] Stoniness was, after all, an old trope for the dispassionate bearing of the Stoic sage. In Elizabeth Carter's translation of Epictetus, an encounter with the Stoic philosopher himself is compared to meeting "a Stone, or a Statue."[56] In 1804, Coleridge wrote to Wordsworth and compared himself to Mortimer from *The Borderers*, confessing that he longed "to retire into stoniness & to stir not, or to be diffused upon the winds & have no individual Existence."[57] Unswayed by pain, pleasure, or any other emotion, the stone in these examples becomes an emblem—almost a caricature—of Stoic detachment. Acknowledging the pleasure he felt in contemplating "the fortitude, independence, persevering spirit, and the general moral dignity of this old man's character," Wordsworth adopts the very fact of his imperturbability as a "stay secure" that might counterbalance an irresolution endemic to the poetic vocation.[58]

By channeling reflections on Stoic detachment through the figure of the stone, Wordsworth separated a philosophical attitude from both its customary rhetoric and its political extremity. His attempt to write about Stoicism in verse bears out Simon Jarvis's sense that Wordsworth's poetic thinking often involves an attempt "to obstruct, displace or otherwise change the syntax and the lexicons currently available for the articulation" of singular philosophical experience.[59] In Henry Crabb Robinson's compressed terms, Wordsworth "reclothes his *idea* in an individual dress which expresses the essential quality, and has also the spirit and life of a sensual object, and this transmutes the philosophic into a poetic exhibition."[60] Displacement and realignment were especially vital to Wordsworth's reflections on Stoicism, for, as I argue above, the revolutionary deployment of its lexicon made it perilous to register a deep interest in Stoicism in the aftermath of the French Revolution. At the same time, transmuting Stoic ideas into a stonelike form put Wordsworth in close proximity to a system that he would take great pains to disclaim in *The Prelude*. In a striking coincidence that unsettles the standard, simplified account of Wordsworth's renunciation of Godwinian rationality, both authors invoked the trope of the stone to account for their evolving perspectives on Stoicism. For Wordsworth, the stone signified a kind of aspiration; for Godwin, it came to represent the overextension of unfeeling rationality in *Political Justice*.

Wordsworth read Godwin's *Things as They Are; or, The Adventures of Caleb Williams* in 1795.[61] Given his intimate acquaintance with Godwin, he might have been familiar with its original unpublished ending, in which a drugged and despondent Caleb claims, "True happiness lies in being like a stone."[62] As a radical examination or "symbolical enactment" of his views in *Political Justice*, *Caleb Williams* captures both the ambition and the austerity of Godwin's benevolent perfectibility.[63] Yet by the time Wordsworth was confronting his own moral crisis over the efficacy of abstract reason, Godwin was significantly qualifying his own philosophical commitments. In revisions to *Political Justice* in 1796 and 1798, Godwin reacted against the "*Principle of the Stoics*" that elevates virtue "into something impossible and unmeaning," and he conceded that disinterested benevolence must be rooted in pleasure, sympathy, and the affections (*PPW* 4:208–9). In *The Enquirer* (1797), he forcefully denounced "an intemperate spirit of philosophy" and warned that the "sect that carried this spirit to the most ridiculous extreme among the ancients, were the Stoics" (*PPW* 5:150). Chastened by the reception of *Political Justice* as well as the death of Mary Wollstonecraft, Godwin vehemently condemned the extreme emotional austerity that he and the Stoics once held in common.

Like Wordsworth, Godwin was enacting a form of self-critique, one that foregrounded his increasingly moderate stance by repressing the severity that had once characterized his deeply held philosophical convictions. In *The Enquirer*, he reframed a sentiment of Hume's to deflate the value of his own Stoic inheritance:

> I can guess very nearly what I should have been, if Epictetus had not bequeathed to us his Morals, or Seneca his Consolations. But I cannot tell what I should have been, if Shakespeare or Milton had not written. The poorest peasant in the remotest corner of England, is probably a different man from what he would have been but for these authors. (*PPW* 5:141)[64]

In closing his Seneca and opening his Shakespeare, Godwin previews his professional turn from philosophical to literary labor and sets himself up as a self-purported new man of feeling.[65] But the transition was never completely effected. Continually negotiating the divide between emotional responsiveness and its antithesis, Godwin often invoked the stone as a mediating trope. Overturning his definition of happiness in *Caleb Williams*, Godwin almost replicates Wordsworth's turn toward emotion in his "Essay on Morals," a move that placed him squarely in the realm of an ethics of sentiment:

> A sound morality requires that *nothing human should be regarded by us as indifferent*; but it is impossible we should not feel the strongest interest for those persons we know most intimately, and whose welfare and sympathies are united to our own. True wisdom will recommend to us individual attachments; for with them our minds are more thoroughly maintained in activity and life than they can be under the privation of them, and it is better that man should be a living being, than a stock or a stone. (*PPW* 2:179)[66]

Qualifying his own earlier conviction that insensibility could foster extensive benevolence, Godwin, like Wordsworth, bids farewell to "the Heart that lives alone."[67] But as Julie Carlson notes so astutely, even Godwin's late-breaking defense of household intimacy insists that the maintenance of detachment remains "central to the home's capacity to facilitate justice."[68] In spite of his clearly articulated "revolutions of opinion," Godwin recognized that a life of straight-up sentiment could be just as hopeless as a life of uncompromising Stoicism.[69] Wordsworth's own uncertainty and irresolution had been allayed by the figure of a stonelike man on top of an eminence, but like Godwin, much of his career would involve accounting for the cost of that security, its value as well as its limitations.

The Purer Element: Essay on Sepulchres *and* The Excursion

Critics often approach *The Excursion* along Victorian lines, allowing its pieties to obscure its revisionary commitments. As such, Wordsworth's invocation of "reason's steadfast rule" in 1814 might seem different in kind from Godwin's appeal to the "calm, sagacious and deliberate effort of reason" in 1793—yet another manifestation of the reduced scope and splendor of Wordsworth's earlier views (*E* 4:91; *PJ* 111). But as the first published installment of Wordsworth's long-deferred *Recluse* project, *The Excursion* takes up the traumas and moral quandaries of the 1790s, exploring latent continuities between his mature ethical outlook and his youthful commitments. Adopting many of the conventions of philosophical dialogue, the poem recounts the lofty conversation that occurs between a Poet, a sagacious pedlar (called the Wanderer), a despondent Solitary, and a rural Pastor—all of whom are imperfect avatars of Wordsworth himself. At once retrospective and self-reflexive, *The Excursion* revisits Wordsworth's early attraction to revolutionary Stoicism while also exploring its modulation and influence over time. This preoccupation was hardly surprising, for the political overtones of ancient philosophy had long been understood as a facet of the *Recluse* project. In 1799, Coleridge had imagined it as "a poem in blank verse addressed to those who, in consequence of the complete failure of the French Revolution, have thrown up all hopes of the amelioration of mankind, and are sinking into an almost epicurean selfishness, disguising the same under the soft titles of domestic attachment and contempt for visionary *philosophes*."[70] While the Solitary conflates Stoic and Epicurean pursuits of "independent happiness," the poem itself fixates on the diffusion of Stoicism in common life, obsessively monitoring its immunities as well as its liabilities (*E* 3:388). In deviating from Coleridge's initial plan, Wordsworth echoes Shaftesbury in distinguishing between an Epicureanism directed toward "inaction and retreat" and a Stoicism that remained attuned to "action, concernment in civil affairs, [and] religion."[71] For Wordsworth, Coleridge's sense of an undifferentiated fall from revolutionary amelioration into unfeeling philosophical solitude was too reductive a vision.

Wordsworth's retrospective investigation of Stoic virtue in *The Excursion* makes a contrasting case for the powerful indeterminacy of unfeeling philosophy. The destabilizing power of Stoic moral autonomy lives on alongside its role in the work of mourning, and a philosophical catalyst for revolution hauntingly coincides with the endurance necessary to surmount that revolution's failure, or failure more generally.[72] Even the "rules and habits" of lives lived "within the sphere of little things" quietly echo the Stoic ethos of Godwin's abstract morality (*E* 3:617–18). At the same time, Wordsworth's aversion to broadcasting his long-standing debts to both Godwin and Stoicism magnifies the significance of seemingly subtle cues—in this case, their shared fascination with the monumental function of "senseless stone."[73]

In 1811, Wordsworth wrote a perfunctory letter to Godwin that ended with a somewhat imperious request: "If you can command a Copy of your book upon Burial, which I have never seen, let it be sent to Lamb's for my use."[74] Duncan Wu questions whether Charles Lamb ever managed to send Wordsworth a copy of Godwin's *Essay on Sepulchres*, but it unquestionably resonates with Wordsworth's reflections in both *The Excursion* and his contemporaneous *Essays upon Epitaphs*.⁷⁵ Godwin calls for an idiosyncratic democratization of Westminster Abbey's memorial project, proposing that a "very slight and cheap memorial" be erected next to the remains of all of Britain's illustrious dead (*PPW* 6:7). Godwin's memorial quest to preserve native virtue for future generations resembles Wordsworth's attempt—in *The Excursion* and its own country churchyard—to depict the mental fortitude and everyday Stoicism that persists amid the trials of ordinary life. Confronting his inability to save the Solitary from his despondency through argument alone, the Wanderer turns to the renovating and didactic potential of "authentic epitaphs" (*E* 5:653), supplementing "abstractions" with "plain pictures" of the virtuous lives of the dead and departed (*E* 5:639–40). In his own *Essay*, Godwin similarly sidesteps "cold generalities and idle homilies of morality" in favor of imaginative access to real lives (*PPW* 6:22).

Both Wordsworth and Godwin identify graveyards as repositories of "plain pictures" that might supplement abstract moral speculation, but the real crux of the essay's confluence with *The Excursion* lies in Godwin's recollection of reading Edmund Spenser's *Epithalamion* near the ruins of the Valle Crucis Abbey. Godwin's vivid impression of the contrast between Spenser's passionate sensibility and monastic austerity prompted an assured footnote, one that subtly incorporates the tension and transformation that had characterized his post–*Political Justice* career:

> Nothing can be more beautiful, than the idea in Grecian Mythology, of the two kinds of fire, and the divinities that presided over each.... The fire of Vulcan was the fire of the forge and of thunder, it was fitful and furious: but the fire of Vesta was the purer element, which burned evenly, and was never extinguished. By this emblem it is signified to us in the most expressive manner, that chastity, a heaven-born resolution, and the sublime pursuit of a determined purpose, is not, "as dull fools suppose," a frigid and languid state of thought, but has in it a fervour and enthusiasm....
>
> Meantime, the moral of this fable is of still wider application. There is, and perhaps always has been, much cant afloat in the world, about *warm hearts*, and *cold hearts* and no doubt there is a real division of human beings into what may be loosely called the *feeling* and the *unfeeling*. But the division is not exactly as it is vulgarly understood. The hottest fire is not that which on every slight incentive blazes on the surface, but that which is close pent up in the recesses of the heart.... In a word, the sincerest warmth is not wild, but calm; and operates

in greater activity in the breast of the stoic, than in that of the vulgar enthusiast. (*PPW* 6:21–22)

Godwin's attempt to differentiate a furious and strangely mechanical passion from its chaste and austere counterpart channels the special kind of frustration that grows out of being misunderstood. For years, friends and critics alike had misconstrued his call for disinterested benevolence as mere indifference, forcing him to endure "the flood of ribaldry, invective and intolerance poured out against me and my writings" (*PPW* 2:165). But here, Godwin forcefully dissects the exclusionary logic implicit in these critiques: Stoicism signifies not the absence of passion but its perfection, and the most vociferous display of emotion rarely coincides with true social concern. Godwin's interest in a warmth "not wild, but calm" falls in line with the Stoic distinction between *pathe* and *eupatheiai*, a distinction between ordinary emotions and "proper feelings."[76] In the *Tusculan Disputations*, for example, Cicero contrasts feelings that elicit "an agitation of the soul alien from right reason and contrary to nature" with a more rational affective experience that "takes place in an equable and wise way."[77] While a Stoic might seek to eliminate delight (*laetitia*), he would dismiss joy (*gaudium*) at his peril.[78] And for good reason: if delight signals false belief, joy for the Stoics corresponds with a meaningful evaluation of the world. Looking past the cant of a false dichotomy—the binary choice between passion and its complete exclusion—Godwin rejects superficial caricatures of Stoic moral psychology and quietly casts his lot with the sublime fire of Vesta. Wordsworth had once condemned Godwin's attempt to "abstract the hopes of man / Out of his feelings, to be fix'd thenceforth / For ever in a purer element" (*Prelude* 10:807–9), but here Godwin himself redefines that "purer element" not as a frigid and "unfeeling" wasteland but as the source of true "fervour and enthusiasm" (*PPW* 6:21).

For Godwin, Stoic virtue is not a form of apathy but an outgrowth of fierce commitment. His footnote coincides with a central question reiterated throughout *The Excursion* and its philosophical dialogue. The most succinct formulation of this ethical quandary occurs in a rare instance of rhetorical humility, one in which the Wanderer ponders the transposition of "naked reason" in a question that even he, for once, hesitates to answer:

> How shall Man unite
> A self-forgetting tenderness of heart
> And earth-despising dignity of soul?
> Wise in that union, and without it blind! (*E* 5:577–80)

Searching for an "inward principle" that might reconcile the "active energy" of social benevolence with a more Stoic and "passive will," the Wanderer echoes Adam Smith's sense of an inherent connection between the amiable virtues of "indulgent humanity" and the awful virtues of "self-denial" and "self-government" (*E* 5:573–75; *TMS* 23). In this sense, Wordsworth's and Godwin's evolving interest in Stoicism and their reassessment of its worldly capacity reflect their inheritance of the impasse between Stoicism and sympathetic exchange discussed in the last chapter. At the same time, Godwin's defense of a union between sensibility and Stoic self-mastery clarifies Wordsworth's preoccupation with a similar correspondence in two concrete ways: his synthesis accords with a pattern of logic Wordsworth had already broached in his first *Essay upon Epitaphs*, and his fiery "emblem" directly informs the Wanderer's description of virtue in *The Excursion*.

A year before requesting a copy of *Essay on Sepulchres*, Wordsworth articulated his own version of the paradoxical connection between feeling and unfeeling natures in his first *Essay upon Epitaphs*, a reflection that he described as "dictated by a spirit congenial to that which pervades" *The Excursion* (*E* 302). The essay focuses on the question of immortality, but it includes a striking contrast between two divergent yet representative responses to bodily remains. Landing in a strange country, the poet Simonides reverently buries an unknown corpse, while an unspecified "ancient Philosopher" regards a dead body with contempt. The moral that Wordsworth expounds from the contrast is not that "tender-hearted Simonides was incapable of the lofty movements of thought, to which that other Sage gave way," nor that the callous philosopher would necessarily be blind to earthly considerations "in a different mood of mind." Instead, he observes that "each of these Sages was in sympathy with the best feelings of our nature; feelings which, though they seem opposite to each other, have another and a finer connection than that of contrast." Since qualities in the natural and moral world "pass insensibly into their contraries," Wordsworth himself adopts "a midway point," one that acknowledges the legitimacy of both positions. Wordsworth's reflections on immortality suggest that he would have been sympathetic to Godwin's point about warm hearts and cold hearts: they "have another and a finer connection than that of contrast."[79]

While Godwin upsets the false binary between vehement sympathy and cool detachment, his own pursuit of a "midway point" ultimately emerges out of his interest in the rehabilitation of Stoicism in the wake of the 1790s. Wordsworth's allusive rendering of Godwin's note in *The*

Excursion captures his interest in a similar revisionary concern. In one of the poem's few extended similes, the Wanderer transposes Godwin's vestal imagery in describing a virtue that persists amid "each vicissitude of loss and gain":

> Within the soul a Faculty abides,
> That with interpositions, which would hide
> And darken, so can deal, that they become
> Contingences of pomp; and serve to exalt
> Her native brightness. As the ample Moon,
> In the deep stillness of a summer even
> Rising behind a thick and lofty Grove,
> Burns like an unconsuming fire of light,
> In the green trees; and, kindling on all sides
> Their leafy umbrage, turns the dusky veil
> Into a substance glorious as her own,
> Yea with her own incorporated, by power
> Capacious and serene. Like power abides
> In Man's celestial Spirit; Virtue thus
> Sets forth and magnifies herself; thus feeds
> A calm, a beautiful, and silent fire,
> From the incumbrances of mortal life,
> From error, disappointment,—nay from guilt;
> And sometimes, so relenting Justice wills,
> From palpable oppressions of Despair. (*E* 4:1055-74)

The chronological history detailed by Mark Reed and the editors of the Cornell Wordsworth holds open the possibility that Godwin's footnote in *Essay on Sepulchres* could have exerted a direct influence on this passage, but irrespective of causality, thematic and linguistic connections are striking.[80] While Godwin turns to mythology and Wordsworth to nature, both use the metaphor of an "unconsuming fire" to account for a constancy or virtue that includes but does not exhaust human passion. Wordsworth's diction is at its most abstract and philosophical here: the soul is equipped with a virtue or "Faculty" that turns obstacles or "interpositions" into paradoxical affirmations of an innate freedom from such obstacles. The "brightness" of this faculty transforms the dark aspect of necessity into its opposite; "incumbrances of mortal life" become nothing more than "contingences of pomp" or, as the *Oxford English Dictionary* puts it, "splendid or impressive display[s]" of one's "freedom from necessity."[81] Such virtue is likened to the light of an "ample moon" impeded by a "thick and lofty grove," but rather than obstructing this light, the trees are absorbed in "an unconsuming fire of light" that only magnifies the "serene power" of the moon itself. Like Godwin's "fire of Vesta," the conflagration that results stands in for a faculty that blends real "fervour and enthusiasm" with Stoicism and its sublime resolve (*PPW* 6:21–22).

In commending a virtue that subverts "incumbrances" to its own glory, Wordsworth validates a Godwinian position he had once criticized: the autonomy of an "individual mind" capable of "shaking off / The accidents of nature, time, and place" (*Prelude* 10:821–22). Wordsworth's extended simile and complex natural imagery point to a possible realignment in his thinking, one that tempers the critique of Godwin in *The Prelude* while also clarifying the nature of the Stoicism that pervades *The Excursion*: far from reactionary, dispassionate virtue precedes life's "interpositions," nor is it defined by them. This subtle realignment of Godwinian Stoicism is more than a passing impression in the poem's philosophical exchange; as Kenneth Johnston has noted, the passage is notably central, an "emblem" of the Wanderer's unfolding argument as well as the image that finally cuts through the Solitary's ironclad skepticism.[82] Even so, the poem's dialogic structure retains this skepticism, ensuring that some of it is Wordsworth's own. For all his initial enthusiasm, the Solitary quickly undercuts the Wanderer's vision of a naturalized and fully rehabilitated Stoic radicalism:

> "But how begin? and whence?—the Mind is free,
> Resolve—the haughty Moralist would say,
> This single act is all that we demand.
> Alas! such wisdom bids a Creature fly
> Whose very sorrow is, that time hath shorn
> His natural wings!" (*E* 4:1075–82)

Echoing an image derived from Coleridge's impossible attraction to Stoicism, the Solitary unsettles the idea that mental resolution itself might elicit independence.[83] The philosophical pride so often associated with Godwin and other Stoic moralists leaves too little room for flawed humanity, not to mention the fact of embodiment itself. For the Solitary, the melancholy impossibility of Stoicism is born out of its inaccessibility. The ethical detachment advocated by both Godwin and the Wanderer might be "Sublime and comprehensive," but it is also eerily inhuman (*E* 1:255). As the Solitary's fast pivot makes clear, the dialogic structure of the poem ensures that any moderation of Godwin's radical Stoicism will exist alongside a continuing mistrust. For Wordsworth, then, philosophical dialogue exceeded even what Sarah Zimmerman has described as the capacity of lyric "to accommodate both his radical and conservative selves, and not just consecutively, but simultaneously, as ambivalence."[84]

A Just Equipoise?

The ethical status of Wordsworth's moderated Stoicism figures prominently in critical estimations of *The Excursion*, and while it is rarely distinguished with a specific philosophical label, it becomes a frequent reference point in the poem's "strong discourse" (*E* 4:256). Jane Worthington noted that while Wordsworth "took up Stoicism with enthusiasm," innumerable passages in *The Excursion* suggest that he "continued to reflect upon it long and carefully."[85] Stoicism frames evaluations of the Wanderer as a character as well as the famous "reconciling addendum" with which he concludes the story of Margaret. Its "grave Philosophy" is both defended and interrogated by the Solitary, prescribed by the Wanderer, and rendered as narrative by the Pastor, whose authentic epitaphs center on those "thoroughly fortified" souls who have "withdrawn from Passion's crooked ways" (*E* 3:344, 5:350–51). Even the landscape takes on a Stoic hue, prompting the Poet to describe the Solitary's vale as "perfectly secure" and unperturbed:

> It could not be more quiet: peace is here
> Or no where; days unruffled by the gale
> Of public news or private; years that pass
> Forgetfully; uncalled upon to pay
> The common penalties of mortal life,
> Sickness, or accident, or grief, or pain. (*E* 2:374, 384–89)

For Adam Potkay, these varied iterations of Stoicism in *The Excursion* exceed the level of content to transform the nature of the verse itself, resulting in a "stoic aesthetic" or "impersonal style" that "waxes classical" and recycles "marmoreal utterances that seem translated from a dead language."[86]

Whether at the level of content or style, Wordsworth's attempts to look past the vulgar distinction between feeling and unfeeling natures are scattered throughout *The Excursion*, with the possibilities and incongruities of Godwin's tempting scheme hovering constantly in the background. But the sidelining of the Godwinian context has made it easy to dismiss the moderated Stoicism in *The Excursion* as a manifestation of indifference or apathy. In a passage that has elicited much commentary, the narrating Poet connects the Wanderer's remarkable sensibility to his decisively Stoic outlook:

>   he kept
> In solitude and solitary thought
> His mind in a just equipoise of love.
> Serene it was, unclouded by the cares
> Of ordinary life; unvexed, unwarped
> By partial bondage. In his steady course
> No piteous revolutions had he felt,
> No wild varieties of joy and grief.
> Unoccupied by sorrow of its own
> His heart lay open; and, by Nature tuned
> And constant disposition of his thoughts
> To sympathy with Man, he was alive
> To all that was enjoyed where'er he went;
> And all that was endured; for in himself,
> Happy, and quiet in his chearfulness,
> He had no painful pressure from without
> That made him turn aside from wretchedness
> With coward fears. He could *afford* to suffer
> With those whom he saw suffer. (*E* 1:382–400)

With a mind held in a "just equipoise of love," the Wanderer resembles the central figure in Oliver Goldsmith's *Citizen of the World*, who counsels that while an "absence of passion" might not be desirable, a mind "influenced by a just equipoize of the passions" can enjoy a true tranquility.[87] Goldsmith's title is apt, for the Wanderer's itinerant existence results in his own kind of cosmopolitan ethos. Choosing a life unanchored by domestic affections, the Wanderer's sphere of influence is an earthly rather than a domestic one. Unencumbered by "partial" affections, his sensibility remains "unwarped," a word that implies not just straightening out but restoration from a state of prejudice.[88] Like Shaftesbury, the Wanderer looks past family and kind in the attempt to reach that "heroic pitch" from which he might experience "an equal, just and universal friendship" (*C* 256). In Adam Smith's terms, he is not "separated and detached" but "a citizen of the world, a member of the vast commonwealth of nature" (*TMS* 140). Though the Wanderer might not have felt any "piteous revolutions," his "open" perspective was revolutionary in its own right. Unencumbered by bondage to "partial" passions, his Stoicism is not unlike that which led the Solitary, prompted by the fall of the Bastille, to set aside "the depths / Of natural passion" only to find his "soul diffused" in "wide embrace" (*E* 3:744–46). The subtle rejection of local ties and prejudice—with all of its Burkean overtones—might even figure the Wanderer as someone who would not be flummoxed by the dilemma of Godwin's burning garret: "unvexed" by partial bondage, he would hardly pause to entertain "coward fears."

Reading the Wanderer against the worn-out contraries of the Revolutionary controversy clearly works against the grain of Wordsworth's self-mythology, and yet the way in which his character synchronizes cosmopolitan detachment and a natural "sympathy with Man" suggests an endorsement of the idea that cold-heartedness might actually be warm. At the least, cosmopolitan rhetoric in the passage makes it difficult to dismiss the Wanderer's renunciation of deep attachment and its consequent sorrow as a simple desire for repose, or a solipsistic antithesis to sensibility. He is, as the narrating Poet puts it, secluded "but not to social duties lost" (*E* 5:52).

At the same time, the Wanderer's de facto salvaging of Godwinian Stoicism within rustic life hardly allayed the misgivings that beset Godwinian rationality in the 1790s. Even Wordsworth's attempt to align Stoicism with a figure often singled out as his philosophical spokesperson fails to circumvent the anxiety that its abstraction might lead to insensibility rather than a just impartiality. As Potkay puts it, the Wanderer's ethical "exceptionality" only underscores his impersonality, not to mention a certain "deafness" to the subtler strains inherent in the still, sad music of humanity.[89] Kevis Goodman's shrewd analysis of the Wanderer's psychic balancing act conveys a similar sense of how precarious such an equilibrium might be. In her terms, "the Wanderer's 'sympathy with man' is very nearly replaced by the achievement of a Stoic *apatheia*, an existence above and free from passion."[90] For Godwin and Wordsworth, however, these moral postures were hardly incompatible, nor was their indeterminacy such a bad thing; the expansivity of sympathy was dependent upon a mode of seeing that was itself "too deep for tears."[91] Wordsworth's stark reprisal of this reality two decades after the publication of *Political Justice* conveys a sense of how central and unavoidable Stoic moral sentimentalism must have been to his ethical imaginings. And yet it would be a mistake to separate this perennial intuition from its accompanying anxiety, or to equate the Wanderer's calm certainty with that of Wordsworth himself. His sublime virtue was prone to the same abstraction and cold indifference that Wordsworth had once critiqued in Godwin's thought. If the Wanderer's Stoicism evoked a faint but resurgent radicalism, it also reprised the difficulty of shaping that vision in a human world.

After all, the last line of Wordsworth's "Ode" speaks to his tendency to define emotional equanimity by its proximity to loss. The death of Mary Wollstonecraft had played into Godwin's reappraisal of the Stoics, just as the loss of his brother John left Wordsworth cleaving to Stoic "fortitude" and "patient chear"—though crucially, in this mournful formulation, a Stoicism that might close the curtain on any heart that "lives alone, / Hous'd in a dream, at distance from the Kind."[92] The Solitary's radical diffusion at the onset of the French Revolution was also the sequel to grievous familial loss, his heart laid open in the worst kind of way. In all of these biographical and poetical cases, the Stoicism of a grief endured affords a new perspective on revolutionary dispassion, if not an antecedent for it. The radical potential of Stoicism could not exist in a conceptual vacuum but was in fact dependent upon an affect-laden life. The ethical power of Stoic detachment was predicated upon the clarity that emerged out of its disruption. Against this background, the Wanderer's own Stoicism is notable for a certain blindness as well as its insight. "Unoccupied by sorrow of its own," and unschooled by "wild varieties of joy and grief," his heart remains distanced from his kind, appropriately alert to the radical power of Stoicism—but for all that, peculiarly insensible to its cost (*E* 1:389-90).

Wordsworth's Commanding Eminence

In its attempt to describe how one might find, in ordinary life and in the wake of calamity, "central peace, subsisting at the heart / Of endless agitation," *The Excursion* explores Stoic detachment while acknowledging, as Wordsworth's Pastor does, that it aspires to a "speculative height we may not reach" (*E* 4:1140-41, 5:484). But like Smith and Godwin, Wordsworth was loath to abandon the imperfect possibilities of Stoicism. In *The Excursion*, he persistently explores a metaphor that links command over the passions to the power of perspective and distance. Throughout the poem, a detached prospect on the world and its variable passions becomes part and parcel of a detached perspective on the self. Without attempting to forge a system from its scattered speculations, I isolate one viable manifestation of Wordsworth's moderated Stoicism at the intersection of Geoffrey Hartman's insight that the poem has deep roots in eighteenth-century topographical poetry and Charles Taylor's notion that modern selfhood involves inhabiting a "moral topography"—of "being able to find one's standpoint" in a moral landscape and achieve "a perspective in it."[93]

In accounting for his early misfortunes, the Solitary calmly describes the stroke of "fatal Power" that shattered his early happiness (*E* 3:646). When both of his children are suddenly caught in the "gripe of Death" (*E* 3:648), he is aggrieved, all the more so when he discovers that this traumatic loss has left his wife "Incalculably distant": she was "Calm as a frozen Lake when ruthless Winds / Blow fiercely, agitating earth and sky" (*E* 3:672, 659–60). While his wife submits to "Heaven's determinations," the Solitary admits that "the eminence on which her spirit stood, / Mine was unable to attain" (*E* 3:667–69). In describing his wife's uncomplaining acceptance as an antecedent of his own apathy, the Solitary deploys another image of an eminence unperturbed by passion and passing necessity. Emerging out of both loco-descriptive poetry and Stoic philosophy, what Pierre Hadot has called "the view from above" affords the disinterested spectator an opportunity to evaluate and better understand his own relation to social existence.[94] In his *Meditations*, for example, Marcus Aurelius advises that "when you are reasoning about mankind, look upon earthly things below as if from some vantage point above them."[95] Yet given the trajectory of the Solitary's political future and the nature of Wordsworth's political past, the composure of the Solitary's wife could also be glossed with Godwin's recognition that a "consequence of the doctrine of necessity is its tendency to make us survey all events with a tranquil and placid temper, and approve or disapprove without impeachment of our self possession." For Godwin, the heights of what he calls a "comprehensive view" render one "superior to the tumult of passion" (*PJ* 173).

In Book 13 of *The Prelude*, Wordsworth turns the prospect trope on its head, trading the visible and comprehensive landscapes in John Denham's *Cooper's Hill* (1642) and James Thomson's *The Seasons* (1730) for a sublime encounter with the "dark deep thorough-fare" where nature had lodged the "Soul, the Imagination of the whole" (*Prelude* 13:64–65). While the prospect trope in *The Excursion* is not entirely dissociated from this "power to commune with the invisible world," its multiple expressions find Wordsworth looking back toward the visible world with the strong desire for a perspective from which contemplation might be reconciled with a life of connection and action (*E* 9:87). A metaphorical prospect like the one on display in Thomson's "A Happy Man" offers a clear sense of how resonant terms from *The Excursion*—all italicized by Thomson—could be reconciled from the right perspective, one

> Where *Judgment* sits clear-sighted, and surveys
> The Chain of *Reason* with unerring Gaze;

> Where *Fancy* lives, and to the bright'ning Eyes,
> Bids fairer Scenes, and bolder Figures rise;
> Where *social Love* exerts her soft Command
> And plays the *Passions* with a tender Hand,
> Whence every *Virtue* flows, in rival Strife,
> And all the *moral Harmony* of Life.[96]

Like the Wanderer's "just equipoise," the view from above holds out the promise of an equilibrium between dispassionate judgment and "*social Love*" (*E* 1:384). As John Barrell has observed, however, the fantasy that a "disinterested viewpoint" might culminate in true social knowledge was beset by contradictions: its ideal of disinterestedness was predicated on economic privilege, and the unified view of society that distance made possible was necessarily a simplified one.[97]

But since the Stoic positioning the prospect trope both accommodates and figures is itself imperfect, Wordsworth's frequent recourse to its power resonates with Amanda Anderson's contention that critical distance can exist only as "a temporary vantage, unstable achievement, or regulative ideal."[98] In *The Convention of Cintra* (1809), Wordsworth described the fleeting nature of detachment in a similar way:

> A man of disciplined spirit, who withdrew from the too busy world—not out of indifference to its welfare, or to forget its concerns—but retired for wider compass of eye-sight, that he might comprehend and see in just proportions and relations; knowing above all that he, who hath not first made himself master of the horizon of his own mind, must look beyond it only to be deceived.[99]

Balancing Stoic self-mastery with sympathy and social concern, Wordsworth suggests that the distancing power of contemplation stands as a necessary precursor to action. He advocates, in other words, what Adam Smith had described as the attempt to "remove ourselves, as it were, from our own natural station" in an effort to view our sentiments and motives "as at a certain distance from us" (*TMS* 110). In inclining toward such a view, Wordsworth followed Godwin, who declared in the second edition of *Political Justice* that "the soundest criterion of virtue is, to put ourselves in the place of an impartial spectator, or an angelic nature, suppose, beholding us from an elevated station, and uninfluenced by our prejudices, conceiving what would be his estimate of the intrinsic circumstances of our neighbor, and acting accordingly" (*PPW* 4:65). In *The Excursion*, Wordsworth turns to such an "elevated station" for the impartiality it might allow rather than the inspiration it might convey. Nor does the poem underestimate the difficulties attendant upon occupying such a perspective. In what might be seen as a tacit critique of his own detachment, the Wanderer contends that

> to relinquish all
> We have, or hope, of happiness and joy,—
> And stand in freedom loosened from this world;
> I deem not arduous:—but must needs confess
> That 'tis a thing impossible to frame
> Conceptions equal to the Soul's desires;
> And the most difficult of tasks to *keep*
> Heights which the Soul is competent to gain. (*E* 4:132–39)

Scaling such heights necessitated "arduous" discipline and vigilant self-practice rather than any easy sense of relinquishment or indifference. Indeed, for both Godwin and Wordsworth, the prospect trope mediates between the claims of self and society, marking the place or metaphorical scene of an ethical self-practice that, in Foucault's own Stoically inflected terms, defines a principle of relation to the self through which both active and contemplative life become possible.[100]

In a telling example, Wordsworth describes the Solitary's attempt to escape the melancholy that followed in the wake of the French Revolution. The Solitary travels to North America—to roam, as he puts it, "at large, to observe, and not to feel" (*E* 3:900). Temperamentally averse to the "Big Passions" on display in American cities, he becomes a "detached Spectator" who seeks in the wild "a composing distance from the haunts / Of strife and folly" (*E* 3:908–9, 913–14). In this venture, he imagines himself as a particularly contemplative noble savage who

> having gained the top
> Of some commanding Eminence, which yet
> Intruder n'er beheld, he thence surveys
> Regions of wood and wide Savannah, vast
> Expanse of unappropriated earth,
> With mind that sheds a light on what he sees. (*E* 3:944–49)

The ideal of a noble savage turns out to be as illusory as the ideal of unmitigated Stoicism, but the Solitary consistently demonstrates a desire, often thwarted, to achieve precisely the "contemplative position" that Coleridge, in *Table Talk*, tied to the genius of Wordsworth's philosophical poetry: "His proper title is *Spectator ab extra*."[101] Hazlitt once claimed that Godwin had placed "the human mind on an elevation, from which it commands a view of the whole line of moral consequences." From such a perspective, Godwin absolved man from the ties of "private and local attachment" so that he might "devote himself to the boundless pursuit of universal benevolence."[102]

The Excursion and its many prospects show Wordsworth as still captivated by a similar pursuit, though it also conveys a sense of how thoroughly he had reimagined the stakes of Godwin's attempt "to pass the Arctic Circle and Frozen Regions, where the understanding is no longer warmed by the affections."[103] Ready to advance human welfare, and thirsty for the certainty of "secure intelligence," Wordsworth first turned to Godwin with a hope that

> man should start
> Out of the worm-like state in which he is,
> And spread abroad the wings of Liberty,
> Lord of himself in indisturb'd delight. (*Prelude* 10:835–88)

Wordsworth's account of that initial desire for transformation is quickly followed by an affirmation of his fidelity to Godwin's aspiration, as well as a sense of how that original vision was amended over time:

> A noble aspiration, yet I feel
> The aspiration, but with other thoughts
> And happier; for I was perplex'd and sought
> To accomplish the transition by such means
> As did not lie in nature, sacrificed
> The exactness of a comprehensive mind
> To scrupulous and microscopic views
> That furnish'd out materials for a work
> Of false imagination, placed beyond
> The limits of experience and of truth. (*Prelude* 10:839–48)

For the ancient Stoics, the restraint of passion was not an end in itself but a corollary to the foundational assertion that an ethical being must live according to nature. Wordsworth's critique of *Political Justice* and its austere morality was not ultimately a repudiation of Stoicism, but a sophisticated insight into the conditions under which its bid for liberty might thrive. Murdering to dissect, Godwin went against nature in his initial pursuit of justice, but like Godwin himself, Wordsworth increasingly linked the liberating potential of Stoicism to its management of distance and perspective. Forsaking "microscopic views" in an attempt to comprehend the world in "its just proportions and relations," Wordsworth's fixation on Stoicism in *The Excursion* attests to his unabated desire for an ethical perspective responsive to "the limits of experience and of truth."[104]

CHAPTER THREE

Coleridge, Lyric Askesis, and Living Form

I might express my outlook by saying that if you conceive philosophy and poetry and therapy in ways that prevent you from so much as seeing their competition with one another then you have given up something I take as part of the philosophical adventure, I mean part of its intellectual adventure.

—STANLEY CAVELL, *IN QUEST OF THE ORDINARY*

IN 1734, DAVID HUME SENT an unsigned letter to an unnamed physician, begging the favor of some medical advice. Hume started by laying out his case history: after a burst of "deep & abstruse thinking," he had unwittingly contracted "the Disease of the Learned." Scurvy spots, general weakness, and "Watryness in the mouth" ensued. To shake his ailment, the eighteen-year-old philosopher tried various remedies: claret wine and a daily ride, "a Course of Bitters," and a round of "Anti-hysteric Pills." After several years of unabated malaise, Hume took steps to trade the scholar's solitary task for a life of "Business & Diversion." But his grasp on a "new Scene of Thought" was not easily set aside. Four years later, after a brief stint as clerk to a Bristol merchant, he published the first books of *A Treatise of Human Nature*.[1]

In the dark days that preceded this philosophical breakthrough, Hume seems to have consulted every physician who came his way, but he remained his own fierce diagnostician. This was only fitting. Claiming "experience and observation" as the only sure foundation for the new science of man, his *Treatise* acknowledged that "we ourselves are not only the beings, that reason, but also one of the objects, concerning which we reason."[2] Taking his own indisposition as an object of that science—but also as a real barrier to its articulation—Hume ascribed his early symptoms to a regrettable enthusiasm for the Stoic moralists. As his letter to a physician makes clear, a wrong philosophical move could take a decisive physical toll:

> There was another particular, which contributed more than any thing, to waste my Spirits & bring on me this Distemper, which was, that having read many Books of Morality, such as Cicero, Seneca & Plutarch, & being smit with their beautiful Representations of Virtue & Philosophy, I undertook the Improvement of my Temper & Will, along with my Reason & Understanding. I was continually fortifying myself with Reflections against Death, & Poverty, & Shame, & Pain, & all the other Calamities of Life. These no doubt are exceeding useful, when join'd with an active Life; because the Occasion being presented along with the Reflection, works it into the Soul, & makes it take a deep Impression, but in Solitude they serve to little other Purpose, than to waste the Spirits, the Force of the Mind meeting with no Resistance, but wasting itself in the Air, like our Arm when it misses its Aim. This however I did not learn but by Experience, & till I had already ruin'd my Health, tho' I was not sensible of it.[3]

Hume had acquired a copy of Shaftesbury's *Characteristics* several years earlier, and here he echoes one of the Third Earl's central insights: however introspective, the ultimate ground of Stoicism was "active Life" in a social world. Removed from that framework, the arduous quest to improve one's temper might backfire, only exacerbating the "Distemper" it sought to moderate. The word that Hume cannot seem to escape here is "waste," a term that balances a needless expenditure of energy and spirit against the reality of physical degradation. "Reflection" outruns "Occasion," leaving a vulnerable body to absorb the regulative attention of an overly fortified mind. But Hume's preoccupation with the Stoics was hardly a waste. It left him, rather, with a sharp conviction: to measure the embodied self against the ancient Stoics and their "beautiful Representations of Virtue & Philosophy" was ultimately to underscore one's own fragility and weakness.

Samuel Taylor Coleridge rarely missed an opportunity to mark his disdain for Hume, and his *Marginalia* was unstinting in its contempt: "as Historian and as Philosopher, Hume has, meo saltem judicio, been extravagantly overrated.—Mercy on the Age, & the People, for whom Lock[e] is profound, and Hume subtle."[4] When it came to the Stoics, however, both thinkers shared a similar skepticism: Coleridge's own scattered but extensive engagement with the Stoics could be seen as an unwitting set of variations on a theme by Hume. In this chapter, I argue that Coleridge balanced a sustained interest in Stoicism against the fact of its rigorous and incapacitating standard. Like Hume, Coleridge was often "smit" by Stoic virtue, but the stubborn fact of his own body could just as frequently prompt a fierce and disenchanted skepticism of its aspirational autonomy. Throughout his work, anxieties about Stoicism's irreligiosity were raised but often overruled. Its forbidding path to perfection seemed only to reinforce its allure. In seven cryptic lines from "Dejection: An Ode," Coleridge set both the possibility of Stoicism as well as the cost of its habitual extremity at the heart of his own poetic existence:

> For not to think of what I needs must feel,
> But to be still and patient, all I can;
> And haply by abstruse research to steal
> From my own nature all the natural Man—
> This was my sole resource, my only plan:
> Till that which suits a part infects the whole,
> And now is almost grown the habit of my Soul. (*PW* 1:700)

For Lionel Trilling, these lines express a simple desire "to escape from the life of emotion."[5] Versions of that desire—to attenuate if not escape the life of emotion—would crop up again and again throughout the sprawling body of Coleridge's poetic and philosophical work.

Testing the axioms of philosophy against his own pulses, Coleridge approached his own life as self-reflexive evidence of the thin line that separated Stoic amelioration from affliction. Too much Stoicism could make one sick, and, like Hume, he translated his philosophical frustration into embodied, tactile terms. For Hume, the mental fortifications of Stoicism were unmeaningful in the abstract, little more than a force of mind "wasting itself in the Air, like our Arm when it misses its Aim."[6] While Hume lamented a lack of resistance, Coleridge was daunted by the disabling resistance of the body itself. He equated the Stoic imperative "Exert your will" with the callous futility of ordering a man with two paralytic arms to "Rub your arms against each other!" (*P Lects* 1:286). Activating too much motion, or none at all, the illusory power of Stoic therapy only compounded its pathology. Hume outgrew a devotion to the Stoics in due course, and his need for medical advice was seemingly short-lived. But Coleridge, who would spend the last eighteen years of his life lodging with a physician, never set aside his ambivalent fascination with Stoicism.

Rarely far removed from more familiar preoccupations, it emerged in ever-varying forms, at one moment an incapacitating ailment, at others an eagerly embraced remedy.

At first glance, an entire chapter on Coleridge's Stoicism might seem an ill-advised extravagance. Taking a cue from Coleridge himself, commentators can rarely resist marking the spectacle of his irresolution, his transient bursts of enthusiasm, and the anguished intensity of his despair. But while Coleridge was one of the least Stoical writers in the period, he spent more time examining the history and efficacy of Stoicism than any other prominent writer in the period. Early and late, from his Bristol lectures of 1795 to the ever-incomplete *Opus Maximum*, questions raised by the Stoics cut across his central philosophical commitments. Like Wordsworth and Southey, he approached Godwin's *Political Justice* as a text that "taught Republicanism and Stoicism," a call for benevolence that did away with "every home-born Feeling, by which it is produced and nurtured."[7] Stoicism was implicit in his formative response to Kant and Spinoza, and it intersected with his reflections on religion, on politics, and on the centrality of the will. In Thomas McFarland's resonant words, "Stoicism crowded hard upon Coleridge's most cherished beliefs."[8] The diversity and range of his Stoic preoccupations kept him from taking his skepticism for granted. Each objection gave rise to new complications, with a hydralike network of philosophical echoes and interconnections sustaining his interest in Stoic precepts that might otherwise have seemed untenable.

In the vast realm of scholarship devoted to identifying his philosophical commitments, Coleridge has been called many things, but he has rarely been described as a Stoic.[9] I will not be making the case for a new philosophical label or strict affiliation in this chapter. Given the broad dispersal of Stoicism in culture, accounting for Coleridge's interest in the Stoics strikes me as more than a matter of classification. Instead, I focus on two central questions: what gravitational pull made a writer doggedly mistrustful of Stoicism so adamant in his exploration of its intricacies, and what relation—if any—did Coleridge's aspirational investment in Stoic tranquility bear to the realm of lyric itself? Answering these questions requires a willing suspension of belief in the influential but often misleading self-mythology that Coleridge vouchsafed to his critics. The strains of duty, desire, and indecision on display in the first, more philosophical part of this chapter unsettle the myth of a poet whose innate irresolution was antithetical to anything resembling Stoicism. Later in the chapter, I complicate the related myth—rehearsed in "Dejection: An Ode"—that unfeeling philosophy might stand in the way of poetry itself.

Since a Stoic accounting of Coleridge's poiesis is an unfamiliar one, I want to sketch out its plausibility with an example at the outset. In 1796, while Sara Coleridge was "dangerously ill, and expected hourly to miscarry," Coleridge wrote some lines on an untimely flower blooming in late winter.[10] The unrhymed lines—twice the length of a sonnet—offer consolation to the doomed flower even as they reflect on the inevitability of loss. At the end of the poem, however, Coleridge looks past the blossom to the origin of the lines themselves, acknowledging that the poetic work of weaving "dim similitudes" in "moral strains" was a therapeutic act, a bid for self-composure or tranquility:

> I've stolen one hour
> From black anxiety that gnaws my heart
> For her who droops far off on a sick bed:
> And the warm wooings of this sunny day
> Tremble along my frame and harmonize
> Th' attemper'd brain, that ev'n the saddest thoughts
> Mix with some sweet sensations, like harsh tunes
> Play'd deftly on a soft-ton'd instrument. (*PW* 1:257)

What might seem obvious is no less important: the poem is not primarily an expression of gnawing anxiety or a record of incipient sadness, but rather an attempt to alleviate or moderate those feelings. In this sense, the poem is oriented toward the mind of the poet rather than the presence of any reader. It is less like an effusion and more like an exercise, a poetic version of what Foucault might describe as "the work of oneself on oneself."[11] Portrayed in musical terms, the poem as "moral strain" works alongside the weather to facilitate the harmonization of an "attemper'd brain," a phrase that captures the cognitive power of poetry to "regulate, control, order, [and] arrange" discordant emotion.[12] In Coleridge's terms, poetry could "elevate the imagination" but it could also "set the affections in right tune."[13] Months later, when Coleridge received news of his son Hartley's birth, he once again turned to poetry as a way of working through the "unquiet Silence of confused Thought / And shapeless feelings" (*PW* 1:272). The emotional regulation on display in these poetic exercises might seem too inchoate to warrant alignment with the Stoics, and yet this zone of philosophical indistinction was, for Coleridge, part of the appeal of lyric itself. It was ultimately in the self-reflexive practice of lyric writing that Stoicism's flexible moral psychology outpaced Coleridge's skepticism to offer a model of the mind in conversation with itself, one in which the poetic processing of "shapeless feeling" and its "unquiet Silence" could yield a new sense of clarity and connection.

Taking his *Lectures on the History of Philosophy* as a jumping off point, I start by tracking Coleridge's intermittent attempt to square Stoicism's alluring freedoms with both his religious convictions and the addiction that underlined his own fraught corporeality. In the latter half of the chapter, I explore the far-reaching implications of this balancing act: the affordances of Stoicism were not altogether different from the affordances of lyric itself. Coleridge tended to define poetry in terms of the readerly pleasure it might elicit, but, like Wordsworth, he traced its origins to a moment of reflective tranquility. Drawing on the tradition of inner dialogue in ancient philosophy, Coleridge approached lyric writing as a kind of practice or regimen that could foster such tranquility or at least result in its extension—a claim that I will rehearse in the context of his groundbreaking conversation poems. At the end of the chapter, I return to Coleridge's beguiling lines from "Dejection: An Ode" with a new perspective on Coleridge's willed rejection of feeling in a poem that seems to lament its loss. The upshot is surprising: there is a long tradition of linking Coleridge's purported poetic decline to the slow onset of Stoic apathy, but in fact a certain strain of Stoic poetics was not prohibitive but sustaining.

Not So Natural: A Stoic Lecture and the "Supplement of All Philosophy"

While the publication of *Biographia Literaria* fueled Coleridge's reputation for speculative bravado, it did little to neutralize his oldest nemesis: financial necessity. This split outcome prompted Coleridge to offer a series of lectures charting "the origin, and progress, the fates and fortunes of philosophy" over the course of more than two millennia (*P Lects* xxxvii). Coleridge delivered his lectures while standing on top of a table at the Crown and Anchor Tavern, making them a literal manifestation of what Philip Sidney called "table talk fashion": unexpected insight adheres in "words as they chanceably fall from the mouth."[14] Coleridge was up-front about the fortuitous contingency that guided him through a discourse. Each of his fourteen lectures reflected the reading and intellectual digestion of a lifetime, but when it came to selection and organization of particular "words, illustrations, &c.," he claimed to know "almost as little as any one of my audience" what "they will be five minutes before the lecture begins."[15] At the same time, Coleridge made it clear that his history of philosophy was an ordered one. He took issue with the immense histories of philosophy compiled by Brucker, Enfield, and Stanley that had informed his own thinking, dismissing them as "massive" volumes that left behind little more than "a dizzy recollection of jarring opinions and wild fancies" (*P Lects* 1:4). The "order of succession" was key to Coleridge's historiographical enterprise, so much so that he urged his auditors to purchase his ready-made "Historical and Chronological Guide," an aid to reflection available for just a sixpence (*P Lects* 1:7). Balancing these competing priorities, the lectures become most suggestive at those flash points in which the dynamics of Coleridge's on-the-spot thoughts rout an expected or preplanned order. In these moments of telling instability, his attempt to trace the universal "striving of a single mind" makes way for the less sublime presence of his own "habit of thought."[16]

Coleridge's exegesis of Zeno and his "Stoic system" is a case in point (*P Lects* 1:278). In his "Prospectus," Coleridge had proposed devoting no less than half a lecture to the Stoics, and an advertisement in the *Courier*—published just two days before the lecture—indicated that they would be his first topic of the evening.[17] But on the night in question, he began by announcing the inversion of his scheduled order. Rather than start with an account of the Stoics, he approached their philosophy as the terminus of his discourse, but a terminus of only four thrifty paragraphs. This was a reduction in size rather than significance, for Coleridge's rearranged lecture placed Stoicism at the pinnacle of what he called "the career of philosophy" (*P Lects* 1:280). As a manifestation of the utmost effort that the "unaided will" could make of philosophy, Stoicism was for Coleridge a breakthrough effort but also an impossible ideal, a limit case for eudaimonistic thinking (*P Lects* 1:283). The Stoics aspired to the perfection of philosophy even as they unwittingly demonstrated its inevitable failure. In both its appeal and its impossibility, Stoicism emerges in the lectures as the most forceful argument for the necessity of religion as a "supplement of all philosophy." For Coleridge, the need for such a supplement was rooted in the recognition that "philosophy itself can only point out a good which by philosophy is unattainable." To emphasize the point, he invoked familiar pathological language. A Stoic who relies on the "supplement" of Christianity is able "to feel that we have a disease," but also "to believe that we have a physician" (*P Lects* 1:287). Not mentioned in the lecture is an unsettling contrast: the unsupplemented Stoic might suffer from a disease without being aware of its existence.

In the newly arranged discourse, Coleridge takes his auditors on an idiosyncratic tour of Skepticism, Epicureanism, and Stoicism that culminates in a "reverential consideration of CHRIST, as a Philosopher" (*P Lects*

1:252). Taken as a whole, Stoicism profits from being set alongside its ancient alternatives. Coleridge is characteristically dismissive of the Epicureans: he ridicules the desire to isolate pleasurable sensation as "the great object of all human thought and action," and he laments the absence of a "universal criterion" for evaluating duty, virtue, and wisdom (*P Lects* 1:263). Implicit but unremarked in all of this is Coleridge's great dissatisfaction with the perceived Epicureanism of contemporary philosophy, what he had described in *The Statesman's Manual* as "that system of disguised and decorous *epicureanism*, which has been the only orthodox philosophy of the last hundred years."[18] The favorably contrasting portrayal of Stoicism makes a tentative case for its contemporary power. If Epicureanism was a kind of "poison," Stoicism could serve as its timely "antidote" (*P Lects* 1:277). While the Epicureans looked to pleasure as both a means and an end, the Stoics routed such expediency in isolating virtue as "an end in itself to which all other things are indifferent except as means" (*P Lects* 1:278). However inexactly, Coleridge aligns Stoic virtue with "the *moral* constituent of genius" and the shape of organic form.[19] The position of Stoicism amid these overlapping commitments even leads him to describe it as the best solution to what he called "the true problem of all true philosophy"—the attempt to take "virtue as a precept in order to render it a nature" (*P Lects* 1:275).

Coleridge's fascination with the attempt to cultivate virtue by circumventing passion becomes a striking moment in the *Lectures*, one in which personal history and self-knowledge intrude upon his more impersonal philosophizing. For all his interest in the "absolutely perfect wisdom" of the Stoics, Coleridge suffered from a self-acknowledged "utter impotence of the *Volition*" that left him deeply skeptical about Stoicism's ability to shape "human nature unaided."[20] Grappling with this split impulse, he connected the Stoic tendency to confound God and nature with a yet more perennial concern:

> The Stoics adopted [the ground error of Socrates], namely, that the definition of virtue is to live according to nature, without considering the double constitution of man, his spirit and his body; in one part indeed the creature of nature, but in another constituted above nature[,] its lord, the master of light and fire who commands its elements and not merely avails himself of them. What then could the Stoics do who had rejected this duplicity? Flatter and idolise nature, make a false nature and thus in [effect] exchange vices and give pride and obduracy for effeminacy and selfishness . . . but alas too often producing despair and

a recklessness of all living from finding that impossible and impracticable which yet was constantly spoken of not only as the true object which man ought to pursue, but as the real prize which man could attain. (*P Lects* 1:279–80)

For Coleridge, the Stoics erred in adopting nature as an ethical ideal without accounting for their own share in its imperfection. His analysis was a melancholy anticipation of Nietzsche's objection to Stoicism and its naturalistic ethics: "Why make a principle of what you yourselves are and must be?"[21] In his own formulation of the critique, Coleridge raised pressing concerns that shaped his reflections on Stoicism throughout his life. Since man was in part a "creature of nature," his embodied condition made Stoicism and its cognitive imperative "impracticable." At the same time, the attempt to subdue the body and its passions left little room for Christianity's welcome circumvention of the will.

The fact of humanity's "double constitution" was, for Coleridge, an endemic concern, one only heightened by the cognitive austerity of Stoic ethics.[22] For figures like Marcus Aurelius and Epictetus, emotions were not "animal urges" or nonrational instincts, but evaluative judgments—choices or opinions about how to view the world.[23] For Coleridge, this cognitive conception of the passions idolized a false, foolishly unrealistic nature, one that failed to account for what the Scottish anatomist Charles Bell would call "the fundamental law of our nature, that the mind shall be subject to the operations of the body, and have its powers developed through its influence."[24] In valorizing spiritual discipline and mental control, the Stoics lost sight of human nature, which was in fact an embodied one. In Coleridge's vivid evocation, the critique of a philosophical school starts to sound like the disappointing experience of a single Stoic practitioner. A blithe Stoic novitiate starts off assured of his own self-mastery, and even fancies himself a modern Prometheus, a "master of light and fire who commands its elements." But such illusions of autonomy could easily be unmasked by the frailty of the body itself. Self-command was necessarily fleeting and unreliable. The Stoic desire to curtail passion was just one version of what Coleridge describes in the lines I have quoted from "Dejection: An Ode" as a vain attempt "to steal / From my own Nature all the Natural Man." Yet as Coleridge charts a course from early pride to "recklessness" and "despair," his description veers from the calm, balanced rhetoric of qualified phrases to a more frantic flurry. The gap between his thrifty notes and his expansive live analysis makes at least one thing clear: Coleridge was a lecturer who could effortlessly evoke the frustration of failing to receive a prize "constantly spoken" of as something he ought to be able to attain.[25]

For Coleridge, the Stoic's presumptuous disavowal of his own embodied nature resulted in a debilitating pride, a kind of self-delusive "deification" that precluded the redemptive possibility of religion as philosophy's supplement. While elevating the project of philosophy to new heights, Stoicism could just as easily collapse into an empty "pride of the human will" and an equally arbitrary "apotheosis of self" (*P Lects* 1:280–81). On this question, Coleridge's critique of prideful Stoic apathy was conventional rather than idiosyncratic. In *The City of God*, Augustine had dismissed the unfeeling advocates of Stoic apatheia who "are so proud and elated in their impiety" that "their haughtiness increases even as their pain diminishes":

> Some of these, with a vanity as monstrous as it is rare, are so entranced by their own self-restraint that they are not stirred or excited or swayed or influenced by any emotions at all. But these rather suffer an entire loss of their humanity than achieve a true tranquillity. For a thing is not right merely because it is harsh, nor is stolidity the same thing as health.[26]

For Augustine, the Stoics almost seem to go against the grain of Christ's own example. Emotion had been a natural facet of his own humanity, an outgrowth of having "the body of a man and the mind of a man."[27] To attempt its negation was to forget the fact of the body, sacrificing tranquility in favor of an empty, self-entrancing pride. This was certainly the stance that Coleridge struck early in his career. Touching on the Stoics in his Bristol lectures, he noted that pride, "the most absurd, and to a wise man, the most disgusting of human Vices, characterized all their Doctrines."[28] But his *Lectures on the History of Philosophy* advanced a more nuanced position. Coleridge recognized the end of Stoic moral psychology as a "true object which man ought to pursue," but like Godwin's rational justice or Kant's moral imperative, he saw it as touching the outer edge of what the human will could accomplish without divine support.

At this point in the lecture, Coleridge confronted a kind of epistemic rupture, one that necessitated a swerve from a philosophical to a theological frame of reference. As he put it in the following week's lecture, "before the birth of our Saviour all philosophy could do or has done had been really achieved" (*P Lects* 1:326). In Coleridge's idiosyncratic lecture, Christ comes fast on the heels of Stoicism to rehabilitate philosophy. But while Augustine described Christ as an inverse of the Stoic ideal, Coleridge portrays him as an intriguingly retrofitted Stoic philosopher: "Again, in opposition to all the pretenders of self-love, with the severity and more than severity of the Stoics we hear him command us to be perfect even as our Heavenly Father is perfect, and yet declaring to men that they must perish, utterly perish, if they rely on themselves" (*P Lects* 1:283). A model of perfection sought through humility, Christ exemplifies the sublime austerity of Stoic moral training without falling into any of its errors. Coleridge's evocation of Christ as the ultimate Stoic gets at a yet more persistent concern. While Christianity retains or subsumes Stoicism's burden of perfection, it also makes room for the reality of human imperfection, which for Coleridge was tied to the fact of the body itself.

Vain Babbling Philosophy and the Pure Precepts of Revealed Religion

The contradictory ideals and potential compatibility of Stoicism and Christianity might have been one of Coleridge's hobbyhorses, but his interest in the question was hardly an aberration. As Marcia Colish has argued, affiliations between Stoic practice and Biblical doctrine have remained a persistent source of controversy over time.[29] Christianity and Stoicism had, early and late, enjoyed periods of mutual accommodation. For centuries, scholars debated the authenticity of *Epistulae Senecae et Pauli*, an apocryphal series of letters in which the apostle Paul was thought to have effected Seneca's conversion. In his notebooks, Coleridge refuted "the Legend respecting the intercourse & acquaintanceship between the Apostle & the Philosopher, and of the apocryphal Correspondences."[30] But the fact of a few forged letters hardly eliminated the allure of their possible coherence. Stoic thinkers navigating Renaissance and Reformation culture worked to reconcile Stoicism and Christianity, a move that required turning a blind eye to the determinism inherent in Stoic cosmology. Justus Lipsius, the most prominent expositor of Stoicism in the period, imagined his influential *De Constantia* (1583) as an attempt to reclaim a "path of Wisdom, so long shut off and overgrown with thorns which certainly is such as (in conjunction with Holy Scriptures) will lead us to tranquillity and peace."[31] Lipsius's insistence that the old Stoic path was actually a Christian one left an indelible mark on European culture in the seventeenth century, but this rapprochement was put under new pressure with the advent of the Enlightenment.

Throughout modernity, the ease with which Stoic ideas could be abstracted from their more comprehensive system helped to ensure their survival and widespread influence. In Christopher Brooke's terms, Stoicism became for many thinkers "a series of philosophical resources or arguments that could be drawn on selectively, indeed eclectically."[32] Stoic moral psychology could, for example, be abstracted from the determinism of Stoic physics, a move that bypassed its irreligious implications. However widespread, Stoic eclecticism was increasingly subject to a withering critique. Spooked or inspired by Spinoza's heterodox substitution of what Coleridge called "a stoical FATE" for "the LIVING GOD," a range of Enlightenment thinkers dismissed such selective Stoicism as an obfuscating eclecticism, one that attempted to take the sting out of what Ralph Cudworth described as "Pseudo-Stoical, or Stoical Atheism."[33]

Though intrigued by Stoic eclecticism, Coleridge was also an heir to this more exacting intellectual tradition. In 1795, he borrowed Cudworth's *True Intellectual System of the Universe* (1678) from the Bristol Library while preparing a series of theological lectures "intended for two classes of men—Christians and infidels."[34] In his *True Intellectual System*, Cudworth split the difference on Stoic theology. He conceded that most Stoics "did indeed religiously worship and honour the supreme God above all their other gods," but he also implied what later critics would make explicit: while individual Stoics might sublimely evoke "our duty towards God," these scattered reflections had to be squared with "the fundamental axioms of their own doctrine."[35] Johann Jakob Brucker made a similar point in the first volume of *Historia Critica Philosophiae* (1742–44), a text that Coleridge had borrowed in William Enfield's English translation from the Bristol Library in 1793:

> Great care should be taken, in the first place, not to judge of the doctrine of the Stoics from words and sentiments, detached from the general system, but to consider them as they stand related to the whole train of premises and conclusions. For want of this caution, many moderns, dazzled by the splendid expressions which they have met with in the writings of the Stoics concerning God, the soul, and other subjects, have imagined that they have discovered an invaluable treasure: whereas, if they had taken the pains to restore these brilliants to their proper places in the general mass, it would soon have appeared, that a great part of their value was imaginary. They who would ascribe to the Stoics tenets which they never held, and affix to the language a modern meaning which they never conceived, must diligently examine their whole system, and explain detached passages in such a sense, as shall be most consistent with their general doctrine, and their fundamental principles.[36]

As a key source for Diderot's *Encyclopédie*, Brucker's account reverberated throughout the Enlightenment, destabilizing the old alliance between Stoicism and Christianity.[37] More to the point, his critique of the attempt to "affix" a "modern meaning" onto an ancient philosophy anticipates Coleridge's own emphasis on the importance of principle and method in philosophy.

Coleridge followed Cudworth and Brucker in his Bristol lectures. Though acknowledging that the Stoics "believed a God indeed or at least seemed to believe one," he was especially attentive to the way their materialism seemed to circumscribe this belief. In a striking metaphor, he compared Stoic apprehension of the deity to the wisdom "with which we might suppose a Mole after turning up a few Inches of Soil might describe [the] central fires, or magnetic Nucleus of this Planet."[38] As Morton Paley has argued, the blindness of the mole was a frequent trope in Coleridge's writing, one he associated with "the partizans of a crass and sensual materialism."[39] Here, he faults the Stoics for their willingness to rest with a shallow, facile belief—a surface-level insight into a matter whose very nature required familiarity and comprehension of the depths. It was vitally important that "schoolboy scraps stolen from the vain babbling of Pagan Philosophy" were not substituted for the "pure precepts of revealed Wisdom."[40]

But Coleridge was rarely content with a straightforward dismissal. Over the course of many years, he read, reread, and annotated *The Emperor Marcus Antoninus: His Conversation with Himself.* Coleridge's text included a "Preliminary Discourse" (1652) by Thomas Gataker, a seventeenth-century Anglican clergyman whose edition of the *Meditations* would later receive high praise from Ralph Waldo Emerson (see *EW* 5:134). Charting a line that Coleridge would follow in his own *Lectures*, Gataker argued that it was "the Opinion of several *Christian Writers* that the Principles of the *Stoicks* come nearer to the Doctrines of the *Gospel*, than any other *Sect* of the *Antient* Philosophers."[41] Almost a century later, Francis Hutcheson and James Moor had struck a similar note in their own translation of *The "Meditations" of the Emperor Marcus Aurelius Antoninus* (1742). In his notes, Hutcheson worked to allay exactly the kind of objection that Coleridge would raise in his *Lectures on the History of Philosophy*. When Marcus suggests that the small amount of his remaining life should be lived "according to nature," Hutcheson intervenes to distinguish this claim from an appeal to a merely natural man:

> It may be remembered here once for all, the life according to nature, in Antoninus, is taken in a very high sense: 'Tis living up to that standard of purity and perfection, which every good man feels in his own breast: 'Tis conforming our selves to the law of God written in the heart: 'Tis endeavouring a compleat victory over the passions, and a

total conformity to the image of God. A man must read Antoninus with little attention, who confounds this with the natural man's life, condemned by St. Paul.[42]

For Coleridge, Hutcheson's defense would have cut two ways. In portraying Stoicism as a call for total "conformity to the image of God," he anticipates Coleridge's own conception of Christ as a manifestation of "the severity and more than severity of the Stoics" (*P Lects* 1:283). For all their differences, both traditions took rigorous perfectibility as an aspirational ideal. But for Coleridge, the genius of Christianity lay in the way it sanctioned the inevitable failure of "that standard of purity and perfection." Nevertheless, Coleridge's own marginalia portray him as keen to effect a Hutchesonesque rehabilitation of the philosophical emperor's inconveniently unchristian assertions. At one point in the *Meditations*, Marcus asserts that one should direct "Worship" to "the best Thing in Nature," that "Being which Manages, and Governs all the Rest." Claims like this risked drawing Coleridge's marginal ire, but here, rather than quibble with the idea of an immanent deity, he argued for the necessity of context and interpretation:

> This Paragraph and the many others of the same kind ought to be remembered as fair interpreters of other Paragraphs in which the Emperor, tho' meaning the same christian Truths, expresses himself in less christian-like phrases. Thus in those passages in which he seems to confound God with the universe, making all Things to be God, it is to be remembered that as a Platonic Stoic he considered matter & the visible world as something below entity or reality / God is the supreme Reality.[43]

In his lecture, Coleridge argued that the Stoics improperly "confounded God and nature," but at this earlier moment, he invokes the explanatory power of a Platonic tendency to conceive of things "not in their accidents or in their superficies, but in their essential powers" (*P Lects* 1:279, 193). In spite of his religious qualms, Coleridge was hesitant to close the door on a philosophical tradition that might lend itself to his own practical amelioration.

Immanuel Kant and the Most "Peccant Part of Stoicism"

Questions about the space between Christianity and Stoicism's "standard of purity and perfection" became a paradigmatic feature of Coleridge's idiosyncratic speculations, a fact borne out by his pointed interest in both

Spinoza and Kant.[44] Historians of philosophy have long noted and debated the debts both thinkers owe to the Stoics. For Coleridge, this obligation was both a recommendation and a liability. His reflections on Kant and Spinoza—much like his response to Stoicism—intersected with his religious position, which was itself related to the trial of his own corporeal existence.

In the *Opus Maximum*, Coleridge argued that the independence of Kant's moral law—its division from desire and inclination—made him "the great restorer of the Stoic Moral Philosophy."[45] In giving Kant such a vaunted title, he was simply taking "the illustrious sage of Königsberg" at his own word.[46] In *The Critique of Practical Reason*, Kant had embraced a connection to the Stoics, arguing that "*morality* alone"—not happiness—"was true wisdom."[47] For Kant this sacrifice was counterbalanced by the tranquil contentment that could result only from the consciousness of virtue:

> Freedom, and the consciousness of an ability to follow the moral law with an unyielding disposition, is *independence from the inclinations*, at least as motives determining (even if not *affecting*) our desire, and so far as I am conscious of this freedom in following my moral maxims, it is the sole source of an unchangeable contentment, necessarily combined with it and resting on no special feeling, and this can be called intellectual contentment.[48]

In his crypto-Kantian "Ode to Duty," Wordsworth had described the desire for such an "unchangeable contentment" as the longing "for a repose which ever is the same."[49] Coleridge intermittently entertained a similar desire, but he remained skeptical of intellectual contentment formed at the expense of the affections:

> I reject Kant's *stoic* principle, as false, unnatural, and even immoral, where in his Critik der Practischen Vernun[f]t he treats the affections as indifferent in ethics, and would persuade us that a man who disliking, and without any feeling of Love for, Virtue yet *acted* virtuously, because and only because it was his *Duty*, is more worthy of our esteem, than the man whose *affections* were aidant to, and congruous with, his Conscience.[50]

On the surface, Coleridge's objection to Kant's unfeeling morality reprises a disenchantment with disinterested benevolence forged in the 1790s, an aversion to "that Pride which affects to inculcate benevolence while it does away every home-born Feeling, by which it is produced and nurtured."[51] But for Coleridge, Kant's austerity prompted a more visceral and individualistic difficulty. In the *Critique of Practical Reason*, Kant takes it for granted that since the will was "determined *by the mere form of law*," it exists apart from "empirical conditions."⁵² For Kant, this was a philosophical presupposition rather than a naïve simplification. He acknowledged outright that humans could "never be altogether free from desires and inclinations" that "rest on physical causes." But Coleridge's hypersensitivity to his own "sensible impulses" and inclinations made him all too aware of Kant's recognition that "the moral law unavoidably humiliates every human being when he compares with it the sensible propensity of his nature."⁵³ Like the Stoics, Kant did not adequately account for the embodied reality of human existence. Pursued to its radical terminus, Kant's ethical theory culminated in what Coleridge described as "a boastful and hyperstoic hostility to NATURE" and an "ascetic, and almost monkish, mortification of the natural passions and desires."⁵⁴

Kant's failure to sync emotion and moral judgment made him, like Godwin, a "wretched Psychologist," a critique that Coleridge easily extended back to the Stoicism that seemed to underwrite Kant's scheme.⁵⁵ All of these figures advanced an idealized and unnatural account of human psychology, one that was radically detached from physiology. In annotating *The Emperor Marcus Antoninus: His Conversation with Himself*, Coleridge described this overestimation of the will's "Priviledge and Power" as the most "peccant part of Stoicism":

> It seems always to suppose, that the mind can act <with> consciousness independent of its bodily organs.—*Recollect*! But what if the Disease has destroyed all power of recollection/ Here it is, that Xtianity is so immeasurably superior in Truth & practical wisdom. The difference between it & Stoicism is that between the roses of a healthy country maiden's cheek, & the puffed flushed Countenance of incipient Dropsy.⁵⁶

In a burst of pathological imagination, Coleridge turns the table on Stoicism and its ameliorative project: in taking a therapeutic cue from the elevation of mind over body, Stoic apatheia risks reinforcing the diseased corporeality it sought to amend. Once again, Coleridge unwittingly echoes Hume's critique: what the Stoics imagine as an antidote is in fact a contagion, the sign of an "incipient Dropsy." Christianity reveals its true practicality by starting with the fact of the body in all its frailty.

Coleridge's frustration with dropsical Stoicism was more than a product of his religious objections. In his late and fragmentary treatise "On the Passions" (1828), he dwells at length on the embodied nature of human emotion. As he puts it, the "separation of Psychology from Physiology" would deprive "the former of all root and objective truth" and reduce "the latter to a mere enumeration of facts & phaenomena without Coupla or living form."[57] Physiology without psychology would result in a reductive or even atheistic materialism, but the reverse exclusion would be just as reductive: Stoic moral psychology was pointless if detached from the passionate bodies of its practitioners.

Coleridge's disenchantment with disembodied Stoicism was just one facet of a much broader concern. Alan Richardson and Jennifer Ford have documented his physiological interest in how dreams and other involuntary processes subjected the mind to the influence of the body.[58] Falling in line with David Hartley, Erasmus Darwin, and Charles Bell, Coleridge was an adamant proponent of "the corporeality of *thought*."[59] Like all of these figures, he disrupted the comfortable Miltonic notion that "the mind is its own place" by exploring the body's ability to thwart conscious volition. For Coleridge, however, the revolutionary alignment of physiology and psychology was demonstrated most convincingly by his own affective experience:

> It should seem, as if certain Trains of Feeling acted, *on me*, underneath my own *Consciousness* . . . & so that all Feelings which particularly affect *myself, as* myself, connect & combine with my bodily sensations, especially the trains of motion in the digestive Organs, & therefore tho' I feel them *en masse*, I do not & cannot make them the objects of a distinct attention. Any one, who witnessed the effects of bad news &c &c on my body, would conclude that I was a creature of diseased Sensibility.[60]

Operating under the radar of consciousness, passions rarely become coherent objects of attention, nor can they be disaggregated from "bodily sensations." For Coleridge, the ability of the mind to single-handedly mitigate a passion seemed as improbable as Godwin's contention that "any effort of the mind can triumph not only over disease, but over death itself."[61]

In throwing cold water on the fire of these possibilities, Coleridge struck a position that would find one of its most compressed articulations in lines by Thomas Bakewell, a reform-minded asylum keeper who doubled as a poet. In "Lines, on Being Told that the Volitions of the Mind Would Overcome the Sense of Bodily Pain," Bakewell captured the limited horizon of Stoicism in an age that increasingly traced the emotions back to a physiological ground:

> Avaunt, thou stoic sophistry,
> So falsely call'd philosophy,

> That would pretend the mind may gain,
> Such power o'er corporeal pain,
> That when we mentally are pleas'd,
> The body may from pain be eas'd.⁶²

Like Bakewell, Coleridge was conversant with the way in which new medical ideas had destabilized classic accounts of volition and autonomy. In his *Domestic Medicine, or The Family Physician* (1796), William Buchan informed his readers that there was a "reciprocal influence betwixt the mental and corporeal parts, and that whatever disorders the one likewise hurts the other."⁶³ Though all too aware of this reciprocity, Coleridge accentuated the incommensurate power of the body over the mind. In the *Biographia*, he mocked Buchan's suggestion that hypochondriacs could improve their condition merely by preserving "themselves uniformly tranquil and in good spirits."⁶⁴ The failure of Buchan, like so many Stoics, to account for the double constitution of man resulted in decisively "impracticable" advice (*P Lects* 1:280).

Coleridge's Lyric Askesis

Arthur Lovejoy once argued that "to *know* Coleridge" it was necessary to understand "the nature and interrelations of those philosophic ideas—abstract, often confused, usually sketchily expressed in any single passage, frequently conflicting with one another—which nevertheless were to him among the most vital things in his existence."⁶⁵ His sustained attempts to weigh the competing claims of Stoicism and Christianity against his own embodied experience capture the intellectual peregrinations that characterized his genius, and yet we sell Coleridge short if we take this spectacle of learning as an end in itself, the philosophical divertissements of a lapsed poet who consigned himself to "the unwholesome quicksilver mines of metaphysic depths."⁶⁶ Coleridge mistrusted the cruel optimism of an inflexible Stoicism, but he remained intrigued by its introspective method, a self-practice that sought to make seemingly passive feelings "the objects of a distinct attention."⁶⁷ For Coleridge, this interest was borne out most substantively, if a bit surprisingly, in the realm of lyric. In grappling with Stoic ideas, Coleridge rarely abstracted their claims from the crucible of his own existence. It was only a short additional jump from his own life to its examination in verse.

At every turn, Coleridge's critical reception has been driven by a few visionary poems notable for their imaginative exuberance: a woman wails for her demon lover, a mariner recounts a supernatural tale with "glittering eye," or a poet laments the slow foreclosure of his "shaping spirit of Imagination." But a vast range of Coleridge's poetic oeuvre—composed across a long life—declines this kind of high-octane Romantic expressivism.[68] Lyric writing was more than a conduit for the expression of passion; it could preside over its modulation or adjustment, setting, in Coleridge's words, "the affections in right tune."[69] While never promoting the outright elimination of emotion, poiesis could subject the affections to the heightened attention of what he called the "self-watching subtilizing mind."[70] In this sense, Coleridge's functional poetics bear some resemblance to what Shaftesbury isolated as Marcus Aurelius's central insight: "All depends on your opinions: These are in your power. Remove, therefore, when thou incline, your opinion; and then, as when one has turned the promontory, and got into a bay, all is calm; so, all shall become stable to you, and a still harbor."[71] If tranquility was a potential by-product of thoughtful self-examination, lyric writing could focalize the active power of mind that might be applied to a deceptively passive realm of feeling. In spite of its etymology, passion did not have to be suffered or endured. For Coleridge, then, lyric designated not just a genre or an artistic artifact but an askesis or practice, a technology of the self by which emotion, opinion, and mental impressions of all stripes could be evaluated, attenuated, or affirmed.[72]

Coleridge broached this "self-watching" account of lyric in the *Biographia*. In delineating the "promises and specific symptoms of poetic power," he had one of Schiller's formulations in mind: a poet must "become alienated from his own self, to disentangle the object of his enthusiasm from his own individuality, to perceive his passion from a tranquil distance."[73] Early and late, this tranquil distance looms as a key aspiration in Coleridge's poetry, but one that destabilizes typical frameworks for understanding the nature and ends of poetry itself. For one thing, the shadow of Stoicism qualifies a cornerstone of lyric theory that Coleridge helped promulgate. After all, the Romantic reinvention of the lyric as a major genre rooted in the representation of subjective experience cedes prime place to the expression of emotion. As M. H. Abrams put it, "those elements in a poem that express feeling become at once its identifying characteristic and cardinal poetic value."[74] At the same time, approaching lyric as a venue for Stoic praxis suggests yet another variation on what it means to claim philosophy as a facet of Coleridge's verse. Taking a page from Simon Jarvis's playbook, Ewan Jones has argued that Coleridge's poetry does more than reflect or anticipate his philosophy. It becomes, rather, "his sole means of thinking in a philosophically significant and original manner."[75] This seems right to an extent, especially in its recognition that poetry involves more than the mere reflection or recapitulation of philosophical ideas. And yet for Coleridge, philosophy did not always entail originality or abstraction, nor did it necessitate voyaging through strange seas of thought alone. In many cases, Coleridge's muse declined the demands of speculative thinking and originality, pursuing instead the quiet yet sustaining tasks of self-reflection and repetitive exercise.[76] Pierre Hadot has argued that living a philosophical life in antiquity did not always entail breaking new intellectual ground; practice was as vital as theory, and cultivating one's garden year after year was enough. Drawing on this tradition, Coleridge equated the postulate of all philosophy with the imperative inscribed on the temple at Delphi: "the heaven-descended KNOW THYSELF!"[77] For Hadot, such an imperative necessitated an acknowledgment of imperfection, of knowing oneself "not as a *sophos*, but as a *philo-sophos*, someone *on the way toward* wisdom."[78] Something of this philosophical aspiration shines through in much of Coleridge's poetry. Setting aside the imaginative sublime, he found in verse a steady way to keep watch over his own mind, which was itself never far removed from the fact of his body. Manifestations of such lyric askesis could seem ancillary even to Coleridge when he accounted for poetry in its most exalted mood, and yet taking them into account drastically alters the conventional wisdom about the fate of his career. Coleridge's Stoicism did not result in an abrupt termination of his poetic vocation; as I will argue below, the Stoic evaluation and mitigation of the passions had long been a feature of his verse.

Of course, Coleridge's own genial and influential criticism tended to emphasize a different conception of the lyric, one that continues to inform the methods and assumptions of contemporary lyric theory. Though working from different perspectives, both Jonathan Culler and Virginia Jackson have drawn attention to just how much our broad conception of the lyric owes to its consolidation in the Romantic period. In Jackson's terms, a variety of recognizable subgenres and modes of transmission were replaced by "an idealized scene of reading progressively identified with an idealized moment of expression."[79] In emphasizing this "moment of expression," both Culler and Jackson take M. H. Abrams's account of the Romantic lyric as paradigmatic.[80] A fast flip through *The Mirror and the Lamp* captures the predominance and ubiquity of emotion in the poetics of this new expressive regime. John Stuart Mill's broad definition of poetry gets aired twice: poetry is, quite simply, "the expression or uttering forth of feeling."[81] Abrams is also fond of an anonymous account that appeared in *Blackwood's Magazine*: "Behold now the whole character of poetry. It is *essentially the expression of emotion.*"[82] Abrams even concedes that the expressive ideal can quickly turn into a parody of itself, an all too "easy effusiveness and loosely articulated impressionism." He takes Hazlitt to task for pursuing the equation of emotion and poetic expression to its logical terminus: "Fear is poetry, hope is poetry, love is poetry, hatred is poetry; contempt, jealously, remorse, admiration, wonder, pity, despair, or madness, are all poetry."[83] At this extreme, seemingly any emotion becomes not just a catalyst, but a poetic equivalent. Rooted in particularity but stripped of its historicity, emotion becomes the great equalizer in all of these formulations, the realm of subjective experience that most clearly bestows upon the expressive lyric its aura of timelessness and universality. To substitute tranquility or detachment for one of the terms on Hazlitt's list would disrupt the sequence of ecstatic states. In redefining the passions as a subset of opinion, Stoic self-reflection would seem to signal not poetry but its antithesis.

But if lyric comes into its majority with the rise of subjective self-consciousness, what accounts for the undue priority of emotion over and above other modes of subjective expression? Surely self-discipline, a desire for clarity, or the achievement of a calm stability can play into expression, too. Hegel's account of the lyric—described by Culler as "the fullest expression of the romantic theory of the lyric"—offers a more nuanced account of its expressive capacity and range.[84] Like Mill and Hazlitt, Hegel plays up the ability of lyric to record and transmit "the whole gamut of feeling": "The momentary and most fleeting mood, the heart's jubilant cry, the quickly passing flashes of carefree happiness and merriment, the outbursts of melancholy, dejection, and lament—in short the whole gamut of feeling is seized here in its momentary movements, or in its single fancies about all sorts of things."[85] At another point, he takes emotional mimesis as the sole criterion for distinguishing a "genuine" lyric from an alternative that he does not even bother to describe: "The genuine lyric, like all true poetry, has to express the true contents of the human heart."[86] All of this comports quite well with the expressive turn as rendered by Abrams, and yet the first paragraph of Hegel's lengthy exposition takes a more qualified view of passion in lyric, one that aligns lyric practice with "the poet's spiritual work":

> If therefore the heart can find relief when its grief or pleasure is put, described, and expressed in words of any sort, a poetic outburst can certainly perform the like service; but it is not confined to its use as an old wife's medicine. Indeed it has on the contrary a higher vocation: its task, namely, is to liberate the spirit not *from* but *in* feeling.

> The blind dominion of passion lies in an unconscious and dull unity between itself and the entirety of a heart that cannot rise out of itself into ideas and self-expression. Poetry does deliver the heart from this slavery to passion by making it see itself, but it does not stop at merely extricating this felt passion from its immediate unity with the heart but makes of it an object purified from all accidental moods, an object in which the inner life, liberated and with its self-consciousness satisfied, reverts freely at the same time into itself and is at home with itself.[87]

Hegel starts off by sweeping a deceptively simplistic account of lyric under the rug in order to magnify the complexity of its task. A "poetic outburst" might work just like "an old wife's medicine," but the contempt evident in both formulations forecloses any serious investigation of poetry's medicinal power.[88] And yet the end goal of "relief" is hardly set aside in his description of lyric in its "higher vocation." Here, expression is not an end in itself, but the catalyst for a self-consciousness that might "deliver" the heart from its "slavery to passion." The psychological delivery that lyric promotes works much like Stoic moral psychology, though Hegel also dismisses the illusory ideal of complete apathy. Lyric holds out the possibility of liberation "not *from* but *in* feeling." Extricated from its "immediate unity with the heart," passion becomes a new object of cognitive attention. As Thomas Pfau has put it, lyric becomes the "medium most suited to extracting the intentionality and lucidity encrypted by a given feeling."[89] Purified from all accidental moods and bodily contingency, feeling becomes an object of the poet's own power. But what I most want to emphasize is that the words of the poem, the artifact itself, are only half the achievement. The poetic work points back toward the poet's work; the relief of a heart made free and "at home with itself" is all too easily overlooked.

Thinking about lyric as a practice, a regimen, or even "an old wife's medicine" seems an awkward endeavor, for it counters deeply engrained intuitions about the lyric mode. It destabilizes the clear though often arbitrary boundary that separates a poem from the life of the poet. At the same time, it makes a critic's interpretive task strangely belated or beside the point. If a cardinal value of the lyric unfolds in the valley of its initial saying, critical retrospection, however acute, becomes all too cold and archaeological. In *Poetry as a Way of Life*, Gabriel Trop makes a case for attending to the "exercise value" inherent in poetry. For Trop, askesis becomes a facet of reception rather than creation: a poem "continually modifies, often imperceptibly, the manifold patterns of being—whether they are perceptual, behavioral, or affective."[90] But for Coleridge lyric askesis was an aspect of private creation and self-formation, a distillation of the "Heart's *Self-commune* & soliloquy" that sometimes started within the confines of his notebooks, occasionally even in cipher (*PW* 2:823). If the act of composition could mark, for Coleridge, the fulfillment of a sustaining introspective process, then many of his poems become residual memoranda, poems whose primary task was neither to mean *nor* be.[91] As we will see, many of Coleridge's lyrics were, like the meditations of Marcus Aurelius, acts of temporary self-coherence; in Hadot's words, "characters traced onto some medium do not fix anything: everything is in the act of writing."[92]

In foregrounding the act of poetic articulation, my argument could be considered an inversion of Catherine Robson's investigation of the memorized poem. Though I focus on composition rather than recitation, my account of Coleridge's poetics squares with Robson's sense that poetry can be a "practice" or "regimen" that is experienced "in and through the body."[93] In this sense, Coleridge's lyric askesis disrupts standard narratives about aesthetic autonomy and the desirable purposelessness of art. It looks uncomfortably out of place amid what David Duff has described as militant Romantic anti-didacticism, a sense of the aesthetic as "an autonomous mode of cognition which can act separately from and even antithetically to the moral sense."[94] And yet as Duff's persuasive argument makes clear, widespread didactic abhorrence coincided with a "relentless" but overlooked demand that literature "perform some function." This split mandate could be a driver for formal innovation. For example, it provoked a revolution in sonnet sensibility, one that turned "a conduit for lachrymose effusion" into what Duff calls "a tool for the analysis of emotion."[95] This account of the sonnet's evolution is especially apropos to Coleridge's poetic development; after all, in his first published volume, he acknowledged that "a considerable number" of his poems could be "styled 'Effusions'"—thirty-six, to be exact (*PW* 1:1196). In adopting this nomenclature, Coleridge aligned his poetic task with an artless and largely indiscriminate deluge of feeling—as the *Oxford English Dictionary* has it, "an 'outpouring' of the author's feelings, genius, etc."[96] The effusion represents the expressive ideal's path of least resistance. In later collections he abjured the designation and never looked back.

Talk amongst Yourselves

Lyric askesis might seem counterintuitive or out of step with Coleridge's expansive sensibility but, then again, for the last forty years of his life, Coleridge was a devotee of another form of sustained, deliberate exercise.

His notebooks, vertiginous and wide-ranging, have been described as covering "every aspect of Coleridge's life—his travels, reading, dreams, nature studies, self-confession and self-analysis, philosophical theories, friendships, sexual fantasies, lecture notes, observations of his children, literary schemes, brewing recipes, opium addiction, horrors, puns, prayers."[97] Unmoored from the conventions of a genre and the communicative expectations of a pleasure-seeking audience, the notebooks furnished a private, conjectural space for the free play of the mind and private self-reflection. On more than a few occasions, Coleridge's meditations in prose make way for fragmentary verse:

> Ills from without extrinsic Balms may heal,
> Oft cur'd & wounded by the self-same Steel—
> But us what remedy can heal or cure,
> Whose very nature is our worst disease. (*PW* 2:863)

In his editorial introduction, J.C.C. Mays has described such notebook poetry as a kind of exercise; lines like these become "notations of a mood," or even "workings out of a passing notion" (*PW* lxxxix). And yet when isolated from its conjectural origins in the notebooks, this self-contained quatrain can seem a not fully realized lyric, its omission of personal emotion and failure to uphold a straightforward rhyme scheme a testament to what many critics describe as Coleridge's lapsed poetic magic. Nevertheless, it starts with an impersonal catalyst: a stray line from the medical philosophy of Paracelsus becomes a self-diagnosis, with versification itself an all-too-imperfect remedy.[98] Tentatively, and in the face of manifest skepticism, verse becomes a regimen that might bring temporary order to, or effect liberation from, the fact of an embodiment that feels like a disease. The exercise, like meter itself, attempts to cultivate a "balance in the mind effected by that spontaneous effort which strives to hold in check the workings of passion."[99]

The *Notebooks* are saturated with Coleridge's recognition that both his affective life and its self-representations were connected with the nonvolitional "motions of the Blood and nerves, and images forced into the mind by the feelings that arise out of the position & state of the Body and its different members."[100] This was the "unfathomable hell within" that lyric askesis worked to assuage. In a poem like "The Pains of Sleep"—written, as Coleridge notes, "as a letter & of course never intended to be published"—a private turn to poetry effects the self-alienation that makes a certain clarity of self-perception or diagnosis possible:

> Fantastic passions! mad'ning brawl!
> And shame and terror over all!
> Deeds to be hid which were not hid,
> Which all confused I could not know,
> Whether I suffered, or I did:
> For all seemed guilt, remorse or woe,
> My own or others still the same
> Life-stifling fear, soul-stifling shame! (*PW* 2:754)

It is tempting to attribute the power of the lines to Coleridge's retrospective mimesis and "faithful portraiture" of embodied and intersubjective negative affect, and yet their real achievement is the clarity that reclaims self and mind from the false and confusing representations inherent in so discrepant a field of passion.[101] Rather than catalog the variety of scattered instances in which Coleridge's poems mimic a kind of Stoic exercise, I want to survey a common dialogic mode that underwrites the impulse to askesis in both Coleridge's poetry and his notebooks.

In a letter to Wordsworth, Coleridge once described his "Pocket books" as his "only full Confidants."[102] At another moment, he addressed his notebook directly: "Ah! Dear book! Sole Confidant of a breaking Heart, whose social nature compels *some* Outlet."[103] In reimaging a solitary and private space as a site of communicative sympathy and exchange, Coleridge's account of his notebook shares much in common with his best-known generic innovation: the conversation poem. Both forms of askesis operate under Coleridge's seemingly paradoxical assumption that self-reflection is not a solipsistic but a conversational practice.

Borrowing the term from a subtitle to Coleridge's "The Nightingale," George McLean Harper was the first to describe eight of Coleridge's more famous lyrics as "conversation poems," a term generally thought to characterize a set of poems notable for both the colloquial tenor of their "intimate speaking voice" and their inclusion of an implied but silent interlocutor.[104] In Bakhtinian terms, a conversation poem was a monologic lyric, but one with clear pretensions to dialogism. Over time, however, Coleridge's conversation poems have drawn critical ire for deploying a conversational ideal without offering any evidence of a bona fide exchange. The seeming deception by which Coleridge advertises dialogue yet delivers up monologue has made poems like "Frost at Midnight" or "The Eolian Harp" paradigmatic case studies of what Nancy Yousef has called "the problematic, symptomatic expression of an aggrandizing, illusorily autonomous ego."[105]

By this logic, Coleridge's egotistical sublimity becomes most intractable at the very point at which he seems to imagine its evanescence by aligning the solitary genre of lyric with something like the radical conversational culture of the 1790s or the accelerating dialogism of the novel. For many critics, Coleridge's attempt to portray a univocal utterance as an instance of conversational dialogism only foregrounds his inadequate grasp of real interchange, a reading intriguingly borne out by recollections of his in-person conversational habits.[106] For Harold Bloom, however, the conversation poems make it clear that Coleridge "preceded Wordsworth in the invention of a new kind of poetry that shows the mind in a dialogue with itself."[107]

Even so, it seems shortsighted to separate a new poetic instance of inner dialogue from the long philosophical tradition informing it. I want to suggest that Coleridge's intermittent engagement with the Stoics offers an alternative way of explaining his generic innovation, one that points toward a therapeutic origin rather than an ineffectual attempt to deploy truly conversational language. Coleridge recorded various marginal reflections in his copy of Marcus Aurelius's *Meditations* over the course of two decades. The title of his particular edition of Marcus is especially striking: *The Emperor Marcus Antoninus: His Conversation with Himself*.[108] Marcus's *hypomnemata*, or notes, have been published over time with many different titles, but the conversational rubric that distinguished Coleridge's edition pointed to what Hadot has described as "the central node of the whole of Stoicism: that of inner discourse, or judgments expressed on the subject of representations."[109] Rather than the negation of all emotion, Stoics like Marcus and Epictetus modeled a form of introspective dialogue that made emotions and impressions a distinct object of attention. Significantly, these judgments took shape amid a conversation that one had with oneself, a kind of soliloquy or "inner dialogue" that Brian Stock has characterized as a literary and pedagogical technique taken up by many different thinkers in the service of philosophy.[110] If Stoic philosophers like Seneca, Epictetus, and Marcus Aurelius were early pioneers of inner dialogue, Coleridge's one-sided conversation poems suggest that he was one of their late and experimental inheritors.

Critics have proposed various ways of accounting for the exact nature or pattern of the meditative inner dialogue at the heart of each conversation poem. In embodied terms, Albert Gérard likened Coleridge's fluctuating attention in each poem to "a heart-beat rhythm of systole and diastole, of contraction and expansion."[111] For Abrams, they enacted the "out-in-out process" by which a mind makes sense of the external world.[112] However the pattern is delineated, it seems vital to note that the conversation poems were not effusions but exercises. When Coleridge evokes an emotion, it is generally attenuated rather than celebrated. Clarity and consolation are the orienting aims of a poet who characterizes himself as "a man, who would full fain preserve/ His soul in calmness" (*PW* 1:470). In "This Lime-Tree Bower My Prison," for example, a sharp sense of loss brought about by injury is famously "sooth'd" and then transformed into joyful contemplation. The broad arc of the poem's meditation falls in line with the Stoic idea than any external prison, even a lime-tree bower, can be subverted by the greater power of what Epictetus called "the Citadel within ourselves."[113] And here, in a poem that takes its origin from the experience of temporary disability—Coleridge's foot was scalded by a pan of boiling milk—he seems to credit the Stoic idea that the mind might gain "power o'er corporeal pain."[114] The whole poem could be glossed with a line that Coleridge marked in his copy of *The Emperor Marcus Antoninus: His Conversation with Himself*: "Accidents are indifferent in themselves, and only good, or bad for us, accordingly as we use them."[115] For all its idealist overtones, this dialogue of the mind with itself reimagines "strange calamity" as a productive limitation, one in which Coleridge's own affective loss is cut down to size by a vision of social interconnection that emerges out of solitude itself. To describe the poem as a species of expressivism is to notice emotions but ignore their trajectory: in a realm "less gross than bodily," loss is expressed but ultimately refigured through poetic meditation as a kind of relinquishment (*PW* 1:352–53).

Though unfolding against a much wider horizon, "Fears in Solitude: Written in April 1798, during the Alarm of Invasion" also foregrounds the mitigation of feeling through inner dialogue. Coleridge himself was forthright about the conversational character of the poem, referencing a motto from Horace to note that it was "sermoni propior" (*PW* 1:469). While Mays translates the motto to suggest a proximity to prose, Daniel White has noted that the Latin *sermo* points more directly to "conversation," or discussion.[116] But here again the conversation is noticeably one-sided. Temporarily ensconced in yet another "quiet spirit-healing nook," Coleridge retreats form the world in an intensively meditative "half sleep," one that is quickly populated by "fear and rage" and thoughts of all the lives undone by "undetermin'd conflict":

> My God! It is a melancholy thing
> For such a man, who would full fain preserve
> His soul in calmness, yet perforce must feel
> For all his human brethren—O my God!
> It is indeed a melancholy thing,

> And weighs upon the heart, that he must think
> What uproar and what strife may now be stirring
> This way or that way o'er these silent hills—(*PW* 1:470–71)

Channeling a state of almost involuntary hypervigilance, Coleridge shows how simply the threat that a distant war might breach Britain's enisled tranquility becomes—as far as his mental tranquility is concerned—already a fait accompli. Much of the poem is given over to a series of "bodings" that are "well nigh" wearying and yet cannot be ignored (*PW* 1:476). Coleridge links the threat of violence to a grievous acknowledgment of complicity, and he punctures the illusion of a peace maintained only by abstracting the "ghastlier workings" of distant war. The instability of this peace wrought by distance results in a paradoxical affective imbalance. The encroaching reality of a "vague and dim" war results in extravagant fear and unwarranted alarm, but this same distance also elicits a corrosive insensibility:

> Boys and girls,
> And women, that would groan to see a child
> Pull off an insect's leg, all read of war,
> The best amusement for our morning-meal! (*PW* 1:473).

For Coleridge, then, the suffering that was too easily confined to the distance or the future produced at once too much feeling and not enough. In 1803, Wordsworth would assuage his fears of invasion by training with the Grasmere Volunteers on the village green. In this earlier poem, Coleridge counters a similar anxiety with a very different kind of exercise, subjecting fear and its equally troubling absence to the dialogic interplay of Stoic self-reflection. But since the fear that Coleridge examines here is—to use Mark Canuel's terms—both a "mental attribute" and a facet of "public order," even Coleridge's internal deliberations and recalibrations search for an order that might reverberate beyond the self.[117]

Coleridge's attempt to pin down personal feeling amid the clamorous "uproar" of a phantom invasion makes "Fears in Solitude" a marquee example of what Lily Gurton-Wachter has described as a Romantic "poetics of attention" inextricably informed by "wartime watchfulness" and the "militarization of attention."[118] She suggests that this deeply engrained habit of wartime vigilance could be reclaimed in various open-ended forms of seeing and attending, an insight potentially borne out in this poem by Coleridge's Stoic turn inward. As Shaftesbury's *Askêmata* made clear, military metaphors pervade Stoic self-practice early and late. But wartime attention could also spill over into empty alarmism. For Gurton-Wachter, "Fears in Solitude" illustrates this latter possibility, fostering alarm by ventriloquizing the "blank assertions" and "empty sounds" that it also calls into question.[119] In this line of analysis, Coleridge's poetry absorbs and replicates—almost against its will—an affective charge from the oratory and rhetorical warmongering that it approaches with deep skepticism. I would not want to dispute this account of the poem's affective resonance, which Gurton-Wachter convincingly tracks all the way to the "empty sounds" and "exclamatory language" of the poem itself.[120] At the same time, Coleridge cross-examines this affective bankruptcy, modeling the kind of self-reflection or examination of "conscience" that might cut through the haziness of fear and its "deep delusion[s]" (*PW* 1:475). The overtones of habit and ritual in this examination resonate with Mary Favret's observation that various lines in "Fears in Solitude" bear more than a passing resemblance to the "rhetorical structure" of sermons occasioned by the General Fast and Humiliation. It is as if the poem's absorption of wartime rhetoric works in two different ways: transmissible feeling's rush to fill the void is imagined against a countervailing manifestation of Stoic askesis that might restore substance to a world of shadow.

Drawing on the work of Silvan Tomkins, Favret has described royally sanctioned days of fasting and humiliation throughout the Revolutionary and Napoleonic Wars as public attempts to "organize disparate, immediate, as well as more archaic feelings into a 'conscious report.'" Two strains of Favret's important account of this pious ritual fallen upon secular times are especially relevant here. Though liable to veer toward performance or "ritualized gesture," the General Fast and Humiliation was, at root, a kind of practice or askesis, a "national examination of conscience" that had—at least in theory—an introspective correlative.[121] At the same time, the contours of its corporate self-discipline were inherently affective, designed to facilitate "the streamlining and buffering of emotion," especially as that emotion was unleashed by war itself.[122] Reading "Fears in Solitude" in light of another regimen for managing the affections suggests that Coleridge's lyric askesis—a poetic channeling of the desire to turn indistinct feelings into a "conscious report"—was just one manifestation of ethical self-practice in Romantic Britain. Not unlike fasting, his internal dialogue held out the promise that "certain Trains of Feeling" could become "objects of a distinct attention."[123] Invoking hollow fear was another way of sounding its depth, for as the plural in Coleridge's title makes clear, fear was hardly a monolithic emotion.

In the *Tusculan Disputations*, Cicero distinguished between precaution (*cautio*) and fear (*metus*). Precaution entailed a rational "turning away" from evil; fear, by contrast, was a kind of caution "alien from reason," an exaggerated "belief of threatening evil which seems to the subject of it insupportable."[124] In "Fears in Solitude," Coleridge works to distinguish between the two, recasting fear as a form of false judgment while isolating a narrower frame of reference in which a rational fear—the kind, for example, occasioned by complicity—could foster a new sense of autonomy or even a "turning away" from evil. To be sure, Coleridge's conversation with himself departs from models of Stoic dialogue in many ways. There is no repetition and reflection on dogma, nor does he ask and then answer questions in a more regimented form of self-inquiry. And yet Coleridge pointedly imagines collective transformation as the outgrowth of private acts of self-examination. The idea that change might come from "constituted power" was a "deep delusion," one that failed to recognize the way in which external government borrowed all its "hues and qualities / From our own folly" (*PW* 1:475). For all his Stoic skepticism, Coleridge was entranced by the individual and collective possibilities that might be unlocked by making the right use of mental impressions. So much of fear was dependent upon judgment and belief. As he would assert in other contexts, self-government was foundational to collective life.[125] This conviction drives the hopeful conclusion of "Fears in Solitude" that lyric askesis—successfully pursued—might lead not just to the mitigation of fear but to cosmic reconnection itself:

> And after lonely sojourning
> In such a quiet and surrounded nook,
> This burst of prospect, here the shadowy Main,
> Dim tinted, there the mighty majesty
> Of that huge amphitheatre of rich
> And elmy Fields, seems like society—
> Conversing with the mind, and giving it
> A livelier impulse and dance of thought! (*PW* 1:476–77)

Emerging from his self-reflexive meditation, Coleridge discovers that his "solitary musings" have reconfigured his relation to the whole world "*imag'd* in its vast circumference" (*PW* 1:263). A private conversation suddenly becomes an enlivening conversation in a broader world. Jon Mee and others have faulted Coleridge for "converting conversation into monologue," but for Stoics like Marcus Aurelius this was inevitably a false distinction.[126] However fleeting and insubstantial, the hope that Stoicism and its introspective mandate might foster even abstract communion in an embodied and deluded world was enough to outweigh—at least occasionally—Coleridge's deep fear of its inadequacy.

"Tranquillity Disappears"

In concluding, I want to take up Coleridge's penultimate conversation poem and pause over the seven self-suppressing lines quoted at the outset of the chapter. Coleridge fixated on and frequently returned to these lines, occasionally copying them into his letters as an intimate but obfuscating affidavit:

> For not to think of what I needs must feel,
> But to be still and patient, all I can;
> And haply by abstruse research to steal
> From my own nature all the natural Man—
> This was my sole resource, my only plan:
> Till that which suits a part infects the whole,
> And now is almost grown the habit of my Soul. (*PW* 1:700)

The lines, from "Dejection: An Ode," immediately follow Coleridge's stark acknowledgement of the unwilled lapse of his own "shaping spirit of Imagination," and this proximity has tended to govern their interpretation, as if they describe the inevitable compounding of a preexisting condition. In trying to reinvigorate or reobtain imagination—so the story goes—Coleridge only hastened its disappearance. I want to advance a different hypothesis by arguing that the trauma of an *unwilled* loss of imagination overshadows, and perhaps defensively so, Coleridge's more than passing interest in a *willed* turn away from feeling itself. After all, these cryptic lines strikingly anticipate his forceful critique of the Stoics in his *Lectures on the History of Philosophy*.

At a certain level, it is hardly surprising that Coleridge would link an elision of feeling to the failure of poetry. His critiques of Stoicism were, after all, variations on a single theme: Stoic apatheia, inadequately embodied, was out of sync with "living form."[127] Given the organic aesthetics that galvanized so much of his poetic thinking, Stoic detachment could seem an unpromising catalyst for poetic creation. As feeling and liveliness lapse, the shaping spirit of imagination recedes: "I see, not feel how beautiful they are" (*PW* 2:699). In its agonistic relationship with the living body, and hence with life itself, Stoicism could almost be called mechanical—a clear disqualifier in the context of Coleridge's aesthetics. His rejection of this poetic mode in "Dejection" is firmly entrenched in literary history. What tends to be overlooked is the adherence that preceded its repudiation.

Coleridge first published "Dejection: An Ode" in the *Morning Post* on the day of Wordsworth's wedding and his own anniversary. For its public debut, he omitted the seven lines I have set at the heart of this chapter. Mays is certainly right to link the elision to Coleridge's impossible passion for Sara Hutchinson, just as Stephen Parrish sensibly ties the omission to the painful vocational transformation that turned an aspiring poet into a self-professed metaphysician.[128] I want to suggest that both accounts overlook Coleridge's own recent fascination with the poetic possibilities of Stoicism. The lines, if printed, could not help but remind readers of a poem published in the *Morning Post* just months before. "Ode to Tranquillity" (1801)—quietly Horatian rather than sublimely Pindaric—is a lyric exercise that entertains the relinquishment of affective immediacy rather than mourning its disappearance. More to the point, it holds out the (faint) hope that Stoic tranquility might be the necessary catalyst for physical health and poetic creativity.

In the classical world, Seneca was the great expositor of tranquility. In "On Tranquility of Mind"—a text that Coleridge referenced in *The Statesman's Manual*—Seneca tries to reason with Nero's police commissioner Serenus, whose determination to follow in the austere footsteps of Greek Stoics like Zeno and Chrysippus leads him into despair and fruitless "wavering."[129] As Serenus puts it, "this weakness of a good mind follows me in every affair." Coleridge would have admired Seneca's response, for he acknowledged the impossibility of attaining complete perfection:

> What you are longing for is a great thing and the highest achievement, near to god: never to be shaken. The Greeks call this stable balance of the mind *euthymia*. . . . I call this tranquility, since we do not have to imitate and transpose their words in the form they use; but the actual thing must be marked by some name that ought to have the meaning, not the form, of the Greek designation. So we are investigating how the mind may always move at an even and favorable pace and be well disposed to itself and glad to see its own qualities and not interrupt this joy, but always remain in a calm condition, neither rearing itself up nor thrusting itself down; this will be tranquility.[130]

Refuting the possibility of perfection, Seneca's aspirational tranquility emphasized health, balance, and the pleasure of moderate emotions. Indeed, he describes tranquility as a remedy that might restore and preserve sound health. In open-minded moments, Coleridge inclined toward a similarly broad interpretation of Stoic apatheia. In annotating Robert Leighton's *Genuine Works*, he echoed Seneca's accommodating perspective: "On what ground can it be asserted that the Stoics believed in the actual existence of their God-like perfection in any individual? or that they meant more than this—'To no man can the name of the Wise be given in its absolute sense, who is not perfect even as his Father in heaven is perfect!'"[131] Short of perfection, and yet aligned with a Senecan stability of mind, tranquility was, for Coleridge, a prerequisite for poetic composition as well as an outgrowth of its exercise. But as his own experience would make painfully clear, it was at best a fleeting attainment.

Coleridge's "Ode to Tranquillity" relies on stately personification to effect a quiet dedication that is also a renunciation. Willard Spiegelman, one of the only critics to address the poem at any length, has criticized its "declamatory, unexplorative, undramatic, and most of all painfully abstract manner," but this line of critique fails to correlate absence with sacrifice.[132] As an exercise in the cultivation of tranquility, the ode knowingly entertains the forfeiture of exploration, drama, and vivid actuality. Spiegelman's inclination to read the ode's formal challenge as an artistic failure or capitulation to "perilous temptation" leads him to a further misreading. Briefly put, he suggests that since tranquility seems to find its own subject, Coleridge "must already have won it if he knows that it will give him respite."[133] The rhetoric of the poem works against such a view, as do Coleridge's tortured letters and agonized notebooks from the same difficult years to which the ode stands as a haunting monument.

In the ode, Coleridge casts himself as an aspirant of tranquility whose health only rarely allows him to enjoy its equanimity:

> Tranquillity! thou better name
> Than all the family of Fame!
> Thou ne'er wilt leave my riper age
> To low intrigue, or factious rage:
> For oh! Dear child of thoughtful Truth,
> To thee I gave my early youth,
> And left the bark, and blest the stedfast shore,
> Ere yet the Tempest rose and scar'd me with its roar.
>
> Who late and lingering seeks thy shrine,
> On him but seldom, power divine,
> Thy spirit rests! Satiety

> And sloth, poor counterfeits of thee,
> Mock the tired worldling. Idle Hope
> And dire Remembrance interlope,
> To vex the feverish slumbers of the mind:
> The bubble floats before, the spectre stalks behind. (*PW* 2:672)

In his initial apostrophe, Coleridge conflates an appeal with an assertion even as Lucretian intimations of inconstancy destabilize his conviction that tranquility will, in fact, preside over his "riper age." Amid the physicality of satiety, sloth, and feverish slumbers, the mind can hardly—to quote Seneca—"be well disposed to itself" or "glad to see its own qualities."[134] And Coleridge's bubble, like those in a *vanitas* still life, only emphasizes the transiency of the body. It is no coincidence that Coleridge invokes tranquility more than thirty times in his letters from these years, almost always in relation to his own precarious health. In a characteristic example, he writes, "I am now only somewhat better / & feel the infinite Importance of the deepest Tranquillity."[135] Later, in a letter to Godwin written just after the ode, he isolated a "want" of self-command as both cause and effect of his own condition:

> If I might so say, I am, as an *acting* man, a creature of mere Impact. "I will" & "I will not" are phrases, both of them equally, of rare occurrence in my dictionary. . . . I ask for Mercy indeed on the score of my ill-health; but I confess, that this very ill-health is as much an effect as a cause of this want of steadiness & self-command; and it is for mercy that I ask, not for justice.[136]

If there was part of Coleridge that was attuned to the body's capacity to thwart Stoic detachment, there was also a part of him that saw Stoic tranquility and self-command as crucial but absent conditions that might bring health and restoration.

But there are other possibilities latent in the ode's aspirational tranquility. If the loss of feeling in "Dejection" threatens the end of poetry, does the surrender of feeling in "Ode to Tranquillity" seek its continuance or restoration? Here I am thinking of a stray phrase in Coleridge's notebooks that chronologically preempts Wordsworth's more famous preface: "poetry . . . recalling of passion in tranquillity."[137] From a Coleridgean perspective, this bulwark of Romantic poetics—the re-collecting power of tranquility—might not be that different from the moderated Stoicism that thrived from Roman times and on through the Enlightenment. In both cases, the aim was the evaluation of passion rather than its elimination. Consider the ode's last stanza:

> The feeling heart, the searching soul,
> To thee [tranquility] I dedicate the whole!
> And while within myself I trace
> The greatness of some future race,
> Aloof with hermit-eye I scan
> The present works of present man—
> A wild and dream-like trade of blood and guile,
> Too foolish for a tear, too wicked for a smile! (*PW* 2:672–73)

When measured against the poetic dialectic of passion and will described in the *Biographia*, "*voluntary* purpose" always defeats "*spontaneous* impulse" in "Ode to Tranquillity"—and that, of course, was the point of the exercise.[138] Renunciation yields self-knowledge, distance, and Ancient Mariner–like isolation, but the terms of the dedication are striking. In Coleridge's choice of "dedicate," I read less emphasis on devotion, and more on surrender; in the *Oxford English Dictionary*'s words, the idea of giving up "earnestly, seriously, or wholly" to a person or purpose.[139] The feeling heart, the searching soul, or even the satisfaction of action in time: the cost of tranquility could be that extensive. In reading poetry after the so-called affective turn, it is easy to lose sight of the fact that Coleridge, at least at times, was ready to pay up: "To see, and not feel" was not just a disabling condition but sometimes, perhaps, the point.

CHAPTER FOUR

The True Social Art

BYRON AND THE CHARACTER OF STOICISM

> *Hail social tube! thou foe to care!*
> *Companion of my easy chair!*
> *Form'd not, with cold and Stoic art,*
> *To harden, but to soothe, the heart!*
> *For BACON, a much wiser man*
> *Than any of the Stoic clan,*
> *Declares thy power to control*
> *Each fretful impulse of the soul;*
> *And SWIFT has said (no common name*
> *On the large sphere of mortal fame)*
> *That he who daily smokes two pipes*
> *The tooth-ache never has,—nor gripes.*
>
> —WILLIAM COMBE, *THE TOUR OF DOCTOR SYNTAX,*
> *IN SEARCH OF THE PICTURESQUE*

ENTRANCED BY PLUTARCH'S *Parallel Lives,* a seven-year-old Jean-Jacques Rousseau fell into the habit of imagining himself not as a Genevan, but as a Greek or a Roman. As he put it in his *Confessions,* "Je devenais le personnage dont je lisais la vie":

> I became the person whose life I was reading: when I recounted acts of constancy and fortitude that had particularly struck me, my eyes would flash and my voice grow louder. One day at table, while I was relating the story of Scaevola, my family were alarmed to see me stretch out my hand and, in imitation of his great deed, place it on a hot chafing-dish.[1]

Another caricature from the Stoic archives, the legendary Roman Gaius Mucius earned the handle Scaevola, "left-handed," when he demonstrated his indifference to pain by shoving his unwavering right hand into an Etruscan fire. In a sharp disjunction, a very young Rousseau gravitates toward the Stoic transcendence of bodily pain that vexed Coleridge in the last chapter. But in reaching out for the hot chafing dish, Rousseau also put his finger on character's discomfiting capacity to turn an abstract philosophy into an inhabitable way of being in the world. Scaevola was born too early to find strength or succor in the particulars of an as-yet unformulated Stoicism, but Seneca later singled out the exemplary power of his "maimed and blistered hand" in his *Moral Epistles*.[2] The symbolic resonance of his self-mastery continued to reverberate within Romanticism. In *Political Justice*, Godwin aligned Scaevola with his own Stoic radicalism and "intellectual resolution," noting that he suffered "his hand to be destroyed by fire without betraying any symptom of emotion" (*PPW* 4:38). Jonathan Sachs has suggested that Scaevola becomes "an emblem" for *Political Justice* in its entirety, and given the prime place I have ascribed to Godwin's Stoicism in this study, Scaevola could be an unexpected but fitting embodiment for the broader sway of "the feel of not to feel it" within Romanticism.[3] But what happens when all the moving pieces of a philosophy like Godwin's or Seneca's are channeled through a mere character? What resources of thought are opened up, and what limitations exposed? Rousseau's case of enthusiastic character shifting foregrounds its tenuous possibilities: character could make a philosophy accessible and inhabitable, but it could also foster a mimesis that outruns thought. If character marks one possible site of philosophy's ultimate realization, it also opens up discursive philosophy to a new level of scrutiny, foregrounding all of the compromises, half-measures, and simplifications that such realization inevitably entails.

In this chapter, I want to suggest that Byron's half-admiring skirmish with Stoicism played out within the ineluctable framework of character. For Byron, Stoicism was an awkward amalgamation realized at the intersection of moral philosophy, romance, and satire. Even his early critics were alert to the way in which its classical contours informed his private and public self-conceptions. Writing in the *Quarterly Review*, Walter Scott emphasized the tendency of Byron's heroes to conceal a "keen susceptibility of injustice or injury, under the garb of stoicism or contempt of mankind."[4] For Scott, the Stoicism on display in the third canto of *Childe Harold* was more like a charade than a philosophical position. But as I will suggest in what follows, Byron consistently belabors a more generative sense of its performative possibilities, cases in which the desire to be seen as Stoical cannot be dismissed as mere dissimulation. At the same time, I want to draw on my excavation of Stoic radicalism in previous chapters to work against the misalignment of Stoicism and justice in Scott's formulation, where the dispassionate face of Stoicism works as if in denial of humanity. Scott took it for granted that Stoicism signals something diametrically opposed to "a keen susceptibility of injustice or injury." For Byron, however, its rhetoric raised anxious questions about any individual's proper affective relation to the world—a point I will revisit in the second half of this chapter by considering Byron's attempt in *Don Juan* to measure the efficacy of Stoicism against the stark reality of slavery.

Even at this ethical extremity, Byron's vision of Stoicism was predicated on the intricacy of character itself, a term that stood at the center of Byron's poetic enterprise. Heightened by the tantalizingly obscure ties that linked his fictional personages to their author's reputation, the escapades of the Byronic hero made character the most conspicuous signature of Byron's legacy. Traces of character's centrality in the Byronic universe are legion. Take, for example, a letter in which his publisher John Murray attempts to placate his lordship even while quibbling with the scandalous ribaldry of *Don Juan*: "Believe me there is no Character talked of in this Country as yours is—it is the constant theme of all classes & your portrait is engraved & painted & sold in every town throughout the Kingdom."[5] Visual representation and social reputation, moral essence and fictional portrayal all converge in the sweeping notion of character at the heart of Murray's reassuring imperative. Self-exiled from England, Byron remained—in almost every sense of the word—a character in absentia. Or take Wordsworth's dour prophecy that "Don Juan will do more harm to the English character, than anything of our time."[6] Both instances of hyperbole speak to the way in which Byron's manipulation of his own character blew open the concept, emphasizing the malleability of a rhetoric of personality in which self-culture and print culture fed into an all-consuming celebrity culture.[7] Much of the pathbreaking work on Byron in recent decades has been absorbed by a vision of his character as both a commodity and the result of a performance, but I want to suggest that Byron could also turn this performative sense of character to more philosophical ends. *Don Juan* is only one of many texts that attest to Byron's sense that characters could deliver philosophy from abstraction, marking the ways in which a formal system of ethics becomes an ethos.

Put in different terms, Byron's approach to Stoicism emphasized the way in which it was at once social and rhetorical. As an inheritor of

Hume's essayistic attempt to render specific schools of ancient philosophy as "a certain Character ... personated," Byron bypassed the philosophical minutiae of Stoicism that preoccupied Coleridge, only to fill his verse with a cast of major and minor but always imperfect Stoic figures.[8] Early in *Don Juan,* for example, the shipwreck of the *Trinidada* becomes something of an ethical thought experiment played out in real time. As the sole survivor of the wreck, a young Juan also receives a crash course in the art of losing—one that will inform his own serial experience of loss over the course of the "Epic Satire" (*DJ* 14:99). As the thirty occupants of a lifeboat are whittled down to one, the narrator takes particular note of a father as he registers the death of his son:

> There were two fathers in this ghastly crew,
>   And with them their two sons, of whom the one
> Was more robust and hardy to the view,
>   But he died early; and when he was gone,
> His nearest messmate told his sire, who threw
>   One glance on him, and said, "Heaven's will be done!
> I can do nothing," and he saw him thrown
> Into the deep without a tear or a groan. (*DJ* 2:87)

Confronted with the death of a child, this first father finds refuge in a reticent Christian Stoicism, exhibiting precisely the kind of apathy that Smith called unnatural and Fielding and Johnson mocked as inhuman. For the sake of this chapter's argument, I want to emphasize two aspects of this seemingly incidental Stoic set piece. First, this example of paternal Stoicism remains a noticeably surface-level phenomenon; the only depths here belong to the ocean. Byron is less interested in tracking the cognitive work of emotional regulation than in detailing the way it plays out in a social field, realized through looks and glances almost as in a theatrical tableau. It is impossible to know whether the external signs of the father's detachment correspond with an authentic interior tranquility. Such Stoic exteriority thwarts a tendency to equate character with the retrieval of deep, emotionally laden interiority. For Byron, the nature or efficacy of consolation seems less important than the social reality of its existence; the correlative of this surface-level Stoicism's simplicity is its legibility.

A second point relates to the conspicuous marginality of a grief that hardly scratches the surface of the poem. This father's appearance is confined to a single stanza of a seventeen-canto poem. But then again, he is not the last one-dimensional Stoic that Juan will run up against. Indeed, it will not be long before he decides to try such Stoicism on for size himself. Juan's close encounters with random Stoic characters seem in many ways a perfect, non-novelistic illustration of Alex Woloch's account of how minor characters have "a particular psychological function within the interior development of the young protagonist, as minor characters stand for particular states of mind, or psychological modes, that the protagonist interacts with and transcends."[9] But as I will suggest in what follows, Juan's strange vacuity—his notable paucity of interiority and resistance to development—complicates this clear account of their functionality. Unaligned with any distinct trajectory of moral development, these minor characters seem more like imperfect glimpses of a livable philosophy than representatives of a mode that must be transcended or overcome.

Stoic characters like this placid, grieving father function, for Byron, as a living shorthand for the habits and dispositions that emanate from doctrine, just as they inhabit a realm in which cut-and-dried principles fade into a more pervasive adjectival existence.[10] At first glance, such a transformation might seem like the airbrushing or abridgement of philosophy, not to mention an occasion for reaffirming Byron's status as "the definitive non-intellectual Romantic."[11] By contrast, I want to register Byron's sense of the complex ramifications attendant upon Stoicism as it spilled past the bounds of private self-culture to become a constitutive feature of life in the social world. Byron's Harrow notebooks as well as records from the sale of his libraries suggest a real familiarity with Epictetus, Seneca, and the Stoic commentary of Cicero.[12] And yet for Byron the textual traces of Stoicism were always superseded by its informal appearance in the midst of travel, on battlefields, or in drawing rooms. Stoicism could be the product of reason and self-discipline, but Byron's special insight was to recognize that it was just as likely to emerge on the scene as pretense or delusion, as a wily tactic, a utopian ideal, or even a momentary stay against trauma and confusion.[13] Byron was fascinated by this dispersal, nor did he imagine it as driving a nail in the coffin of its ethical possibility. Byron's interest in the flattening out of Stoicism put it in closer proximity to self-fashioning than self-culture. In this rhetorical or performative sense, Byron's exploration of Stoicism in and through character anticipates Amanda Anderson's account of the way in which contemporary theory and philosophy often take shape in characterological form, presenting "themselves as ways of living." For Anderson, the characterizations that adhere to various theories or philosophies are ubiquitous but often unacknowledged, forceful even as they operate "below the radar, or with only half-lit awareness."[14] Byron's rendering of Stoicism also resembles Rita Felski's account of the debt critique owes to the rhetorical "cultivation of an intellectual persona." Like critique, Stoicism is as much an attitude as a "relentlessly hardheaded and dispassionate practice."[15] Both of these recent critical reassessments can help us see Byron's characterological Stoicism as an intensification rather than an adulteration: playing up its adaptability as well as its cosmopolitan ethos, Byron reclaimed Stoicism by foregrounding the power unleashed even in the performance of its impossibility.

The chapter that follows occasionally indulges the digressions by which Byron's thought moves and lives, but it unfolds in three major movements. First, in a discussion opened up by *The Corsair*, I describe Byron's rehabilitation of Stoicism as a surface-level, exteriorized phenomenon by aligning it with his celebration of the performative nature of character and identity. Next, I highlight Byron's discovery—primarily in *Don Juan*—that a literary character could work much like a classical commonplace, an abridgement of philosophy that plays up commensurability by obliterating depth and specificity. Here I focus on his recurrent invocation of Horace's *nil admirari*, a Stoical adjuration to "admire nothing" that Byron traces from the corners of empire to the heart of the English character itself. Finally, I grapple with Byron's attempt to unlock via irony the ethical possibility of a Stoicism whose figure in the world owes as much to the endurance of suffering as it does to cosmopolitan detachment. Cutting through what he called the cant of sympathy and sentimentality, Byron's Stoic characters—running the gamut from pirates and sultans to soldiers and slaves—fostered an austere vision of commonality, one in which "changing persons and characters" (to adapt a phrase from Adam Smith [*TMS* 317]) could illuminate the power as well as the absurdity of Stoicism in an interconnected world.

Playing the Stoic

At first glance, Stoicism might seem an unlikely impetus for Byron's characterological reflection, for he is often approached as a living metonym for passion. Just before Byron's death, Hazlitt described him as the opposite of a Stoic, a writer who "obstinately and invariably shuts himself up in the Bastile of his own ruling passions."[16] The title of Benita Eisler's biography—*Byron: Child of Passion, Fool of Fame*—is similarly unambiguous. An unceasing fascination with the pageant of Byron's bleeding heart has led both readers and critics to fetishize a passionate intensity that the poet himself approached more equivocally. Like Adam Smith, Byron knew all too well that life in the (commercial) world made Stoic reserve a prerequisite for emotional expression and connection. His poetry explores the choreography of affect and indifference in life, for as Byron himself noted, a life of uninterrupted passion was as inconceivable as "a continuous earthquake, or an eternal fever" (*BLJ* 8:146). Regulation could be just as desirable as expression.

While often associated with a realm of passionate excess, Byron's particular brand of heroism was just as often presumed to hail from a place beyond astonishment. The two realms are hardly antithetical, and scholars have been alert to the way in which the Byronic hero can feel nothing precisely because he has already felt everything. The catalyst behind Childe Harold's pilgrimage—"the fulness of satiety"—exemplified the way in which passionate expenditure could result in a kind of affective bankruptcy (*CW* 2:9, ll. 34). At points, Byron himself owned up to the inescapability of such indifference.[17] In a letter to the future Lady Byron, he observed that "Apathy—disgust—& perhaps incapacity have rendered me now a mere spectator" (*BLJ* 3:179).

While the experience of such detachment could imply a sidelining of action and agency, Byron also remained alert to the way in which a Stoic perspective could reverse the polarity of indifference by making its passivity the ground for a new, critical clarity: as in criticism, a fine line separated indifference from disinterestedness. Byron's mistress Teresa Guiccioli captured this vein of critical dispassion in her *Vie de Lord Byron en Italie*, where she detailed his surprising interest in the sort of Stoic askesis that Coleridge relished. She recounts Byron's sporadic habit of retiring to his rooms "in the silence of his nights" to keep up a "fascinating Journal." Summoning himself "to his own judgement-seat," Byron's late-night bouts of self-critique added up to "an examination of conscience worthy of a Stoic—or an earnest Christian."[18] This portrait of dispassionate, self-reflective piety might seem overly earnest if not far-fetched, but it resonates with Byron's account of his attempt to make *Don Juan* a "moral model" by ensuring that "all passions" would be "in their turn attack'd" (*DJ* 5:2). The Stoic and the satirist were both self-reflexive occupants of "the judgement-seat," self-appointed arbiters of individual and collective opinion that could misrepresent the nature of reality. At least from this angle, *Don Juan* could seem like a public correlative to the private work of Stoic self-analysis.[19]

A more characteristic account of Byron's own conception of Stoicism is on display in an enticing anecdote from the Countess of Blessington's *Conversations of Lord Byron* (1834). Sitting on a balcony in Genoa, Byron was unexpectedly moved to tears when a group of English sailors started to sing "God Save the King":

When the song ceased, Byron, with a melancholy smile, observed, "Why, positively, we are all quite sentimental this evening, and *I—I* who have sworn against sentimentality, find the old leaven still in my nature, and quite ready to make a fool of me. 'Tell it not in Gath,' that is to say, breathe it not in London, or to English ears polite, or never again shall I be able to *enact* the stoic philosopher."[20]

Claimed here as a surface demeanor rather than a reordering of interior depths, Stoicism is not all imposture but rather a counterbalance to sentimentality's own expressive regime. Casting himself as a Stoic character even at a moment of nostalgic reverie, Byron validates a dual sense of disposition—a natural tendency or bent of the mind that is also, in rhetorical terms, the reflection of something ordered and arranged. Borrowing a well-known formulation from Judith Butler, we might say that Byron imagines Stoicism as something "tenuously constituted in time, instituted in an exterior space through a *stylized repetition of acts.*"[21] In aligning Stoicism with habitual performance, Byron jettisons the anxiety about Stoic hypocrisy that was legion in the Enlightenment and its fictions: unmoored from any strict sense of coherence, what counts as Stoic for Byron is intimidatingly broad. Years earlier, he had shrugged off his liaison with Mary Shelley's stepsister Claire Clairmont in similar terms: "I could not exactly play the Stoic with a woman—who had scrambled eight hundred miles to unphilosophize me" (*BLJ* 5:92). While setting sexual appetite above Stoic aversion in this particular case, Byron off-handedly styled Stoicism as a surface-level phenomenon, a philosophy in which performance and articulation were just as important as essence.

Like Robespierre and other Jacobins discussed in chapter 2, Byron intuited that part of Stoicism's power lay in its easy alliance with pageantry and public spectacle. At the same time, his emphasis on surface and enactment points to a broader ambivalence about interiority that had both literary and philosophical manifestations. My thought here has been galvanized by Susan Manning's account of how the Scottish Enlightenment supercharged the significance of character by foregrounding its power across the broad spectrum of "the science of man." For Manning, this centrality made character inherently rhetorical and essentially relational:

> Even at its most "private" in eighteenth-century writing, in diaries and commonplace books, "character" was understood discursively, at points of transaction where projected identity encountered a social context. Never straightforwardly a textual mirror for some essential extratextual reality of personal identity, character might be "produced" in

a reader by imitation of good models in literature. Eighteenth-century Rhetoric placed character at the juncture of social, political, and ethical formations, rather as gender has been more recently construed: learned, performative, and conditioned.[22]

Manning's account of the transactional nature of character raises the interesting prospect that Byron's Stoic journaling was no less rhetorical or performative than his desire to "*enact*" the Stoic for "English ears polite." But then again, Byron's public or private Stoic enactments were only a small facet of his freewheeling "projected identity." By almost any standard, Byron and his textual doppelgangers represent a quintessential example of performative character. From Jerome Christensen's account of "the performance of lordship" to Jerome McGann's analysis of his rhetorically staged sincerity, Byron's unstinting flair for performance has been recognized as a constitutive fact of his genius.[23] Like all performance, this notion of character was dependent upon an audience, and the dialogic nature of Byronism has been celebrated for qualifying a strain of Romantic egoism while also foregrounding the social dimensions of subjectivity. Thomas Carlyle might have been averse to Byron's "brawling theatrical insincere character," but contemporary accounts of Byronic performance tend to celebrate the creative power of his self-representations rather than lament their falsity or inherent dissimulation.[24]

Why, then, does a seemingly unlimited approbation for Byronic performance—the enactment of a self unmoored from any stable interior essence—run intriguingly aground when it comes to the performance of dispassion? Drawing on an ambivalence in Byron's own portrayals, critics have often approached the Byronic hero's tendency to "*enact* the stoic philosopher*"* as a kind of pathology, if not a troubling form of false consciousness. In *The Corsair*, for example, the swashbuckling pirate Conrad is a paradigmatic Byronic figure with all the requisite dark mystery and alluring austerity. True to form, Conrad's placid external semblance belies—but only just—a core of passionate intensity:

> Sun-burnt his cheek, his forehead high and pale
> The sable curls in wild profusion veil;
> And oft perforce his rising lip reveals
> The haughtier thought it curbs, but scarce conceals.
> Though smooth his voice, and calm his general mien,
> Still seems there something he would not have seen:
> His features' deepening lines and varying hue
> At times attracted, yet perplexed the view,

>   As if within that murkiness of mind
>   Worked feelings fearful, and yet undefined;
>   Such might it be—that none could truly tell—
>   Too close enquiry his stern glance would quell. (*CW* 3:157, ll. 203-14)

At first glance, the emotional regulation that inheres in a smooth voice and calm mien works against an unkempt machismo seemingly born of nature itself. But "close enquiry" scuttles any clear correlation between external bearing and internal reality: Conrad's stern ascendency over "feelings fearful" is more rhetorical than actual. Lacking definition, his feelings hardly rise to the level of cognitive evaluation and judgment. Confronted with the sentry-like force of Conrad's "stern glance," it is easy enough to read his projected placidity as a deceptive performance, one that might even circumscribe his own self-knowledge.

At the end of *The Corsair*, and after Conrad loses his wife Medora to an unnecessary grief, Byron figures the obfuscating disjunction between Conrad's inner and outer life in distinctly Stoic terms: "Full many a stoic eye and aspect stern / Mask hearts where grief hath little left to learn" (*CW* 3:211, ll. 636-37). The proposition is a simple one: Stoicism is a deceptive performance, one meant to obscure the palpable feelings of a heart that has been thoroughly schooled in grief. Many critics have seen this mismatch between Conrad's Stoic exterior and his turbulent inner life as a sign of unhealthy repression. Peter Manning's "composite portrait" of the Byronic hero foregrounds such sublimation: he is "a thwarted figure, ignorant of his essential self, who represses his inner dismay under a shell of sternness."[25] The negative, self-obfuscating aura of repression in a post-Freudian context only exacerbates an older charge of Stoic hypocrisy. In both cases, the privileged authority of authentic self-expression subverts that of the performed Stoic self. But why should a poet celebrated for his performative mobility bar Stoicism from that creative praxis? So much of the sense of these lines depends on the connotations of "mask." In *The Mask of Anarchy*, Shelley vividly captures the way a "mask" can hide cruelty and indifference from itself. But Byron—an enthusiastic connoisseur of the Venetian carnival—also relished the possibilities of life "*en masque*."[26]

As Conrad mourns Medora at the end of the poem, his Stoic façade is out of sync with his interior life. He is, after all, caught up in his grief, an adventurer who "deserved his fate / But did not feel it less" (*CW* 3:211, ll. 629-30). But isn't this disjunction precisely the privilege of rhetorical performance, the *articulation* of a self and an ethos rather than a reflection of some correspondent reality? Conard is not a perfect Stoic in any philosophical sense. His Stoicism is inherent in expression—almost an attribute of the eye itself—rather than the reflection of an antecedent psychological reality. As an exteriorized aspiration, it resembles the Stoicism that Jacques-Louis David glimpsed in his famous sketch of Marie Antoinette en route to the guillotine, just as it parallels Charles I's slow progress to the scaffold "without the least sign in his countenance of any discomposure of mind."[27] In all of these cases, perfect apathy would seem an impossibility, but representation of "the indistinctness of the suffering breast" would hardly keep up the last vestiges of a fading sovereignty. Unmoored from interiority, the performance of philosophy could be more powerful than its perfect realization. In *The Corsair*, Conrad almost seems to think in tactical terms, playing up the ambiguity of a lip that "reveals" and "scarce conceals" almost as if his attempt to regulate emotion was meant to be less obvious than the futility of that effort.

The allure of Byron's many self-referential characters is often attributed to the fleeting glimpse they offer of a secret Byronic self, a dense if ineffable core of interiority made strangely personal to readers through what Tom Mole has called a "hermeneutic of intimacy."[28] In this sense, Byron represents a special case of the literary and social distinctiveness made possible by what Deidre Lynch has called the "romantic faith in unsoundable depths."[29] Byron did not always sketch out these subjective depths, and his reticence allowed readers to revel in the sensation of their own uncommon ability to access the inner lives of uncommon characters. This narrative tells us something about Byron's commercial savvy in a shifting literary field, but I want to suggest that the trajectory of his career toward *Don Juan* evinces a countervailing interest in an old-school, surface-level sense of character as a device that might, to use Lynch's terms, "fabricate a sense of the typical and so a sense of social coherence."[30] Sidestepping the idiosyncratic singularities of an affect-laden inner life was an implicit bid for commonality. Byron's Stoicism resembles the much-vaunted concept of Byronic mobility in that it was, as McGann has put it, "a structure of social relations and not simply a psychological characteristic."[31] Stoicism might have been an aspect of individual character, but its performance worked against solipsism by imagining the self as sovereign and yet part of something broader.

The Prohibition of Admiration

Days after finishing the second canto of *Don Juan* in April 1819, Byron was struck by the nineteen-year-old Countess Teresa Guiccioli at a *conversazione* in Venice. In short order, he dispatched a stealthy letter assuring her that she would be his final passion, "l'ultimate mia Passione" (*BLJ* 6:110). In Byron's telling, the sudden onslaught of love turned his philosophical world upside down, negating a Stoicism that he had been half-heartedly performing for years: "For some years I have been trying systematically to avoid strong passions, having suffered too much from the tyranny of Love. *Never to feel admiration*—and to enjoy myself without giving too much importance to the enjoyment itself—to feel indifference towards human affairs—contempt for many, but hatred for none,—this was the basis of my philosophy" (*BLJ* 6:118). Byron's urgent desire results in an unfamiliar self-portrait, and the sudden onset of sincerity prompts him to sidestep a well-established mistrust of systemization. He had once warned Thomas Moore that "when a man talks of system, his case is hopeless" (*BLJ* 6:46). In many ways, the only thing systematic about Byron's time in Venice up to this point had been his serial pursuit of women, an exercise in detached "enjoyment" that led to at least two hundred conquests before Byron lost count.[32] But as his letter to Teresa has it, this detached pursuit of carnal knowledge was part of a broader austerity campaign, a philosophical outlook that framed a turn away from passionate connection as a bid for liberty. Like so many before him, Byron evoked this elusive equanimity with a hint from Horace: "Nil admirari prope res est una, Numici, / solaque quae possit facere et servare beatum ["Marvel at nothing"—that is perhaps the one and only thing, Numicius, that can make a man happy and keep him so]."[33]

Byron's casual importation of Horace's motto into an urgent love letter speaks to its outsized significance in literary culture, as well as its easy availability as a shorthand for equanimity and virtuous detachment. In translating the phrase, Byron emphasized admiration, but the exact sense of Horace's interdiction has been variously understood as an advisory against wonder and surprise, a clear bid against the insecurity that comes from being astonished. In *Tom Jones*, a key precursor to *Don Juan*, Henry Fielding deployed the phrase in picaresque quarters, referencing "the famous *nil admirari* of Horace."[34] Alexander Pope adopted the Horatian tag line as the epitome of his project in *An Essay on Man*, literally emblazoning it on the ornate header that precedes that poem's first epistle. Christopher Yu goes so far as to suggest that Horace's maxim "may be said to constitute a motto for the English Augustans."[35] Byron's eagerness to claim the mantle of his eighteenth-century poetic precursors explains his marked interest in the concept. Indeed, his fascination with the *nil admirari* was always channeled through "the little Queen Anne's man" and his *Imitations of Horace*:

> "Not to Admire, is all the Art I know,
> To make men happy, and to keep them so."
> [Plain Truth, dear MURRAY, needs no flow'rs of speech,
> So take it in the very words of *Creech*.]³⁶

Enacting the clear vision and perspicuity championed by Horace, Pope declined to make an old saw newly elaborate, ratifying instead Thomas Creech's rendition of the lines from 1684. The simple virtue of a life freed from fear and admiration could speak for itself. In *Don Juan*, Byron followed suit, breaking apart Pope's heroic couplets to meet the demands of his own *ottava rima*:

> "Not to admire is all the art I know
>   (Plain truth, dear Murray, needs few flowers of speech)
> To make men happy, or to keep them so;
>   (So take it in the very words of Creech)."
> Thus Horace wrote we all know long ago;
>   And thus Pope quotes the precept to re-teach
> From his translation; but had *none admired*,
> Would Pope have sung, or Horace been inspired? (*DJ* 5:101)

Characteristically, Byron can't help but undercut the *nil admirari* precept by arguing from extremity: without admiration, there would be little impulse to creation. But his fast reversal does little to unsettle an ever-lengthening chain of citation, one that points to a timeless bequest, something "we all know."

Drawing undue, almost perverse attention to lines of poetic transmission, Byron plays up the perils and possibilities of relying on commonplaces, those "everlastingly repeated" old saws that balance the sanction of long-experience against an embarrassing sense of redundancy.³⁷ Jerome Christensen and Stephen Cheeke have analyzed the many well-worn scraps from Horace that abound in *Don Juan*, manifestations of an anxious "citation compulsion" that Christensen reads as "the symptom of a bookish existence unattached to a community of ethical phrases."³⁸ Almost as though salvaged from a vanished context, a commonplace could seem an empty remainder, a mantra made vapid by its detachment from the thick complexity of its origins. Cheeke is quick to connect the commonplace to Byron's own ambivalence about his classical education at Harrow, an origin in which commonplaces were embedded in a context and community, but also an epicenter of the "drill'd dull lesson," a master site of mechanical learning (*CW* 2:149, l. 674). For Hazlitt, this classical bequest meant that Byron most frequently dwelt on what was "familiar to the mind of every schoolboy": he "thinks by proxy," and he "talks by rote."39

The dogmatic repetition of the *nil admirari* solidified a familiarity of reference, but an imprecision of thought. As a shorthand for Stoicism, it was at once pervasive and indistinct. Later in the century, Walter Savage Landor would write his own epigrammatic objection to what struck him as commonplace made empty by overuse:

> Horace and Creech!
> Thus do you teach?
> What idle speech!
> Pope! and could you
> Sanction it too?
> 'Twill never do!
> One idle pen
> Writes it, and ten
> Write it again.40

Brushing aside the "idle" replication of commonplace wisdom, Landor reclaims wonder, taking it for granted that "Sages require / Much to Admire."41 Without the amplification of astonishment, how would the everyday make a claim on art or wisdom? Landor recapitulates Byron's own critique of the *nil admirari* doctrine in *Don Juan*, and yet both writers simply replicate Pope's and Horace's own equivocation in setting them up as straw men. As Pope's imitation made clear, to think of the *nil admirari* was already to land in a place in which moral idealism ran into irony. At the same time, the commonplace was also—in Cheeke's terms—a site of "inherent doubleness," a linguistic formulation that balanced the cliché with a sense of "vividly recurring authenticity."42 The power of the phrase lay in its perennial ability to evoke, even through language itself, a feeling or pattern of thought in ever-new contexts.43 Hazlitt's and Landor's critique could also cut two ways: trafficking in known quantities rather than idiosyncratic expression privileged relationality over originality. A commonplace insists on the priority of legibility, foregrounding this even at the expense of conveying one's distinctive experience or essence. As such, the commonplace stands in analogic relation to the notion of character I have been describing, one in which a preoccupation with the revelation of depth gives way to alignment with a surface that retains signifying power in the social realm.

Though occasionally inclined to make merry with the *nil admirari*, Byron approached the concept as one whose moral seriousness had not been adulterated by its overarticulation. The capaciousness of its still-resonant signaling capacity owed much to the cachet of Pope's example. Byron's adoption of Pope as an ethical and poetical idol has always been something of an aberration that sets him apart from his contemporaries. The streamlined histories that underpin literary periodization typically figure Pope as antithetical to Romanticism, even as his strong example prompts its formation.[44] Censuring his poetic diction as well as a purported lack of pathos and sublimity, Wordsworth once quipped that Pope was admirable in treading his way "but that way lies almost at the foot of Parnassus."[45] By contrast, Byron's advocacy of his Augustan idol in the "Pope controversy" that convulsed the literary sphere in the 1820s led to his self-critical conclusion that he and his poetic contemporaries were "all in the wrong—one as much as another—that we are upon a wrong revolutionary poetical system—or systems—not worth a damn in itself" (*BLJ* 5:265).

Byron's call for a turn back to Pope and his master Horace arose in part out of a preference for a plain and moderate style that might curtail the "system of prosaic raving" and reverie that he felt had hijacked contemporary British poetics.[46] As James Chandler has argued, Byron's defense of Pope was just one of several attempts to reclaim Pope's cosmopolitan poetics in the face of an ascendant and provincializing literary nationalism. To make a case for Pope was to embrace "a classical canon that cuts across national boundaries and rises above national interests."[47] But as Jonathan Sachs has noted, Byron's own classical vision in the Pope controversy was a distinctly Roman one focused most intensively on a "concept of poetic permanence" that might outlast a moment of frightening poetic decline.[48]

As the shorthand for a long-sanctioned ideal of worldliness, Horace's *nil admirari* encapsulated the aesthetic and ethical values that Byron defended most strenuously in the Pope controversy. But in leaning on the famous commonplace, Byron also landed on a de facto defense of characterological Stoicism. Jerome McGann has written at length about Byron's decision to cast *Don Juan* in the plain and decorous style of Horace, a determination that emphasized conversation, an embrace of the ordinary, and the possibility of instruction.[49] McGann traces this Horatian ideal of propriety back to its origins in Cicero's *De Officiis*, a text that addresses aspects of rhetorical style within an ambient field of ethics. For Cicero, the practice of avoiding "exhibitions of passion" and excessive "mental excitement" in daily life had a conversational correlative. As he put it, "our conversation ought to be free from such emotions: let there be no exhibition of anger or inordinate desire, of indolence or indifference, or anything of the kind."[50] Situated at the intersection of style and ethics, Stoic reserve could be a deep-seated ethical practice, but it could also shape social interchange and even the way one exhibited one's self in the world. The proper place of emotion in discourse was not altogether different from its proper place in life. In poetic terms, this correlation of style and ethics stood behind Byron's interest in reclaiming for Pope an epithet that was often offered up in derision. Pope was the "Poet of reason," a virtue equally evident in the style of his verse as well as its content. As his thoughts evolved, Byron's alignment of Pope and Horace transcended the realm of style to enter the realm of ethics. Pope was most notable in his character as an ethical poet, a task that Byron described as "the highest of all poetry." He was, quite simply, "the moral poet of all Civilization."[51] Byron's double move—setting up Pope as an unrivalled ethical poet, and then firmly aligning him with the *nil admirari* doctrine—suggests a deep investment in the motto's ethical signification.

Isolating the exact philosophical impetus for Horace's *nil admirari* has been as elusive as pinpointing the philosophical angle of Pope's imitation; scholars have connected both texts to a panoply of philosophical positions.[52] In his letters, Shaftesbury took the Stoic option, noting that while Horace's *Epistle* sounded the occasional Epicurean note, it was "strongly of the other sort, and means quite another thing, as I could show you at leisure out of Cicero, Seneca."[53] Shaftesbury was on solid ground in intuiting Stoic intimations in the epistle. Horace's *nil admirari* was just a hair's breadth away from Cicero's "nihil admirari" in the *Tusculan Disputations*, a pivotal account of Stoic moral psychology that Byron would have known from his days at Harrow. Cicero's Stoic delineation of the passions, as well as his sense of how the danger of admiration could be precluded by anticipation, were both firmly entrenched in Horace's and Pope's epistles. Cicero, for example, suggests that the emotions attendant upon unanticipated distress retain a special power to unbalance the mind and "snatch the Man away" (in Pope's resonant phrase) precisely because they are unexpected. Equanimity resulted from "the ideal of that wisdom which excels and is divine, namely in the thorough study and comprehension of human vicissitudes, in being astonished at nothing when it happens, and in thinking, before the event is come, that there is nothing which may not come to pass."[54] Stoic moral psychology is predicated on the constant work of counterfactual imagination. Nothing should provoke astonishment because it has all been imagined before. As Philip Fisher has put it, "Stoicism could be called a training in expectation."[55] Byron was cognizant of these finer points of Stoic moral psychology. Indeed, Juan's gradual attunement to the dangers of admiration in a world "full of strange vicissitudes"—his own Stoic training in expectation—might be the cardinal manifestation of his development in the poem (*DJ* 4:51).

But Byron would censure the pedantry of textual sleuthing that purports to expound a phrase by tracing its bookish origins. The power of the commonplace ultimately derived from the way in which the solid stuff of moral philosophy had been sublimed into a diffuse but influential ethos and cultural reference. As an outgrowth of classical exemplarity, it fostered a universal vision of human nature by which the past might continuously stake a claim upon the present.[56] Nietzsche, for example, would later flag *nil admirari* as a phrase that encompassed for ancient philosophers "the whole of philosophy," an impulse that bridged many different doctrines.[57] Often exceeding the boundaries of philosophy itself, it could also evoke a standard of deportment and worldliness. In an early letter to Robert Southey, Coleridge opined that "Nil admirari is the quintessence / of Politeness as well as of Wisdom."[58] A characterological abridgement of philosophy, it marked an indistinction between a way of seeing the world and a way of being in the world. James Boswell described another facet of its worldly uptake in his *Life of Johnson*. Over a meal, Johnson and his garrulous biographer debate the relative merits of Horace's *nil admirari*:

> I maintained that Horace was wrong in placing happiness in *Nil admirari*, for that I thought admiration one of the most agreeable of all our feelings; and I regretted that I had lost much of my disposition to admire, which people generally do as they advance in life. JOHNSON. "Sir, as a man advances in life, he gets what is better than admiration—judgement, to estimate things at their true value." I still insisted that admiration was more pleasing than judgement, as love is more pleasing than friendship. The feeling of friendship is like that of being comfortably filled with roast beef; love, like being enlivened with champagne. JOHNSON. "No, Sir; admiration and love are like being intoxicated with champagne; judgment and friendship like being enlivened."[59]

While acknowledging admiration's inevitable evanescence, Boswell's opening salvo makes a case for its power and pleasure as a "disposition." For Johnson, however, the agreeable sensation of admiration gives way to something more valuable: a faculty of judgment that allows one to "estimate things at their true value." But it is hard to parse the difference in distinct terms, for Boswell and Johnson's competing claims both rest on figuring the particulars of philosophy as the sentiments of characters who eat, love, drink, and judge. Johnson's *nil admirari* adherent appears on the scene like a critic or a connoisseur, not a sadder but a wiser man whose first feelings have been superseded by an enlivening judgment.

Byron would depict a similar account of judgement displacing the heart's illusions in *Don Juan*, but he would also take up Boswell and Johnson's collaborative intuition that the gradations of cold philosophy might best be charted in relation to the intoxicating power of champagne. Appropriately enough, Byron's most comprehensive theorization and thick description of Horace's *nil admirari* occurs in the English Cantos of *Don Juan*, at a point in the poem in which detachment is suddenly legion. Turning back to England after a long exile, Byron rejects a nostalgic impulse to admire, announcing instead a Johnsonian resolution to "show things really as they are" (*DJ* 12:40). From this disenchanted height, he is alert to a pervasive cultural malaise, one in which "fashion" has effectively absorbed "passion."[60] Nor is Juan immune from this broad pivot away from admiration. Though he wastes no time on casuistry or "the moral lessons of mankind," his arrival in England corresponds with the onset of an ascendant indifference:

> A little "*blâsé*"—'tis not to be wondered
>   At, that his heart had got a tougher rind:
> And though not vainer from his past success,
>   No doubt his sensibilities were less. (*DJ* 12:81)

These various coordinates of emergent insensibility pale in comparison to Byron's analysis of Lady Adeline Amundeville, a portrait that doubles as a pivotal articulation of Romantic Stoicism and its contradictions. In this single passage, several of the threads I have been pursuing in this chapter come together. Horace's *nil admirari* becomes the anchor for an improvisatory character sketch even as anxious commentary on the commonplace tradition intervenes. At the same time, the whole vignette links Stoicism—evoked figuratively rather than directly—to "aspects," "manner," and other forms of exteriority:

> There also was of course in Adeline
>   That calm Patrician polish in the address,

Which ne'er can pass the equinoctial line
    Of any thing which Nature would express;
Just as a Mandarin finds nothing fine,—
    At least his manner suffers not to guess
That anything he views can greatly please.
Perhaps we have borrowed this from the Chinese—

Perhaps from Horace. His "*nil admirari*"
    Was what he called the "Art of happiness;"
An art on which the artists greatly vary,
    And have not yet attained to much success.
However, 'tis expedient to be wary:
    Indifference *certes* don't produce distress;
And rash Enthusiasm in good society
Were nothing but a moral Inebriety.

But Adeline was not indifferent: for
    (*Now* for a common place!) beneath the snow,
As a volcano holds the lava more
    Within—*et cetera*. Shall I go on?—No!
I hate to hunt down a tired metaphor:
    So let the often used volcano go.
Poor thing! How frequently by me and others,
It hath been stirred up till its smoke quite smothers.

I'll have another figure in a trice:—
    What say you to a bottle of champagne?
Frozen into a very vinous ice,
    Which leaves a few drops of that immortal rain,
Yet in the very centre, past all price,
    About a liquid glassful will remain;
And this is stronger than the strongest grape
Could e'er express in its expanded shape:

'Tis the whole spirit brought to a quintessence;
    And thus the chilliest aspects may concentre
A hidden nectar under a cold presence.
    And such are many—though I only meant her,
From whom I now deduce these moral lessons,
    On which the Muse has always sought to enter:—
And your cold people are beyond all price,
When once you have broken their confounded ice. (*DJ* 13:34–38)

Taken as a whole, the passage seems to posit—at least at first glance—a central discrepancy between Adeline's "calm, patrician polish" and the "quintessence" of her being. There is a gap between "address" and essence, one that could be variously diagnosed as hypocrisy or repression.[61] Borrowing a line from Walter Scott, we might say that Adeline is yet another Byronic character whose "keen susceptibility" is concealed "under the garb of stoicism or contempt of mankind."[62] This is a significant rather than an arbitrary gloss, for the passage owes its figuration to yet another of Scott's attempts to distinguish the "generous feeling" of Byron's characters from the aura of dispassion that often obscured it. For Scott, the Byronic hero's inner core of ardent feeling constantly belied "the frozen shrine in which false philosophy had incased it, glowing like the intense and concentrated alcohol, which remains one single but burning drop in the centre of the ice which its more watery particles have formed."[63] At first glance, Scott's prompt seems to support a rough schematic parsing of Adeline's character in which Stoicism is simply a "false philosophy," a wholly exterior dissimulation negated by a dense but hidden affectivity.

But as I have been arguing throughout, the trajectory of this reading goes against the grain of Byron studies in stripping the performative of all its power. A more complicated exposition of the *nil admirari* is at stake here, one that catches the subtle logic of the commonplace by mapping its possibilities in characterological terms. As with Conrad, or Napoleon, or Byron himself, Adeline's cold philosophy is constituted by performance. Since character is rhetorical and relational, exterior forms and motions are as determinative as any moot speculation about essence. Adeline's "manner" and "address"—her way of being in the world—effect the formation rather than the erasure of a self. The "tired metaphor" of the snow-packed volcano fizzles out not from overuse but because it posits a stark discrepancy between exterior semblance and interior reality: lava at the heart of things with snow on top. Better by far is the bottle of champagne with its single substance, where the exteriorization of a self—those "chilliest aspects"—also results in a determinative concentering of being. The play of the surface precedes the formation of depths, and there is no real disjunction between the two. Byron's improvisatory figure gestures toward predictable if somewhat paradoxical ends. Adeline's habitual but unnamed Stoicism—a living enactment of Horace's *nil admirari*—results not in indifference, but in a powerful and concentrated sensitivity. The transit here is from the intoxication of admiration to the enlivening of judgment, but the image is also a second-generation variation on Godwin's attempt to dispute all of the easy distinctions "afloat in the world, about *warm hearts*, and *cold hearts*." As Godwin put it, "the sincerest warmth is not wild, but calm; and operates in greater activity in the breast of the stoic, than in that of the vulgar enthusiast" (*PPW* 6:21–22).

In chapter 2, I described Godwin's sentiment as part of his long, beleaguered attempt to defend his Stoic radicalism in the years of reaction that followed the French Revolution. Byron's uptake of the sentiment might seem far removed from the days of *liberté, égalité, fraternité*, for Stoicism is distinctly classed in Byron's portrait. Manifest in Adeline's "patrician polish," it is implicit in the disaffected outlook of the mandarin, a "manner" that takes shape in "good society." Equated with the finest wine, "cold people" like Adeline are "beyond all price," incommensurate with the logic of any market. Byron's point here anticipates John Barrell's account of a link between disinterestedness and the wealth and property that fostered it.[64] But the sheer variety of inhabitable, exteriorized Stoicism in *Don Juan* suggests a more destabilizing insight, one that posits the Stoic refusal of fellow feeling as particularly suited to a world of difference. Early in the passage, Byron is equivocal about the origins of Adeline's Stoic ethos: it might have come from Horace, but in a shift from first-person singular to a more disorienting first-person plural, he suggests that "perhaps we have borrowed this from the Chinese." However extemporized or glancing, this unexpected genealogy advanced a destabilizing possibility, reorienting a classical commonplace toward a yet wider commonality. A certain kind of temperament—"Cool, and quite English; imperturbable" (*DJ* 13:14)—was not an essential facet of national character but a product of cross-cultural borrowing and exchange. If the Stoical character was a deeply engrained aspect of Englishness, it was also a commonplace form of detachment borrowed from various Others at the edge of empire. Byron's ironic theorization of this resonance would echo throughout the century.

Nil Admirari at the Margins

In an 1844 issue of *Fraser's Magazine*, Captain Orlando Sabertash took aim at the engrained hypocrisy that both pervaded and vitiated fashionable manners. The nom de plume of Major General John Mitchell, Sabertash was a Scottish near-contemporary of Byron's who had served in the West Indies before returning to Europe to finish out the Napoleonic wars.[65] Writing twenty years after Byron's death, Sabertash took up a version of his lordship's campaign against affectation and social cant, reserving especial ire for what he called the "*Sliding Scale of Manners*," a calculated distribution of attention and condescension especially "adapted to the character of modern and fashionable society."[66] The sliding scale was Sabertash's shorthand for the way in which persons of fashion parceled out courteous attention to those around them on the sole basis of class and position. Defined by this downward thrust, Sabertash held that a great cooling of social relations had unsettled the fashionable world. Like Byron, Sabertash equated aristocratic equanimity with a kind of "*nil admirari* stoicism," and he formulated an account of its provenance to argue against its profusion. Simultaneously racist and revealing, Sabertash's attempt to pin down the origins of a pervasive and empowered Stoic posture points to the prominence of its caricatured form at society's margins:

> Forgetting that it is far more meritorious to be beloved than admired, we go into society to astonish the natives, to excite wonder, but rarely, indeed, with the least intention of evincing a particle of admiration for any one else, the stoicism of the *nil admirari* school being looked upon as the very perfection of high breeding. And from whom does the reader suppose this boasted tone of fashion has been derived? From the high, accomplished, and cultivated of the earth? No, faith! from the very opposite class; from the dull, the ignorant, and the savage. We who write have seen this species of fashionable stoicism displayed in the highest perfection by Arowak Indians, who deem it beneath their dignity to evince surprise or admiration on any occasion, as they wish it to be believed that they are perfectly familiar with all that is most excellent and most exalted in the world. By the united testimony of all African travellers, every petty Negro despot excels in the same style of fashionable deportment, and retains as much apparent composure at the sight of a scarlet-bay's cloak and bottle of rum, that make his very heart throb again, as he would on beholding a bowl of palm wine, or ordinary piece of Negro-worked cloth. The merit of the *nil admirari* system is not, therefore, of a very high order or brilliant origin.[67]

Trading on reductive stereotypes—the Stoic noble savage and the despotic African king—Sabertash angles to expose what he views as the sliding scale's ultimate misprision: the aristocracy borrows its manners from the colonial margins, extending the corrosive sway of *nil admirari* "breeding" and "deportment." What looks like sophistication is in fact a covert form of savagery. For Sabertash, an unpalatable ancestry should rule Stoicism out of court.

Laced with all the irreverent conviction of John Bull triumphalism, Sabertash unwittingly (and certainly uncritically) stumbles upon foundational postcolonial insights: the relational nature of identity, or the way in which mimicry foregrounds the performative nature of identity even in its reversal.[68] The ultimate privilege of inhabiting the pinnacle of the imperium might be—to invert one of Gayatri Spivak's formulations—the anxious constitution of the Self as the Other's shadow.[69] Byron's contention that Adeline's "fashionable stoicism" might represent a borrowing from the Chinese seems a clear antecedent to Sabtertash's logic, though Byron is noticeably more sanguine about the characterological possibilities latent in the collision of cultures. Byron was alert to the way in which a global outlook fostered by trade, travel, colonization, and war foregrounded Stoicism's prominence at points of cultural intersection. As an aspect of character, Stoicism facilitated what Nigel Leask has described as Byron's attempt to reduce "the imperialist Self to a level with its oriental Other."[70] Keen from an early moment to imagine himself as "a Citizen of the World" stamped by nature in "the Die of *Indifference*," Byron intuited—and, indeed, interrogated—the way in which a Stoic ethos could blur social distinctions by forging lines of affinity between the haut monde and the wretched of the earth (*BLJ* 1:112, 114). This unlikely consonance was significant and destabilizing, a coincidence worthy of examination and an irony that could not be easily dismissed.

In pondering the entangled affinities of global dispassion, Byron was the belated inheritor of what Julie Ellison has described as a shift in the culture of sensibility, one that turned a mode of interrelation operating amongst like-minded equals into an outlook premised on inequality: "Sensibility increasingly is defined by the consciousness of a power difference between the agent and the object of sympathy. The literary victim is typically marked by racial, social, or national disadvantages: the deep-feeling Moor, the dying Indian, the impoverished veteran, the slave, the vagrant."[71] Quite a few of these stock characters make their way into Byron's verse (and the ones that do not seem to be comfortably ensconced in Wordsworth's blank verse and lyrical ballads). In both cases, characters confront their "disadvantages" with the familiar arsenal of Stoic postures that Ellison—following Shaftesbury and Smith—sees as integral to the circuit of sensibility. For Ellison, these displays of Stoic severity become occasions for the proliferation of sensibility itself, exhibitions of magnanimous reserve that provoke a "sensitive masculinity hyperconscious of imperial and colonial frameworks."[72] By contrast, Byron writes with an especial attentiveness to the way in which the proliferation of sensibility had become a sign of its vacuity, a mechanical kind of social cant. Instead of serving as catalysts for a sentimental exchange, his Stoic characters remain eerily without depth, drawn as if in denial of affective identification. Unlikely to elicit sympathetic tears, they model an unastonished response to great suffering, an outlook forged by trauma and the traumatic knowledge that, as Cicero put it, there is "nothing which may not come to pass."[73] At the same time, *nil admirari* endurance of suffering gestured, however obliquely, toward an ethics that might bring about its redress.

Byron's linkage of moors, slaves, and Indians under the sign of Stoicism entailed more than a philosophical twist on sentimental exoticism, for Stoicism holds forth an alternative ideal of sovereignty that might flourish even when political freedom threatens to fall into abeyance. The reach of Britain's imperial project meant that this threat was omnipresent on multiple fronts. Leask has noted that poems attentive to colonialism in the Americas and the Far East often reflected similar concerns and political messaging. Orientalism could fade into New World primitivism, a transit certainly on Byron's mind: why else turn from Juan at the siege of Ismail to digress at length on Daniel Boone in the "free-born forest"? (*DJ* 8:65). In the context of both continents, Stoicism cleaves to the category of race precisely because it so often straddles the bounding line of sovereignty. As a perennial source of *constantia in publicis malis* (constancy in times of public calamity), Stoicism was—in Srinivas Aravamudan's terms—a readily available if imperfect form of anticolonial "virtualization," a bastion of moral autonomy for the disempowered and dispossessed.[74] At the same time, Byron's racialized Stoic characters weigh the theoretical invulnerability of Stoic sovereignty against the real possibility of its inefficacy. To borrow a line from Jonathan Elmer, sovereignty—like the perfect apathy of the Stoic sage—names a fiction that "has never coincided with practice." Both ideals were fleeting, visions of autonomy out of sync with things as they are. This compromised vision gives rise to a central paradox: at the margins of empire, the enactment of Stoicism was particularly necessary but especially inefficacious, a philosophical hedge against a pressing material reality. For Byron, this mismatch left Stoicism not just compromised but susceptible to an irony that he would bend back toward England and his own detached pretensions. The accessibility, but also the frustrating instability of Stoic detachment only amplifies Elmer's sense that the "enduring power" of racialized sovereign individuals "comes from their capacity, in varying measures, to absorb projection, identification, and disavowal."[75]

Byron's tendency to isolate a vein of Stoicism in a diverse array of sovereign characters should be seen as a correlative of his attempt to reclaim but also re-envision the moral seriousness of the commonplace. The step back from "a community of ethical phrases"—say Harrow, or the elite world of classical education, or even Great Britain—could also be a step into a wider commonality, one in which a "truth" held in common might exceed any particular instance of its articulation. If characters were, as Deidre Lynch has argued, "devices for thinking about typicality" in the service of "social coherence," a character and a commonplace could undertake a similar kind of work.[76] In both cases, something other than comprehensive mimesis was at stake: the representation of interior psychology or the full context of a detailed philosophy falls by the wayside. If what emerges instead is delimited or even schematic, it is also more easily shared.

Genealogical accounts of Byron's own signature character type give some indication of how suggestive he found this realignment to be. In his study of the Byronic hero, Peter Thorslev finds early intimations of the type in the "neoclassical and stoic Noble Savage," a figure he suggests was often portrayed as "stoically laconic."[77] The Byronic hero retained something of the calm austerity that Rousseau attributed to humans in the savage state: "not even the unperturbed tranquility of the Stoic approaches his profound indifference."[78] Adam Smith thought in similar terms, noting that the magnanimity and self-command cultivated by "rude and barbarous nations" were "almost beyond the conception of Europeans" (*TMS* 205). Though hardly stepping outside a Eurocentric perspective, such a characterological genealogy suggests that Stoicism could be a node of imaginative correspondence rather than a marker of inherent difference. More to the point, it fostered a relativism in which the superiority of British values could hardly be taken for granted. On this front, Byron again falls in line with Rousseau in his *Discourse on the Origin and Foundations of Inequality among Men* (1755): "When I see multitudes of utterly naked savages scorn European pleasures and brave hunger, fire, sword, and death, simply to preserve their independence, I sense that it is inappropriate for slaves to reason about liberty."[79] Europeans, in other words, enjoy liberty in name only; their moral slavery colors all. Manifesting the contempt that Wendy Lee has tied to the figure of the insensible, Rousseau's savages—scorning European incursion with *nil admirari* rigor— call the very notion of European autonomy into question.[80] The failure to exercise an integral freedom available even in a state of nature suggests that the "cultivated of the earth" might really be the slaves.[81]

"Determined Scorn of Life"

Byron's interest in the way Stoicism works as an interface between self and world is on full display at various junctures in *Don Juan*. At the tail end of the siege of Ismail, Byron's narrator loses sight of Juan to detail the fate of two Turkish figures whose Stoic enactments emerge out of war even as they foreground its inherent "butchery" (*DJ* 7:69). In a rendition of an episode from Tasso's *Gerusalemme Liberata*, a sultan "flanked by *five* brave sons" refuses to stand down in spite of Juan's entreaties (*DJ* 8:105). His sons are struck down around him in sequence until he finds himself alone. In emulation of "Heroic, stoic Cato," the Tartar khan pours forth his soul by flinging his breast "upon the Russian steel" (*DJ* 6:7, 8:118). Byron's interest lies less with the action than its aftermath:

> 'Tis strange enough—the rough, tough soldiers, who
>   Spare neither sex nor age in their career
> Of carnage, when this old man was pierced through,
>   And lay before them with his children near,
> Touched by the heroism of him they slew,
>   Were melted for a moment; though no tear
> Flowed from their blood-shot eyes, all red with strife,
> They honoured such determined scorn of life. (*DJ* 8:119)

The khan's suicide inches asymptotically close to the dynamic sketched out by Ellison, in which decorous suffering prompts vicarious tears. But in the context of battle, the "rough, tough soldiers" have no occasion for crying and just time enough to melt for a moment. The sentimental circuit remains incomplete, and yet a moment is enough to prompt a wry sense of the disparity between an honor ethic and the ethos of "career" soldiers—mercenaries, really—who flirt with sentimentalism but will "spare neither sex nor age in their career / Of carnage." Byron uses the concluding ottava rima couplet to good effect, cleverly undercutting what comes before while also opening it up to a new level of critique. Determined "scorn of life" suddenly becomes ambiguous, at once a Stoic assessment of the essential nature of existence, but also a callous contempt for the life of others.

As a character, the khan strips Stoicism of any of its finer distinctions; the supposition of a philosophical attitude rests solely on a single action. Like Burke's vision of French legislators who ape Cato with bare feet and savage looks, it is almost as if he acts out a commonplace, or becomes one. The example of his sovereignty lies in its simplicity. His death is immediately followed by the evocation of a minor Stoic character who, in a noticeable repetition, crosses the narrative's path twice. First brought to Juan's attention through dialogue, he is identified as an old pasha who "sits among some hundreds dead, / Smoking his pipe quite calmly, 'midst the din / Of our artillery and his own" (*DJ* 8:98). When the pasha reappears more than twenty stanzas later, his calm vigil amid the unliving remains uninterrupted:

> In the mean time, cross-legged, with great sang froid,
>   Among the scorching ruins he sat smoking
> Tobacco on a little carpet;—Troy
>   Saw nothing like the scene around;—yet looking
> With martial stoicism, nought seemed to annoy
>   His stern philosophy; but gently stroking
> His beard, he puffed his pipe's ambrosial gales,
> As if he had three lives as well as tails. (*DJ* 8:121)

The stanza begins by carving out an alternate temporality, a "mean time": not the frantic pace of a conflict in which soldiers are only "melted for a moment" but the slow time of spectatorship and ruination. For the space of a stanza, the forward thrust of narrative ebbs in an example of what Elisha Cohn calls lyrical suspension, a "still life" made "vibrant in its absorptive movelessness."[82] It is as if a historical timescale is grafted onto the pasha's sense of the present. With the dead piled around his carpet, it might as well be Troy that burns. Named outright, Stoicism is prominently aligned with the body. Manifest in a look, it is also—as sangfroid—present in the blood. Amid "scorching ruins," the pasha remains paradoxically cold-blooded. Seemingly insulated from the heat of Byron's own satire, the reader is left to puzzle over the implication of this dereliction from immediacy, a state of inaction as incongruent in battle as it is in narrative.

Activating readerly suspension, the pasha's Stoic smoking break draws attention to two vivid actualities latent in the characterization of his "stern philosophy." Most obviously, an austere philosophy is rendered as a familiar habit or regimen, facilitating in the process the immersive changing "of persons and characters" (*TMS* 317). Puffing on his "pipe's ambrosial gales" becomes a metonym for the Stoic "scorn of life," an external sign of an internal sovereignty. Even at this catastrophic juncture, the pasha's pipe renders an austere philosophy ordinary and inhabitable, but also visible. In the epigraph from *Doctor Syntax* at the start of this chapter, the tobacco pipe is hailed as a "social tube," a daily ritual—endorsed by the likes of Bacon and Swift—that takes the cold reserve of the "Stoic clan" and warms it ever so slightly into a soothing English geniality.[83] In this episode from *Don Juan*, the pipe becomes a "social tube" in a different sense, a conduit that connects discrepant Stoicisms, or at least makes the pasha's "stern philosophy" familiar without quite eliminating its foreignness.

The reduction of philosophy to a familiar regimen gives rise to a more capacious signifying power, one that activates a wider sense of its availability and correspondence. Orientalized here, a classical school of philosophy finds its main mode of expression in a popular habit instigated by a new world commodity. The broad distribution of the pipe as an object correlates with the similarly far-reaching availability and modularity of the philosophical attitude it encodes. In juxtaposing an almost gestural Stoicism against the reality of a "sea of slaughter" (*DJ* 8:122), Byron's pasha recalls Aphra Behn's Oroonoko, another racialized sovereign individual who remains untouched, smoking while suspended within a death sentence:

> He had learnt to take tobacco, and when he was assured he should die, he desired they would give him a pipe in his mouth ready lighted, which they did, and the executioner came, and first cut off his members, and threw them into the fire; after that, with an ill-favoured knife, they cut his ears, and his nose, and burned them. He still smoked on, as if nothing had touched him. Then they hacked off one of his arms, and still he bore up, and held his pipe; but at the cutting off the other Arm, his head sunk and his pipe dropped, and he gave up the ghost without a groan or a reproach.[84]

Mustering an almost inhuman composure, Oroonoko's ability to endure mortal torture "without a groan" contrasts with the unfeeling inhumanity of his executioners. Stoicism was often linked with a meditative practice of the self, but in its characterological existence the demand for legibility means that it is always relational and performative. In James Eli Adams's terms, an "ascetic self is an observable self," an assertion especially pertinent when one kind of character (ethos) is being converted into another (literary personage).[85] As with Byron's pasha, Oroonoko's ability to "smoke on" foregrounds a visibility that supports the mobility of "*nil admirari* stoicism." Signified again by a common habit, Oroonoko's capacity to resist the infringement of his sovereignty becomes the paradoxical occasion of its most vehement enactment.

But as with representations of Stoicism more generally, Oroonoko's exemplary display of virtue anticipates its habituation in common life. In the digressive universe of *Don Juan*, the figure of the pasha calmly smoking "among some hundreds dead" becomes, for the narrator, a kind of wake-up call for those "Cockneys of London" also sitting and reading—though at a distance—"among some hundreds dead":

> Think how the joys of reading a Gazette
>   Are purchased by all agonies and crimes:
> Or if these do not move you, don't forget
>   Such doom may be your own in after times. (*DJ* 8:125)

Juxtaposed by the sequential nature of the narrative, one unmoving character implicitly challenges the unmoved reader of the gazette, or perhaps even the detached reader of *Don Juan*, calmly digesting "sketches of love, tempest, travel, war" (*DJ* 8:138).[86] Byron himself was not insulated from the pasha's unmoving virtue. Three years before the Ismail cantos were published, a military commandant was gunned down outside his villa in Ravenna. Shaken by the incident, he had the body transported to his quarters. A letter to Murray describing the aftermath suggests that in some ways the pasha's inscrutable Stoicism might have originated in Byron's own intimate domestic space. As he put it in a letter, "The Lieutenant who is watching the body is smoking with the greatest Sangfroid—a strange people" (*BLJ* 7:248).

"Things to Shake a Stoic"

In reducing Stoicism to a commonplace that was also an attitude, Byron foregrounded its characterological existence, a move that opened up its austerity by marking the range of its global diffusion. Within this expanded scene, Byron seems pulled by two discrepant impulses: a sense of Stoicism's strange otherness—its almost primordial divergence from the mannered culture of sensibility—but also a clear unwillingness to separate that strangeness from his own conception of a mannered self. For Byron, both impulses converged in the figure of the slave, a crystallization of abjection and otherness that synchronized an omnipresent historical reality with a set of disruptive philosophical questions about the nature of autonomy.

Jane Stabler has described *Don Juan* as a poem "hospitable to many different voices," but Juan himself pays the cost of this catholicity and hardly speaks at all in the first four cantos of the poem that bears his name.[87] His first recorded conversation—in fact, his lengthiest and most sustained in the poem—occurs at the beginning of canto V, just after he wakes from his elysian interlude with Haidee to find himself a slave. The stakes and tone of Byron's "Epic Satire" modulate here, for Juan's amours and mock-heroic travails spill past the bounds of romance to merge with the traumatic realities of history (*DJ* 14:99). His enslavement in the Cyclades evokes the Barbary slave trade that loomed over Britain's imperial and mercantile expansion in the Mediterranean throughout the seventeenth and eighteenth centuries. At the same time, narratorial nods to William Wilberforce serve as a reminder that *Don Juan* is a product of two timescales, one of which postdates Parliament's abolition of the slave trade. In this sense, Juan and his "fellow captives" become anachronistic embodiments of the economics of scarcity born out of regulation:

> Twelve negresses from Nubia brought a price
>   Which the West Indian market scarce would bring;
> Though Wilberforce, at last, has made it twice
>   What 'twas ere Abolition (*DJ* 4: 80, 115)

In juxtaposing the Atlantic and Barbary trades, Byron foregrounds the urgent and intractable reality of race slavery while also conjuring up an older context in which slavery was not delimited by race. Chronicled in Defoe's *Robinson Crusoe* as well as Rousseau's unfinished sequel to *Emile*, the Barbary system of capturing Europeans in quest of exorbitant ransoms exerted a strong pull on the British popular imagination. Linda Colley's revisionist account vividly documents the way in which it forced Britons to confront slavery as "never something securely and invariably external to themselves."[88] In *Don Juan*, Byron exploits the narrative possibility of this history, one in which there is no clear line of distinction between one's own fate and that of the other.

Grappling with the vision of autonomy inherent in Byron's entangled perspective on slavery and Stoicism seems important, for recent scholarship has emphasized the significant resonance of his work for African American writers and abolitionists in the nineteenth century, especially at the level of the citational commonplace. Jared Hickman has described the way in which abolitionists transformed key lines from *Childe Harold's Pilgrimage* into a radical and influential refrain: "Hereditary bondsmen! Know ye not / Who would be free themselves must strike the blow" (*CW* 1:69, ll. 720–21). Written in the hope that Greece might rise up and resist "the scourge of Turkish hand," the lines are another example of the overlapping affinities that connected poetry written about the Orient and the Americas (*CW* 1:69, l. 709). In Hickman's terms, writers and orators "converted Byron's high-Romantic couplet into a radical colloquialism."[89]

Henry Highland Garnet used the couplet in an address urging a bid for insurrection at the African American National Convention in 1843, which was barely defeated, and Frederick Douglass "claimed these lines as a personal mantra," deploying them at the end of a key chapter in which he resists his overseer in *My Bondage and My Freedom*.[90] If allusion is a fair barometer, Byron's uptake suggests that when it came to slavery, he was—as James McCune Smith put it—a radical "evangel of freedom."[91]

But Byron's Stoic reflections insinuate that the exact nature of that freedom could be more complicated. In his initial evocation of the slave market at Constantinople, the commerce in flesh goes hand in hand with the practice of philosophy:

> A crowd of shivering slaves of every nation,
>   And age, and sex, were in the market ranged;
> Each bevy with the merchant in his station:
>   Poor creatures! their good looks were sadly changed.
> All save the blacks seem'd jaded with vexation,
>   From friends, and home, and freedom far estranged;
> The negroes more philosophy display'd,—
> Used to it, no doubt, as eels are to be flay'd. (*DJ* 5:7)

The crowded slave market is Byron's ironic inversion of Enlightenment cosmopolitanism and the idea that commerce might yield prosperity and connection. At the same time, Byron's disillusioned nod to philosophy stands as a reminder that Stoicism had been integral to the ethical project of cosmopolitanism from its origins. As a citizen of the world, the Stoic looks past national claims toward ethical ideals born out of common humanity. In the space of a single stanza, Byron charts the way in which an aspirational, universalizing ethic gives way to mere forbearance. His equation of persons and "creatures" emphasizes the reduction of common humanity to bare life, even as the figurative alignment of black slaves to eels skinned alive marks the subtle transposition of abjection into critique.

The trope of the eel flayed alive was a common figure for the naïve assumption that habitual suffering breeds indifference. It was also a perfect target in Byron's broad satirical campaign against cant and affectation, what he saw as the "primum mobile" of England.[92] In waging war on cant, Byron loves to evoke—but only to undercut—hollow sentiments that hint at the vacancy of sentimental morality, or empty phraseology taken up for fashion's sake. Boswell describes the figure as a "striking instance of human insensibility" in the *Life of Johnson*, and Peter Beckford's *Thoughts upon Hunting* (1781) tells of a gentleman who sees a girl skinning eels alive and asks about the cruelty of the practice. Her response is blithely self-damning: "'O, not at all, sir,' replied the girl, *'they be used to it.*'"[93] In both cases, the naïve assumption that repetitive suffering breeds indifference conflates aggregate and individual experience, as though all eels might be inured to suffering because of the intensity of any one individual's experience. The sentiment glides over the reality of suffering, as well as the possibility of its amelioration. At the same time, it points inadvertently to the more dangerous detachment of those who inflict harm.

The only respectable use of the eel trope was to invoke its inanity in the service of abolition. In 1792, the Whig statesman William Windham called on the trope to argue against any delay in the full implementation of abolition:

> With regard to delaying the period for abolition, no real argument had been offered for that point; and he trusted it would not be said that the period of a few years for abolition is nothing, when compared to the space of time in which they have been accustomed to slavery; arguing thus, that because they had long suffered under their misfortunes, there was no great harm in continuing the trade a little longer; like the person who, when charged with cruelty for skinning eels alive, answered, "they are used to it."[94]

Windham casts doubt on the idea that suffering long endured might result in indifference, marking it down as an obfuscating rationalization of harm rather than an accurate depiction of psychology. I take Byron's invocation of the eel trope under the auspices of satire as a similarly knowing refutation. Like abolitionist poets across the political spectrum, he rejected the idea that cultivated indifference or Stoic reflection could make slavery and the loss of freedom anything other than an evil. His thinking here falls in line with a rhetorical question posed in Hannah More's poem "Slavery": "Did ever slave less feel the galling chain, / When Zeno prov'd there was no ill in pain?"[95] The answer, of course, is no, though an acknowledgment of its inability to blunt pain hardly exhausted the possibilities of Stoicism. As I have argued throughout, Byron was almost always attuned not to the inner workings of Stoic moral psychology but to the shape it cut in the world. It was—in Susan Manning's resonant terms—not some "reality of personal identity" but an aspect of character realized "at points of transaction where projected identity encountered a social context."[96] In this regard, the key fact about the Stoicism attributed to the black slaves at the market in Constantinople is that it is a "philosophy display'd." While the indexing of inner lives by outward "looks" admits the real possibility of a gap between inward conviction and outward performance, this uncertainty had never really bothered Byron. As with Conrad, authentic consolation was less important than rhetorical force, a sense of what Stoicism might do in the world. Byron's stance on *nil admirari* Stoicism seems clear: you fake it even if you might not make it, but in the meantime the enactment itself becomes a new starting point for social connection—not a desire for the condescension of sympathy, but the presumption of sovereignty.

As the scene plays out, Byron literalizes the suggestive *nil admirari* connection that links his protagonists to the dispossessed. Juan finds himself thrown into the company of an English gentleman named John Johnson. Their respective life trajectories and responses to enslavement give rise to a philosophical debate about the nature and efficacy of Stoicism. For both characters, Stoicism is tied to the body, a bearing or posture more than an intellectual position. Johnson—thirty, stout, hale, and "with curling rather dark brown hair"—bears a striking resemblance to Byron himself (*DJ* 5:11). The name equivalency of John and Juan also suggests another kind of doubling, with both characters representing different aspects of the same Byronic self.[97] For his part, Juan experiences "things to shake a stoic," but his "carriage"—a register of bearing and deportment—remains "serene" (*DJ* 5:9). Prone to vacillation, he will burst into tears later in the canto only to call "back the stoic to his eyes" (*DJ* 5:121). Johnson's Stoicism is similarly ocular—he appears on the scene with "resolution in his dark gray eye" (*DJ* 5:10)—but like the Tartar khan at the siege of Ismail it is also in his blood. Johnson stands amid the slave market "with such *sang-froid* that greater / Could scarce be shown even by a mere spectator" (*DJ* 5:11). The ideal of cold-blooded spectatorship summons up thoughts of Adam Smith's admonition to see our own concerns "in the light in which any other citizen of the world would view us" (*TMS* 140–41). For Byron, however, the ethical intensity of this demanding self-spectatorship was preempted by the more urgent knowledge that all the world's a stage.

All the same, I'm hesitant to dismiss these Stoic enactments as self-fashionings devoid of any ethical significance. What Juan describes as an impulse to "take things coolly" isn't the point, for if Stoicism is to have any correlation with justice, it must—as Johnson puts it—set "things in their right point of view" (*DJ* 5:23). This is a very Godwinian project, a turn from one's partial passions toward those other equally important parts of a vast system. Following the Stoics, the Byronic tenor of Johnson's perspective suggests that the best way to confront the injustice of slavery might be to stage an exit from the affective realm itself. Johnson gets to this thought right as the machinations of the plot draw his dialogue with Juan to a screeching halt:

> "But after all what *is* our present state?
>   'Tis bad and may be better—all men's lot:
> Most men are slaves, none more so than the great,
>   To their own whims and passions and what not;
> Society itself, which should create
>   Kindness, destroys what little we had got:
> To feel for none is the true social art
> Of the world's stoics—men without a heart." (*DJ* 5:25)

Ranging through several common Stoic ideas, Johnson's evocation of "our present state" effects a sleight of hand, one that aligns his and Juan's perilous legal enslavement with a broadly shared human condition. Such a realignment reflected two divergent tenets of Stoic ethics. On the one hand, the Stoics held that a common rationality resulted in the kinship of all people, master or slave. In a letter from the *Moral Epistles* on slavery, Seneca asks Lucilius to remember that the "man whom you call your slave was born of the same seeds as you—enjoys the same sky—breathes, lives, dies, just as you do."[98] Given this common capacity, anyone could become the master of his fate, or the captain of his soul.[99] On the other hand, human beings rarely live up to the potential of their rationality, resulting in a pervasive and incapacitating moral slavery. In suggesting that "most men are slaves" to their own passions, Johnson alludes to a famous Stoic paradox: "Only the wise man is free, and every fool a slave." Drawing on a distinction between legal and moral slavery, the paradox posited the kind of social inversion that Rousseau and Byron both relished.[100] Prone to circumstance and desire, almost all neglect the fact of their own autonomy, falsely attributing it to external things elusive of control. By contrast, a slave who learned not to be astonished or surprised by the shifting and often cruel realities of existence could become an exemplar of sovereignty.[101]

Juan and Johnson's dialogue ends inconclusively, cut off by the spectatorship of a potential buyer who "seem'd to mark their looks and age, / And capabilities, as to discover / If they were fitted for the purposed cage" (*DJ* 5:26). Given this reminder of material constraint, it might seem that the paradoxical autonomy of the Stoic slave was nothing more than a pipe dream, especially for Juan, who "cared not a tobacco-stopper / About philosophy" (*DJ* 10:60). But if autonomy born of wisdom was elusive, its display was not. As so many Byronic characters seem to intuit, the power of the paradox lies in its performance and the transvaluation of feeling it might effect. As such, the impact of the dialogue hangs on the declamatory power of its final couplet: "To feel for none is the true social art / Of the world's Stoics—men without a heart." Frederick Beaty has described these concluding lines as a "contrived sign-off" that undercuts Stoicism by suggesting that "cool detachment from life is purchased only at an extraordinarily high price."[102] In this vein, it seems clear enough that reference to the "social art" of the world's Stoics is a sly one, a formulation meant to draw attention to the near proximity of contrivance and hypocrisy. Nevertheless, this strikes me as a stanza in which the ottava rima's concluding couplet effects not a deflating critique but a careful elevation of the seemingly absurd into the realm of unexpected insight. It is, after all, a *"true social art,"* a strange phrase that encapsulates Byron's penchant for performance by aligning affectation with something more aesthetic, the creative application of principle. It is only a short jump from the "true social art" of Byron's Stoics to Michel Foucault's account of ancient philosophy as an "art of living."[103] Nor do these lines sanction a solipsistic ideal. To be a Stoic, here, is to be affiliated with the world; it is just that the mechanism of affiliation is a rejection of fellow-feeling rather than its embrace. What looks like apathy from one angle is justice from another. Living without heart—admiring nothing—was not cruel indifference but a different way of imagining commonality. Like Shaftesbury, Byron claims Stoicism as a truly social philosophy, the outlook of those who are aligned with the world. Casually and quietly—and maybe too quietly—the end of Juan's dialogue turns a charge against Stoicism into a testament of its power.

But then again, has Byron really strayed all that far from the comedic realm in which Swift and other eighteenth-century writers unmasked the hollow pretensions of the world's Stoics? Byron's Romantic irony puts pressure on the sympathetic localism that informs so much of Romanticism and its famed moral imagination, but that same ironic impulse seems already poised to qualify the easier-said-than-done idealism of the world's Stoics, those "men without a heart." Byron's real insight seems to lie in bringing Stoicism and irony into closer proximity, letting irony preserve the ethical possibilities of Stoicism by checking its vast pretensions. In this sense, *Don Juan* opens a window onto the predicament of many writers after the French Revolution, invested in the possibility of Stoic cosmopolitanism but painfully aware of its culpabilities.

In the last canto of *Don Juan*—incomplete but important, like the Mutabilitie Cantos at the end of the *Faerie Queene*—Byron reflects on the misunderstandings and "sad usage" suffered by trailblazing "sages" like

Socrates and Galileo. This line of thought gives rise to reflection on his own intermittent Stoic enactments:

> If such doom waits each intellectual Giant,
>   We little people in our lesser way,
> To Life's small rubs should surely be more pliant,
>   And so for one will I—as well I may—
> Would that I were less bilious—but, oh, fie on't!
>   Just as I make my mind up every day,
> To be a *"totus, teres,"* Stoic, Sage,
> The wind shifts and I fly into a rage. (*DJ* 17:10)

With a healthy dose of self-effacement, Byron casts his lot not with the sages but the "little people," prompting his literal positioning of Stoicism as an ever-evanescent philosophy of the "every day." Unsettling the Horatian ideal of a wise man "totus teres atque rotundus"—complete in himself, entirely smooth and rounded—this last trace of Stoicism in *Don Juan* belabors its susceptibility to all kinds of winds and humors.[104] Its very irresolution would seem to preclude any new or consequential "social art." But this need not have been the last word. Shortly after dispatching the manuscript with Juan and Johnson's Stoic dialogue to England, Byron sent Murray an account of his future plans for his evolving epic: "The 5th. is so far from being the last of D.J. that it is hardly the beginning.—I meant to take him the tour of Europe—with a proper mixture of siege—battle—and adventure—and to make him finish as *Anacharsis Cloots*—in the French Revolution" (*BLJ* 8:78). A "citizen of the world by choice," Anacharsis Cloots imagined without any irony at all that a universal republic might encompass the whole globe and stretch to the moon. In his *La republique universelle*, he claimed "a universal apostleship for the gratuitous defence of the millions of slaves, who groan from one pole to the other."[105] His embrace of revolutionary cosmopolitanism put him at odds with Robespierre, and he delivered a series of philosophical harangues at the guillotine as he faced his end. Elizabeth Boyd was surely right to suggest that Byron would have relished such a character, a "mixture of cosmopolitanism, rugged independence, fiery love of liberty, freedom of thought, stoical endurance, and prophetic oratory."[106] If Byron had lived, perhaps Juan would have met his end in quest of such a sublime ethic, another revolutionary figure left without a head because he dared to live "without a heart."

CHAPTER FIVE

Stoic Futurity in Sarah Scott and Mary Shelley

NEAR THE MIDDLE of Jane Austen's *Persuasion*, Anne Elliot finds herself placed "rather apart" with Captain Benwick, a grief-stricken naval officer with "very strong feelings" and a penchant for poetry.[1] In their memorably bookish conversation, Anne quickly claims "seniority of mind" and attempts to steer Benwick away from the excessive Romanticism of figures like Byron who wallow in "impassioned descriptions of hopeless agony." To her mind, better ballast was available in the last century's best prose moralists. It is tempting to imagine this meta-literary moment as Austen's attempt to carve out her own preferred place in literary history, or an effort—just at the end of the Napoleonic Wars—to venture an early critical retrospect on the emergent poetic tradition that has been the focus of the last three chapters. But Anne's attempt to "preach patience and resignation" while working up a "particularized" reading list also engages the variable fate of Stoicism within a system of literary genre, emblematized here by the distinction between poetry and prose. For Anne, divergent conventions and expectations meant that different genres were unequally suited to the work of emotional representation, which was itself a precursor to emotional regulation. Nor were poetry and prose equally "calculated to rouse and fortify the mind" of any reader. For one thing, poetry gave too much sway to feelings liable to "burst their usual restraints." The emotional intensity requisite for the appreciation of poetry initiated a precarious feedback loop, one in which the cultivation of proper poetic feeling was perilously close to a destabilizing enthusiasm. As Anne put it, "it was the misfortune of poetry, to be seldom safely enjoyed by those who enjoyed it completely; and that the strong feelings which alone could estimate it truly, were the very feelings which ought to taste it but sparingly." Prose is described in a contrastingly therapeutic light. Like an apothecary dispensing a drug, Anne recommends "a larger allowance of prose" in Benwick's "daily study."[2]

Based on the argument I have been pursuing over the course of several chapters, it would be easy enough to quibble with the way Anne sets Stoicism and poetry at loggerheads. In my telling, Byron was just as preoccupied by the characterological power of Stoicism "to rouse and fortify the mind" as many eighteenth-century moralists, and for Coleridge, the lyric was just as likely to incite Stoic askesis as any memoir or essay. But as Anne herself notes in a later conversation about the gendered reality of constancy and strong feeling, literary precedent is a misleading realm for considering the propinquity of Stoicism and poetry, for men "have had every advantage of us in telling their own story. Education has been theirs in so much higher a degree; the pen has been in their hands."[3] Anne's sense of Stoicism's alignment with the expectations of genre seems superseded by the clear contours of gender that inform those expectations. Her conviction that prose and not poetry is the proper habitat for Stoic reflection points to a striking disjuncture in the period: while there is a long tradition of women writers looking to Stoicism as an avenue for empowerment and what Martha Nussbaum describes as the "radical criticism of conventional belief," little of that critical Stoic tradition finds its way into Romantic poetry written by women.[4]

Affirming the common rationality of all human beings, the ancient Stoics held that men and women were equally capable of acquiring virtue and living a philosophical life. In his lost *Republic*, Zeno eliminated common gender distinctions from his ideal community, stipulating that men and women should "wear the same clothes."[5] Epictetus's own teacher Musonius Rufus argued that since men and women were born with the same virtues, they deserved identical philosophical educations. Indeed, Musonius offers qualified praise for women who "let their housework go and come into the middle of the company of men and get involved in arguments and make sophistical distinctions and take apart syllogisms."[6] Mary Robinson foregrounded the fact of this educational equality in her *Letter to the Women of England, On the Injustice of Mental Insubordination* (1799), noting that the Stoics (along with the Epicureans) "delivered their lessons freely to both sexes, and all conditions."[7] Long before Mary Wollstonecraft arrived on the scene, women writers were drawn to the Stoics not for their willingness to "preach patience and resignation" but for their encompassing ethos and critical potentiality.

And yet little of this critical Stoic ethos shows up in Romantic women's poetry. As Isobel Armstrong has argued most persuasively, the lion's share of poetry by women in the period is less invested in the suspension of affect than in turning it "to *analytical* account." For Armstrong, these poets were more typically interested in challenging "male philosophical traditions that led to a demeaning discourse of feminine experience."[8] In a cultural moment still engrossed by the gendered conventions of sensibility, it was more productive to deconstruct "affect with affect" than to step out of the affective realm altogether.[9] Besides, the plummeting of Mary Wollstonecraft's posthumous reputation foregrounded the danger of female Stoic assertion, as did the vehement condemnation of Anna Barbauld's *Eighteen Hundred and Eleven*, a notably Stoic poem whose dismal reception marked the end of Barbauld's poetic career.[10] Coleridge's glib commentary on Barbauld focalizes the strikingly gendered inequity of poetic expectations, for he mocks Barbauld for a Stoic coldness that he himself cultivated in his own poetry. When told that Barbauld's husband had complained of his wife's coldness, Coleridge replied that he "must have had a very warm constitution, for he had clasped an icicle in his arms for forty years before he found it was cold."[11] E. J. Clery reads this as less a sexual slur than a philosophical one; as she notes, Coleridge was prone to throw the term around in expressing his condescension for bluestockings more generally.[12]

Rather than explore poetry's lack of hospitality for female Stoicism in the period, I want take Anne Elliot's own advice and suggest—though with a swerve—that the most penetrating accounts of Stoicism's ability to foster autonomy for women occur not in poetry but in the heteroglossic space of the novel. Looking at an early intimation of Romanticism and its late sequel, I argue that Sarah Scott's *Millenium Hall* (1762) and Mary Shelley's *Lodore* (1835) portray Stoic autonomy as a model for the future even as they erect various buffers to qualify the intensity of that vision. As we will see, the dialogic form of the novel—open to a range of overlapping voices and perspectives—easily accommodates the intensive questioning that often accompanies the deployment of Stoicism in women's writing. But as both novels make clear, this careful work of qualification and mitigation often resulted not in the reduction but the extension of Stoicism and its power.

It is worth tarrying for another moment with Anne Elliot's "seniority of mind," for she is not just an advocate of the turn to prose in quest of Stoicism but a quiet exemplar of that philosophy's future-oriented temporality. From a certain angle, *Persuasion* might seem more like a cautionary tale about the damage wrought by Stoicism than an exploration of its potentialities. Compelled by a "severe degree of self-denial," Anne's decision to set duty above inclination in ending her engagement with Frederick Wentworth occurs long before the novel begins.[13] Austen makes it abundantly clear that Anne's turn away from Captain Wentworth—her "great act of submission to duty and propriety"—comes at an equally great cost.[14] But rather than condemn all of the protocols of dispassion inaugurated by that loss, Austen belabors their centrality, folding them into the narrative itself. Throughout the novel, Anne's Stoicism underwrites the autonomy her disappointment perversely affords. When Wentworth threatens to descend upon Uppercross, Anne tries to "teach herself to be insensible." Forced to endure her sister's inanities, she draws on vast reserves of "forced cheerfulness" and musters "perseverance in patience." Our access to her interior life confirms that she has not outlived "the age of emotion," and yet her existence is punctuated by its management.[15]

In all of these daily moments, *Persuasion* offers less an endorsement of Stoicism than a penetrating depiction of how it plays out in real time: a sense of the composure it affords, but also a vivid rendering of its liabilities—its inconvenient failure at moments of greatest need, or the very instability of its security. As John Wiltshire has noted, the first half of *Persuasion* limns Anne's recapitulation of the various exercises and practices "through which the stoics both guarded and constituted the self." Though motivated by deep feeling in herself and others, "she seeks means, through the exertion of 'reason,' to combat her feelings, and to generate, if possible, an independent, autonomous self."[16] When Wentworth comes to her aid in a moment of undeniable tenderness, Stoic self-culture ensures that all of her "disordered feelings" will be "arranged." Later, Anne's Stoic training in expectation offers ballast and even a relational edge when Wentworth stumbles upon her in a pastry shop:

> He was more obviously struck and confused by the sight of her, than she had ever observed before; he looked quite red. For the first time, since their renewed acquaintance, she felt that she was betraying the least sensibility of the two. She had the advantage of him, in the preparation of the last few moments. All the overpowering, blinding, bewildering, first effects of strong surprise were over with her. Still however, she had enough to feel![17]

Even in the moment, Anne weighs her mental impressions, cross-referencing them with belief. Subduing, like Byron, her own astonishment, what remains is just feeling enough to solidify her control. In affective terms, it is a repetition of that fateful moment on the Cobb in Lyme in which Anne—to borrow a line from William Galperin—takes on "the poise and self-control ordinarily characteristic of the captain."[18] But, as in that moment, all of these affective recalibrations can seem like little more than a "program of repression and self-censorship," the proliferating echoes of a pivotal act of Stoic self-denial.[19] And yet in a novel so drawn toward what Emily Rohrbach has called "the implications of an unpredictable futurity," it seems shortsighted to imagine the questioning of Stoicism as a sign of its ultimate disavowal.[20] In parsing these moments when Anne brings Stoicism to bear on "bewildering" feeling, I gravitate toward Wendy Lee's sense that something more generative might be isolated within the "affective chainmail" that Austen forges for her characters.[21] In *Persuasion*, the affirmative power of insensibility seems less like reticence as a form of care than the promise of autonomy, a self-authorizing space in the present, even what Galperin has described as an "egress from the heteronormative economy and its strictures."[22] In this sense, the trajectory of Anne's withholding is more determinative than its origin. Waiting out a reduced present, Anne's quietly radical Stoic autonomy does not just set the pattern for a happy future, it makes that future possible.

In turning from Austen's familiar terrain to focus on novels separated by an interval of seventy years, I want to capture not the unfolding of an influence but rather the consistent recourse to Stoicism as an avenue for imagining women's empowerment across the period. There is no trace of Sarah Scott in Shelley's record of her own reading, but both Scott and Shelley turn to Stoicism in reconciling propriety with a radicalism whose full significance seems just over the horizon. Published shortly after Elizabeth Carter's influential translation of Epictetus and Smith's *Theory of Moral Sentiments*, Scott's *Millenium Hall* lodges an early objection to Smith's gendered portrayal of the "awful" virtues of self-denial and self-government. It also demonstrates how the resources of fiction can nullify much of the skittishness that surrounded Stoicism in the period. By linking Stoicism to characters whose conversation and extended backstories contextualize their philosophical commitment, Scott shows how the mitigation of Stoicism only amplifies its power. Though Scott herself would greet the French Revolution with deep skepticism, *Millenium Hall* clears the ground Wollstonecraft would more forcefully occupy in the 1790s.

In a kind of contrast, Wollstonecraft's daughter Mary Shelley wrote *Lodore* at the far outer edge of most Romantic chronologies. Shelley originally planned to mark the historicity of her penultimate novel, composed between 1831 and 1833, with a distinctly chronological subtitle: "Lodore—a tale of the present time."[23] Though the novel looks back through two Romantic generations to the American War of Independence, the overt presentism of the subtitle points to its emergence alongside the First Reform Bill.[24] Poised at this epochal hinge, *Lodore* turns back to reevaluate Romantic Stoicism, raising the ghost of Wollstonecraft while also revisiting Stoic republicanism and Coleridgean tranquility.[25] Though Shelley herself imagined the novel as a strong affirmation of "the genuine affections of the heart," all of its major characters gravitate toward Stoicism at one point or another.[26] Galvanized by the success of silver-fork fiction, Shelley paid due attention to the manners of modern aristocratic life, capturing in the process a sense of how thoroughly and equivocally those manners bore traces of Stoicism. More than a few characters, for instance, exhibit the "calm Patrician polish" and *nil admirari* Stoicism that captured Byron's attention (*DJ* 13:34). But for all its interest in the past and present, *Lodore* remains preoccupied with "the secrets of futurity" (*L* 69). Though Shelley hatches two companionate marriages before the novel concludes, she gives the last word to Fanny Derham, a "Quixotic" Stoic whose queer and selfless desire cannot be adequately encapsulated "in a few tame lines" (*L* 323, 448).

The character of Fanny Derham is interesting in her own right, but her unknown future suggestively falls in line with that of Romanticism itself. *Lodore* makes it clear that the Stoic vision that held so much sway with Shelley's parents' generation was less a burden of the past than the shape of things to come. At the same time, these sequential glimpses of Stoic futurity—separated by such a broad swath of time—cannot help but draw attention to a future endlessly forestalled. If the risk of this fundamentally anticipatory stance is an autonomy that never materializes, both texts hold open the possibility that Stoicism works even in anticipation, facilitating new arrangements or ways of living within the present. In this sense, both novels could be seen as manifestations of what Rohrbach and Jonathan Sachs have described as a shift in the experience of temporality itself, one in which the status of the present—or even "the affective history of the present moment"—was increasingly imagined or even "reconceived" from the "projected vantage of some future time."[27] Working toward its own perfection, Stoicism becomes not just the promise of a future liberation but a way of existing within the imperfect present, or even a way of bringing that future about.

Sarah Scott's Stoic Reformers

Even from the outset, the narrator of *Millenium Hall* is alert to the possibilities latent in a paradox: How is it that retirement, the conscious turning away from "the great world," might furnish the "means of mending mankind"? (*MH* 64, 53). Touring Britain after twenty years in Jamaica, an unnamed narrator and his fashionable sidekick are waylaid in Cornwall only to find themselves wandering through a "truly pastoral" landscape redolent of "the days of Theocritus" (*MH* 56). This orderly, aesthetic agrarianism is only a warm-up act to the ideality they will discover upon meeting the inhabitants of the hall, an encounter that prompts the narrator to imagine himself "in the Attick school" (*MH* 58).[28] The experimental domestic arrangements he describes in his long epistolary account are so impressive and strikingly unconventional that he cannot help but indulge in extra adverbs to capture their exceptionality: the ladies united at Millenium Hall were "so uncommon a society," or later, "a family so extraordinary" (*MH* 59, 62). Pooling their financial resources to obtain tranquility while spreading benevolence abroad, six women "qualified both by nature and fortune to have the world almost at command" strike out on their own. Turning away from the masculine world and its disempowering mores, they "make as it were a new one for themselves," a world in which the sentimental narratives of heterosexual romance are consigned to the past in favor of a life of virtuous retirement and general usefulness (*MH* 76). Borrowing Mary Louise Pratt's term for an idealized world "of female autonomy, empowerment, and pleasure," Felicity Nussbaum describes Millenium Hall as a "feminotopia of domesticity," one in which "enclosure paradoxically brings freedom from tyranny."[29] This last note—of nuns who fret not at their convent's narrow room—speaks to the Stoic character that pervades the volume as a whole. Zeno of Citium sits off in the corner of Raphael's magisterial painting of the Attic School, but his philosophical proclivities stand at the very heart of *Millenium Hall*.

Informed by its significant cachet in bluestocking culture, the character of Stoicism in *Millenium Hall* is noticeably dual. In its most recognizable guise, it emerges as the fortitude and resignation so often requisite for women navigating a world in which their agency and desires were circumscribed by male tyranny. All of the proprietors of Millenium Hall have occasion to draw on Stoicism in their precollective life. Avoiding dangers and accepting disappointment, each of them learns like Miss Louisa Mancel "to submit patiently to her fate, and to support her present trial with constancy" (*MH* 145). After all, the Stoics offered a resonant model for enjoying liberty within when it was unattainable without.

But while feminine Stoicism as a resource for bearing up against the wrongs of woman plays more than a cameo role in the novel, it also materializes as a more destabilizing force, a philosophical outlook or dispassionate commitment that turns private empowerment into extensive benevolence. The freedom of the inner citadel gives way to an experiment in collectivity, an "assured asylum" with a shared and "entirely rational" agenda for extending its influence abroad. As the narrator's fashionable sidekick puts it, "if any people have a right to turn reformers, you ladies are best qualified, since you begin by reforming yourselves" (*MH* 58, 159, 166). Though Scott's novel emerges from a very different set of political commitments, there is a clear line of connection between *Millenium Hall* and the Stoic cosmopolitanism that would inform Mary Wollstonecraft's call for "a revolution in female manners," one that would make women "as a part of the human species, labour by reforming themselves to reform the world."[30]

In envisioning a utopia actuated by Stoic restraint, the "female Arcadia" at the heart of Scott's novel anticipates Anahid Nersessian's vision of a Romanticism whose divestment from "regimes of comprehensive gratification" becomes the "source of politically efficacious joy."[31] At least their own mode of life corresponds to the lineaments of this restrained model: rejecting all the self-indulgence that might accompany a great fortune allows the hall's proprietors to enact small-scale reforms while also "enjoying in a supreme degree, the happiness they dispersed around them" (*MH* 222). The neighborhood surrounding their manor is transformed by utopian projects. Aged cottagers—previously unable to eke out a living wage in the local economy—are united together in a subsidized community of mutual care. When an impoverished local mother has more than four children, the ladies of Millenium Hall adopt, support, and educate her future children as soon as they can walk. They offer the privacy and tranquility of an enclosed garden community to men and women whose disabilities and deformities had once been exploited as a public spectacle, and they operate a kind of hostel for "indigent gentlewomen" whose excessive education and diminished funds leave them without a place in the world. Aiming for "extensive good" in all things, their arrangements ensure that "as large a part of mankind as possible should feel the happy influence of their bounty" (*MH* 219, 160). Confronted with example after example of such orderly yet imaginative benevolence, the narrator reflects that there "was something so whimsically good in the conduct of the ladies in these particulars, as at first made me smile; but when I considered it more thoroughly, I perceived herein a refinement of charity, which, though extremely uncommon, was entirely rational" (*MH* 169). His sense of a whimsical method suggests an early intimation of "fancy," the faculty for envisioning and re-envisioning the world that Julie Ellison has linked to the "reorientation of sensibility to the needs of global culture" as well as "women's literary ambition."[32] But by definition whimsy also speaks to a "deviation from the ordinary," and the disorienting swerve in this novel entails a profusion of benevolence without any of the sensibility, enthusiasm, or demonstrable sympathy often thought to accompany it.[33] If the ladies exhibit any "natural affection," it takes shape in the Stoically inflected Shaftesburian form I described in chapter 1, "that high & principal Natural Affection, wch in a Mind soundly rational is, as it were, in the Place of all" (*A* 254).

This cosmopolitan vision might seem too abstract a stance for fictionality, but the novel's inset narratives explore the emergence of this rational utopian vision out of trauma, ensuring that the dispassionate rationality regnant at Millenium Hall never descends to a Houyhnhnm-like level of caricature or insensibility. As Gary Kelly puts it, the alternation of history and description shows how "the oppression and exploitation of women in the world outside Millenium Hall paradoxically produced its feminized and feminist utopia" (introduction to *MH*, 30). The back and forth between these two different components of the narrative drives home the overarching trajectory of Stoicism in the novel. Though it starts as a self-regulative resource for virtuous and intellectually inclined women, it grows into a collective and startlingly cosmopolitan perspective, one that redefines what a "family" might entail.

But if this redefinition was whimsical and philosophical, it was also rooted in Scott's own unconventional biography. Just over a decade before her novel's publication she married George Lewis Scott, a Fellow of the Royal Society who was also a tutor to the Prince of Wales. The marriage collapsed within a year, and Sarah Scott left her husband to establish an unconventional household with her companion Lady Barbara Montagu. As in *Millenium Hall*, though on a decidedly less extravagant scale, queer desire and economic partnership conspired to replace heterosexual domesticity with an intimate but outwardly focused arrangement.[34] Describing their intertwined finances, Scott once noted that she spoke "of Ly Babs Pension as if it were my own, & in truth it is as much mine as hers, we having as little distinction of property as any married couple."[35] Their house at Bath became "the centre of a network of like-minded women, dedicated to relieving poverty, educating poor children and providing a Sunday school."[36] To make their always scanty ends meet, Scott translated French works and wrote histories and novels. A letter in which Elizabeth Montagu, "Queen of the Bluestockings," chronicles her sister's life with Lady Bab makes it clear that Scott's own choice of life reflected a clear divestment from Montagu's genteel values as well as the gentry capitalism that figures so prominently in *Millenium Hall*:

> My sister rises early, and as soon as she has read prayers to their small family, she sits down to cut out and prepare work for twelve poor girls, whose schooling they pay for; to those whom she finds more than ordinarily capable, she teaches writing and arithmetic herself.... These good works are often performed by the Methodist ladies in the heat of enthusiasm, but thank God, my sister's is a calm and rational piety. Her conversation is lively and easy, and she enters into all the reasonable pleasures of society ... [though] as their income is small, they deny themselves unnecessary expenses. My sister seems very happy, it has pleased God to lead her to truth, by the road of affliction.... Lady Bab Montagu concurs with her in all these things, and their convent, for by its regularity it resembles one, is really a very chearful place.[37]

In Montagu's rendering, Scott's life falls in line with the narrative pattern she would sketch out five times over in *Millenium Hall*: the road of affliction leads not to enthusiasm but "a calm and rational piety." But to end with the convent is to lean too heavily on renunciation, as if self-culture yielded only a cloistered virtue. As even a hazy picture of Scott's own life makes clear, her interest in interrogating the naturalness of so many presumed natural affections leads to a strikingly expansive view.[38]

Elizabeth Carter's Ruse

That Scott's interest in a more rational rejoinder to sentimentalism took shape in a distinctly Stoic form was hardly surprising, for Elizabeth Carter's groundbreaking translation of Epictetus meant that Stoicism enjoyed an especial prominence in bluestocking culture. At the same time, Carter's subtle reframing of Stoicism offers a clear sense of why such a significant influence appears so fleetingly and ambiguously in *Millenium Hall*. In 1758, Carter published the first complete translation of Epictetus in English, one that would serve as the standard edition of his works for more than a century.[39] Trained in the classical languages by her father, Carter famously adopted extreme measures to advance her scholarship. Waking before sunrise, she took snuff and chewed green tea to stay awake while studying late into the night.[40] It is hard not to imagine Carter as the model for Harriot Trentham in *Millenium Hall*, one of the community's initial proprietors who studies with "such unwearied diligence" that she becomes "the perfect mistress of the living languages, and no less acquainted with Greek and Latin. She was well instructed in the ancient and modern philosophy, and in almost every branch of learning" (*MH* 227). Similarly wide-ranging in her languages and learning, Carter's intellectual reputation was legendary; in a letter to his pupil, the tutor of William Pitt the Younger once described Carter as "not only the most learned Woman of any age but one of the most learned Persons of that in which She lives: The pure sublime Genius which never swerves from Virtue."[41] Carter began translating *All the Works of Epictetus* in 1749 at least in part to assuage the grief of her friend Catherine Talbot. Anticipating Anne Elliot's recommended regimen of consoling prose, Carter dispatched her amassing translation to Talbot in installments, "rather like a series of medical prescriptions."[42] Shortly after its publication, Carter became a friend and intimate correspondent of Scott's sister Elizabeth Montagu, and Scott herself is mentioned early and often in their correspondence.

For Carter, the task of making Epictetus available to a broad audience was perilous on two levels: if the prideful reputation of Stoicism diverged from Christian piety and respectability, its presentation by a woman writer only threatened to amplify its intractability. Anticipating the dilemma that weighed so heavily on Coleridge's mind, Carter was forced to confront the disparities between what she called the "Stoical Doctrine" and the "Christian System."[43] Talbot in particular urged Carter to be wary of "those points" in which Epictetus's philosophy was "false, wild, and defective" in its divergence from Christianity, "the only true philosophy."[44] In her introduction, Carter addresses the affinities between Stoicism and Christianity as well as their points of departure. Though sometimes "strongly tempted to think, that *Epictetus* was acquainted with the New Testament," Carter makes it clear that his teachings are ill-suited to the reality of "human Imperfection." After all, the attempt to abide by Stoic principles that ran afoul of the true "Nature of Man" all too often resulted in "Pride" and "Hardheartedness."[45] But as Jennifer Wallace has argued, Carter risked exacerbating this prideful and pedantic reputation by presuming to enter the decidedly male sphere of classical learning. In Wallace's terms, Carter had to tread a careful line between "the chastening and virtuous qualities of classicism" and "the 'pedantic' or exhibitionist associations of classical learning."[46]

For Carter, part of this balancing act entailed a thorough campaign of "moralizing the classics," of censoring through translation some of Epictetus's more objectionable imagery while also extolling his compatibility with Christian virtue.[47] In her introductory discourse, for example, Carter gives the Stoics due credit for being "the clearest and most zealous

Assertors of a particular Providence." Approaching belief in providence as "the Foundation of all true Piety," Carter suggests that the Stoics "are intitled to the highest Honour for their steady Defence of it."[48] Toward the end of the discourse, she makes it clear that Stoicism can be happily reconciled with a life of social virtue and Christian duty:

> Even now, their Compositions may be read with great Advantage, as containing excellent Rules of Self-government, and of social Behaviour; of a noble Reliance on the Aid and Protection of Heaven, and of a perfect Resignation and Submission to the divine Will: Points, which are treated with great Clearness, and with admirable Spirit, in the Lessons of the Stoics; and though their Directions are seldom practicable on the Principles, in trying Cases, may be rendered highly useful in Subordination to Christian Reflexions.[49]

Suddenly useful and perfectly proper, Epictetus was scrubbed of his atheistic sting, becoming in the process the stuff of daily devotionals, the crux of an idiosyncratic but respectable conduct manual. This "subordination" might seem like a capitulation or at least a strong containment of Stoicism and its radical, reordering possibilities. But Harriet Guest's account of the way in which the familiar channel of religious discourse could empower women writers by overriding "the modesty appropriate to femininity" more accurately explains the dynamic of Carter's discourse. As Guest puts it, religious language "creates a peculiar context which sweeps aside the conventions of gendered identity to invoke from educated women a liberal moral authority and comprehensiveness of vision reminiscent of that appropriate to public men."[50] The aura of devotion makes transgressive ideas palatable even as it puts traditionally masculine tasks or topics within reach of women writers. In Carter's introduction, the presence of piety signals not the closing down of Stoicism but a strengthening of its power. Richard Polwhele's *The Unsex'd Females* offers one sign of this strategy's ability to disarm. While Wollstonecraft is skewered for "affecting to dismiss the heart" and drawing precepts "cold from sceptic Reason's vase," Carter—the preeminent translator of unfeeling philosophy—remains a paragon of modest virtue, diffusing "with a milder air / The moral precepts of the Grecian Muse."[51]

The Stoics at Home (in the Universe)

Given their near proximity in the bluestocking network, it is hard to believe that Sarah Scott was blind to the phenomenon of Carter's *Epictetus*. And while it is probably a stretch to imagine that Elizabeth Montagu tucked her own subscribed copy of *All the Works of Epictetus* into one of the hampers of partridge and eel she sent to Scott and Lady Bab, Carter's strategy of veiling feminist and Stoic assertion in Christian piety pervades *Millenium Hall*.[52] This split potential of Stoicism to be at once trenchant and pious is especially notable in the novel's most extensive backstory, the history of the hall's initial cofounders, Miss Mancel and Miss Melvyn. Thrown together at boarding school, their shared propensity for rational sociability, self-denying virtue, and Christian piety conspires to create a deep intimacy, one that outlasts the trials they confront together. Betrayed by a scheming stepmother, Miss Melvyn is compelled to marry a debauched and "extremely disagreeable" gentleman several decades her senior (*MH* 107). Miss Mancel barely escapes her own guardian's attempted seduction, only to run up against daunting contingencies in her attempt to navigate the world without fortune, prospects, or known parentage. Scott's novel risks extravagance in evoking almost ad nauseam the ironclad constancy such virtue testing elicits. Adhering "to every duty" and bearing "all the trials she might meet with in the married state," Miss Melvyn is a veritable fount of "entire faith and resignation" (*MH* 127–28, 100). Louisa Mancel deploys an equally proficient self-discipline, keeping "so strict a watch over herself" that she is seemingly capable of supporting all trials "with constancy" (*MH* 139, 145).

Throughout the novel, Scott makes it clear that this strong aura of fortitude and constancy is not just temperamental or spiritual but decisively intellectual, an outgrowth of shared reading and rigorous study. Scott goes so far as to suggest that Mrs. Selvyn, another of the hall's inhabitants, was not just deeply conversant with "the doctrine of the ancient moralists" but was "bred a philosopher from her cradle" (*MH* 200). Miss Mancel and Miss Melvyn obtain their own philosophical credentials at school. Early in their friendship, the former's guardian bestows upon both friends a "very pretty library," one that we might reasonably assume contained a copy of Carter's *Epictetus*. Engaging in a course of study with the older Miss Melvyn, Louisa becomes adept "in such parts of philosophy of which her age was capable" (*MH* 90–91). If these motherless daughters had turned to Sarah Pennington's contemporaneous *An Unfortunate Mother's Advice to Her Absent Daughters* (1761), they would have found Epictetus, Seneca, and Cicero all described as worthy of a young lady's attention. But as Carter's model made clear, such classical learning was most useful "in Subordination to Christian Reflexions."[53] As such, it is only fitting that Miss Mancel and Miss Melvyn do not pick up any impious Stoic proclivities while reading; their virtuous self-possession remains void of that philosophic "pride which often conceals itself under the name of spirit and greatness of soul" (*MH* 92).

This balancing act between Stoic morality and Christian propriety becomes especially clear at the only juncture in the novel in which Stoicism is specifically registered by name. Embracing poverty in order to preserve her virtue, Miss Mancel remains unperturbed by her fate, for "all the evils that attend it then appeared to her so entirely external, that she beheld them with the calm philosophy of a stoic, and not from a very contrary motive; the insensibility of each arose from a ruling passion; the stoic's from pride, her's from love" (*MH* 147). It is a striking moment: prompted by similar motives, apatheia and agape seem like interchangeable realities, at least as far as appearances are concerned. What looks like insensibility might just as well be love. Figured as less insular and self-involved, Stoicism is directly aligned with the "humility and calmness of a true christian disposition" (*MH* 194). Such a realignment opens up a powerful sense of commensurability: while seemingly ordinary or even conservative, the Stoic outlook cultivated by the Misses Mancel and Melvyn quietly advances a transgressive agenda, one that reimagines a society based on the logic of heterosexual domesticity.

Shaftesbury might as well join Carter as one of Millenium Hall's patron saints, for its "sisterhood" seems ever preoccupied by the kind of Stoic transit he charts from the family-centric realm of partial affections to the more extensive needs of a vast system. In chapter 1, I argued that Shaftesbury gradually redefined natural affection, linking it not with zeal for "the propagation and nurture of the young" but with the staunchly dispassionate perspective "*of a rational creature*, capable of knowing Nature, and of considering the Good & Interest of the Whole" (*C* 192, *A* 78). The proprietors of Millenium Hall embrace this rational vision with a feminist twist, emphasizing in particular the way in which marriage constrains not only autonomy and desire but also a woman's ability to take part in the framing of "an equal, just and universal friendship" (*C* 256). In Scott's rhetoric, Shaftesbury's distinction registers as the difference between a "narrow" and an "extensive" perspective. Miss Melvyn's debauched husband, for example, becomes a caricature of the confining force of partial affections: "He lived intirely in the country, and seemed to be totally insensible to the pleasure of contributing to the happiness of others. All his tenderness was confined within the narrow circle of himself" (*MH* 155). Bound to such delimited partiality by legal and moral ties, Miss Melvyn's marriage implicates her in this narrowness, even as it circumscribes her active power to redress the wrongs of the world. The utopian experiment at Millenium Hall established after her husband's death noticeably inverts this confinement, for its model of friendship and "rational society" supersedes all partial affections, prioritizing "extensive good" and the hope that "as large a part of mankind as possible should feel the happy influence of their bounty" (*MH* 236, 160).

These suggestive parallels between Shaftesbury's reflections and the bookish Stoicism cultivated by the unconventional protagonists in *Millenium Hall* speaks to Scott's investment in a moral philosophical discourse attuned to the proper apportionment of ethical attention. But her own important corollary—reflected in the novel, but also born out of her own experience—lay in the suggestion that Stoicism's challenge to sensibility could elicit not just a mental recalibration but a social reconfiguration. Epictetus's own foregrounding of any being's inherent separateness from child, spouse, or family made Stoic autonomy especially compelling for anyone averse to the trappings of domestic life.[54] It could be an alternative to the affective protocols of marriage and domesticity, a source of legitimizing virtue for figures like Miss Mancel or Mrs. Selvyn who make "so strange a resolution in favour of a single life" (*MH* 207). It is certainly the case that Scott's Stoic decentering of heterosexual domesticity opens up space for queer desire, even as it becomes—in Susan Lanser's resonant terms—a kind of ascetic performance that authorizes "female intimacy."[55] When Miss Melvyn is forced to marry, the pain of her separation from Miss Mancel is compared to that which might accompany the division of body from soul. Miss Mancel similarly laments that "a second paradise could not recompense her for the loss of her society" (*MH* 129). But as this last turn of phrase suggests, such personal desire is always linked in *Millenium Hall* to a larger aggregate vision. If the Stoic disavowal of partial affection results in a broadened sense of what love might entail, it also gives rise to new forms of commonality, friendship, and even family through which that love might cohere. After all, a "second paradise" or "female Arcadia" will—by the end of the novel—be more than abundant recompense for everything that Miss Mancel has to endure along the way (*MH* 223). To borrow a formulation from Claudia Johnson, the collective cultivation of Stoicism at Millenium Hall is itself one of those "idyls of *female* society" that "challenge the sentimental premise that heterosexual affect is the basis for virtue."[56] If Shaftesbury redefined natural affection along Stoic lines, Scott's vision reimagines family and domesticity in a similarly radical way: powered by Stoic rationality and upheld by Christianity, these sites of possible partiality and confinement become spaces for a newly extensive vision of autonomy.

In a certain light, *Millenium Hall* might seem a modest vision. Dropping men from the marital equation fosters an autonomy that collectivity amplifies, and yet domesticity remains the rule of the day. The narrator first describes the community he has stumbled upon as simply an "amiable family" anxious "to conceal their virtues in retirement." His decision to "nominate" the place "Millenium Hall" claims this familial model as a premonition of Christ's thousand-year reign on earth, but then again, the thought of that far-off moment balances yearning with a future as-yet unsecured (*MH* 53). Nevertheless, the Stoic rationality in effect at Millenium Hall reframes the concept of family itself, linking intimacy to autonomy and equality while also extending that vision outward in practical terms. The concealment of Stoic virtue by domesticity itself paradoxically gives that vision amplitude and range. Here again Carter was a useful model. Famous for her scholarly and domestic multitasking, she emphasized her domestic responsibilities to disarm in advance negative reactions to her intellectual pursuits. So omnipresent were these two competing priorities that Samuel Johnson remained convinced that she could do it all, once observing that his "old friend, Mrs Carter, could make a pudding as well as translate Epictetus."[57] While domestic life could put a cramp on the exertion of intellect and agency, that same domesticity also sanctioned such exertion. In this sense, the task of ordering and running a large country estate is one of many strategies that Scott adopts to put forward but also conceal the Stoic cosmopolitanism that provides "excellent Rules of self-government" for so many of her protagonists.

After all, who exactly does the narrator mean to include in describing this "amiable family"? Is it limited to the six inhabitants of the hall who have managed to blend a single life with "the social comforts of friendship" (*MH* 110)? Or does it encompass the many persons—the indigent, the overlooked, and the maimed—who come under their sway? Early in their philosophically charged friendship, Miss Mancel and Miss Melvyn share all of their property "in one undistinguished common," breaking down "the boundaries and barriers raised by those two watchful and suspicious enemies, Meum and Tuum" (*MH* 93). In envisioning a world recreated in the image of their own familial model, the sisterhood at Millenium Hall tears down further boundaries enforced by social convention, ever in pursuit of such commonality. Though hierarchy remains, Miss Mancel looks to a "future" in which "there may probably be no inequality" (*MH* 245). In the meantime, the careful attention they lavish on their rational "household arrangements" resonates with the rhetoric of domesticity that is, after all, the "main point" of reference for Zeno's own cosmopolitan vision, though with a crucial caveat. At Millenium Hall, it is not just men but women who become "fellow-citizens":

> The much admired *Republic* of Zeno ... is aimed at this one main point, that our household arrangements should not be based on cities or parishes, each one marked out by its own legal system, but we should regard all men as our fellow-citizens and local residents, and there should be one way of life and order, like that of a herd grazing together and nurtured by one law. Zeno wrote this, picturing as it were a dream or image of a philosopher's well-regulated society.[58]

For what is Millenium Hall itself but a dream or image of a philosopher's well-regulated society? Central to the history of its founders, Stoicism—a kind of self-reform that could reorder the world—was also vital to its future. As Miss Mancel puts it, "God's mercy and bounty is universal, it flows unasked, and unmerited; we are bid to endeavor to imitate him as far as our nature will enable us to do it. What bounds then ought we to set to our good offices, but the want of power to extend them farther?" (*MH* 244–45).

Mary Shelley's Errand into the Wilderness

Despite its strict attention to propriety, *Millenium Hall* is almost always described as a novel that dips into the future in quest of a vision of what the world might be, one in which domesticity is detached from matrimony, making it a public and empowering site in which philosophy and active benevolence converge. By contrast, Mary Shelley's career as a novelist is typically described as following a general trajectory toward increasing conformity and propriety, a trade-off in which what Barbara Johnson describes as the "unresolvable contradictions" inherent in her earliest novels are set aside for tidier narratives that take family relations as the widest horizon available for understanding the self.[59] On a practical level, Shelley's narrower preoccupation with bourgeois domesticity can be seen as a bid for the financial security that might come along with respectability. Noting that her first and last novels almost seem to be the work of different writers, Mary Poovey has suggested that Shelley's later fiction intentionally courts "the approval of a middle-class, largely female audience."[60] This practicality is often thought to come at a philosophical cost, one in which Shelley's heightened interest in the domestic affections entails a turn away from the more extensive views that characterized the radicalism of her parents. But as *Millenium Hall* makes clear, propriety need not correspond with the retrenchment of a radical vision. As Julie Carlson has noted most powerfully, Shelley's apparent swerve toward Victorian conformity obscures her emergent interest in female characters "who have made, or will make, the future."[61]

In excavating Shelley's prophetic vision in *Lodore*, I want to foreground the minor but conspicuous character Fanny Derham, a Wollstonecraftian figure of pure "female potentiality" who consistently attracts the attention of the novel's few critics.[62] Fanny resembles the ladies who flock to Millenium Hall, and her Stoicism is as radical and disruptive as her intellectual prowess and aversion to marriage. If a break with sentimental morality makes Scott's reformers "whimsically good," the same rupture leads Shelley to describe Fanny as "Quixotic" (*MH* 169, *L* 323). But to dismiss Stoicism as an eccentric aberration is to miss Shelley's point: like a lightning rod, Fanny is simply the most obvious manifestation of a Stoic ethos that Shelley distributes throughout the text precisely because she finds it distributed so complexly throughout life itself.

In *Lodore*, Fanny's future perfect Stoicism emerges of out sustained narrative reflection on the instability of emotional detachment as a way of escaping the past. After a turbulent youth and a failed marriage, Lord Lodore and his young daughter tread a path carved out by Wordsworth's Solitary and take up shelter in the "primeval quiet" of the American wilderness (*L* 56). Establishing a secluded homestead in Illinois, Lodore reroutes all of the interest he took in his tabula rasa wife to his tabula rasa daughter, Ethel. Lodore and Ethel's twelve-year errand into the wilderness resonates throughout the novel as an early source of Stoic potentiality. When most of his neighbors decamp to a more prosperous village, Lodore treats this further seclusion as a happy accident, one that ensures his local terrain will be "left to those who courted tranquility, and desired the necessaries of life without the hope of great future gain" (*L* 56). Set apart from the novel's persistent marriage plotting as well as the *Bildung* that plays out in a social field, prairie existence becomes a cul-de-sac in the novel, a turn away from the future in which narrative progression gives way to isolated character formation.

In this tranquil zone, Lodore's own turn to Stoicism is juxtaposed with Shelley's suggestive epigraphs, a convergence that points to the way in which the eddying of the plot in Illinois facilitates a retrospective look back to an earlier Romantic moment, one in which Stoicism was linked to rural retirement by the lyric itself. The first chapter that dwells on life in Illinois features a short excerpt from Andrew Marvell's translation of Seneca's tragedy *Thyestes*:

> Settled in some secret nest,
> In calm leisure let me rest;
> And far off the public stage,
> Pass away my silent age. (*L* 54)

Shelley's choice of epigraph suggests the whole chapter unfolds under the sign of Stoicism, but her letters indicate that her original intention was to include not Seneca but "the whole or greater part" of Coleridge's "Ode to Tranquillity," a lyric I discuss at length in chapter 3.[63] The substitution of Seneca for Coleridge offers tantalizing confirmation of the Stoic ethos Romantic readers found in that ode, but its presence in this chapter also points to a persistent rift in the Romantic imagination of Stoicism: was it at heart a retired or an active virtue? Like the Senecan epigraph, Coleridge's ode stages a self-conscious turn away from public work to private self-cultivation. While Shelley herself desired tranquility and had long admired Coleridge's ode, it is hard not to detect an element of critique in a chapter that sets a Stoic republican ethos against the vision of virtuous but insular retirement that Lodore himself strives to uphold.[64]

Drawn to serenity but unused to solitude, Lodore is an uncomfortable convert to life in the big woods. Tranquility in Illinois was all too easily "allied to loneliness," and though he attempts to regulate his affairs "by the strictest regard to republican plainness and simplicity," the promise of equality could just as quickly turn into "the dominion of *sameness*" (*L* 54, 57). Peopling his solitude with "the elegant philosophy of the ancients," Lodore orders chest after chest full of books. But in the desert solitaire of his Illinois existence, books turn into "friends," their presence more real than most of the beings he meets in human form. Imaginary conversation with ancient philosophers becomes a matter of course: "Plato could elevate, Epictetus calm, his soul" (*L* 59–60).[65] Though Lodore's engagement with the Stoics aligns him with a certain Godwinian intensity, signs of its inadequacy are apparent well before Shelley introduces the contrasting example of Fanny Derham. Unlike the inhabitants of *Millenium Hall*, Lodore cannot drag his philosophy out of "Closets and Libraries" so that it might dwell in "Clubs and Assemblies."[66] A notably solipsistic affair, it does little to broaden the distribution of his attention: amid republican terrain, Lodore takes little interest in res publica. His concerns remain strikingly domestic, focused almost entirely on an insular plan of education designed to turn Ethel into an angel in the house. But just as the future opens up, Lodore loses "all command over himself" and is killed in a duel (*L* 158).

At this moment of rupture and transatlantic leave-taking, the novel's tight focus on the failed family triangle gives way to a marriage plot, a transition that Mellor has described as symptomatic of Shelley's own tendency to imagine her life in "exclusively relational terms."[67] The second volume of *Lodore* is almost entirely taken up by a tight focus on the courtship and eventual marriage of Ethel and Edward Villiers, not to mention all of the fortitude and self-denial necessary to endure their persistent financial insecurity. When imagining that dire financial straits might render marriage impossible, Edward vows to "stoically banish every pleasant dream" of life with Ethel (*L* 233). Newly married, Ethel faces privation and social pretense with equanimity, navigating "the crooked and sordid ways of modern London" with the same fortitude that had "adorned heroines of old, as they wandered amidst trackless forests, and over barren mountains" (*L* 300). And yet in this vast stretch of narrative, Ethel's tender pertinacity makes it difficult to keep tabs on her ethical development. The equation of modern London and the trackless forest is telling: though tested by experience, the uninterrupted alignment of Ethel's virtue with natural affection makes it seem—for better or worse—as delimited as it was in Illinois. Though dependent upon the dialogic give and take that the novel form fosters, Shelley's attempt to wrest from the past a viable Stoic vision ultimately points beyond narrative itself.

A Few Tame Lines: The History of Fanny Derham

In *Millenium Hall*, tales of Stoic resolve become the guarantor of future good. Theory grows out of practice, with the power of Stoicism to set convincing terms for a rational future of "extensive good" dependent upon the stories of its past upholding (*MH* 160). In *Lodore*, by contrast, Fanny Derham becomes the source of a Stoic future whose story remains untold. The manner in which she "leaps off the pages of *Lodore*" owes as much to her peculiar relation to narrative as it does to her alternative model of agency.[68] Put simply, how can a character who occupies so little space in the novel weigh so heavily on the sense of its unfolding? Though Fanny meets Ethel prior to her father's death, her early appearance in the novel is brief and tentative. She drops out of the narrative as soon as they disembark in London and reappears only at the very end of the novel's second volume.

While other characters are revealed by their relation to event, Fanny is strangely insulated from circumstance, at once always herself and entirely unformed. When first introduced to Lodore and Ethel, she is described as "unlike every other child" precisely because she "never was a child" (*L* 144).

Like Mrs. Selvyn in *Millenium Hall*, she seems to have been "bred a philosopher from her cradle" (*MH* 200). Instantaneously aligned with the adult world of scholarship and the life of the mind, she has no need—at least at first glance—for any interceding *Bildung*. Just as quickly, however, Fanny is situated on the other side of narratability, all of her story yet to be told: "Intelligence, or rather understanding, reigned in every feature; independence of thought, and firmness, spoke in every gesture. She was a mere child in form and mien—even in her expressions; but within her was discernible an embryo of power, and a grandeur of soul, not to be mistaken" (*L* 145). In this latter description, the fact of Fanny's intelligence outweighs its demonstration; words need not convey what every gesture speaks. Her power coheres in its resistance to ordinary language and "the business of life," a model of generative withholding that characterizes her deployment in the novel as well (*L* 144). This sense of a potential not yet assimilated to circumstance lasts even through the novel's ending, in which Fanny is portrayed as embryonic as ever, just ready to enter "upon life":

> One only remains to be mentioned: but it is not in a few tame lines that we can revert to the varied fate of Fanny Derham. She continued for some time among her beloved friends, innocent and calm as she was beautiful and wise; circumstances at last led her away from them, and she has entered upon life. One who feels so deeply for others, and yet is so stern a censor over herself—at once so sensitive and so rigidly conscientious—so single-minded and upright, and yet open as day to charity and affection, cannot hope to pass from youth to age unharmed. Deceit, and selfishness, and the whole web of human passion must envelope her, and occasion her many sorrows ... still she cannot be contaminated—she will turn neither to the right nor left, but pursue her way unflinching; and, in her lofty idea of the dignity of her nature, in her love of truth and in her integrity, she will find support and reward in her various fortunes. What the events are, that have already diversified her existence, cannot now be recounted; and it would require the gift of prophecy to foretell the conclusion. (*L* 448)

Destined to confront the "web of human passion" with a stern and upright soul, it is as if Fanny is at the start of a journey that might one day lead to Millenium Hall. As in that novel, the evocation of prophecy, however rational, gestures to a moment not yet arrived. Shelley's simultaneous calling forth of prophecy and deferral of its gifts suggest that the ending of *Lodore* might be another version of what Orianne Smith has described as Shelley's interest in accessing but also displacing the subversive power of female prophecy.⁶⁹ But if Fanny speaks most powerfully as a figure of the untold future, her perspective also seeps into the more familiar narrative terrain she inhabits. Toiling in a comfortless boarding house and "patching up the casualties of heterosexual life," her Stoic virtue transcends but also rehabilitates those domestic spaces.⁷⁰

Though most critics of *Lodore* emphasize the suggestive possibility of Fanny Derham, Lisa Vargo is the only one to dwell on her Stoicism at any length, paying particular attention to the way in which Fanny's self-possession subverts the romance plot.⁷¹ But as in *Millenium Hall*, autonomy is only half of the story, for Fanny's unnarrated futurity is inherently linked to her Stoicism and the hope that it might reconcile tranquility and self-possession with sallies of benevolence. Like Lodore on the prairie, Fanny lives in a world of her own making, one in which she engages in perpetual conversation with books. In her telling, philosophical immersion effects a liberation from worldly constraint: "while I converse each day with Plato, and Cicero, and Epictetus, the world, as it is, passes before me like a vain shadow" (*L* 317). Later in the novel, she is glimpsed in a solitary corner "with her Cicero," reading "the Tusculan Questions" from which Percy Shelley had once plucked out an epigraph for *Prometheus Unbound* (*L* 415). But when approached in conversation, Fanny eagerly lays Cicero aside. Stoic self-dialogue might insulate her from life's trials, but, unlike Lodore, it also draws her toward the world. For Fanny, Stoicism is antithetical to escapism. Shortly after her unexpected reunion with Ethel, she lays out a vision of her own life, one that blends what is past and passing with that which is to come:

> It was my father's lesson, that I should never fear any thing but myself. He taught me to penetrate, to anatomize, to purify my motives; but once assured of my own integrity, to be afraid of nothing. Words have more power than any one can guess; it is by words that the world's great fight, now in these civilized times, is carried on; I never hesitated to use them, when I fought any battle for the miserable and oppressed. People are so afraid to speak, it would seem as if half our fellow-creatures were born with deficient organs; like parrots they can repeat a lesson, but their voice fails them, when that alone is wanting to make the tyrant quail. (*L* 316)

Though often inaccessible to narrative, Fanny's own imagination of her future plays out in language and centers upon an imperative to speak. In her vision, daily converse with Epictetus decimates fear and solidifies mind and motive, culminating in the self-integrity that makes truth-telling possible. Here, the radical vision of disinterested judgement and private inquiry that Godwin and Wollstonecraft shared eclipses the gradual reform and gentry capitalism that Stoicism elicits in *Millenium Hall*.

But in a different sense the model of *Millenium Hall* is prescient, for Shelley belabors the way in which Stoic self-possession leads not just to active virtue but the imagination of a life outside of heterosexual domesticity itself. This facet of Fanny's future is illustrated most convincingly in relation to Ethel, whose "sexual education" in the wilds of America taught her to "give herself away with unreserved prodigality" first to a father and then a husband (*L* 321–22). By contrast, Fanny learns to guard "her individuality and would have scorned herself could she have been brought to place the treasures of her soul at the disposal of any power, except those of the moral laws which it was her earnest endeavour never to transgress. Religion, reason, justice—these were the landmarks of her life" (*L* 322). While Ethel places her soul at the disposal of Edward Villiers, Fanny's deepest commitment is to the moral law itself, an alignment that once again sets her at odds with the conventions of narrative. Averse to the "landmarks" of life made conspicuous by the marriage plot that unfolds around her, her own "landmarks"—the events "which mark a period or turning-point in the history of a thing"—are hardly events.[72] Who is to say when or how reason and justice begin? Like Emerson in my next chapter, Fanny is a figure whose very existence seems to suggest "a closer sympathy with Zeno and Arrian, than with persons in the house" (*EW* 2:163).

While Fanny's "way of life by abandonment" seems to foreground benevolence above all, Shelley also follows Scott in belaboring a link between disinterested love and a queer desire that will not be coaxed into narrow or conventional channels.[73] Described as someone "more made to be loved by her own sex than by the opposite one," Fanny's Stoic outlook is portrayed at various points in the novel as a parody of heterosexual marriage itself (*L* 317). Committed to a "single existence," she is described as both "more wedded . . . than ever" to the pursuit of Greek learning and "too wedded" to "notions of the supremacy of mind" (*L* 307, 409). At the same time, this parodying of marriage works toward a vision of female friendship and community. Ethel's unexpected announcement that she has to leave London makes Fanny—ever the Stoic—cry. Though trying to explain away her tears, what she calls foolishness is surely a reflection rather than a subversion of her quixotic vision: "I am a fool—but pardon me, for the folly is already passed away. For the first time you have made it hard for me to keep my soul firm in its own single existence" (*L* 331). For Fanny, the brief respite of Ethel's friendship is its own kind of prophecy, the vision of a space or solidarity in which "individuality" need not be zealously guarded and integrity is assured.

Forever Unvanquished

At the end of *Lodore*, Shelley salvages some certainty from the abyss of Fanny's prophetic future, acknowledging that in "after times" the "life of Fanny Derham" will serve as a "useful lesson" of Stoic resolve and "human excellence" (*L* 448). But as with any utopian prospect, these future imaginings can occlude Shelley's subtle attempt to show how Fanny's radical example infiltrates and transforms even the seemingly conventional fixtures of her present world. Though the narrative frustrates our desire as readers to access Fanny's story, Ethel herself is privy to at least a partial "narration" of Fanny's "own history" (*L* 308). The most striking aspect of this private exchange is the quiet transference it prompts. Reimagining her own vexed affairs in light of Fanny's example, Ethel takes up Epictetus in her own delimited terms: "Can I not bear those cares with equanimity for Edward's sake, which Fanny regards as so trivial, merely because Plato and Epictetus bid her do so?" (*L* 308). Almost as she speaks, Fanny's uncompromising world view drifts into the mainstream of the marriage plot. Ethel, of course, bends this world view to her own ends. Fanny's trust in the power of her own mind gives way to Ethel's trust in a power "superior to any earthly authority" (*L* 309). This might seem like a clear deflation of Fanny's radical vision, and yet it also strikes me as a tentative version of the transposition effected by both Carter and Scott, one in which a moralizing strain actually pushes back at conventionality to authorize a bold "comprehensiveness of vision."[74]

Before Fanny Derham is folded back into the novel at the end of the second volume, Ethel unequivocally dismisses the reasoning of "a cold and meaningless philosophy" that would describe her natural affection for Edward as a form of selfishness. Young and in love, she has no desire to walk back her partial affection in favor of some Stoic or Shaftesburian view of the immense system. But after extensive conversation with Fanny, Ethel adopts a strikingly different stance:

> Where we establish ourselves, and look forward to the passage of a long interval of time, we form ties with, and assume duties towards, many of our fellow-creatures, each of which must diminish the singleness of the soul's devotion towards the selected one. No doubt this is the fitting position for human beings to place themselves in, as affording a great scope for utility: but for a brief space, to have no occupation but that of

contributing to the happiness of him to whom her life was consecrated, appeared to Ethel the very heaven upon earth. It was not that she was narrow-hearted: so much affection demands a spacious mansion for its abode; but in their present position of struggle and difficulty, there was no possibility of extending her sphere of benevolence, and she gladly concentrated her endeavours in the one object whose happiness was in her hands. (*L* 329)

In the space of thirty pages, it is as if Ethel has become a qualified convert to the Stoic doctrine of *oikeiosis*, or at least has had occasion to peruse some Adam Smith. Fanny's radical perspective has unsettled her own domestic complacency, prompting a new line of thought about how a limited amount of ethical attention might be distributed in a world whose scale vastly exceeds her own establishment. Narrow inhabitation vies with extensive benevolence. The claims of "the selected one" are understood in relation to the duties owed to "fellow-creatures." There is nothing particularly radical about what Ethel is saying here. She is still devoted to Edward, and it seems telling that her central figure for imagining her outlay of affective attention is a "spacious mansion"—a house. But there might be a more radical idea working in the background. The immediate effect of Fanny's conversation on Ethel's ethical framing of the world represents a strong endorsement of her own sense that "words have more power than any one can guess," which is itself an echo of Godwin's contention that "if there be such a thing as truth, it must infallibly be struck out by the collision of mind with mind" (*PJ* 15).

Mary Poovey once suggested that Shelley's late novels "reveal the way in which stereotypical feminine propriety could disguise—and even accommodate—the kind of unladylike aggression she had expressed in the productions of her youth."[75] More striking yet is the way in which this same propriety offers a sly road back not just to a radicalism foreclosed but to the urgent Romantic question of how to build a Stoic future out of the ruins of a revolutionary past. Was Stoicism compatible with a life of tranquility, retirement, and domestic affection? Or did its uncompromising severity demand a new prophecy? Looking back to the origins of Romanticism from a moment that might have already seemed like a curtain call, Shelley found in the novel a way of balancing out the books, of pulling together a vision that might be useful for the future. In this sense, what is ultimately striking about Shelley's treatment of Stoicism is less the superlative, anticipatory reality of Fanny than its tentative alignment with Ethel, and the emergent sense of both figures as two sides of the same coin:

Ethel, as well as her friend, was elevated above the common place of life; she also fostered a state of mind, "lofty and magnificent, fitted rather to command than to obey, not only suffering patiently, but even making light of all human cares; a grand and dignified self-possession, which fears nothing, yields to no one, and remains for ever unvanquished." When Fanny, in one of their conversations, while describing the uses of philosophy, had translated this eulogium of its effects from Cicero, Ethel had exclaimed, "This is love—it is love alone that divides us from sordid earth-born thoughts, and causes us to walk alone, girt by its own beauty and power." (*L* 330–31)

It is as if these two distinctly different characters—the newlywed angel in the house and the rationalist ready to jump into the "world's great fight"—are of the same mind (*L* 316). What one friend describes as Stoic virtue appears to the other as love, a telling repetition of Miss Mancel's reappraisal of Stoicism in *Millenium Hall*. Stranger yet, both are equally accommodated by the sublime lines adapted from Cicero's *De Finibus*. When it came to the competing ethical visions offered up by her father's generation, this portrait of Ethel and Fanny talking over the "uses of philosophy" suggests that for Shelley it was not a choice *between* but *of*. At the end of the novel, Fanny is still waiting for a far-off future in which something like Millenium Hall's radical re-envisioning of collective life is not a utopian prototype but the norm. In the meantime, the path toward that Stoic future plays out amid the domestic affections themselves. As a bequest for the future, this makes sense. After all, *Lodore* was not the last novel to puzzle over the question of sympathy while also setting its sight on the years leading up to the Great Reform Bill. George Eliot's *Middlemarch* notebooks attest to her own deep interest in Cicero's *Tusculan Disputations* as well as Epictetus and Marcus Aurelius.[76] Indeed, no less a figure than Dorothea Brooke will be surprised to find in "a nearer introduction to the Stoics" some "people who had ideas not totally unlike her own."[77]

CHAPTER SIX

Emerson, Stoic Cosmopolitanism, and the Conduct of Life

WRITERS MAKING SENSE of Ralph Waldo Emerson from across the Atlantic could not shake a sense of his Stoicism. For Charles Baudelaire, Emerson was the "trans-atlantic moralist" with "a certain touch of Seneca about him."[1] Matthew Arnold disputed Emerson's literary greatness even as he forged a Stoic comparison to describe a more substantial kind of authority. Emerson was neither "a great poet, a great writer" nor "a great philosophy-maker," and yet he served a higher function: "His relation to us is more like that of the Roman Emperor Marcus Aurelius. Marcus Aurelius is not a great writer, a great philosophy-maker; he is the friend and aider of those who would live in the spirit. Emerson is the same."[2] Discarding the typical caricature of its austerity, Arnold's Emersonian Stoicism is not forbidding but friendly, an art of living rather than an abstract philosophy. More surprisingly, Emerson's proximity to Stoicism becomes not an indication of complacence or indifference, but a sign that he had transcended the familiar vocations of poet and philosopher to emerge within a new category altogether.

It would take an eminent Victorian like Leslie Stephen—Virginia Woolf's father, and first editor of the *Dictionary of National Biography*—to evoke the contradictory possibilities of a Stoic vision that could seem at once trenchant and naïve. Noting that Emerson was often compared to moralists like Epictetus and Marcus Aurelius, he drew on an "amusing fiction" to depict Emerson's ability to "serenely front the trials of life."[3] Two travelers of different philosophical persuasions enter a village plagued by smallpox. Drawing on the inductive method, an empirically inclined traveler hands out vaccinations. The Stoic traveler simply "assures the villagers that to the wise man disease and the loss of friends is no evil." For Stephen, the Stoic's blithe reply echoed Emerson's assertion that the "isolated facts" of tragedy make sense when seen as part of a larger whole. His moral tale validates the power of this Stoic vision while dismissing its more exaggerated aspirations:

> While such things [as disease] remain with us, some sort of moral discipline will have its uses; and if the Stoic paradoxes when taken literally are hard of acceptance by anybody who has had the toothache, they were exaggerations of principles which have formed noble characters and even had their utility in the world. . . . The wise man of the Stoics is to become independent of chance and change by identifying himself with reason; and Emerson's disciple is to perceive that in all evils there is compensation when we look upon the world as the evolution of divine ideas.[4]

In a world structured by strict utility rather than "divine ideas," vaccination outweighs consolation. But then again, Stephen paints Stoic detachment itself in strangely utilitarian terms, acknowledging the ennobling force of Emerson's perspective. Imperfect practice need not annul Stoic aspiration and, as Byron discovered, the characterological force of Stoicism could be just as formative as its doctrine.

In reading Emerson under the sign of Stoic paradox, Stephen put forward a model for interpreting Emerson's unbending maxims, the seemingly inhuman assertions that crop up throughout the essays. For Emerson, self-reliant rejoinders signal a tactical exaggeration of principle even as they advance a serious claim. In "Experience," Emerson deploys his own infamous rendition of the idea that "the loss of friends is no evil," but only, I will argue, as a high-water mark of his own striving, a view from some commanding eminence toward which the soul might aspire. The effect of these grand claims lies not in the possibility of literal adherence, but in the figurative thinking and self-formation that occurs in the space between ideal and everyday perspectives. In this sense, Emerson absorbs Stoicism and its cosmopolitan ethics along the distinctly Romantic lines I have been describing throughout the book. The extremity of his Stoic rhetoric draws attention to a position that finds its proper home not in an abstract or exceptional realm, but amid what Cavell describes as common or ordinary life.[5]

Emerson's wide-angled perspective on the world resulted in an expansive range of interest and action, but this perspective was predicated on an aspirational relinquishment, a cultivated austerity in which "all worldly relations" might "hang very loosely about him" (*EW* 2:72). Recent attempts to account for this broad positioning have enlisted Emerson in a cosmopolitan discourse, though this attempt to understand him in a transnational context has noticeably shortchanged Emerson's significant interest in the austere Stoic origins of cosmopolitan thought. For Emerson, the concentrated self-focus of Stoicism gives rise to a paradoxically expansive ethical stance; as he put it, "in listening more intently to our own reason, we are not becoming in the ordinary sense more selfish, but are departing more from what is small" (*JMN* 3:199). Worked out and explored in a range of journals and essays that stretch from *Nature* (1836) to *The Conduct of Life* (1860), Emerson's cosmopolitan Stoicism bears out Foucault's claim that self-culture both precedes and informs ethical awareness, social commitment, and political action.[6]

Placing Emerson's Stoicism

Early in his essay "From Edwards to Emerson" (1940), Perry Miller acknowledged that the universalizing tendency of transcendentalism was out of step with a modern investment in particularity, which informed his own historicist scholarship. Singled out for especial ire is a passage from "The Transcendentalist" (1842), a famous early lecture in which Emerson defends the notion that it is best to be "self-dependent" or "self-sustained" (*EW* 1:203–4). Emerson characterizes this idealist strand of thought as perennial and pervasive rather than specific to a group of genteel philosophers in New England:

> This way of thinking, falling on Roman times, made Stoic philosophers; falling on despotic times, made patriot Catos and Brutuses; falling on superstitious times, made prophets and apostles; on popish times, made protestants and ascetic monks, preachers of Faith against the preachers of Works; on prelatical times, made Puritans and Quakers; and falling on Unitarian and commercial times, makes the peculiar shades of Idealism which we know. (*EW* 1:206)

In this extravagant intellectual genealogy, Emerson makes Stoicism the first philosophical manifestation of his own "way of thinking." In its next incarnation, that same way of thinking animated the hyper-Stoic Roman republican ethos that loomed so significantly in revolutions on both sides of the Atlantic. For Miller, however, Emerson grows increasingly disingenuous as he traces his historically conditioned perspective back to a diffuse, classical source. Impatient with this "undiscriminating eclecticism," Miller confined his own attention to the "laboratory" of New England, linking his national exceptionalist narrative to what Emerson called "the great camp and army of the Puritans" (*EW* 10:153).[7]

More recent critics have had less trouble squaring Emerson's centrality in American literary emergence with his philosophical eclecticism. In *Emerson: The Mind on Fire*, Robert Richardson contends that Stoicism had "an enormous impact on Emerson and his circle, probably greater than that of Puritanism, whether direct or indirect." This insight leads him to describe *Nature* as itself "a modern Stoic handbook," a distinct manifestation of "Marcus Aurelius in New England."[8] In a related vein, Sharon Cameron has qualified traditional accounts of Emerson's egotism by dwelling on his fascination with impersonality.[9] But in an intriguing bend toward abstraction, Cameron's influential account of Emerson's mistrust of personal feeling sidesteps the demonstrable centrality of Stoic philosophy to his intellectual world view. The broader category of the impersonal underscores the lingering effects of a critical tendency to treat any sign of Emerson's Stoicism as the anesthetization of an early optimism brought about by his own increasing familiarity with tragedy, limitation, and life's adamantine laws. In Lawrence Buell's crisp digest of this view, "a burst of energetic affirmation" was transformed after his son Waldo's death into mere "stoic acquiescence."[10] I will contend that this familiar narrative inverts the arc of Emerson's development. Informed by his Unitarian background, Emerson's idealism was Stoic from the outset. The tragedies he encountered put to the test a regulative ideal forged in his earliest work, one that outlasted the skeptical vein of his later essays to inform—however imperfectly—his public response to slavery and other manifestations of human suffering. Neither rhetorical embellishment nor acquiescent reaction formation, the "Stoical *plenum*" that Emerson saw as a characteristic of genius became one of his most persistent philosophical preoccupations (*EW* 1:104).

Rethinking the trajectory of Emerson's Stoicism entails following a rough pattern established in earlier chapters: the fact of Emerson's sustained engagement with the Stoics challenges conventional narratives of his intellectual development, just as it puts pressure on easy assumptions about his political commitments and motivations. But in crossing the Atlantic to end this book with Emerson, I am envisioning a larger provocation. Emerson's documented interest in approaching British Romanticism from the Stoic side invests his own articulation of Stoic Romanticism with unique explanatory power. His affinity with but distance from his British predecessors highlights—by an exaggeration of both time and temperament—an overlooked Stoic proclivity foundational to Romantic expression from the 1790s forward. Emerson's essays become occasions for retrospection, with his own emphasis on impersonality serving as a rearview mirror capable of magnifying, and even clarifying, British Romanticism's more inconspicuous critique of the passions. While the fallout of the French Revolution prevented many Romantic writers from claiming this disenchantment as a distinctly Stoic phenomenon, the wide temporal and geographic interval separating Emerson from that revolutionary moment allowed him to formulate his own critique of "the importunacy of passion" more forthrightly (*JMN* 3:9). My argument bears out Leon Chai's more general point that Emerson and his American compatriots make visible the "strains and tensions" inherent in the Romantic movement. In Chai's terms, "after certain aesthetic or conceptual norms attain the level of conscious expression" they become "fraught with extraordinary tensions that prevent the possibility of their perpetuation."[11] American Romanticism makes the fissures that had long destabilized sympathetic ethics and affective poetics visible in a new way. By the same token, the outsized significance of Stoicism in Emerson's essays attests to its importance in Romantic writing all along.

Emerson's encounters with Wordsworth and Coleridge at a watershed moment in his own career have led to a broad emphasis on the formative role that British Romantic ideas played in his writing.[12] This is an important insight, but the promise of continuity often results in claims that lose sight of what is excluded in the transatlantic crossing. In forging a connection between transcendentalists and old-world Romantics on the question of emotion and its expression, critics have sidestepped the Stoic side of British and European Romanticism, not to mention its effect on Emerson's own moral psychology. Indeed, it has been all too easy to imagine that Emerson's well-established interest in the Stoics was an idiosyncratic, sui generis fixation rather than a real point of convergence with his transatlantic precursors. By contrast, one of Emerson's commonplace Harvard notebooks captures the entanglement of Stoicism and Romanticism in his mind: in the space of just two pages, he interleaves quotations from James Hogg, Byron, Scott, and Coleridge with both a list of Stoic philosophers and selected maxims from the Roman Stoics Arrian (who recorded the *Discourses of Epictetus*) and Marcus Aurelius (see *JMN* 1:225–26). Emerson's ability to balance the Stoics and the Romantics on the same page points toward an important facet of his intellectual inheritance. Looking to the British Romantics, Emerson discovered a version of what he would later attribute to Plutarch's *Lives*: "a stoicism not of the schools, but of the blood" (*EW* 2:147). In elevating disposition over doctrine, this resonant phrase goes some way toward defining Stoicism in its Romantic guise. In an irony of literary history, Emerson was the most substantive analyst of the fusion of Stoicism and Romanticism that pervaded his own work. Though this fusion informed prominent essays like *Nature*, "Self-Reliance," and "Experience," its first emergence was intimately connected to Emerson's Unitarianism, a movement whose temporal correspondence with British Romanticism resulted in a similar preoccupation with the ethics of emotion in an increasingly global world.

Cosmopolitan Prospects, Romantic Reflections

Over the past three decades, studies of Emerson have been preoccupied by three critical agendas: the uncovering of Emerson's substantial interest in social reform, the reassessment of his philosophical project, and the triangulation of his cosmopolitan position in a transnational literary field. Emerson's sustained interest in Stoicism intersects with all three critical modes, though it significantly qualifies the way in which his cosmopolitan commitments are typically portrayed. Always attuned to the paradoxical overlap of the "individual man" and the "universal mind," Emerson is often linked to the cosmopolitan notion that universal affinity need not come at the cost of local detachment (*EW* 2:4). Emersonians have been making this point for over a century. In 1885, George Willis Cooke declared that Emerson was "at the same time an American and a cosmopolitan; he believed equally in humanity and in his own country."[13] Like Cooke, recent critics have described Emerson as invested in a form of cosmopolitan discourse that acknowledges the hybridity of local and universal attachments while remaining capacious enough to accommodate the inescapability of place, nation, patriotism, and clan. Gregg Crane, T. Gregory Garvey, and Johannes Voelz all strike similar notes by emphasizing Emerson's attempt to square cosmic detachment with his own local loyalties.[14] Though capturing the way in which Emerson imagined himself as both "Man Thinking" and "American Scholar," this perspective plays up Emerson's geographic expansivity without taking into account the prominent role of Stoic thought in cosmopolitan ethics. In a reprisal of issues first raised at the beginning of the book, I want to suggest that Emerson follows Shaftesbury and Smith in his tendency to draw on Stoic thought when puzzling out the ethical implications of "worldly relations."

Emerson's conviction that every soul was constantly "quitting its whole system of things, its friends, and home, and laws, and faith" points toward his investment in the Stoic origin of cosmopolitanism, but his interest in this earlier facet of moral philosophical speculation has been obscured by the shifting fate of cosmopolitanism in literary and cultural studies (*EW* 2:72). In its classical form, cosmopolitanism represented a turn away from the confined and particular interests of the polis in favor of a broader identification with rational humanity. Reclaimed by Martha Nussbaum in the early 1990s, this "exclusionary" model of cosmopolitanism was premised on the transcendence of local passions and affiliations.[15] Critical interest in cosmopolitan universalism was quickly followed by vehement critiques of both its detachment from feeling and its evasion of responsibility and political action. Over the past two decades, however, this dispassionate substructure has been obscured by more "inclusive" reclamations of cosmopolitanism that foreground global commitment or connection without abandoning the importance of local rootedness.

The dispassionate aura of Emerson's cosmopolitanism stands as a powerful contrast to inclusive forms of cosmopolitanism, one that might clarify how the overextension of the term in recent discourse has turned an ethical aspiration into what Bruce Robbins has called a "comfortable piety."[16] In *Perpetual War*, Robbins worries that cosmopolitanism has "been evacuated of all ethical substance, leaving nothing more than a marker of transnational movement." In its Stoic and normative form, the creation of a just human community was predicated on the subversion of emotion and local attachment. In its less rigorous afterlife, "the truth of cosmopolitanism no longer seemed to preclude the emotions, even emotions as particularistic and apparently inconsequential as rooting for a local team."[17] *Perpetual War* thus takes up a twenty-first-century version of a Romantic-era problem: the realization that for all the sympathy it can produce, the expansion of affect is ultimately incommensurate with ethical action.[18] Emerson was enthralled by the difficulty of this disproportion, and his essays are marked by its reality. Accounts of Emerson's cosmopolitanism that emphasize his transnationalism risk losing sight of its ethical stakes. After all, Emerson's cosmopolitan perspective does not result in a conspicuous outpouring of sympathy, affective connection, or heightened fellow feeling. Emerson imagined himself as a citizen of the universe, but he gravitated toward a Stoic elaboration of what that global citizenship entailed. If his cold cosmopolitanism thwarts contemporary expectations, its exacting price should nevertheless clear his Stoicism from the charge of acquiescence.

Laura Dassow Walls emphasizes the stakes of cosmopolitanism in transcendentalist literature with a striking claim. For Walls,

"Cosmopolitanism's most pressing dilemma is not how to imagine connections to the other but how to *feel* them: how to go from loving one's family, friends, and neighbors to experiencing bonds of affection with distant foreigners and seemingly repulsive aliens."[19] This model of feeling's distribution reflects a position endorsed by Edmund Burke, one in which the love of one's own "little platoon" gives rise to the "public affections" that lead toward a love of country and mankind.[20] Emerson adopted a different approach to the problem. In "The Over-Soul," he describes his adherence to an alternative model, one in which a wider perspective comes not by riding the concentric waves of affection and affiliation, but through a refusal to cling to the visible, the local, and the domestic: "With each divine impulse the mind rends the thin rinds of the visible and finite, and comes out into eternity, and inspires and expires its air. It converses with truths that have always been spoken in the world, and becomes conscious of a closer sympathy with Zeno and Arrian, than with persons in the house" (*EW* 2:163). Like Shaftesbury, Emerson takes the Stoic critique of partial affections and makes it shockingly vivid. Stoic "truths" take shape in strikingly personal form, displacing—almost to a person—domestic ties. He will return to this idea in "Experience": the full ethical stakes of Stoic cosmopolitanism become most vivid as they are brought into close relation with "persons in the house." Articulated at the convergence of local and expansive perspectives, Emerson's "closer sympathy" signals not the end of sympathy but its conversion into something unalloyed by private interest, a version of what Shaftesbury called "a sympathizing of the Whole" (*A* 92).

In describing the expansion of affect in circular terms, Burke and Walls invert the cosmopolitan logic implicit in the Stoic idea of *oikeiosis*. Connecting a responsibility to self with an imperative for justice, *oikeiosis* attests to the reality that human affection diminishes in direct proportion to concentric distance.[21] Its empirical logic is relatively straightforward: more often than not, the affection one feels for one's family or neighbors will overshadow the affection one could conceivably feel for the unknown inhabitants of distant continents. Emerson would have encountered Cicero's articulation of the concept in *De Officiis*, and yet Hierocles explains *oikeiosis* more succinctly:

> Each of us is as it were entirely encompassed by many circles, some smaller, others larger, the latter enclosing the former on the basis of their different and unequal dispositions relative to each other. The first and closest circle is the one which a person has drawn as though around a centre, his own mind. . . . Next, the second one further removed from

the centre but enclosing the first circle; this contains parents, siblings, wife, and children. The third one has in it uncles and aunts, grandparents, nephews, nieces, and cousins. The next circle includes the other relatives, and this is followed by the circle of local residents, then the circle of fellow-tribesmen, next that of fellow-citizens, and then in the same way the circle of people from neighbouring towns, and the circle of fellow-countrymen. The outermost and largest circle, which encompasses all the rest, is that of the whole human race.[22]

For Burke, this empirical reality offers a scheme for assigning moral priority; for Adam Smith, it represents an existential challenge that obstructs well-meaning extensions of sympathy. Indeed, from Smith forward, *oikeiosis* increasingly becomes either a model of sympathy's existent and inevitable distribution, or a guide for determining how it might naturally be apportioned.

For Hierocles and the Stoics, however, this empirical reality necessitated a proactive ethical rearrangement: "Once these [circles] have all been surveyed, it is the task of a well tempered man, in his proper treatment of each group, to draw the circles together somehow towards the centre."[23] The moral agent at the center of the circle does not radiate affection out toward more distant circles. On the contrary, such agents replace the affection they feel toward their nearest relations with reason, until all humanity abides in the same circle of concern. In Forman-Barzilai's evocative terms, the "Stoic activity of cultivating apathy and contracting the circles is like collapsing a telescope."[24] *Oikeiosis* fostered a change of perspective whereby individuals in the outermost circle—encompassing no less than the "whole human race"—were to be seen as though they were, in Emerson's terms, "persons in the house" (*EW* 2:163). Striving to limit his habitual sympathies rather than work toward their extension, Emerson's cosmopolitanism was starkly opposed to the Burkean model. His approach was noticeably congruent with what Smith described as a Stoic cosmopolitan mode:

> Among the moralists who endeavour to correct the natural inequality of our passive feelings by diminishing our sensibility to what peculiarly concerns ourselves, we may count all the ancient sects of philosophers, but particularly the ancient Stoics. Man, according to the Stoics, ought to regard himself, not as something separated and detached, but as a citizen of the world, a member of the vast commonwealth of nature. To the interest of this great community, he ought at all times to be willing that his own little interest should be sacrificed. Whatever concerns

himself, ought to affect him no more than whatever concerns any other equally important part of this immense system. We should view ourselves, not in the light in which our own selfish passions are apt to place us, but in the light in which any other citizen of the world would view us. (*TMS* 140)

Like the Stoics, Emerson endeavored to "sacrifice" or extinguish "his own little interest," but while the former had imagined cosmopolitan detachment as a process of centripetal retrenchment—an attempt to bring all of humanity into one's closest circle—Emerson imagined this retrenchment in paradoxically centrifugal terms. In "Circles," Emerson famously describes the life of man as "a self-evolving circle, which, from a ring imperceptibly small, rushes on all sides outwards to new and larger circles, and that without end" (*EW* 2:180). Unconfined by convention or sentiment, however, this extension was decisively *not* an expansion of sympathy. Emerson dwelt on the immensity that Smith emphasized in the Stoic model. As he put it, "immense and innumerable expansions" of perspective surpassed convention and replaced affection in pressing eagerly onward "to the impersonal and illimitable" (*EW* 2:181, 186).

As an impersonal ideal, the challenge implicit in cosmopolitanism turned on a question of reason rather than feeling. In his *Republic*, Zeno had claimed that logos, or reason, was inherent in all persons as part of their own nature, and that this common rationality stood as the foundation for a global community. Plutarch—one of Emerson's favorite writers—described Zeno's vision in these terms:

> The much admired *Republic* of Zeno ... is aimed at this one main point, that our household arrangements should not be based on cities or parishes, each one marked out by its own legal system, but we should regard all men as our fellow-citizens and local residents, and there should be one way of life and order, like that of a herd grazing together and nurtured by a common law. Zeno wrote this, picturing as it were a dream or image of a philosopher's well-regulated society.[25]

As a realization of what Emerson once called "the admirable science of universals," the promise of this shared world threatened to weaken the hold of more "partial interests" (*EW* 3:143, 2:100). Wider prospects did not *necessitate* a sacrifice of local attachments, but in this new world order, their importance could easily be attenuated or abridged. As Byron also discovered, life as a citizen of the world was its own kind of exile, an insight that Nussbaum has traced to a certain loneliness in the writings of Marcus Aurelius.[26] This outgrowth of Stoic cosmopolitanism captures a mood that is inherently Emersonian, particularly when read in light of Branka Arsić's contention that almost all of Emerson's essays tackle both "the question of leaving and the repercussions that the idea of universal fluctuation has for our everyday lives."[27] As Emerson put it, "our affections are but tents of a night" (*EW* 2:109).

Like that of many other writers in this study, Emerson's interest in Stoic cosmopolitanism raised central questions about the place of emotion in aspirational visions of society's operation and arrangement. As I argued in chapter 2, the French Revolutionary contours of this dissension made Stoicism a seemingly requisite fixture of Romantic discourse. While Burke held that "passions instruct our reason," Godwin and Wollstonecraft took the opposite view, defining morality as a quest for "*reason without passion*."[28] Without entirely disavowing the force of moral sentiment, Emerson inclined toward a Godwinian position, one that looked past personal and local considerations. Godwin once asked what magic in the pronoun "my" allowed it to overturn everlasting truths (*PJ* 50). In "Intellect," Emerson broached a similar question, invoking both cosmopolitan and scientific language to highlight the limitations of even positive affects:

> Intellect separates the fact considered from *you*, from all local and personal reference, and discerns it as if it existed for its own sake. Heraclitus looked upon the affections as dense and colored mists. In the fog of good and evil affections, it is hard for man to walk forward in a straight line. Intellect is void of affection, and sees an object as it stands in the light of science, cool and disengaged. The intellect goes out of the individual, floats over its own personality, and regards it as a fact, and not as *I* and *mine*. (*EW* 2:193–94)

In emphasizing the function of intellect, Emerson characteristically overstates the division between reason and passion. After all, a delicate reminder that every intellect is housed in a body might serve as a natural rejoinder to the intensity of this detachment, but Emerson was hardly a staunch partisan of bodily transcendence. Nor was this particular "cool and disengaged" state a constant substratum of existence. It could be interspersed with love or friendship, but for Emerson, even love bore a trace of this "mature philosophy" and its impersonality. It is not difficult to see how Emerson, like Godwin, could incur "the imputation of unnecessary hardness and stoicism from those who compose the Court and Parliament of Love" (*EW* 2:99). In more philosophical moments, he traced this dispassionate stance all the way back to a distinctively Stoic and cosmopolitan source: "Morals is the direction of the will on universal ends. He is immoral who is acting to any private end. He is moral,—we say it with Marcus Aurelius and with Kant,—whose aim or motive may become a universal rule, binding on all intelligent beings" (*EW* 10:448). Detaching the self from others and all the affections that intervened, Emerson described another, less transcendent version of mean egotism's disappearance. His persistent and multifaceted attempt to understand the power of this disappearance might, in its magnitude, illuminate previous Romantic iterations of this desire for desire's eradication.

American Unitarianism, British Romanticism, and the Ethics of Feeling

In one of the last journals he kept, Emerson imagined the discussion that would ensue if "the noblest saint among the Buddhists, the noblest Mahometan, the highest Stoic of Athens, the purest & wisest Christian, Menu in India, Confucius in China, Spinoza in Holland" were all to meet in one place. He predicted that conversation would lead to a new sense of commonality, one that would dwarf "country traditions," making them seem merely "childish" (*JMN* 16:91). Emerson's investment in Stoic cosmopolitanism prompted him to evaluate local standpoints from a more universal perspective, but this impulse was the ultimate outgrowth of a Stoic tendency implicit in Unitarianism itself.

Emerson's Stoicism—like Godwin's—had a complex religious origin, and like Coleridge and Carter, he resisted Enlightenment orthodoxy in acknowledging the shared aspiration of Stoicism and Christianity (see *JMN* 3:21–22, 61, 134). His most innovative reflections on Stoic thought emerged after he traded his pulpit for a lyceum podium, but this mature perspective was predicated on an earlier religious position. In an early sermon, he declared that since the "Stoic was the forerunner of the Christian," both versions of "truth" were intrinsically valuable:

> More than this, I think, brethren, that we should be more likely to honour our Christian profession if we would look a little into the lives and instructions of some of the old heathen Stoics. We should there find the picture of a life which would shame the common life we lead ourselves. It would reveal to us a most important truth, that the whole value of Christianity to us is prospective; that in time past whilst we have rested in its accidental advantages, it has not made us such good men as many

heathens; that its superiority can only be shown by the adoption of its rules in practice, by living on earth with our Father in heaven.[29]

Emerson's sermons appeal to the centrality of the affections and occasionally dismiss "the boastful spirit of a stoical philosophy." At the same time, he thinks in Coleridgean terms in connecting "Jesus, the instructer [sic] not of a nation but of human nature" with "the teachers of wisdom among the Greeks and Romans, especially of the Stoic sect."[30]

Untangling the Stoic and sentimental strands of Unitarian thought is no easy task. The primacy of ethics in Unitarianism was part of a renewed interest in moral philosophy that spanned Enlightenment and Romantic thought. As skepticism undermined old theological certainties, ethics emerged as a more stable or tenable focus of religious speculation.[31] Few of Emerson's published sermons failed to touch on the question of virtue, and William Ellery Channing, the most prominent expositor of American Unitarianism, described "power over ourselves" as "the beginning and end of virtue."[32] More importantly, Stoicism fell clearly in line with the Unitarian emphasis on self-culture. Both demanded what Francis Bowen called "the cultivation and control of proper affections."[33] Indeed, Channing's most evocative description of self-culture's disinterestedness deploys a trope that I have characterized as omnipresent at the point where Romantic and more dispassionate values collide: "A man, who rises above himself, looks from an eminence on nature and providence, on society and life."[34]

These intimations of emotional regulation and disinterested virtue seem to validate Emerson's retrospective caricature of Unitarianism and its "corpse-cold rationalism," but they overlook the equally vital role that emotion and affection played in Unitarian thought. Though Channing advocated intellectual self-culture, he also ridiculed preachers who had "forgotten, that affection is as essential to our nature as thought, that action requires motive, that the union of reason and sensibility is the health of the soul."[35] For all its rationalism, Unitarianism was also a religion of the heart, one whose social outlook was predicated on a propensity for letting benevolent affections serve as a guide to action. But as I established in chapter 1, even Shaftesbury's and Smith's foundational account of moral sentimentalism was hardly an uncomplicated celebration of affectivity.[36] Indeed, the Stoic genealogy of the moral sentiment suggests that Emerson's mature ethical austerity was an outgrowth rather than a rupture from his Unitarianism. Though never entirely removed from the realm of emotion, even his early Unitarian reflections on moral sentiment gesture beyond it. In 1822, Emerson suggested that the moral sentiment "differs from the affections of the heart and from the faculties of the mind" (*JMN* 2:49–50). Years later, he would define it as "the most impersonal of all things."[37]

In broader terms, Emerson's inheritance of the Unitarian attempt to reconcile Stoic wisdom with human emotion illuminates Unitarianism's noticeable proximity to British Romanticism when it comes to moral psychological questions. Though separated by the Atlantic, British Romantics and early American Unitarians were the product of similar historical and intellectual upheavals. In 1822, William Ellery Channing met Wordsworth, Coleridge, and Southey in England.[38] As a tutor on a Virginia plantation, he read Godwin's *Political Justice* and *Caleb Williams* in the 1790s, and his admiration for Wordsworth's *Excursion* was so extensive that he claimed he "never read anything but Shakespeare more."[39] Like Wordsworth and Godwin, Channing vacillated between different ways of imagining the proper role of the emotions. At the beginning of the French Revolution, David Tappan welcomed Channing and the rest of the class of 1794 to Harvard with a Burkean sentiment. He encouraged the new class "not to set aside or extinguish [their] affections, like the unnatural and barbarous system of the stoics, but to rectify their disorders" and restore them to their "original end, namely, the service of God, and the moral perfection and happiness of man."[40] Several years later, however, an encounter with one of Robert Southey's sonnets prompted Channing to approach an insight like Tappan's more critically:

> The other day, I handed to a lady a sonnet of Southey's, which had wrung tears from me. "It is pretty," said she, with a smile. "Pretty!" echoed I, as I looked at her; "pretty!" I went home. As I grew composed, I could not help reflecting that the lady who had made this answer was universally esteemed for her benevolence. I knew that she was goodness itself. But she still wanted feeling. "And what is feeling?" said I to myself.... I found that the mind was just as passive in that state which I called "feeling," as when it received any impressions of sense. One consequence immediately struck me, that there was no *moral merit* in possessing feeling. Of course there can be no crime in wanting it.... I then went on to consider whether there were not many persons who possessed this boasted feeling, but who were still deficient in *active* benevolence. A thousand instances occurred to me. I found myself among the number. "It is true," said I, "that I sit in my study and shed tears over human misery. I weep over a novel. I weep over a tale of human woe. But do I ever relieve the distressed? Have I ever lightened the load of

affliction?" ... a cloud of error burst from my mind. I found that virtue did not consist in feeling, but in *acting from a sense of duty*."⁴¹

For Channing, a discrepancy in aesthetic response illuminates a difficulty of ethical evaluation, one that underscored an unnerving gap between affection and action. Galvanized by nothing less than a Romantic lyric, Channing—like so many of the writers I have considered in this study—was suddenly alert to the ethical insufficiency of feeling without more dispassionate forms of apprehension.

For Emerson, the ultimate affinity between Stoicism and Christianity lay in their ability to elicit this disinterestedness. Five years before the death of his wife Ellen in 1831, Emerson made a note in his journal:

> What is Stoicism? What is Christianity? They are for nothing (that is to say the human mind at its best estate & the Divine mind in its communication with the human), are for nothing, if they cannot set the soul on an equilibrium when it leans to the earth under the pressure of calamity. I bless God there *is* virtue in them. (*JMN* 3:45)

After the calamity of Ellen's death, Emerson moved away from Christianity and entertained Stoicism more affirmatively. In the "Divinity School Address," he dismisses "historical Christianity" and embraces sublimity excited by "the great stoical doctrine, Obey thyself" (*EW* 1:82).

Hours of Clear Vision: Nature, Self-Reliance, and Other Early Essays

For all its Romantic effulgence and philosophical idealism, *Nature* (1836) is also a celebration of Stoic indifference. Emerson's transformation into a "transparent eye-ball" on a bare common has become one of his most revered figurations, but the immediate sequel to that moment of radical transcendence is framed in quasi-dispassionate terms:

> There I feel that nothing can befal me in life,—no disgrace, no calamity, (leaving me my eyes,) which nature cannot repair.... The name of the nearest friend sounds then foreign and accidental. To be brothers, to be acquaintances,—master or servant, is then a trifle and a disturbance. I am the lover of uncontained and immortal beauty. (*EW* 1:10)

Though the passage starts by privileging feeling and intuition over mere understanding, Emerson quickly turns to signal the evacuation or irrelevancy of feeling. In a striking formation, a supersaturation of affect—being "glad to the brink of fear"—points precisely to the limitations of affect itself. The rhapsodic moment preaches what Emerson, in his more sober essay "Experience," will call "indifferency" (*EW* 1:288, 3:35). In such a moment of natural insight, the bonds of family and friendship seem accidental or even expendable. The sudden estrangement of friends close at hand registers the vertigo that results from being quickly "uplifted" to cosmopolitan heights. Viewed from "infinite space," even life's storehouse of potential tragedy and disgrace strikes Emerson, as it did the ancient Stoics, as an unremarkable threat incapable of disrupting self-possession. Emerson boldly asserts—as he will again, with much pathos, in "Experience"—the inability of "calamity" to touch him (*EW* 1:10, 3:29).

In seeking to extract an ethical ideal from nature, Emerson elevated a Stoic line of reasoning over a prominent line of nineteenth-century critique. In his *Lectures on the History of Philosophy*, Coleridge's religious sensibility led him to bristle against the Stoic imperative that all things should be done "according to nature." Later in the century, John Stuart Mill was equally dismissive on secular grounds, arguing that since nature exercised "a supercilious disregard both of mercy and of justice," it was not to be followed but rather amended.[42] For Emerson, however, the supercilious "absence of private ends" in nature was a clear symptom of its "ethical character," the effect of a moral law that penetrated "the bone and marrow of nature, as to seem the end for which it was made" (*EW* 1:206, 26). In the face of nature's disinterested method, all griefs would seem merely local and "impertinent" (*EW* 1:9).

For the ancient Stoics, the *naturam sequi* ethic—the imperative to follow nature—was an outgrowth of their perspective on the physical world. In a deterministic universe, they took up the model of nature's imperturbability as a logical way of responding to a life that eluded control. For Emerson, however—at least in his early thought—the tendency to see sublime dispassion as a constitutive part of nature's ethical character stems not from the fixed determinations of nature but from its disinterested eclipse of private drama and concern. Nature becomes a model for the cosmopolitan subject who must subvert personal claims in favor of what Smith called the "immense system" (*TMS* 140). Such, at least, is his contention in "The Method of Nature":

> In short, the spirit and peculiarity of that impression nature makes on us, is this, that it does not exist to any one or to any number of

particular ends, but to numberless and endless benefit, that there is in it no private will, no rebel leaf or limb, but the whole is oppressed by one superincumbent tendency, obeys that redundancy or excess of life which in conscious beings we call *ecstasy*. (*EW* 1:126–27)

Curbing the "private will" of every rebel individual or leaf, nature's methodical and inherently disinterested dispensation becomes a model for cosmopolitan thinking. In a kind of irony, its nonconscious, natural inevitability illustrates how one might live out a strenuously moral existence by dispassionately prioritizing the "endless benefit" of the whole above any particular end. But as Adam Smith argued most forcefully, a cosmopolitan frame of reference is most often apprehended from a position of locality. For Emerson, too, unmediated universality can become a kind of "waste abyss" until it is localized or "housed in an individual" (*EW* 1:127). In this sense, his cosmopolitanism demands not just the inhabitation of wider horizons but an intensified relationship with the self. This familiar paradox of the necessary locality of the universal accounts for the considerable heft of Stoic rhetoric in "Self-Reliance." Mobilizing a slightly unexpected concept, Emerson suggests that the dispassionate pattern of nature available for emulation by "conscious beings" is experienced most often as "*ecstasy*."

If the mystical orientation of *Nature* seems to prepare the way for a transcendent or trancelike sense of "ecstasy," Emerson's rare italicization points toward a deeper semantic complexity that informs the shared Stoicism of *Nature* and "Self-Reliance." Etymologically, "ecstasy" derives from *ekstasis*, with its sense of standing outside of one's self. As in the transparent eyeball moment, what looks at first glance like rapturous apotheosis is also a paring down to a more restrained state. A muted precursor of Emersonian "double consciousness," this disengagement of the self from the self—a crucial aspect of Greek ethical practice—prepares the way for an understanding of nature's more universal concerns.[43] Put another way, the comprehensive perspective made visible in nature ultimately depends upon the flourishing of one's "essential" or aboriginal self (*EW* 2:49). The most compressed particularity becomes the key to the broadest kind of universality. Such paradoxical logic informs his imperative in "Self-Reliance": "Let a Stoic open the resources of man, and tell men they are not leaning willows, but can and must detach themselves" (*EW* 2:43).

In this sense, Emersonian self-reliance is yet another version of what Charles Taylor has described as the disengaged self's tendency to stand apart not just from the natural world but from its own emotions and inclinations, "achieving thereby a kind of distance and self-possession."[44] This distanced perspective is both a foundation of "Self-Reliance" and one of its "highest truths":

> Fear and hope are alike beneath it. There is somewhat low even in hope. In the hour of vision, there is nothing that can be called gratitude, nor properly joy. The soul raised over passion beholds identity and eternal causation, perceives the self-existence of Truth and Right, and calms itself with knowing that all things go well. Vast spaces of nature, the Atlantic Ocean, the South Sea,—long intervals of time, years, centuries,—are of no account. (*EW* 2:39-40)

In an early journal, Emerson had cited Edmund Burke's praise of "that elevation of reason which places centuries under our eye," obscuring passion and party so that "the spirit & moral quality of human actions" might become visible (*JMN* 3:28). A similar metaphor of elevation reigns in this passage, where original self-possession results in a prospect view that opens up wider temporal and spatial coordinates. There is a kind of danger to this detachment: from too great a distance, the elevation of Stoic rationality might find not just vast stretches of the Atlantic but the historical traumas it facilitated "of no account." But this line of critique lands too quickly on detachment as denial, losing sight of Emerson's critical project. Stretching out across deep time and cosmopolitan terrain, his self-reliance transcends not only the imaginative uncertainties of fear and hope but less equivocal emotions like joy and even gratitude. The upshot of self-reliance is not fulfilment or security but clear vision.

Different variations of the urge to be "unaffected" recur throughout the essay, but Emerson's call for the displacement of emotion and imagination seems a means toward some end rather than an objective in itself (*EW* 2:29). In the logic of "Self-Reliance," passion leads to the pledges and commitments we make to others, which in turn ensure that the affections of others must always enter into our own accounting. In *Emerson and Self-Reliance*, George Kateb pursues this line of thought in describing Emerson's repudiation of "all social and personal encrustation" as an "unmistakable" manifestation of his Stoicism.[45] While Emerson's celebration of autonomy has made him a backbone of American liberalism, this intense level of detached self-cultivation cannot be equated with self-absorption in any simplistic sense. It becomes, rather, a ground for the wider, dispassionate panoramas that stand at the heart of both *Nature* and "Self-Reliance." For Emerson, emotional regulation is a practice of the self, but its delimitations are not inherently self-interested. Self-reliance demands "something godlike in him who has cast off the common motives of humanity, and has ventured to trust himself," but this relinquishment of human motives was hardly inhumane (*EW* 2:43).

In Emerson's characteristic fashion, "Self-Reliance" courts philosophical inconsistency to ensure its own misunderstanding. The essay concludes by attributing peace to the "triumph of principles," but Emerson also makes the contradictory exhortation that one should simply "obey thy heart" (*EW* 2:51, 47). My emphasis of the austere bedrock of self-reliance plays down its affective tendencies, but Emerson split his bet and entertained both principled and sentimental accounts of how individual self-possession might lead to a more universal perspective. Indeed, other early essays qualify the strenuous virtue that seemed deceptively simple to attain in the "hour of vision." "Spiritual Laws," for example, starts by reprising an insight from "Self-Reliance." Balancing extreme negations with equally drastic affirmations, Emerson begins the essay with a chain of paradoxical assertions that paint a portrait of imperturbable Stoicism:

> If in the hours of clear reason we should speak the severest truth, we should say, that we had never made a sacrifice. In these hours the mind seems so great, that nothing can be taken from us that seems much. All loss, all pain, is particular: the universe remains to the heart unhurt. Neither vexations nor calamities abate our trust. No man ever stated his griefs as lightly as he might. Allow for exaggeration in the most patient and sorely ridden hack that ever was driven. For it is only the finite that has wrought and suffered; the infinite lies stretched in smiling repose. (*EW* 2:77)

In hours of vision or clear reason, measure and proportion give way to the kind of definitive and superlative statements that Emerson typically approached warily. In this exalted reasoning, infinite truth conciliates any finite grief. Three pages later, however, Emerson foregrounds this temporal framework by emphasizing its evanescence. Since the world is ultimately finite, Stoicism remains an ideal achieved only intermittently:

> There is no permanent wise man, except in the figment of the stoics. We side with the hero, as we read or paint, against the coward and the robber; but we have been ourselves that coward and robber, and shall be again, not in the low circumstances, but in comparison with the grandeurs possible to the soul. (*EW* 2:81)

In his journal, Emerson's reflections on his own attempt to achieve permanent wisdom referenced two of his poetic predecessors. One might follow

Milton in aspiring to "moral perfection," but the soul was "only superior at intervals to pain, to fear, to temptation." The intermittent, discontinuous reality of emotional austerity in ordinary life also brought to mind lines from Wordsworth's *Excursion* that Emerson, like Thoreau, both quoted and admired: "Tis the most difficult of tasks to keep / Heights which the soul is competent to gain" (*JMN* 4:87).[46] Yet in spite of all these qualifications, Emerson was unambiguous about the intellectual roots of self-reliance. In an overlooked journal entry from 1855, he stated the case quite simply: "If one reduce the doctrine of Zeno & the Stoic sect, who were the pre-Christians, the religions of the Greek & Roman states; you will find not many thoughts, but a few thoughts; one thought, perhaps;—self-reliance" (*JMN* 13:463).

"Experience" and Stoic Paradox

For many critics, the death of Emerson's son Waldo in 1842 stands out as one of the few crucial flash points that transformed his intellectual life, an important encounter with life's "immovable limitations" that turned his enthusiastic self-trust into a variety of Stoic apathy (*EW* 6:2). In this narrative, Emerson's experience of the intransigence of the universe is thought to have resulted in his own intellectual calcification. At a deeper level, however, "Experience" is a record of Emerson's attempt to reconcile his own trauma with the Stoic assumptions he put forward in earlier essays. His reflection on the insubstantiality of Waldo's death dealt in distinctly Stoic terms. This was not a new or chastened perspective, but the recursion to a loss imagined in advance. By 1842, Emerson had already endured not only the death of his wife and brother, but the repeated and disconcerting experience of grief's dissipation over time. In "Compensation," he channeled these early losses through the same dispassionate framework he would later evoke in "Experience":

> The death of a dear friend, wife, brother, lover, which seemed nothing but privation, somewhat later assumes the aspect of a guide or genius; for it commonly operates revolutions in our way of life, terminates an epoch of infancy or of youth which was waiting to be closed, breaks up a wonted occupation, or a household, or style of living, and allows the formation of new ones more friendly to the growth of character. (*EW* 2:73)

For all its melancholy, release from the "household" and its domestic ties opens up new "formations," alternative visions and scales of inhabitation.

"Experience" advances a sentiment that was constitutive of his earlier thought, not a departure from it, one that vividly reiterates how very loosely "all worldly relations" hang about him (*EW* 2:72).

The death of a child has long been a stark limit case to detachment, the ultimate trial that makes or breaks a Stoic's self-mastery. Epictetus famously counseled that one should never "say of anything, 'I have lost it;' but, 'I have restored it.' Is your Child dead? It is restored."[47] When Addison's Cato lost his son in battle, his simple response bore no sign of equivocation: "I'm satisfied."[48] The shocking proximity of theory and practice manifested in this detachment became a prominent fixture of modern critiques of Stoicism. In Johnson's *Rasselas*, a venerable sage versed in the "conquest of passion" agrees to share his insight with the young Prince of Abyssinia. When the prince returns for his first discourse, he finds the erstwhile Stoic entirely unhinged by the unexpected death of his daughter.[49] Smith adopted a similar position in *The Theory of Moral Sentiments*, arguing that the "unnatural indifference" of a man who felt nothing at the death of his son would "incur our highest disapprobation" (*TMS* 142). For all the ways in which Smith saw mitigated Stoicism as constitutive of social morality, he nevertheless admits that emulating the indifference of nature would be paradoxically unnatural.

Given this broad condemnation of Stoicism's unnatural grief management, the terse autobiographical onset of "Experience" strikes an unregenerate and ambiguous chord. It seems at once a perverse or calculated response to grief, as well as an acknowledgment of being undone by it:

> Grief too will make us idealists. In the death of my son, now more than two years ago, I seem to have lost a beautiful estate,—no more. I cannot get it nearer to me. If tomorrow I should be informed of the bankruptcy of my principal debtors, the loss of my property would be a great inconvenience to me, perhaps for many years; but it would leave me as it found me,—neither better nor worse. So it is with this calamity: it does not touch me: something which I fancied was a part of me, which could not be torn away without tearing me, nor enlarged without enriching me, falls off from me, and leaves no scar. It was caducous. I grieve that grief can teach me nothing, nor carry me one step into real nature. (*EW* 3:29)

The passivity of Emerson's language is striking, so much so that fancy and empty grief represent the most active forms of self-assertion in the passage; everything else is nonvolitional and simply happens to a vulnerable self. Yet this latent passivity is not prompted by identifiable passion, an absence that, etymologically speaking, points to the way in which Emerson makes a lack of suffering look like control. Even so, this rendition of Waldo's death is marked by too much incredulity and affective background noise for it to stand as a straightforward example of Emerson's contention "that nothing can be taken from us that seems much" (*JMN* 5:19). After all, Robert Richardson describes Emerson's grief at the loss of his son Waldo as "deep, real, and immediate."[50] At the same time, his studiously unconcerned rhetoric shows Emerson courting Stoicism at its extreme edges. Grief is not entirely disclaimed, but nor is it acknowledged as a useful perspective or permanent foothold on reality. The gnomic complexity of the passage derives in part from the indeterminacy of its feeling, but also from the clash of agency and disempowerment that Emerson stages. Is this touchstone of Emersonian criticism a register of the absence of feeling, its suppression, or—in elegiac terms—a sign of its displacement?

Like Coleridge, but more overtly, Emerson acknowledges here the contiguity of tranquility and dejection, the subtle correspondence whereby one's freedom not to feel can turn precipitously into an inability to feel. In the context of his son's death, Emerson conceded that both kinds of emotional poverty would strike his contemporaries as "scandalous" (*EW* 3:46). In a remarkable essay, Sharon Cameron has identified several sources of the scandal: for instance, not only does "Experience" conceal the omnipresence of feeling that Emerson insistently denies, but Emerson himself seems to "mourn the loss of his affect more than the loss of his son."[51] Why, then, does Emerson "hold hard to this poverty" (*EW* 3:46), disavowing sentimental consolations as if in spite of scandal?

I take Emerson to be rehearsing a version of Stoic cosmopolitanism, though not in any naïve or mindless sense. The famous passage in the essay draws on two related Stoic tenets to describe how the dispossession of his son did not result in the dispossession of his self. First, in comparing Waldo's death to the loss of an estate, Emerson ventured a wrenching adaptation of Epictetus's claim that nothing external to the self defines the self. None of the essay's many commentators have noticed Emerson's indebtedness to Epictetus in the *Enchiridion*: "NEVER say of any thing, 'I have lost it;' but, 'I have restored it.' Is your Child dead? It is restored. Is your Wife dead? She is restored. Is your Estate taken away? Well: and is not that likewise restored?"[52] Emerson's perception of the affective interchangeability of losing a son or an estate has been described as both "dreadful" and deliberately vulgar, but this view overlooks the way in which Emerson pours his own grief into Epictetus's Stoic mold.[53] Yet for Emerson, the insubstantiality of owning farms and estates that he had ridiculed in *Nature* made the comparison all the more incisive. The death of Waldo felt immaterial precisely because, like the landscape or the horizon, he could never have been possessed in the first place. Second, Emerson's description of the way in which Waldo's death shattered an illusion of ownership exemplifies the Stoic idea that one is just a temporary beneficiary of persons and things that ultimately belong to the universe. Epictetus, for example, counseled that one should take care of any object that one possessed, "but as of something not your own, as Passengers do of an Inn."[54] Emerson had imagined his "ownership" or affinity with Waldo as so forceful that it seemed more like embodiment, but his quick shift to "caducous" detachment, with its botanical and zoological connotations, retrospectively testifies to the ephemeral and unspiritual nature of corporeal life.

Since Emerson's reflection on the death of Waldo represents one of the most substantial autobiographical aberrations in the impersonal facade of the essays, more hinges on its interpretation than the mere identification of a muted Stoical sentiment. I see Emerson's intentional subversion of conventional sentimental morality as evidence of his careful exploitation of a stylistic mode perfected by the ancient Stoics. Richardson has described Emerson's grief at the failure of grief in "Experience" as a piece of "Thoreauvian contrariness and paradox," but the propensity for enigmatic formulations shared by both writers has a deeper rhetorical ancestry.[55] In making assertions that would strike most of his readers as "not a little repugnant to common understanding," Emerson styled his own unorthodox assertions after what Plutarch, following Cicero, called Stoic paradox.[56] For both Cicero and Plutarch, the Stoics stretched the connotation of paradox beyond mere logical contradiction to engage more directly with its etymological origins: a Stoic paradox was simply a premise that stood in distinct opposition to *doxa*, or pervasive opinion. Emerson would have been familiar with the mode from a range of examples in Plutarch, whose *Moralia* contained both a catalog and a critique of those "celebrated doctrines" that the Stoics themselves, "gently admitting their absurdity, style paradoxes."[57]

For Plutarch, Stoic maxims perverted "common conceptions" and made a farce of "common sense."[58] Framed in intentionally disquieting rhetoric, the initially rebarbative quality of these utterances relies on defamiliarization to carve out a conceptual space that might be filled in only with further meditation. In search of an easy example, Plutarch proposed, "only wise men are kings," and "they only are rich."[59] Though clearly incongruous with common experience, the extremity of these maxims concealed a more nuanced significance, one that might ultimately reorient conventional expectations. For example, all political sovereigns are not wise. But like Shelley's Prometheus, all truly wise men must exercise sovereignty over themselves. More to the point, such self-possession is itself a kind of wealth, the most valuable sort of possession imaginable. It is not difficult to see how this paradoxical mode might have a bearing not just on Emerson generally, but on "Experience" in particular. So many of Emerson's own formulations take perplexity as the prompt for a reformed understanding that this stylistic proclivity cannot be solely attributed to Stoic rhetoric. That said, approaching some of Emerson's counterintuitive affirmations as intentionally modeled on Stoic paradoxes might go some way toward decoding the complex work of statements that overturn "common conceptions." Take, for example, his assertion that "love, which is the deification of persons, must become more impersonal every day" (*EW* 2:107). Here, as in Plutarch's example, readerly alienation counterbalances the possibility of an emergent ethical awareness.

For Emerson, as for Cicero, this new awareness required more than reversion to an antiquated system of ethics. Cicero's *Paradoxa Stoicorum* explored old pronouncements in new essays, finding what one translator describes as "a new context and justification for Stoic ethics in the social, political, and economic life of the late Republic."[60] In transplanting aspects of Stoic doctrine into more contemporary moral terrain, essays like "Experience" undertake a similar repositioning. In her analysis of "Experience," Cameron describes "contradiction" as an effect of the essay's strategy, but like Stoic paradox, that contradiction was particularly well suited to an essay that sought to unmask "custom and gross sense" while also articulating an ethics that could thrive "within the actual horizon of human life" (*EW* 3:28, 30).[61] Waldo's appearance in the essay dramatically magnifies Emerson's Stoic reassessment of the relations that govern ordinary morality.

On this front, Cicero's *Paradoxa Stoicorum* is a particularly apt counterpoint for Emerson's detachment in the essay. Like Emerson, Cicero sets himself the arduous task of reconciling extreme Stoic doctrine with common opinion and understanding. He describes his task as that of bringing "amazing" doctrines "into the light" to see whether it might be possible "to expound them in a way which would make them acceptable."[62] Implicit in this articulation of his method is a sense that *paradoxa* obtain their significance only against the *doxa* they contravene. Put in different terms, an experimental moralist or essayist must anchor even his most intractable claims in a common and tractable language. In Richard Poirier's terms, the paradox of "self-erasure"—with all of its Stoic implication—can be understood only "within the system of signs, the community of words and sounds, by which human beings have identified themselves as human."[63]

This constraint illuminates a strange tension in the essay, one felt even at the level of tone: Emerson's dispassionate stance emerges out of a reigning *doxa* of sentiment. Like Cicero, Emerson grounds his appeal to the virtue of dispassion in a strikingly emotional register.[64] In "Experience," Emerson at first contests the blithe world view of the Stoics by foregrounding the moral and psychological bankruptcy that an affectless existence might imply. For example, he prefaces his meditation on Waldo's death with the thought that in certain moods, reality might be found only by courting suffering against the "sharp peaks and edges of truth" (*EW* 3:29). The aspiration to a place beyond emotion plays out against a nostalgic and ambivalent desire for feeling itself. I take it for granted that Emerson's attempt to unsettle such a sentimental perspective was inherently related to his own investment in it.

Emerson followed his meditation on Waldo's death with an allusion to Robert Southey's *The Curse of Kehama*: "The Indian who was laid under a curse, that the wind should not blow on him, nor water flow to him, nor fire burn him, is a type of us all" (*EW* 3:29). Barbara Packer has described this as Emerson's "grimmest assessment of the human condition," but Emerson himself had been casting similar spells in earlier essays, long imagining a place beyond sympathy and affective reciprocity.[65] The paradoxical emptiness of grief results in a turn toward a more general reconsideration of sympathy, which Emerson describes as "a little eager and sentimental" (*EW* 3:36). The life of truth is cold and mournful, but it is not "the slave of tears, contritions, and perturbations" (*EW* 3:46). This prompts what strikes me as the real cosmopolitan trajectory of the text, a passage that is almost entirely overlooked in commentary on the essay:

> All private sympathy is partial. Two human beings are like globes, which can touch only in a point, and, whilst they remain in contact, all other points of each of the spheres are inert; their turn must also come, and the longer a particular union lasts, the more energy of appetency the parts not in union acquire. (*EW* 3:44)

Rendering the two-dimensional concentric circles of Stoic *oikeiosis* in three-dimensional terms, Emerson visualizes the global disproportion that results from heightened local sensibility. The tendency of affect to delimit perspective is inevitable and only human, and yet the precarity of these private sympathies illuminates by contrast the wider sway of impartial reason. Since it is "the eye which makes the horizon," a particular focal point is always set against the curving line of a wider world (*EW* 3:44). Cameron has suggested that Emerson's valorization of the impersonal entails a failure to acknowledge not only the suffering of others but "his own suffering, which is never very real to him."[66] This is a strangely motivated misreading. It is not that Emerson failed to feel the loss of his son, but that the evanescence of this feeling only confirmed an old intuition. Not without melancholy, Waldo's death made a cosmopolitan perspective seem not just necessary but feasible.

Pure Sympathy with Universal Ends

Emerson's vision of partial sympathy as the delimiting convergence of two globes speaks to the way in which his evocation of Stoicism is never just a salve for personal trauma. Like Smith, he turns again and again to its demanding vision of how ethical attention might be disciplined and thereby apportioned for life in an "immense system" (*TMS* 140). All of the natural points of convergence that result from the "private sympathy" of domestic life are counterbalanced by the infinite other points that make up our ensphered existence. Over the course of the chapter, I have emphasized the Stoic register of Emerson's long-standing theoretical gravitation toward those other impersonal points that stretch out across the globe. Drawing on this earlier engagement, Emerson's Stoic griefwork in "Experience" becomes an understated philosophical rationale for his slow turn toward "ethical engagement" and questions of social reform.[67] But like so many other radical, outward-facing manifestations of Stoicism lurking within Romanticism, this kind of dispassionate aspiration was easily mischaracterized. To borrow a phrase from Larissa MacFarquhar, Emerson's impartial outlook could easily seem to be "the antithesis of what we value about deep human attachment."[68] This general mistrust of Emerson's impartiality was only exacerbated by the evolution of his later work, in which Stoicism could easily seem like the reaction to a world whose "tyrannous circumstance" undercut human action in advance (*EW* 6:8).

In concluding, I want to suggest that *The Conduct of Life* finds Emerson turning back to explore his enduring Stoic commitments even as he attempts to forge a connection between ethical self-culture and social reform. At the same time, this suggestive reorientation hovered just shy of practice. Emerson's claim from another late essay has some bearing on the trajectory of Stoicism in his work: "The astonishment of life, is, the absence of any appearance of reconciliation between the theory and practice of life" (*EW* 4:101).

Published four months before the start of the Civil War, the essays that make up *The Conduct of Life* draw unambiguous attention to Emerson's fascination with the Stoics. He is, for example, demonstrably preoccupied with Marcus Aurelius, who shows up no fewer than five times in the essays. In *Sartor Resartus* (1836), Carlyle had called for a recalibration of literary culture, urging his readers to "Close thy *Byron*" and "Open thy *Goethe*."⁶⁹ In *The Conduct of Life*, a similar timeliness inheres in Emerson's call to "Open your Marcus Antoninus," an imperative that casts Stoicism as central not just to the "Spirit of the Times" but to the more "practical question" of how those times might be inhabited in an ethical way (*EW* 6:1). For many critics, however, Emerson's interest in Stoic self-culture is upstaged by the fatal, self-limiting realities of existence that he explores throughout the volume, most directly in his unstinting essay "Fate." Capturing the way in which human autonomy is boxed in by temperament, physiology, history, natural law, and inexplicable disaster, Emerson paints a picture of an indifferent world resistant to human intervention:

> Nature is no sentimentalist,—does not cosset or pamper us. We must see that the world is rough and surly, and will not mind drowning a man or a woman; but swallows your ship like a grain of dust. The cold, inconsiderate of persons, tingles your blood, benumbs your feet, freezes a man like an apple. The diseases, the elements, fortune, gravity, lightning, respect no persons. (*EW* 6:3–4)

Emerson's disenchanted account of the objective world and its inexorable limitations can easily seem like a swerve away from his idealism, a touchstone in the arc his essays trace from "unceasing affirmation" to a Stoic recognition of limit and law.⁷⁰ In this common narrative, Stoicism represents a new mode of thought for Emerson, and one that arrives in a decidedly minor key. As one contemporary reviewer put it, "Mr. Emerson is a stoic . . . in his quiet acquiescence in all powerful Fate and in the sovereign self-reliance with which he confronts the movements of destiny."⁷¹ Abstracted from its slow development and exposition in his earlier work, the Stoicism on display in *The Conduct of Life* could seem like fatalism or mere endurance. And yet signs of Emerson's more radical Stoic vision are present even in this account of nature's indifferency. In describing nature as "no sentimentalist," Emerson aligns nature itself with an antithetical morality, one that rides roughshod over the personal in its pursuit of broader systemic concerns. In *Nature*, he had observed that the "ethical character so penetrates the bone and marrow of nature, as to seem the end for which it was made" (*EW* 1:26). In offering a penetrating description of that dispassionate natural ethic, *The Conduct of Life* follows Emerson's earlier essays in describing the "method of nature" as an apt model for Stoic cosmopolitan ethics. *The Conduct of Life* could even be seen as an extended commentary on a line from Marcus Aurelius: "Imperturbability in the face of what comes upon you through an external cause; righteousness in activities caused from within you, that is, an impulse to act which culminates in socially useful actions—this is being for you in accord with nature."[72]

In these later essays, the example of nature's disinterested operation cuts through the "deceptions of the passions, and the structural, beneficent illusions of sentiment" (*EW* 6:170). As part of a broader trajectory in Emerson's thought, this Stoic vision of what acting in accordance with nature might entail should be seen as an inchoate vision in quest of a future: "The right use of Fate is to bring up our conduct to the loftiness of nature" (*EW* 6:13). Indeed, Emerson goes so far as to suggest that the "fatal strength" of natural law is nothing less than the "moral sentiment itself" (*EW* 6:117). But what does acting on such imperturbability actually look like, and how does the thought of approximating nature's impersonality inform Emerson's turn toward ethical engagement and social reform?

In *The Theory of Moral Sentiments*, Smith made up a hypothetical earthquake in China to posit in vivid terms the feeble power of sympathy in an ever-widening world. In "Fate," Emerson adopts a similar tack, recalling the earthquake at Lisbon "that killed men like flies" and the more recent Neapolitan convulsion in which "ten thousand persons were crushed in a few minutes" (*EW* 6:4). Later, he evokes the millions of slaves and immigrants who were "ferried over the Atlantic" to "ditch and to drudge . . . and then to lie down prematurely to make a spot of green grass on the prairie" (*EW* 6:9). Like Smith, Emerson describes sympathy as a "ridiculously inadequate" response to such suffering. By foregrounding the personal it "amounts to little more than a criticism or a protest made by a minority of one, under compulsion of millions" (*EW* 6:10). A sense of the delimited power of sympathy also pervades Emerson's cautious, late-onset contributions to the push for abolition. His rage against the Fugitive Slave Law leads, in his "Address to the Citizens of Concord" (1851), to a denunciation of mawkish piety: "Only persons who were known and tried benefactors are found standing for freedom: the sentimentalists went down stream."[73] In a later "Lecture on Slavery" (1855), Emerson takes up water imagery again to distinguish between the variable "tides of public sentiment" and the fact of slavery's continued subsistence.[74] In all of these cases, meaningful reform has to derive from something more powerful than feeling. Fighting the injustice of slavery means cultivating the indifference of a hurricane, not the false personification of its rage.

If Emerson's work toward social reform was catalyzed by his Stoicism, his public advocacy never quite replicates the cool intensity of the philosophical vision that enabled it.[75] Like so many other forms of Romantic Stoicism from the French Revolution forward, there was a mismatch between Emerson's austere Stoic vision and the reality of its worldly uptake. This, of course, was not a condemning novelty but the extension of a much older gap between Stoic theory and practice. As Godwin knew all too well, the Stoic's cool façade was often misunderstood, his radical vision "pent up in the recesses of the heart" (*PPW* 6:22). Stoic self-culture could give rise to a bold cosmopolitan ethic, but such self-culture was not ideally suited to its transmission outside of the philosophical context of the essays. Even so, Emerson's turn to nature in the Stoic attempt to find a "pure sympathy with universal ends" put him in good company (*CW* 6:15). In *Perpetual Peace*, Kant himself made a similar move, arguing that "with regard to the ideal of perpetual peace" it is "our duty to make use of the mechanism of nature for the realization of that end."[76] Then there was Henry David Thoreau, who claimed—early in the journal that Emerson inspired him to write—that "Zeno the stoic stood in precisely the same relation to the world that I do now."[77] Aided by Thoreau, Gandhi's vision of nonviolent resistance has been described as a kind of Stoic experiment. In Richard Sorabji's terms, Gandhi follows Thoreau and the Stoics in reconciling emotional detachment with an attempt to extend "*love* to all humans" and an imperative "to engage in *politics*."[78]

But Emerson's Stoic cosmopolitan vision was not simply a philosophical dead end, nor a position lying in wait for the far-off future. Thomas Wentworth Higginson had always outstripped Emerson in his radical abolitionism. One of the Secret Six who helped raise funds for John Brown's raid on Harper's Ferry, he was also the commander of one of the Union's first Black regiments. Wounded toward the end of the war, Higginson wrote to Emerson as he readjusted to civilian life. In his response, Emerson held out hope that "the appearance of an enthusiastic moral genius, a new Zeno or Buddh, thinking and acting with simplicity, would crystallize the chaos, and begin the new world."[79] Responding to Emerson's call in his own way, Higginson looked back to the mid-eighteenth century and decided to revise Elizabeth Carter's translation of *The Works of Epictetus*. In the preface to that work, Higginson draws a straight line from his own fight for abolition and equality back to the Stoic-inspired revolutions that rocked Haiti and France in the 1790s:

> It has not seemed to me strange, but very natural, to pass from camp life to the study of Epictetus. Where should a student find contentment in enforced withdrawal from active service, if not in "the still air of delightful studies"? There seemed a special appropriateness, also, in coming to this work from a camp of colored soldiers, whose great exemplar, Toussaint l'Ouverture, made the works of this his fellow-slave a favorite manual. Moreover, the return of peace seems a fitting time to call anew the public attention to those eternal principles on which alone true prosperity is based; and, in a period of increasing religious toleration, to revive the voice of one who bore witness to the highest spiritual truths, ere the present sects were born.[80]

If the Stoics offered consolation in times of war, they also advanced a vision of the principles and high spiritual truths that could make those wars worth the fight. In his review of the translation, Henry James took the classic line that the Stoicism of Epictetus "fosters apathy and paralyzes the sensibilities."[81] But Higginson's own look back to the 1790s speaks to the still-resonant radicalism of a Stoic Romanticism that might bring about a revolution, or challenge the status quo. In Emerson's terms, some new Zeno searching for the pattern of a "new world" need only look back to Romanticism itself. Writing two decades after Emerson's death, Higginson linked him to this enduring Stoic legacy, one whose power and availability lay in its lack of systematicity:

> The great English, Scotch, French, and German philosophers pass in review, and we see how they succeed and replace one another. But Epictetus, Marcus Antoninus, Seneca, still live; their detached maxims outlast the systems of others; they did not displace each other; new versions of them constantly appear, perhaps to remind us that it is, after all, the fragmentary and unsystematic teacher that we most need. Renan's fine remark about the works of Marcus Antoninus, that "they will never grow antiquated, because they embody no dogma," might have been made for Emerson.[82]

Almost a breathing of the common wind, Emerson's Stoic thought could fall in line with that of Louverture or Kant, Carter or Wordsworth, ready to inspire even in its fragmentary form the new "teacher that we most need."

NOTES

Introduction

1. Mooallem, "Megafire," 50–51.
2. Mooallem, 53.
3. Mooallem, 38, 53.
4. Charles Taylor gives a compelling account of how the Romantic "idea that we find the truth within us, and in particular in our feelings" plays into modern notions of authenticity. See C. Taylor, *Sources of the Self*, 368–69, and *Secular Age*, 473–504, especially 473 where this phrase occurs.
5. Brooke, *Philosophic Pride*, 207.
6. The phrase is Ian Watt's, from *Rise of the Novel* (60). But here I am thinking in particular of William Galperin's account of the everyday as a "category in process" whose emergence is crucially facilitated by "romantic literature's altogether unique role as both text and context" (*History of Missed Opportunities*, 23).
7. Wordsworth, *Prose Works*, 1:148.
8. Lillian Furst gives pride of place to passion and its expression in her account of Romanticism: "That the personal feelings of the imaginative individual form the basis of art was unanimously accepted by the Romantics. There is indeed hardly any other tenet in the Romantic credo on which so remarkable a degree of agreement is found throughout Europe" (*Romanticism in Perspective*, 228).
9. Wenley, *Stoicism and Its Influence*, 163.
10. Aravamudan, *Tropicopolitans*, 104 (quote), 106.
11. Weinbrot, *Britannia's Issue*, 62.
12. R. Adams, *Roman Stamp*, 203.
13. Blake, *Poetry and Designs*, 70.
14. Harold Bloom's use of the term to describe poets who wrestle and appropriate in pursuit of their own imaginative vision represents another example of Stoicism's sidelining in the pursuit of a canonical version of Romanticism. Stoicism does not, apparently, earn you a place in the "visionary company." See *Anxiety of Influence*, 5–6.
15. See Rieff, *Freud*, 17.
16. I borrow the terms for these two "powerful challenges" to Stoicism from A. A. Long, *Stoic Studies*, 179–81.
17. Hegel, *Phenomenology*, 115; Kojève, *Introduction*, 53–54.
18. See Moyn, *Last Utopia*, 11–15, and Edelstein, *On the Spirit of Rights*, 7–9, 107–14.
19. See Pascoe, *Romantic Theatricality*, 40–41, 63–64. For Pitt's "Reign of Alarm," see Johnston, *Unusual Suspects*.
20. Cited in Whatmore, *Republicanism and the French Revolution*, 94.
21. Hazlitt, *Collected Works*, 3:156.
22. Hadot, *Inner Citadel*, 192.
23. Cited in Millingen, *Recollections*, 274.
24. S. Swift, "Stoicism and Romantic Literature," 303.
25. Cicero, *On Moral Ends*, 3.74, pp. 88–89. For an account of this systematicity, see Schofield, "Stoic Ethics," 236–39.
26. Seneca, "On the Constancy of the Wise Person," in *Hardship and Happiness*, 10.4,

p. 159. For the most significant contemporary account of the place of emotion within Stoicism, see M. Graver, *Stoicism and Emotion*.

27. Burton, *Anatomy of Melancholy*, 251.
28. Landor, *Imaginary Conversations*, 2:97.
29. P. Shelley, *Complete Works*, 9:33, 35.
30. *Oxford English Dictionary Online*, s.v. "stoical, *adj.*," March 2021, https://oed.com/view/Entry/190674.
31. Nehamas, *Art of Living*, 34.
32. Strange and Zupko, *Stoicism*, 1–2.
33. Wallace, *Shelley and Greece*, 5. Sachs makes a comparable point in *Romantic Antiquity*, arguing that Roman classicism "was not a static tradition but an available set of examples that could be deployed to make authorized statements about the present" (20).
34. C. Taylor, *Sources of the Self*, 361.
35. See Epictetus, in Carter, *All the Works of Epictetus*, 1.1.2, p. 35.
36. Connor, *Giving Way*, 206, 3.
37. Pfau, *Romantic Moods*, 21.
38. Baucom, *Specters of the Atlantic*, 240.
39. Pfau, *Romantic Moods*, 21.
40. Favret, *War at a Distance*, 145.
41. Cox, *Romanticism*, 3.
42. Here I am thinking of Caruth's generative *Unclaimed Experience: Trauma, Narrative, History*.
43. Wordsworth, *Poems, in Two Volumes*, 84–86.
44. Ramsey, *Military Memoir*, 15–18.
45. François, *Open Secrets*, xviii–xix.
46. Nersessian, *Utopia, Limited*, 2, 6.
47. K. Singer, *Romantic Vacancy*, xxxii.
48. Faflak and Sha, *Romanticism and the Emotions*, 2.
49. In this sense, it is no surprise that one of the five sections in Gregg and Seigworth's *The Affect Theory Reader* is titled "Managing Affects."
50. Hume, *Treatise of Human Nature*, 386.
51. Gregg and Seigworth, *Affect Theory Reader*, 4. See Coleridge, *Shorter Works*, 2:1419–53.
52. See Reddy, *Navigation of Feeling*.
53. Faflak and Sha, *Romanticism and the Emotions*, 1.
54. Berlant, *Cruel Optimism*, 5.
55. Massumi, *Parables*, 35; Sedgwick, *Touching Feeling*, 21.
56. Massumi, *Parables*, 43.
57. Long, *Epictetus*, 28.
58. Cohen-Vrignaud, "Love Actually," 301.
59. See Faflak and Sha, who see the affective turn as an interdisciplinary project "directly traceable" to—but also a continuation of—Romanticism (*Romanticism and the Emotions*, 7). Other important assessments of affect theory in relation to the period include Favret, "Study of Affect and Romanticism," and Yousef, "'Emotions that Reason Deepens.'"
60. Sedgwick, *Touching Feeling*, 18.
61. B. Graver, "Romanticism," 81.
62. See C. Jones, *Radical Sensibility*; Pinch, *Strange Fits of Passion*; Stauffer, *Anger, Revolution, and Romanticism*; and Chandler, *Archaeology of Sympathy*.
63. See B. Graver, "Wordsworth and the Stoics," and Potkay, *Wordsworth's Ethics*.
64. See C. Johnson, *Equivocal Beings*, 16. For Barbauld's Stoicism, see in particular

McCarthy, *Anna Letitia Barbauld*, 51–58, and Clery, *Eighteen Hundred and Eleven*, 67–85. For Wollstonecraft, see Vernon, "Mary Wollstonecraft," 58–80.
65. Peacock, *Four Ages of Poetry*, 16.
66. P. Shelley, *Complete Works*, 6:141.
67. Yeats, *Poems*, 235.
68. P. Shelley, *Complete Works*, 1:231.
69. P. Shelley, 1:232.
70. P. Shelley, 2:179.
71. Cicero, *Tusculan Disputations*, 2.25.60, p. 214.
72. Cicero, 2.24.58, p. 213.
73. Cicero, 2.25.60, pp. 214–15.
74. Wasserman, *Shelley*, 282–85.
75. P. Shelley, *Complete Works*, 2:171.
76. P. Shelley, 2:172.
77. P. Shelley, 2:193–94.
78. P. Shelley, 2:179.
79. P. Shelley, 2:188.
80. Cicero, *Tusculan Disputations*, 3.34.82, p. 323.
81. P. Shelley, *Complete Works*, 1:240–41.
82. P. Shelley, 2:219, 224.
83. P. Shelley, 2:242.
84. Long and Sedley, *Hellenistic Philosophers*, 1:429.
85. Peacock, *Four Ages of Poetry*, 15, 16–17.
86. P. Shelley, *Complete Works*, 7:118, 140.
87. Cassirer, *Myth of the State*, 168.
88. Wordsworth, *Prose Works*, 1:103.
89. Coleridge, *Lectures 1795*, 164.
90. De Quincey, *Works*, 2:54–55.
91. Coleridge, *Collected Letters*, 3:477.
92. Coleridge, *Marginalia*, 1:172.
93. Keats, *Selected Letters*, 37.
94. T. S. Eliot, *Selected Essays*, 10–11.

Chapter 1: Stoic Moral Sentimentalism from Shaftesbury to Wollstonecraft

1. Mee, *Romanticism, Enthusiasm, and Regulation*, 7.
2. See, for example, Siegel, "Should Literature Be Useful?" and Paul, "Reading Literature."
3. Kames, *Essays*, 17.
4. Beattie, *Elements of Moral Science*, 1:180.
5. S. Goldsmith, *Blake's Agitation*, 22.
6. Lamb, *Essays of Elia*, 134.
7. Pagden, *Enlightenment*, 75. See also the many references to Stoicism in Peter Gay's *Enlightenment*.
8. I want to belabor the prominence of Stoicism within moral sentimentalism, for it seems very often eclipsed by the notoriously Stoic outlook of Immanuel Kant, a figure who gave "full weight" to the "utterances of the Stoics" in distinguishing rational duty from the promptings of sensibility itself. Since scholars of Romanticism frequently connect Kant's account of moral self-mastery to the "*humilitas animi* of the Stoics," I have let his thought

linger on the sidelines of this project. But in a roundabout way the minimization of Kantian dispassion only foregrounds the shared Stoic substratum that connects the two wildly divergent moral philosophical outlooks that predominate in the period. See Kant, *Lectures on Ethics*, 323, 355. For Kant as an exemplar of the Stoic side of Romantic ethics, see Lockridge, *Ethics of Romanticism*, 74–80.

9. Pope, *Poems*, 519, II.101–4.
10. Hume, *Essays: Moral, Political, and Literary*, 539.
11. Hume, 159–80, quote 172.
12. Coleridge, *Poetical Works*, 1:700.
13. Swift, *Gulliver's Travels*, 217–18. For a compelling account of how the Houyhnhnms out-Stoic the Stoics, see Nuttall, "Gulliver among the Horses," 51–67.
14. Swift, *Gulliver's Travels*, 226.
15. Swift, 228.
16. Swift, 231.
17. Swift, "Thoughts on Various Subjects," in *Prose Works*, 1:244.
18. S. Johnson, *Yale Edition of the Works*, 3:174.
19. Potkay, *Passion for Happiness*, 78, 113.
20. S. Johnson, *Yale Edition of the Works*, 2:39.
21. Johnson himself was not immune to these Stoic deflations. See *Rasselas* in S. Johnson, 16:70–76.
22. Addison and Steele, *Spectator*, 1:44.
23. S. Johnson, *Yale Edition of the Works*, 3:280.
24. Hume, *Essays Moral, Political, and Literary*, 138n.
25. Festa, *Sentimental Figures of Empire*, 16.
26. Ellison, *Cato's Tears*, 46.
27. M. Nussbaum, *Cosmopolitan Tradition*, 193–97.
28. Carter, *All the Works of Epictetus*, 27.
29. Carter, 21, 27.
30. Cited in Guest, "Bluestocking Feminism," 68.
31. S. Pennington, *Unfortunate Mother's Advice*, 38–39.
32. C. Macaulay, *Letters on Education*, 130.
33. C. Jones, *Radical Sensibility*, 8. Mee also notes that Shaftesbury's ideas in *Characteristics* "were extended and debated by others who often wished to make its model of politeness less socially exclusive" (*Romanticism, Enthusiasm, and Regulation*, 42).
34. De Quincey, *Works*, 15:223–42.
35. Burke, *Writings and Speeches*, 1:230.
36. Marcus Aurelius, in Hutcheson and Moor, "Meditations," 4.59, p. 57.
37. Burke, *Writings and Speeches*, 1:230.
38. Voitle, *Third Earl*, 135.
39. Hirschman, *Passions and the Interests*, 47.
40. For the legacy of Shaftesbury's attitudes within Romanticism, see Engell, *Creative Imagination*, 22–25.
41. Wordsworth, *Prose Works*, 3:72.
42. Simpson, *Wordsworth, Commodification, and Social Concern*, 33.
43. Yousef, *Romantic Intimacy*, 21.
44. Yousef, 46.
45. Hobbes, *Leviathan*, 126, 157.
46. Shaftesbury, *Life, Unpublished Letters*, 359. Lawrence Klein notes that for Shaftesbury "this grand opposition between stoic and Epicurean absorbed the entire variety of ancient opinion" (*Shaftesbury*, 60).
47. Mandeville, *Fable of the Bees*, 133.

48. Cited in Rivers, *Reason, Grace, and Sentiment*, 2:152.
49. Hume, *Treatise of Human Nature*, 386.
50. Philippe Lejeune cited in Genette, "Introduction to the Paratext," 261.
51. Cited in Paknadel, "Shaftesbury's Illustrations," 297.
52. See Brooke, *Philosophic Pride*, 120.
53. Marcus Aurelius, in Hutcheson and Moor, *"Meditations,"* 12.22, p. 148.
54. In *Characteristics*, Shaftesbury describes this ruling faculty, or "governing part," of the mind as a faculty that "superintends and manages its own imaginations, appearances, fancies, correcting, working and modelling these as it finds good" (*C* 302). See also Jaffro, Maurer, and Petit, "Pathologia," 231–32.
55. S. Johnson, *Yale Edition of the Works*, 4:309.
56. Klein, *Shaftesbury*, 74. I am borrowing Long's translation from *Epictetus* (34). Elizabeth Carter's translation refers to a power suited to "the Use of the Appearances of Things" (*All the Works of Epictetus*, 1.1.2, p. 35).
57. Marcus Aurelius, in Hutcheson and Moor, *"Meditations,"* 7.54, p. 90.
58. Marshall, *Figure of Theater*, 38.
59. Hadot, *Inner Citadel*, 84.
60. For an important analysis of the oblique role of Stoicism in Shaftesbury's *Characteristics*, see Rivers, *Reason, Grace, and Sentiment*, 2:91–96, 118–20.
61. Schneewind, *Invention of Autonomy*, 301.
62. *Oxford English Dictionary Online*, s.v. "immane, *adj.*," March 2021; https://oed.com/view/Entry/91795.
63. Potkay, *Story of Joy*, 98.
64. Pfau, *Minding the Modern*, 237–38.
65. Arnold, *Complete Prose Works*, 9:51.
66. Kames, *Essays*, 55.
67. C. Jones, *Radical Sensibility*, 8.
68. Phillipson, *Adam Smith*, 19–23, 181. See A. Smith, *Correspondence*, 58.
69. A. Smith, *Lectures on Rhetoric*, 56.
70. Hume, *Treatise of Human Nature*, 368.
71. See McKeon, *Secret History of Domesticity*, 377. Pfau also emphasizes this virtuality in "Certain Mediocrity," 59–61.
72. Marshall, *Figure of Theater*, 168; Duncan, *Scott's Shadow*, 119–21; Greiner, *Sympathetic Realism*, 9.
73. P. Shelley, *Complete Works*, 7:118.
74. See Ian Baucom's account of the contradiction whereby Smith entertains a systematic vision of capital and yet commends a countersystematic approach to sentiment: "The more he commands a global knowledge of capital, in other words, the more Smith demands a parochial territory of moral vision and knowledge" (*Specters of the Atlantic*, 239).
75. Introduction to *TMS*, 6.
76. David Marshall acknowledges—but ultimately looks past—this apparent divide. See Marshall, *Figure of Theater*, 184–85. For other important accounts of Smith's Stoicism, see Forman-Barzilai, *Adam Smith*; Griswold, *Adam Smith*; Justman, *Autonomous Male of Adam Smith*; M. Nussbaum, *Cosmopolitan Tradition*; and Vivenza, *Adam Smith and the Classics*.
77. Rothschild, *Economic Sentiments*, 133; Baker, "Scott's Stoic Characters," 457–59.
78. Rothschild, *Economic Sentiments*, 133.
79. Fairclough *Romantic Crowd*, 27–28.
80. See Soni, *Mourning Happiness*, 310.
81. Epictetus, in Carter, *All the Works of Epictetus*, 3.12.4, p. 187.
82. M. Shelley, *Last Man*, 52; *PPW* 3:425, 4:32, 4:65; and Hazlitt, *Collected Works*, 1:33.

83. Bakhtin, *Problems of Dostoevsky's Poetics*, 120. See Klein's reference to Bakhtin in *Shaftesbury* (89n), as well as Marshall's account of Smith's dialogism in *Figure of Theater* (175–78).

84. M. Nussbaum, *Cosmopolitan Tradition*, 181.

85. Rothschild notes Smith's tendency to use the word tranquility "amazingly often," especially in his discussion of duty (*Economic Sentiments*, 302n93).

86. Wordsworth, *Prose Works*, 3:71n.

87. Palumbo-Liu, *Deliverance of Others*, 10.

88. Bender, *Imagining the Penitentiary*, 224–25.

89. Pfau, "Certain Mediocrity," 54. I part ways with Pfau in his sense that "emotion in Smith's *Theory* proves to be altogether extra-rational and non-propositional" (56). On this front, Greiner's account of "Smith's cognitive model" in which emotions are a form of judgment is more compelling. See Greiner, *Sympathetic Realism*, 4.

90. Forman-Barzilai, *Adam Smith*, 50.

91. Molesky, *This Gulf of Fire*, 6.

92. Hayot, *Hypothetical Mandarin*, 8. Robbins addresses the global and literary implications of Smith's example in "Is Literature a Secular Concept?"

93. See Forman-Barzilai's important reading of Smith's *oikeiosis* in *Adam Smith* (1–26, 120–34).

94. See Cicero, *De Officiis*, 1.15.46 to 1.18.60, pp. 49–63. For more on *oikeiosis*, see M. Nussbaum, "Kant and Stoic Cosmopolitanism," 9; Brennan, *Stoic Life*, 154–68; and Striker, *Essays on Hellenistic Epistemology*, 281–97.

95. Greiner, *Sympathetic Realism*, 21.

96. This passage, introduced in the second edition of 1760, appeared up to the fifth edition of *TMS* but was replaced in the sixth.

97. See Rothschild, *Economic Sentiments*, 133–34.

98. A. Smith, *Correspondence*, 46–47. See also *TMS* 58–60.

99. Burke, *Writings and Speeches*, 8:132.

100. Wollstonecraft, *Works*, 7:320.

101. Wollstonecraft, *Vindication*, 214–15.

102. Kay, "Canon, Ideology, and Gender," 72.

103. B. Taylor, *Wollstonecraft and the Feminist Imagination*, 211.

104. Polwhele, *Unsex'd Females*, 10.

105. Wollstonecraft, *Vindication*, 6; *TMS* 136.

106. Wollstonecraft, *Vindication*, 74.

107. Wollstonecraft, 29–30.

108. Wollstonecraft, 39, 17, 21.

109. Pushing his auditors to become "citizens of the world," Price argued that the noblest principle of human nature entailed "the regard to general justice, and that goodwill which embraces all the world" (*Discourse on the Love*, 10).

110. Wollstonecraft, *Vindication*, 17, 33.

111. Wollstonecraft, 113.

112. C. Johnson, *Equivocal Beings*, 30, 16.

113. Wollstonecraft, *Vindication*, 277, 271, 127.

114. Wollstonecraft, 131.

Chapter 2: Wordsworth and Godwin in "Frozen Regions"

1. H. Robinson, *Diary*, 2:18.

2. H. Robinson, 1:41.

3. Garrod, *Wordsworth*, 138.
4. Ferguson, *Language as Counter-Spirit*, xv.
5. M. Cooke, *Romantic Will*, 216.
6. McFarland, *Romanticism*, 148.
7. Batho, *Later Wordsworth*, 341.
8. M. Shelley, *Journals*, 1:25.
9. Wordsworth, *Letters*, 1:126.
10. Frye, "Defining an Age of Sensibility," 144.
11. B. Graver, "Romanticism," 81. See also Graver's "Wordsworth and the Stoics," 145–60.
12. Worthington, *Wordsworth's Reading of Roman Prose*, 45.
13. Trilling, *Opposing Self*, 119.
14. Pope, *Poems*, 515, I.294.
15. Francis, *Subversive Virtue*, 42.
16. Hegel, *Phenomenology*, 115; see Kojève, *Introduction*, 53–54.
17. Wu, *Wordsworth's Reading: 1770–1799*, 165–66, and B. Graver, "Duncan Wu's *Wordsworth's Reading*." Wordsworth's familiarity with Stoicism far exceeded any regime of classical reading in school or after. In this sense, his familiarity with ancient philosophy mirrors James Castell's sense of his familiarity with classical verse: "The classical is entangled with the English, and the classics are not an alternative source for Wordsworth but part of an aesthetic tradition that is made up of various literatures and histories" ("William Wordsworth," 331).
18. Godwin, "The Principal Revolutions of Opinion," in *Collected Novels and Memoirs*, 1:53.
19. For Godwin's Sandemanianism, see White, *Early Romanticism*, 94–97.
20. Spiegelman, *Wordsworth's Heroes*, 173. Drawing on his own dissenting background, Hazlitt convincingly described Godwin as "a mixture of the Stoic and of the Christian philosopher" (*Collected Works*, 11:19).
21. Canuel, *Shadow of Death*, 71.
22. Coleridge, *Lectures 1795*, 164.
23. J. Wordsworth, *Borders of Vision*, 267.
24. Wordsworth, *Prose Works*, 1:103.
25. Wordsworth, 1:126.
26. Hazlitt, *Collected Works*, 11:23.
27. Chandler, *Wordsworth's Second Nature*, xviii.
28. See Graham, *William Godwin Reviewed*, 70.
29. Chandler, *Wordsworth's Second Nature*, 29.
30. Southey, *Collected Letters*, no. 387.
31. Southey, no. 1246.
32. C. Jones, *Radical Sensibility*, 89.
33. Burke, *Writings and Speeches*, 8:218–19.
34. Burke, 8:217; Wordsworth, *Prose Works*, 1:122.
35. Horace, *Epistles* 1.19.12–14, cited in Burke, *Writings and Speeches*, 219.
36. Outram, *Body and the French Revolution*, 69. For Outram, the move to align one's public identity with "Stoic-republican virtue" (77) often obscured "the complex doctrines of classical Stoicism," nor were most revolutionaries keen "to take on board the whole freight of the consideration which the ancient world had devoted to the control of the passions" (69).
37. Robespierre, Speech to National Convention on May 7, 1794, cited in Millingen, *Recollections*, 272, 274.
38. Parker, *Cult of Antiquity*, 139–42. See also Sachs, *Romantic Antiquity*, 13–16.

39. "Decree on Worship of the Supreme Being," in Maclear, *Church and State*, 88–90.
40. *Whitehall Evening Post*, July 15, 1794–July 17, 1794, 2.
41. *Sun*, April 17, 1794, 3.
42. *Sun*, April 18, 1794, 2. See also Fox, *Speeches during the French Revolution*, 162–63.
43. In his autobiography, Godwin recalled wearing the wig of a venerable ancestor while "representing the character of Cato in my father's barn, agreeably to the costume of the original frontispiece to [Addison's] play" (Godwin, *Collected Novels and Memoirs*, 1:5).
44. Burke, *Writings and Speeches*, 8:131.
45. See Singer, Cannold, and Kushe, "William Godwin," 67–86.
46. Hazlitt, *Collected Works*, 11:16.
47. B. Williams, *Moral Luck*, 18.
48. Wordsworth, *Prose Works*, 1:123.
49. Wordsworth, *Poems, in Two Volumes*, 124.
50. Wordsworth, 126.
51. Wordsworth, *Prose Works*, 2:187.
52. Hobbes, *Leviathan*, 190.
53. Wordsworth, *Prose Works*, 3:33.
54. Fry, *Wordsworth*, 72.
55. Fry, 106, 6, and 74.
56. Epictetus, in Carter, *All the Works of Epictetus*, 3.9.1, p. 182.
57. Coleridge, *Letters*, 2:1116.
58. Wordsworth, *Letters*, 1:367.
59. Jarvis, *Wordsworth's Philosophic Song*, 4.
60. Cited in Jarvis, 23.
61. See Wu, *Wordsworth's Reading: 1770–1799*, 66–67.
62. Godwin, *Collected Novels and Memoirs*, 3:340.
63. Clemit, *Godwinian Novel*, 45.
64. For Hume's original sentiment, see Godwin's quotation of it in *Thoughts of Man* (*PPW* 6:83).
65. For Godwin's turn from Stoicism to the "empire of feeling," see Weston, "Godwin's Critique of Enlightened Modernity," 445–70.
66. Don Locke notes that this passage appears three times without alteration in Godwin's published writings between 1798 and 1801. See Locke, *Fantasy of Reason*, 145–46.
67. Wordsworth, *Poems, in Two Volumes*, 268.
68. Carlson, *England's First Family*, 87–88. While Carlson does not puzzle over Godwin's Stoicism per se, her rehabilitation of Godwin's chilly indifference as "a type of humanity intimately tied to justice" (67) has been formative to my own account. See *England's First Family*, 66–91.
69. Godwin, *Collected Novels and Memoirs*, 1:52.
70. Coleridge, *Letters*, 1:527.
71. Shaftesbury, *Life, Unpublished Letters*, 359.
72. For an incisive account of Stoic tranquility and social freedom in *The Excursion*, see Michael, *British Romanticism* (193–202). The interplay of Stoicism and Epicureanism is also central to Boyson's account of the poem in *Wordsworth* (153–87).
73. Wordsworth, *Prose Works*, 2:54.
74. Wordsworth, *Letters*, 2:469–70.
75. See Wu, *Wordsworth's Reading: 1800–1815*, 93–94.
76. The translation is from Margaret Graver, *Stoicism and Emotion* (51).
77. Cicero, *Tusculan Disputations*, 4.6.11–12, pp. 339–41.
78. See Potkay, *Story of Joy*, 5–6.

79. Wordsworth, *Prose Works*, 2:52–53.
80. See *E* 426–27 and Reed, *Chronology of the Middle Years*, 23–24.
81. *Oxford English Dictionary Online*, s.vv. "pomp, *n.*," December 2020, https://oed.com/view/Entry/147528, and "contingence, *n.*," December 2018, https://oed.com/view/Entry/40246.
82. Johnston, *Wordsworth and "The Recluse,"* 273–74.
83. For a more thorough account of Coleridge's presence in these lines, see Risinger, "*Excursion* as Dialogic Poem," 435–37.
84. Zimmerman, *Romanticism, Lyricism, and History*, 84.
85. Worthington, *Wordsworth's Reading of Roman Prose*, 71.
86. Potkay, *Wordsworth's Ethics*, 149, 161, 164, 163.
87. O. Goldsmith, *Collected Works*, 2:201.
88. *Oxford English Dictionary Online*, s.v. "unwarp, *v.*," June 2019, https://oed.com/view/Entry/219444.
89. Potkay, *Wordsworth's Ethics*, 162, 168.
90. Goodman, *Georgic Modernity*, 123.
91. Wordsworth, *Poems, in Two Volumes*, 277.
92. Wordsworth, 268.
93. See Hartman, *Wordsworth's Poetry*, 296, and C. Taylor, *Sources of the Self*, 111–12.
94. See Hadot, *Philosophy*, 238.
95. Cited in Hadot, 244.
96. Thomson, *"Liberty,"* 285.
97. See Barrell, *English Literature in History*, 51–109.
98. Anderson, *Powers of Distance*, 32.
99. Wordsworth, *Prose Works*, 1:342.
100. See Foucault, *Care of the Self*, 86.
101. Coleridge, *Specimens of the Table Talk*, 186.
102. Hazlitt, *Collected Works*, 11:18–19.
103. Hazlitt, 11:23.
104. Wordsworth, *Prose Works*, 1:342.

Chapter 3: Coleridge, Lyric Askesis, and Living Form

1. Hume, *Letters*, 1:12–18, quotes 18, 14, 17, 13.
2. Hume, *Treatise of Human Nature*, 4.
3. Hume, *Letters*, 1:13–14.
4. Coleridge, *Marginalia*, 4:75.
5. Trilling, *Liberal Imagination*, 135.
6. Hume, *Letters*, 1:14.
7. Coleridge, *Letters*, 3:316; *Lectures 1795*, 162.
8. Coleridge, *Opus Maximum*, xlv.
9. Coleridge himself never adopted the label, though riffing on his residence in Nether Stowey during the annus mirabilis of 1797–98, he wittily aligned himself with "the Stowics." See *Letters*, 3:58.
10. Coleridge, *Letters*, 1:188.
11. Foucault, *Care of the Self*, 51.
12. *Oxford English Dictionary Online*, s.v. "attemper, *v.*," December 2020, https://oed.com/view/Entry/12750.
13. Coleridge, *Letters*, 1:397.
14. Sidney, "Defence of Poesy," 12.

15. Coleridge, *Letters*, 4:924.
16. Coleridge, *P Lects*, 1:5; *Letters*, 4:923.
17. See *P Lects* 1:252.
18. Coleridge, *Lay Sermons*, 108.
19. Coleridge, *Friend*, 1:415.
20. Coleridge, *P Lects* 1:278; *Letters*, 3:477; and *P Lects* 1:275.
21. Nietzsche, *Beyond Good and Evil*, 15.
22. I survey this argument in Risinger, "Coleridge, Politics," 647–67.
23. M. Nussbaum, "Poetry and the Passions," 106.
24. Bell, *Essays*, 16. Discussed in A. Richardson, *British Romanticism*, 29–34.
25. For Coleridge's notes, see *P Lects* 1:288–98.
26. Augustine, *City of God*, 602.
27. Augustine, 599.
28. Coleridge, *Lectures 1795*, 156–57.
29. Colish, "Stoicism and the New Testament," 334–79.
30. Coleridge, *Notebooks*, 4:5072.
31. Cited in Cooper, "Justus Lipsius," 12.
32. Brooke, *Philosophic Pride*, 145.
33. Coleridge, *Aids to Reflection*, 168–69; Cudworth, *True Intellectual System*, 1:198.
34. Coleridge, *Lectures 1795*, 83.
35. Cudworth, *True Intellectual System*, 2:113, 119.
36. Enfield, *History of Philosophy*, 1:342. Coleridge also borrowed the original Latin text from the Bristol library in 1797.
37. For Brucker, see Brooke, *Philosophic Pride*, 146–48, and Sellars, *Stoicism*, 147–48.
38. Coleridge, *Lectures 1795*, 156–67, quotes 156, 157.
39. Paley, *Coleridge's Later Poetry*, 49. In *The Friend*, Coleridge describes Rousseau as a Stoic mole: "the crazy Rousseau, the Dreamer of lovesick Tales, and the Spinner of speculative Cobwebs; shy of light as the Mole, but as quick-eared too for every whisper of the public opinion; the Teacher of stoic *Pride* in his principles, yet the victim of morbid *Vanity* in his feelings and conduct!" (1:132).
40. Coleridge, *Lectures 1795*, 209. Compare this phrase to his evocation of "vain Philosophy's aye-babbling spring" in "The Eolian Harp" (*PW* 1:234).
41. Gataker, "Preliminary Discourse," 1.
42. Hutcheson and Moor, *"Meditations,"* 91.
43. Coleridge, *Marginalia*, 1:179.
44. Hutcheson and Moor, *"Meditations,"* 91.
45. Coleridge, *Opus Maximum*, 39–40.
46. Coleridge, *Biographia Literaria*, 1:153.
47. Kant, *Critique of Practical Reason*, 93.
48. Kant, 98.
49. Wordsworth, *Poems, in Two Volumes*, 106.
50. Coleridge, *Letters*, 4:791–92.
51. Coleridge, *Lectures 1795*, 162.
52. Kant, *Critique of Practical Reason*, 28.
53. Kant, 71, 63–64.
54. Coleridge, *Biographia Literaria*, 1:159–60.
55. Coleridge, *Notebooks*, 1:1717. For another account of Coleridge's dissatisfaction with Kant's Stoicism, see Harding, *Coleridge*, 165–69.
56. Coleridge, *Marginalia*, 1:172–73.
57. Coleridge, *Shorter Works*, 2:1421.

58. See A. Richardson, *British Romanticism*, 39–65, and Ford, *Coleridge on Dreaming*, 158–82.
59. Coleridge, *Letters*, 1:137.
60. Coleridge, *Letters*, 2:1046.
61. Graham, *William Godwin Reviewed*, 82.
62. Bakewell's poem, originally published in *The Moorland Bard*, is cited in Faubert (*Rhyming Reason*, 1–2). For more on Bakewell, see Faubert, 75–97.
63. Buchan, *Domestic Medicine*, 112.
64. Coleridge, *Biographia Literaria*, 1:234.
65. Lovejoy, "Coleridge and Kant's Two Worlds," 341.
66. Coleridge, *Biographia Literaria*, 1:17.
67. Coleridge, *Letters*, 2:1046.
68. I am drawn to what Mays describes as the way in which conventional Romantic preoccupations have kept critics from properly assessing the totality of Coleridge's oeuvre. See Mays, *Coleridge's Experimental Poetics*, 6–7.
69. Coleridge, *Letters*, 1:397.
70. The phrase is from an alternate, rejected draft of "Frost at Midnight." See *PW* 1:454n.
71. Marcus Aurelius, in Hutcheson and Moor, *"Meditations,"* 12.22, p. 148.
72. See Foucault, *Technologies of the Self*, passim.
73. Coleridge, *Biographia Literaria*, 2:19, 22n.
74. Abrams, *Mirror and the Lamp*, 88.
75. E. Jones, *Coleridge*, 4.
76. Among the Romantics, Coleridge was hardly alone in imagining philosophy as a work in progress rather than a settled position or commitment. Discussing Keats, for example, Susan Wolfson contends that "philosophy is no settled creed for Keats; it is always the work of philosophy" (*Reading John Keats*, 60).
77. Coleridge, *Biographia Literaria*, 1:252.
78. Hadot, *Philosophy*, 90.
79. Jackson, *Dickinson's Misery*, 7.
80. See Culler, *Theory of the Lyric*, 73, 76, as well as Abrams's prominence in Jackson and Prins, *Lyric Theory Reader*, 86–90, 140–43.
81. Abrams, *Mirror and the Lamp*, 23, 48.
82. Abrams, 48, and 150. Abrams attributes the review to one Alexander Smith of Banff, Scotland.
83. Abrams, 154; Hazlitt, *Collected Works*, 5:2.
84. Culler, *Theory of the Lyric*, 92.
85. Hegel, *Aesthetics*, 1114–15.
86. Hegel, 1123.
87. Hegel, 1112.
88. Hegel's sense of poetry as an "old wife's medicine" is not unlike Byron's complaint that Shelley "used to dose me with Wordsworth physic even to nausea" (quoted in Medwin, *Journal*, 192).Yet one crucial difference stands out: for Hegel it is the writing, and not the reading, of poetry that brings relief.
89. Pfau, *Romantic Moods*, 67.
90. Trop, *Poetry*, 4. Like Coleridge, Trop approaches the work of art as something that can "graft itself onto mental and bodily practices or become a focal point for patterns and styles of life" (6).
91. See MacLeish, *Collected Poems*, 106–7.
92. Hadot, *Inner Citadel*, 51.

93. Robson, *Heart Beats*, 6, 8, 14.

94. Duff, *Romanticism*, 104.

95. Duff, 108, 109.

96. *Oxford English Dictionary Online*, s.v. "effusion, *n.*," December 2020, https://oed.com/view/Entry/59835.

97. Holmes, *Coleridge: Early Visions*, 91n.

98. "Philosophiae etenim meae ea doctrina est, quod natura ipsa morbus sit [For that is the teaching of my philosophy, that nature is itself a disease]" (quoted in *PW* 2:863).

99. Coleridge, *Biographia Literaria*, 2:64.

100. Coleridge, *Notebooks*, 2:2543.

101. Coleridge, *Letters*, 3:495.

102. Coleridge, 3:408.

103. Coleridge, *Notebooks*, 3:3325. Seamus Perry draws attention to this striking characterization in his introduction to *Coleridge's Notebooks: A Selection*, vii.

104. Abrams, "Structure and Style," 531.

105. Yousef, *Romantic Intimacy*, 126.

106. See Charles Lamb's evocation: "In him was disproved that old maxim, that we should allow every one his share to talk. He would talk from morn to dewy eve, nor cease till far midnight; yet who ever would interrupt him,—who would obstruct that continuous flow of converse, fetched from Helicon or Zion?" (quoted in Coleridge, *Table Talk*, 1:xli).

107. Bloom, *Ringers in the Tower*, 31.

108. When Coleridge reclassified these conversation poems for *Sibylline Leaves* (1817), they were called "Meditative Poems in Blank Verse"—perhaps another echo of Marcus Aurelius.

109. Hadot, *Inner Citadel*, 84.

110. See Stock, "Soliloquy," 371–472.

111. Gerard, "Systolic Rhythm," 314.

112. Abrams, "Structure and Style," 528.

113. Epictetus, in Carter, *All the Works of Epictetus*, 4.1.12, p. 239.

114. Bakewell, cited in Faubert, *Rhyming Reason*, 1.

115. Coleridge, *Marginalia*, 1:194.

116. White, *Early Romanticism*, 141.

117. Canuel, "Romantic Fear," paragraph 27.

118. Gurton-Wachter, *Watchwords*, 25–26.

119. Gurton-Wachter, *Watchwords*, 74–83. This first phrase is Coleridge's; see Gurton-Wachter, 79.

120. Gurton-Wachter, 81.

121. Favret, "General Fast," 133, 140.

122. Favret, 139.

123. Coleridge, *Letters*, 2:1046.

124. Cicero, *Tusculan Disputations*, 4.6.13 through 4.7.14, pp. 341–43.

125. See Coleridge's claim that the "necessity for external government to man is in an inverse proportion to the vigor of his self-government. Where the last is most complete, the first is least wanted" (*Table Talk*, 1:387).

126. Mee, *Conversable Worlds*, 190.

127. Coleridge, *Shorter Works*, 1:1421.

128. See *PW* 2:696 and Parrish, *Coleridge's Dejection*, 17–18.

129. See Coleridge, *Lay Sermons*, 23, and *Marginalia*, 1:818.

130. Seneca, *Hardship and Happiness*, 1.15, 2.3–4, pp. 184–85.

131. Coleridge, *Marginalia*, 3:531–32.

132. Spiegelman, *Majestic Indolence*, 62.
133. Spiegelman, 62.
134. Seneca, *Hardship and Happiness*, 2.4, p. 185.
135. Coleridge, *Letters*, 2:945.
136. Coleridge, 2:782–83.
137. Coleridge, *Notebooks*, 1:787.
138. Coleridge, *Biographia Literaria*, 2:65.
139. *Oxford English Dictionary Online*, s.v. "dedicate, v.," March 2021, https://oed.com/view/Entry/48546.

Chapter 4: The True Social Art: Byron and the Character of Stoicism

1. Rousseau, *Confessions*, 9.
2. Seneca, *Letters on Ethics*, 66.51, p. 200.
3. Sachs, *Romantic Antiquity*, 72.
4. W. Scott, "Childe Harold's Pilgrimage, Canto III," 183.
5. Cited in MacCarthy, *Byron*, 349–52.
6. Wordsworth, *Letters*, 3:579.
7. Some of the most penetrating Byron scholarship from the twenty-first century has been focused on the way in which Byron shaped and was shaped by celebrity culture. See Mole, *Byron's Romantic Celebrity*, and Tuite, *Lord Byron and Scandalous Celebrity*.
8. See Hume, "Advertisement," in *Essays Moral and Political*, 2:iii.
9. Woloch, *One vs. the Many*, 29.
10. Warren's *The Orient and the Young Romantics* has been a useful guide to the many ways in which Byron and other Romantic writers are drawn to "ideological, aesthetic, and ethical positions which are instantiated in various characters, narrators, references, and styles" (16).
11. A. Howe, *Byron*, 1.
12. See Byron, *Complete Miscellaneous Prose*, 198.
13. For other notable accounts of Byron's Stoicism, see in particular Michael Cooke's *Blind Man Traces the Circle* (181–83), and Richard Lansdown's "Byron's Relativism" (101–10).
14. Anderson, *Way We Argue Now*, 3.
15. Felski, *Limits of Critique*, 6, 25. Indeed, Felski casts the practitioner of critique as an especially Byronic character, a dandy whose "debonair stoicism combines knowing distance and aesthetic flair" (49).
16. Hazlitt, *Complete Works*, 11:71.
17. See Gray, *Poetry of Indifference*, 47–71.
18. Guiccioli, *Lord Byron's Life in Italy*, 265.
19. In "Byron's Imitations," Beaty links this passage directly to Byron's sense of himself as an ethical satirist, describing "his denunciation of 'all passions'" as "essentially the philosophy of Stoicism" (347).
20. Blessington, *Conversations of Lord Byron*, 65–66.
21. Butler, *Gender Trouble*, 191.
22. S. Manning, *Poetics of Character*, 23.
23. Christensen, *Lord Byron's Strength*, xix; McGann, *Towards a Literature*, 38–40.
24. Carlyle and Carlyle, *Letters*, April 28, 1832, to Macvey Napier.
25. P. Manning, *Byron and His Fictions*, 61.
26. See McGann, *Byron and Romanticism*, 141–59.

27. George Bate, *Elenchus motuum nuperorum in Anglia: or, A Short Historical Account of the Rise and Progress of the Late Troubles in England*, cited in Lee, *Failures of Feeling*, 94.

28. Mole, *Byron's Romantic Celebrity*, 22–77 and passim. See also Elfenbein, *Byron and the Victorians*, 13–46.

29. Lynch, *Economy of Character*, 133.

30. Lynch, 54. For a comparable account of character as something other than a fixed, interior essence, see Omri Moses's account of "modernism's vitalist-inspired conception of character," one in which character is predicated on taking the "complexity and open-endedness of life as a conceptual starting point" (*Out of Character*, 4).

31. McGann, *Beauty of Inflections*, 273.

32. See *BLJ* 6:66.

33. Horace, *Satires, Epistles* 1.6.1–2, pp. 286–87.

34. Fielding, *Tom Jones*, 276.

35. Yu, *Nothing to Admire*, 19.

36. Pope, *Poems*, 630, brackets in original. "Queen Anne's man" quote at *BLJ* 5:265.

37. Hazlitt, *Collected Works*, 8:147.

38. Christensen, *Lord Byron's Strength*, 327. See also Cheeke, "Byron and the Horatian Commonplace."

39. Hazlitt, *Collected Works*, 11:73 and 4:137.

40. Landor, "Nil Admirari, Etc.," in *Poems*, 2:231.

41. Landor, 2:231.

42. Cheeke, "What So Many Have Told," 523.

43. For a vivid evocation of preexistent language's ability to foster thought in new contexts, see Pinch's account of Charlotte Smith in *Strange Fits of Passion* (51–71).

44. Robert Griffin argues that Romantic literary history "originates with, and continues to function in relation to, an anxiety about Pope" (*Wordsworth's Pope*, 25).

45. Quoted in Field, *Memoirs of Wordsworth*, 37.

46. Byron, "Preface to Cantos I and II," in *Don Juan*, 38.

47. Chandler, "Pope Controversy," 503.

48. Sachs, *Romantic Antiquity*, 115–31, quote 129.

49. McGann, *Don Juan in Context*, 68–79.

50. Cicero, *De Officiis*, 1.38.136, p. 139.

51. Byron, *Complete Miscellaneous Prose*, 111, 143, 150.

52. For a survey of attempts to link Horace's *nil admirari* to "many divergent philosophical systems," see McCarter, *Horace between Freedom and Slavery*, 108. For attempts to weigh Pope's own philosophical agenda in his imitation, see Stack (*Pope and Horace*, 202–10) and Noggle (*Skeptical Sublime*, 134–42).

53. Shaftesbury, *Life, Unpublished Letters*, 365.

54. Cicero, *Tusculan Disputations*, 3.14.30, p. 263.

55. Fisher, *Wonder*, 59.

56. On the nature of classical exemplarity and its disruption by the French Revolution, see Koselleck's *Futures Past* (21–38) and Sachs's *Romantic Antiquity* (29–30 and throughout). In this particular case, it is striking that Byron's embrace of classical exemplarity and the commonplace is linked to a polemical turn away from Romantic poetics to an older, Augustan model.

57. Nietzsche, *Daybreak*, 129.

58. Coleridge, *Letters*, 1:98.

59. Boswell, *Life of Samuel Johnson*, 454.

60. See *DJ* 11:33–34. See also Tucker's account of the "disturbing continuity" of these terms in *Epic* (231).

61. See Franklin's account of Adeline's "self-repression" in *Byron's Heroines* (160–62).

62. W. Scott, "Childe Harold's Pilgrimage, Canto III," 183.
63. W. Scott, "Childe Harold's Pilgrimage, Canto IV," 220. See McGann's note in *DJ* 756, and Stabler, *Byron, Poetics, History*, 166–69.
64. See Barrell, *English Literature in History*, 51–109.
65. See "Memoir of the Author" in Mitchell, *Biographies of Eminent Soldiers*, vii–xviii.
66. Sabertash, "Sliding Scale of Manners," 580.
67. Sabertash, 587–88.
68. See Bhabha, *Location of Culture*, 85–92.
69. See Spivak, *Critique of Postcolonial Reason*, 266.
70. Leask, *British Romantic Writers*, 4.
71. Ellison, *Cato's Tears*, 18.
72. Ellison, 18.
73. Cicero, *Tusculan Disputations*, 3.14.30, p. 263.
74. Aravamudan, *Tropicopolitans*, 106. Byron's interest in Stoicism as a surface-level, characterological phenomenon might be seen as an outgrowth of Aravamudan's "virtualization," a term that he uses to describe "colonialist representations that acquire malleability because of a certain loss of detail, a process that enables readier identification and manipulation by readers" (17).
75. Elmer, *On Lingering and Being Last*, 2, 4.
76. Lynch, *Economy of Character*, 54.
77. Thorslev, *Byronic Hero*, 27, 29.
78. Rousseau, *Basic Political Writings*, 90.
79. Rousseau, 82.
80. Lee, *Failures of Feeling*, 2–3, 15–19.
81. Sabertash, "Sliding Scale of Manners," 588.
82. Cohn, *Still Life*, 5.
83. Combe, *Tour of Doctor Syntax*, 267.
84. Behn, *Oroonoko, and Other Writings*, 72.
85. J. Adams, *Dandies and Desert Saints*, 35.
86. Byron's point here is just one example of what Mary Favret has described as the way in which military violence was for many Romantic readers "at once strange and familiar, intimate and remote, present and yet not really here" (*War at a Distance*, 15).
87. Stabler, *Byron, Poetics, History*, 107.
88. Colley, *Captives*, 63.
89. Hickman, *Black Prometheus*, 356.
90. Hickman, 361. Daniel Hack has analyzed the similarly prominent though differently modulated citation of the lines in W.E.B. Du Bois's *The Souls of Black Folk* (*Reaping Something New*, 181–83).
91. James McCune Smith, cited in Hickman, *Black Prometheus*, 360.
92. Byron, *Complete Miscellaneous Prose*, 128.
93. Boswell, *Life of Samuel Johnson*, 729; Beckford, *Thoughts upon Hunting*, 116.
94. *Parliamentary History of England*, 1258. Byron once described Windham as "one of those who governed nations," "the first in one department of oratory and talent." Quoting Hamlet after Windham's death, Byron said, "But he is gone, and Time 'shall not look upon his like again'" (*BLJ* 3:219).
95. More, "Slavery, A Poem," in A. Richardson, *Verse*, 117.
96. S. Manning, *Poetics of Character*, 23.
97. For more on these suggestive parallels, see Lansdown, "Byron's Relativism," 100, and Barton, *Don Juan*, 47–49.
98. Seneca, *Letters on Ethics*, 47.10, p. 136. For a concise account of the Stoic perspective on slavery, see Garnsey, *Ideas of Slavery*, 128–52.

99. William Ernest Henely's "Invictus" might seem only tangentially related to my point here, and yet Henley edited one volume of an ultimately abandoned edition of Byron's prose that he hoped might advance "a more intimate understanding of Byron's character" (Henley, in Byron, *Works*, ix).

100. Byron drew on the Stoics to blur the boundaries between legal and moral slavery in a contemporaneous journal entry: "The Stoics Epictetus & Marcus Aurelius call the present state 'a Soul which drags a Carcase'—a heavy chain to be sure, but all chains being material may be shaken off" (*BLJ* 9:45).

101. My account of Byron's attempt to forge a meaningful, political connection between legal and moral slavery has been galvanized by Klausen's reading of the connection between Rousseau's philosophical account of slavery and primitivism and the empirical realities of colonial modernity. See Klausen, *Fugitive Rousseau*, esp. 80. For the "anti-imperial" possibilities of Stoicism in relation to literal and metaphoric slavery, see Pasanek's *Metaphors of Mind* (110–13, 134–36).

102. Beaty, "Byron's Imitations," 350.

103. See Nehamas's *Art of Living* for a compelling investigation of ancient philosophy as an "art of living," as well as Sellars's *Art of Living* for an important discussion of Stoicism in these terms.

The idea of Stoicism as an art of living is manifest in Elizabeth Carter's translation of Epictetus, which Byron owned: "Philosophy, answered *Epictetus*, doth not promise to procure any thing external to Man; otherwise it would admit something beyond its proper Subject-matter. For the Subject-matter of a Carpenter is Wood; of a Statuary, Brass; and so, of the Art of Living, the Subject-matter is each Person's own Life" (Carter, *All the Works of Epictetus*, 1.15.1, pp. 65–66).

104. Horace, *Satires, Epistles*, 2.7.86, p. 230–31.

105. "Anecdotes of Persons Connected with the French Revolution," 727–8. See Schama, *Citizens*, 753.

106. Boyd, *Byron's Don Juan*, 40. Alexander Bevilacqua offers a full account of Cloots's political philosophy while also addressing the intellectual proximity of Cloots and Godwin. See Bevilacqua, "Conceiving the Republic of Mankind."

Chapter 5: Stoic Futurity in Sarah Scott and Mary Shelley

1. Austen, *Persuasion*, 81, 84.
2. Austen, 84–85.
3. Austen, 188.
4. M. Nussbaum, *Therapy of Desire*, 318. See, for example, Wright, "Women Reading Epictetus," 321–37.
5. Diogenes Laertius in Long and Sedley, *Hellenistic Philosophers*, 1:430. See Schofield, *Stoic Idea of the City*, 43–46.
6. Cited in M. Nussbaum, *Therapy of Desire*, 325.
7. M. Robinson, *Letter to the Women*, 54.
8. Armstrong, "Gush of the Feminine," 15–16.
9. Armstrong, "Msrepresentation," 11.
10. Clery, *Eighteen Hundred and Eleven*, 67–85.
11. Coleridge, *Table Talk*, 1:564–55.
12. See Clery, *Eighteen Hundred and Eleven*, 81–82, 246.
13. Austen, *Persuasion*, 17.
14. Pinch, *Strange Fits of Passion*, 139.
15. Austen, *Persuasion*, 47, 37, 44.

16. Wiltshire, *Jane Austen and the Body*, 175–76.
17. Austen, *Persuasion*, 69, 142.
18. Galperin, *Historical Austen*, 228.
19. Davidson, *Hypocrisy*, 152.
20. Rohrbach, *Modernity's Mist*, 106.
21. Lee, *Failures of Feeling*, 128, 135.
22. Galperin, *Historical Austen*, 223. See Lee's account of "reticence as a mode of care or consideration" in *Failures of Feeling* (125–62).
23. M. Shelley, *Letters*, 2:196.
24. See Stafford, "*Lodore*: A Tale," 181–93.
25. See McInnes, *Wollstonecraft's Ghost*, 160–68.
26. M. Shelley, *Letters*, 2:185.
27. Sachs, *Poetics of Decline*, 117, 16, 93.
28. See Crystal Lake's account of the way in which the novel's progressive, feminist vision is informed by a typically masculine antiquarianism that embeds "the edifying tenets of classicism within a domestic topography" ("Redecorating the Ruin," 668).
29. Pratt, *Imperial Eyes*, 163, and F. Nussbaum, *Torrid Zones*, 152, 160.
30. Wollstonecraft, *Vindication*, 113.
31. *MH* 223; Nersessian, *Utopia, Limited*, 13.
32. Ellison, *Cato's Tears*, 100, 122.
33. *Oxford English Dictionary Online*, s.v. "whimsical, *adj.* and *n.*," December 2020, https://oed.com/view/Entry/228368.
34. See Susan Lanser's careful account of Scott's desire, particularly for the way in which the "performance of an ascetic and pious philanthropy" might serve "as the cover story for Sarah Scott and Barbara Montagu's cohabitation, turning a discourse of personal fulfilment toward altruistic ends" ("Tory Lesbians," 178).
35. S. Scott, *Letters*, 1:314.
36. S. Scott, *History of Cornelia*, vii.
37. Montagu, *Letters*, 3:336–37.
38. Attentive to Scott's discomfort with the increasing prestige of moral sentimentalism by midcentury, Deborah Weiss reads *Millenium Hall* as a critique of Shaftesbury's "emotionalizing of morality" as well as an early critical response to Smith's recently published *Theory of Moral Sentiments*. Weiss is surely correct to belabor Scott's ethical deemphasis of affect, but my own sense of the Stoic cross-currents churning through Shaftesbury's and Smith's moral philosophy suggests that her relation to their work might be characterized as an especially canny penetration rather than the "clear opposition" of critique. See Weiss, "Sarah Scott's 'Attick School,'" 464, 479.
39. For a broader sense of Carter's significance in the reception and dissemination of Epictetus, see Long, *Epictetus*, 261–62.
40. Hawley, "Carter, Elizabeth."
41. Cited in Guest, *Small Change*, 100.
42. Wallace, "Confined and Exposed," 325.
43. Carter, *All the Works of Epictetus*, 25.
44. Catherine Talbot, in Pennington, *Series of Letters*, 2:139.
45. Carter, *All the Works of Epictetus*, 30, 24, 27.
46. Wallace, "Confined and Exposed," 317.
47. Wallace, 322.
48. Carter, *All the Works of Epictetus*, 19.
49. Carter, 27.
50. Guest, *Small Change*, 146.

51. Polwhele, *Unsex'd Females*, 7, 12, 32.
52. See Hill, "Tale of Two Sisters," 222.
53. Carter, *All the Works of Epictetus*, 27.
54. See Epictetus, in Carter, 4.1.1–12, pp. 232–42.
55. Lanser, "Tory Lesbians," 177.
56. C. Johnson, *Equivocal Beings*, 16.
57. C. Williams, "Poetry, Pudding, and Epictetus," 3.
58. Long and Sedley, *Hellenistic Philosophers*, 1:429.
59. B. Johnson, *Life with Mary Shelley*, 25.
60. Poovey, *Proper Lady*, 117.
61. Carlson, *England's First Family*, 98.
62. Mellor, *Mary Shelley*, 208.
63. M. Shelley, *Letters*, 2:196.
64. Her journal, for example, notes that Percy repeated Coleridge's "poem to tranquility" in January 1815. See M. Shelley, *Journals*, 1:59.
65. See Carlson's account of how the "performative status of reading" complicates a sense of Shelley's later fiction as merely conservative in *England's First Family* (93–98).
66. Addison and Steele, *Spectator*, 1:44.
67. Mellor, *Mary Shelley*, 178.
68. Mellor, 206.
69. O. Smith, *Romantic Women Writers*, 190–218.
70. Gonda, "*Lodore* and Fanny Derham's Story," 340.
71. Vargo, "Aikins and the Godwins," 84–98.
72. *Oxford English Dictionary Online*, s.v. "landmark, *n*.," March 2021, https://oed.com/view/Entry/105499.
73. I borrow this great phrase from Cameron's "The Way of Life by Abandonment: Emerson's Impersonal" (in *Impersonality: Seven Essays*, 79–107).
74. Guest, *Small Change*, 146.
75. Poovey, *Proper Lady*, 159.
76. G. Eliot, *Middlemarch Notebooks*, 30, 33–35, 72.
77. G. Eliot, *Middlemarch*, 79.

Chapter 6: Emerson, Stoic Cosmopolitanism, and the Conduct of Life

1. Baudelaire, *Selected Writings on Art*, 372.
2. Arnold, *Complete Prose Works*, 10:177. Emerson shared Arnold's sense that Marcus Aurelius lacked philosophical rigor: "But that excellent Stoic was not an intellectual but a moral speculator. His studies were directed not to the search of new truth but to a sublime yet simple theory of duties. His studies were rather in religion than in philosophy so that he did not find a distraction in business but endeavored to execute on the throne the pious conclusions of his closet" (Emerson, *Early Lectures*, 1:186).
3. Stephen, *Studies of a Biographer*, 142. Stephen's "amusing fiction" is first broached by Thomas Macaulay in "Lord Bacon" (*Critical and Historical Essays*, 2:400–401).
4. Stephen, *Studies of a Biographer*, 141, 143.
5. See Cavell, *Emerson's Transcendental Etudes*, 20–32.
6. See Foucault, *Care of the Self*, 42, 86.
7. Miller, "From Edwards to Emerson," 592.
8. R. Richardson, *Emerson*, 233. For a contrasting picture of Emerson's Stoicism, see Woelfel, "Beautiful Necessity."

9. See Cameron, *Impersonality*. Writing in a similar vein, Branka Arsić's engagement with Stoic logic in *On Leaving* represents a notable divergence from the tendency to dismiss Emerson's Stoicism out of hand. Arsić also draws attention to Emerson's interest in "Stoic self-making," and to the way in which he follows the Stoics in approaching "ontological questions as ethical" (esp. 19–23 [quotes 20, 21], 293–302).

10. Buell, *Emerson*, 98.

11. Chai, *Romantic Foundations*, xii.

12. See, for example, Greenham, *Emerson's Transatlantic Romanticism*; Harvey, *Transatlantic Transcendentalism*; and Wesibuch, *Atlantic Double-Cross*.

13. G. Cooke, "Emerson's View of Nationality," 310.

14. See Garvey, "Simular Man," 513–42; Crane, *Race, Citizenship, and Law*, 87–104; and Voelz, *Transcendental Resistance*, 221–22. Ian Finseth sounds a dissenting note in suggesting that Emerson held an "irreducibly humanist belief that the biological and spiritual bonds linking humanity into one whole were more important and more fundamental than national allegiance" ("Evolution," 731).

15. For inclusionary and exclusionary forms of cosmopolitanism, see McKillop, "Local Attachment and Cosmopolitanism," 191–218, and Anderson, "Cosmopolitanism," 267–68.

16. Robbins, *Perpetual War*, 32.

17. Robbins, 14.

18. For an important take on the mismatch between empathy and action in literature, see Fisher, *Hard Facts*, 87–127.

19. Walls, "Cosmopolitical Project," 111.

20. Burke, *Writings and Speeches*, 8:97.

21. See Cicero, *De Officiis*, 1.15.46 to 1.18.60, pp. 49–63.

22. Long and Sedley, *Hellenistic Philosophers*, 1:349.

23. Long and Sedley, 1:349.

24. Forman-Barzilai, *Adam Smith*, 122.

25. Long and Sedley, *Hellenistic Philosophers*, 1:429.

26. M. Nussbaum, "Kant and Stoic Cosmopolitanism," 11.

27. Arsić, *On Leaving*, 9.

28. Burke, *Writings and Speeches*, 8:131, and Hazlitt, *Collected Works*, 11:20.

29. Emerson, *Complete Sermons*, 3:20–21.

30. Emerson, 2:45, 4:245.

31. See Lockridge, *Ethics of Romanticism*, 21; Van Cromphout, *Emerson's Ethics*, 30–32; and D. Howe, *Unitarian Conscience*, 7, 100–113.

32. See Brown, *Always Young for Liberty*, 168.

33. Francis Bowen cited in D. Howe, *Unitarian Conscience*, 112.

34. W. E. Channing, *Selected Writings*, 231.

35. W. E. Channing, *Works*, 3:21. See D. Howe, *Unitarian Conscience*, 151–60.

36. For Emerson's relation to Shaftesbury and other counter-Lockean Enlightenment thinkers, see Dolan, *Emerson's Liberalism*, 60–62.

37. Emerson, *Early Lectures*, 2:346.

38. See Beer, *Providence and Love*, 98–115.

39. See Delbanco, *William Ellery Channing*, 30–31, and Eckel, "'Empire of the Muse,'" 1–9 (quote 5).

40. Tappan, *Sermons*, 15. For the connection between Tappan and Channing, see Brown, *Always Young for Liberty*, 22.

41. W. H. Channing, *Life*, 60–61.

42. Mill, *Three Essays on Religion*, 81.

43. See Van Cromphout, *Emerson's Ethics*, 9.

44. C. Taylor, *Sources of the Self*, 21.

45. Kateb, *Emerson and Self-Reliance*, 76. See also Buell's account of self-reliance's "emotional austerity" in *Emerson* (70–73).

46. See also *JMN* 4:274.

47. Epictetus, in Carter, *All the Works of Epictetus*, XI, p. 288.

48. Addison, *Cato*, 83.

49. S. Johnson, *Yale Edition of the Works*, 16:70–76.

50. See R. Richardson, *Emerson*, 358–60. Richardson includes Louisa May Alcott's childhood recollection of calling at the Emerson house the day after Waldo's death: "his father came to me, so worn with watching and changed by sorrow that I was startled and could only stammer out my message. 'Child, he is dead' was the answer. That was my first glimpse of a great grief" (359).

51. Cameron, *Impersonality*, 54.

52. Epictetus, in Carter, *All the Works of Epictetus*, XI, p. 288.

53. See Bishop, *Emerson on the Soul*, 198, and Packer, *Emerson's Fall*, 168.

54. Epictetus, in Carter, *All the Works of Epictetus*, XI, p. 288.

55. R. Richardson, *Emerson*, 359.

56. Plutarch, *Morals*, 4:375. For Emerson's particular engagement with Plutarch's "Of Common Conceptions, against the Stoics," see *JMN* 5:368 and Berry, *Emerson's Plutarch*, 41, 235.

57. Plutarch, *Morals*, 4:374.

58. Plutarch, 4:374–75.

59. Plutarch, 4:374.

60. M. R. Wright, introduction to Cicero, *On Stoic Good and Evil*, 17–18.

61. Cameron, *Impersonality*, 70. See also Cameron's assertion that in Emerson's essays "contradictory propositions" are "the solvent that dissolves personality" (95).

62. Cicero, *On Stoic Good and Evil*, 77.

63. Poirier, *Renewal of Literature*, 192, 29.

64. Wallach points to Cicero's tendency to take "a Stoic method of reasoning and rhetoricize it," noting in particular that his arguments in the *Paradoxa Stoicorum* tend to rely more on emotion than logic. See "Rhetoric and Paradox," 176.

65. Packer, *Emerson's Fall*, 167.

66. Cameron, *Impersonality*, 107.

67. Robinson, *Emerson*, 3.

68. MacFarquhar, *Strangers Drowning*, 67.

69. Carlyle, *Sartor Resartus*, 146.

70. Whicher, *Freedom and Fate*, 139, 109 (quote).

71. Noah Porter Jr., "Ralph Waldo Emerson on the Conduct of Life," reprinted in Myerson, *Emerson and Thoreau*, 303.

72. Marcus Aurelius, *Meditations* (trans. Grube), 9.31, p. 93.

73. Emerson, *Emerson's Antislavery Writings*, 55.

74. Emerson, 92.

75. See Hanlon's convincing account of how Emerson's abolitionist discourse illuminates his attempt to reconsider "the virtues of cool distance" as well as "the 'cold-handed, cold-hearted' indifference from which he was in the process of resuscitating himself" (*Emerson's Memory Loss*, 46–85, quotes 78, 81).

76. Kant, *Perpetual Peace*, 146.

77. Thoreau, *Journal*, 1:26.

78. Sorabji, *Gandhi and the Stoics*, 2.

79. Emerson to Thomas Wentworth Higginson, July 18, 1864, cited in Higginson, "Personality of Emerson," 223.

80. Higginson, in Epictetus, *Works*, x. See also Sacks's brief account of Higginson and his sense of Stoicism "as a symbol of liberation" in "Stoicism in America" (336).

81. James, *Notes and Reviews*, 173–87, quote 179.

82. Higginson, "Personality of Emerson," 223.

BIBLIOGRAPHY

Abrams, M. H. *The Mirror and the Lamp*. New York: W.W. Norton, 1958.

———. "Structure and Style in the Greater Romantic Lyric." In *From Sensibility to Romanticism*, edited by Frederick Hilles and Harold Bloom, 527–60. Oxford: Oxford University Press, 1965.

Adams, James Eli. *Dandies and Desert Saints: Styles of Victorian Masculinity*. Ithaca, NY: Cornell University Press, 1995.

Adams, Robert. *The Roman Stamp: Frame and Facade in Some Forms of Neoclassicism*. Berkeley: University of California Press, 1974.

Addison, Joseph. *Cato: A Tragedy and Selected Essays*. Edited by Christine Dunn Henderson and Mark Yellin. Indianapolis: Liberty Fund, 2004.

Addison, Joseph, and Richard Steele. *The Spectator*. Edited by Donald Bond. 5 vols. Oxford: Clarendon, 1965.

Anderson, Amanda. "Cosmopolitanism, Universalism, and the Divided Legacies of Modernity." In *Cosmopolitics: Thinking and Feeling beyond the Nation*, edited by Pheng Cheah and Bruce Robbins, 265–89. Minneapolis: University of Minnesota Press, 1998.

———. *The Powers of Distance: Cosmopolitanism and the Cultivation of Detachment*. Princeton, NJ: Princeton University Press, 2001.

———. *The Way We Argue Now: A Study in the Cultures of Theory*. Princeton, NJ: Princeton University Press, 2006.

"Anecdotes of Persons Connected with the French Revolution." *Scots Magazine*, November 1796, 727–28.

Aravamudan, Srinivas. *Tropicopolitans: Colonialism and Agency, 1688–1804*. Durham, NC: Duke University Press, 1999.

Armstrong, Isobel. "The Gush of the Feminine: How Can We Read Women's Poetry of the Romantic Period?" In *Romantic Women Writers: Voices and Countervoices*, edited by Paula R. Feldman and Theresa M. Kelley, 13–32. Hanover: University Press of New England, 1995.

———. "Msrepresentation: Codes of Affect and Politics in Nineteenth-Century Women's Poetry." In *Women's Poetry, Late Romantic to Late Victorian: Gender and Genre, 1830–1900*, edited by Isobel Armstrong and Virginia Blain, 3–32. Basingstoke, UK: Macmillan, 1999.

Arnold, Matthew. *The Complete Prose Works of Matthew Arnold*. Edited by R. H. Super. 11 vols. Ann Arbor: University of Michigan Press, 1960–73.

Arsić, Branka. *On Leaving: A Reading in Emerson*. Cambridge, MA: Harvard University Press, 2010.

Augustine, *The City of God*. Edited and translated by R. W. Dyson. Cambridge: Cambridge University Press, 1998.

Austen, Jane. *Persuasion*. Edited by James Kinsley. Oxford: Oxford University Press, 2004.

Baker, Samuel. "Scott's Stoic Characters: Ethics, Sentiment, and Irony in *The Antiquary, Guy Mannering,* and 'The Author of *Waverley.*'" *MLQ: Modern Language Quarterly* 70, no. 4 (December 2009): 443–71.

Bakhtin, Mikhail. *Problems of Dostoevsky's Poetics.* Edited and translated by Caryl Emerson. Minneapolis: University of Minnesota Press, 1984.

Barrell, John. *English Literature in History, 1730–80: An Equal, Wide Survey.* London: Hutchinson, 1983.

Barton, Anne. *Landmarks of World Literature: Byron, Don Juan.* Cambridge: Cambridge University Press, 1992.

Batho, Edith. *The Later Wordsworth.* New York: Macmillan, 1933.

Baucom, Ian. *Specters of the Atlantic: Finance Capital, Slavery, and the Philosophy of History.* Durham, NC: Duke University Press, 2005.

Baudelaire, Charles. *Selected Writings on Art and Artists.* Edited by P. E. Charvet. Cambridge: Cambridge University Press, 1981.

Beattie, James. *Elements of Moral Science.* 2 vols. Edinburgh: T. Cadell, 1790.

Beaty, Frederick. "Byron's Imitations of Juvenal and Persius." *Studies in Romanticism* 15, no. 3 (Summer 1976): 333–55.

Beckford, Peter. *Thoughts upon Hunting, in a Series of Familiar Letters to a Friend.* Sarum [Salisbury, UK]: E. Easton, 1782.

Beer, John. *Providence and Love.* Oxford: Clarendon, 1998.

Behn, Aphra. *Oroonoko, and Other Writings.* Edited by Paul Salzman. Oxford: Oxford University Press, 1994.

Bell, Charles. *Essays on the Anatomy and Philosophy of Expression.* London: John Murray, 1824.

Bender, John. *Imagining the Penitentiary: Fiction and the Architecture of Mind in Eighteenth-Century England.* Chicago: University of Chicago Press, 1987.

Berlant, Lauren. *Cruel Optimism.* Durham, NC: Duke University Press, 2011.

Berry, Edmund G. *Emerson's Plutarch.* Cambridge, MA: Harvard University Press, 1961.

Bevilacqua, Alexander. "Conceiving the Republic of Mankind: The Political Thought of Anacharsis Cloots." *History of European Ideas* 38, no. 4 (December 2012): 550–69.

Bhabha, Homi. *The Location of Culture.* London: Routledge, 1994.

Bishop, Jonathan. *Emerson on the Soul.* Cambridge, MA: Harvard University Press, 1964.

Blake, William. *Blake's Poetry and Designs.* Edited by Mary Lynn Johnson and John E. Grant. New York: Norton, 2008.

Blessington, Marguerite. *Conversations of Lord Byron with the Countess of Blessington.* London: Henry Colburn, 1834.

Bloom, Harold. *The Anxiety of Influence: A Theory of Poetry.* Oxford: Oxford University Press, 1997.

———. *The Ringers in the Tower.* Chicago: University of Chicago Press, 1971.

Boswell, James. *The Life of Samuel Johnson.* Edited by David Womersley. London: Penguin, 2008.

Boyd, Elizabeth French. *Byron's Don Juan: A Critical Study.* New York: Humanities Press, 1958.

Boyson, Rowan. *Wordsworth and the Enlightenment Idea of Pleasure.* Cambridge: Cambridge University Press, 2012.

Brennan, Tad. *The Stoic Life: Emotions, Duty, and Fate.* Oxford: Clarendon, 2005.

Brooke, Christopher. *Philosophic Pride: Stoicism and Political Thought from Lipsius to Rousseau*. Princeton, NJ: Princeton University Press, 2012.
Brown, Arthur. *Always Young for Liberty: A Biography of William Ellery Channing*. Syracuse, NY: Syracuse University Press, 1956.
Buchan, William. *Domestic Medicine, or The Family Physician*. Cambridge: Cambridge University Press, 2014.
Buell, Lawrence. *Emerson*. Cambridge, MA: Harvard University Press, 2003.
Burke, Edmund. *The Writings and Speeches of Edmund Burke*. Edited by Paul Langford. 9 vols. Oxford: Oxford University Press, 1989–2015.
Burton, Robert. *Anatomy of Melancholy*. Edited by Holbrook Jackson. New York: New York Review Books, 2001.
Butler, Judith. *Gender Trouble: Feminism and the Subversion of Identity*. New York: Routledge, 2006.
Byron, George Gordon. *Byron's Letters and Journals*. Edited by Leslie Marchand. 13 vols. Cambridge, MA: Harvard University Press, 1973–94.
———. *The Complete Miscellaneous Prose*. Edited by Andrew Nicholson. Oxford: Clarendon, 1991.
———. *The Complete Poetical Works*. Edited by Jerome McGann. 7 vols. Oxford: Clarendon, 1980–93.
———. *Don Juan*. Edited by T. G. Steffan, E. Steffan, and W. W. Pratt. London: Penguin, 2004.
———. *The Works of Lord Byron*. Edited by William Ernest Henley. London: William Heinemann, 1897.
Cameron, Sharon. *Impersonality: Seven Essays*. Chicago: University of Chicago Press, 2007.
Canuel, Mark. "Romantic Fear." In *Secularism, Cosmopolitanism and Romanticism*, edited by Colin Jager. Romantic Circles Praxis Series. Romantic Circles, August 2008. https://romantic-circles.org/praxis/secularism/canuel/canuel.html.
———. *The Shadow of Death: Literature, Romanticism, and the Subject of Punishment*. Princeton, NJ: Princeton University Press, 2007.
Carlson, Julie A. *England's First Family of Writers*. Baltimore, MD: Johns Hopkins University Press, 2007.
Carlyle, Thomas. *Sartor Resartus*. Edited by Kerry McSweeney and Peter Sabor. Oxford: Oxford University Press, 1987.
Carlyle, Thomas, and Jane Welsh Carlyle. *The Carlyle Letters Online*. Edited by Brent E. Kinser. Durham, NC: Duke University Press, 2007–16. https://carlyleletters.dukeupress.edu/home.
Carter, Elizabeth. *All the Works of Epictetus*. Edited by Judith Hawley. Vol. 2 of *Bluestocking Feminism: Writings of the Bluestocking Circle, 1738–1785*. Edited by Gary Kelly. 6 vols. London: Pickering and Chatto, 1999.
Caruth, Cathy. *Unclaimed Experience: Trauma, Narrative, History*. Baltimore, MD: Johns Hopkins University Press, 1996.
Cassirer, Ernst. *The Myth of the State*. New Haven, CT: Yale University Press, 1966.
Castell, James. "William Wordsworth." In *The Oxford History of Classical Reception in English Literature*, vol. 4, edited by Norman Vance and Jennifer Wallace, 325–46. Oxford: Oxford University Press, 2015.

Cavell, Stanley. *Emerson's Transcendental Etudes*. Edited by David Justin Hodge. Stanford, CA: Stanford University Press, 2003.

———. *In Quest of the Ordinary*. Chicago: University of Chicago Press, 1988.

Chai, Leon. *The Romantic Foundations of the American Renaissance*. Ithaca, NY: Cornell University Press, 1987.

Chandler, James. *An Archaeology of Sympathy: The Sentimental Mode in Literature and Cinema*. Chicago: University of Chicago Press, 2013.

———. "The Pope Controversy: Romantic Poetics and the English Canon." *Critical Inquiry* 10, no. 3 (March 1984): 481–509.

———. *Wordsworth's Second Nature: A Study of the Poetry and Politics*. Chicago: University of Chicago Press, 1984.

Channing, William Ellery. *William Ellery Channing: Selected Writings*. Edited by David Robinson. New York: Paulist, 1985.

———. *The Works of William Ellery Channing*. 6 vols. Boston, MA: American Unitarian Association, 1903.

Channing, William Henry. *The Life of William Ellery Channing, D.D.* Boston, MA: American Unitarian Association, 1899.

Cheeke, Stephen. "Byron and the Horatian Commonplace." *Byron Journal* 36, no. 1 (June 2008): 5–17.

———. "'What So Many Have Told, Who Would Tell Again?': Romanticism and the Commonplaces of Rome." *European Romantic Review* 17, no. 5 (December 2006): 521–41.

Christensen, Jerome. *Lord Byron's Strength: Romantic Writing and Commercial Society*. Baltimore, MD: Johns Hopkins University Press, 1993.

Cicero. *De Officiis*. Translated by Walter Miller. Cambridge, MA: Harvard University Press, 1913.

———. *On Moral Ends*. Edited by Julia Annas. Translated by Raphael Woolf. Cambridge: Cambridge University Press, 2001.

———. *On Stoic Good and Evil: "De Finibus" 3 and "Paradoxa Stoicorum."* Translated by M. R. Wright. Warminster, UK: Aris and Phillips, 1991.

———. *Tusculan Disputations*. Translated by J. E. King. Cambridge, MA: Harvard University Press, 1960.

Clemit, Pamela. *The Godwinian Novel*. Oxford: Clarendon, 1993.

Clery, E. J. *Eighteen Hundred and Eleven: Poetry, Protest, and Economic Crisis*. Cambridge: Cambridge University Press, 2017.

Cohen-Vrignaud, Gerard. "Love Actually: On Affect Theory and Romantic Studies." *Wordsworth Circle* 51, no. 3 (Summer 2020): 300–321.

Cohn, Elisha. *Still Life: Suspended Development in the Victorian Novel*. Oxford: Oxford University Press, 2016.

Coleridge, Samuel Taylor. *Aids to Reflection*. Edited by John Beer. Vol. 9 of *The Collected Works of Samuel Taylor Coleridge*. Princeton, NJ: Princeton University Press, 1993.

———. *Biographia Literaria*. Edited by James Engell and W. Jackson Bate. 2 vols. Vol. 7 of *The Collected Works of Samuel Taylor Coleridge*. Princeton, NJ: Princeton University Press, 1983.

———. *Coleridge's Notebooks: A Selection*. Edited by Seamus Perry. Oxford: Oxford University Press, 2002.

———. *Collected Letters of Samuel Taylor Coleridge*. Edited by Earl Griggs. 6 vols. Oxford: Clarendon, 1956–71.

———. *The Friend*. Edited by Barbara Rooke. 2 vols. Vol. 4 of *The Collected Works of Samuel Taylor Coleridge*. Princeton, NJ: Princeton University Press, 1969.

———. *Lay Sermons*. Edited by R. J. White. Vol. 6 of *The Collected Works of Samuel Taylor Coleridge*. Princeton, NJ: Princeton University Press, 1972.

———. *Lectures 1795: On Politics and Religion*. Edited by Lewis Patton and Peter Mann. Vol. 1 of *The Collected Works of Samuel Taylor Coleridge*. Princeton, NJ: Princeton University Press, 1971.

———. *Lectures 1818–1819: On the History of Philosophy*. Edited by James Robert de Jager Jackson. 2 vols. Vol. 8 of *The Collected Works of Samuel Taylor Coleridge*. Princeton, NJ: Princeton University Press, 2000.

———. *Marginalia*. Edited by H. J. Jackson and George Whalley. 6 vols. Vol. 12 of *The Collected Works of Samuel Taylor Coleridge*. Princeton, NJ: Princeton University Press, 1980–2001.

———. *The Notebooks of Samuel Taylor Coleridge*. Edited by Kathleen Coburn, Merton Christensen, and Anthony John Harding. 5 vols. Princeton, NJ: Princeton University Press, 1957–2002.

———. *Opus Maximum*. Edited by Thomas McFarland. Vol. 15 of *The Collected Works of Samuel Taylor Coleridge*. Princeton, NJ: Princeton University Press, 2002.

———. *Poetical Works*. Edited by J.C.C. Mays. 6 vols. Vol. 16 of *The Collected Works of Samuel Taylor Coleridge*. Princeton, NJ: Princeton University Press, 2001.

———. *Shorter Works and Fragments*. Edited by H. J. Jackson and James Robert de Jager Jackson. 2 vols. Vol. 11 of *The Collected Works of Samuel Taylor Coleridge*. Princeton, NJ: Princeton University Press, 1995.

———. *Specimens of the Table Talk of Samuel Taylor Coleridge*. Edited by Henry Nelson Coleridge. London: John Murray, 1851.

———. *Table Talk*. Edited by Carl Woodring. 2 vols. Vol. 14 of *The Collected Works of Samuel Taylor Coleridge*. Princeton, NJ: Princeton University Press, 1990.

Colish, Marcia. "Stoicism and the New Testament: An Essay in Historiography." *Aufstieg und Niedergang der romischen Welt* (*ANRW*), II, 26, no. 2 (1992): 334–79.

Colley, Linda. *Captives: Britain, Empire, and the World, 1660–1850*. New York: Anchor Books, 2002.

Combe, William. *The Tour of Doctor Syntax: In Search of the Picturesque: A Poem*. London: R. Ackermann's Repository of Arts, 1812.

Connor, Steven. *Giving Way: Thoughts on Unappreciated Dispositions*. Stanford, CA: Stanford University Press, 2019.

Cooke, George Willis. "Emerson's View of Nationality." In *The Genius and Character of Emerson: Lectures at the Concord School of Philosophy*, edited by F. B Sanborn, 310–38. Boston, MA: J. R. Osgood, 1885.

Cooke, Michael. *The Blind Man Traces the Circle: On the Patterns and Philosophy of Byron's Poetry*. Princeton, NJ: Princeton University Press, 1969.

———. *The Romantic Will*. New Haven, CT: Yale University Press, 1976.

Cooper, John. "Justus Lipsius and the Revival of Stoicism in Late Sixteenth-Century Europe." In *New Essays on the History of Autonomy*, edited by Natalie Brender and Larry Krasnoff, 7–29. Cambridge: Cambridge University Press, 2004.

Cox, Jeffrey N. *Romanticism in the Shadow of War: Literary Culture in the Napoleonic War Years*. Cambridge: Cambridge University Press, 2014.
Crane, Gregg D. *Race, Citizenship, and Law in American Literature*. Cambridge: Cambridge University Press, 2002.
Cudworth, Ralph. *The True Intellectual System of the Universe*. Translated by John Harrison. 3 vols. London: Thomas Tegg, 1845.
Culler, Jonathan. *Theory of the Lyric*. Cambridge, MA: Harvard University Press, 2015.
Davidson, Jenny. *Hypocrisy and the Politics of Politeness: Manners and Morals from Locke to Austen*. Cambridge: Cambridge University Press, 2004.
Delbanco, Andrew. *William Ellery Channing: An Essay on the Liberal Spirit in America*. Cambridge, MA: Harvard University Press, 1981.
De Quincey, Thomas. *The Works of Thomas De Quincey*. Edited by Grevel Lindop. 21 vols. London: Pickering and Chatto, 2003.
Dolan, Neal. *Emerson's Liberalism*. Madison: University of Wisconsin Press, 2009.
Duff, David. *Romanticism and the Uses of Genre*. Oxford: Oxford University Press, 2009.
Duncan, Ian. *Scott's Shadow: The Novel in Romantic Edinburgh*. Princeton, NJ: Princeton University Press, 2007.
Eckel, Leslie. "'Empire of the Muse': American Encounters with Wordsworth." *Literature Compass* 1, no. 1 (2004). https://doi.org/10.1111/j.1741-4113.2004.00134.x.
Edelstein, Dan. *On the Spirit of Rights*. Chicago: University of Chicago Press, 2019.
Eisler, Benita. *Byron: Child of Passion, Fool of Fame*. New York: Vintage, 2000.
Elfenbein, Andrew. *Byron and the Victorians*. Cambridge: Cambridge University Press, 1995.
Eliot, George. *Middlemarch*. Edited by David Carroll. Oxford: Oxford University Press, 1996.
———. *Middlemarch Notebooks: A Transcription*. Edited by John Clark Pratt and Victor Neufeldt. Berkeley: University of California Press, 1979.
Eliot, T. S. *Selected Essays, 1917–1932*. New York: Harcourt, Brace, 1950.
Ellison, Julie. *Cato's Tears and the Making of Anglo-American Emotion*. Chicago: University of Chicago Press, 1999.
Elmer, Jonathan. *On Lingering and Being Last: Race and Sovereignty in the New World*. New York: Fordham University Press, 2008.
Emerson, Ralph Waldo. *The Collected Works of Ralph Waldo Emerson*. Edited by Robert E. Spiller, Alfred R. Ferguson, Joseph Slater, Jean Ferguson Carr, Wallace E. Williams, Douglas Emory Wilson, Philip Nicoloff, et al. 10 vols. Cambridge, MA: Harvard University Press, 1971–2013.
———. *The Complete Sermons of Ralph Waldo Emerson*. Edited by Albert J. von Frank, Teresa Toulouse, Andrew Delbanco, Ronald A. Bosco, and Wesley T. Mott. 4 vols. Columbia: University of Missouri Press, 1989–92.
———. *The Early Lectures of Ralph Waldo Emerson*. Edited by Robert Spiller, Stephen Whicher, and Wallace Williams. 3 vols. Cambridge, MA: Harvard University Press, 1959–72.
———. *Emerson's Antislavery Writings*. Edited by Len Gougeon and Joel Myerson. New Haven, CT: Yale University Press, 1995.

---. *The Journals and Miscellaneous Notebooks of Ralph Waldo Emerson*. Edited by William H. Gilman, Alfred R. Ferguson, George P. Clark, Merrell R. Davis, Merton M. Sealts, Jr., Ralph H. Orth, A. W. Plumstead, et al. 16 vols. Cambridge, MA: Harvard University Press, 1960–82.

Enfield, William. *The History of Philosophy from the Earliest Times to the Beginning of the Present Century; Drawn Up from Brucker's Historia Critica Philosophiae*. 2 vols. Dublin: P. Wogan, P. Byrne, A. Grueber, W. McKenzie, J. Moore, J. Jones, R. McAllister, W. Jones, J. Rice, R. White, and G. Draper, 1792.

Engell, James. *The Creative Imagination*. Cambridge, MA: Harvard University Press, 1981.

Epictetus. *The Works of Epictetus, Consisting of His "Discourses" in Four Books, "The Enchiridion," and "Fragments": A Translation from the Greek Based on That of Elizabeth Carter*. Translated by Thomas Wentworth Higginson. Boston: Little, Brown, 1865.

Faflak, Joel, and Richard C. Sha, eds. *Romanticism and the Emotions*. Cambridge: Cambridge University Press, 2014.

Fairclough, Mary. *The Romantic Crowd: Sympathy, Controversy, and Print Culture*. Cambridge: Cambridge University Press, 2013.

Faubert, Michelle. *Rhyming Reason: The Poetry of Romantic-Era Psychologists*. London: Pickering and Chatto, 2009.

Favret, Mary. "The General Fast and Humiliation: Tracking Feeling in Wartime." In *Romanticism and the Emotions*, edited by Joel Faflak and Richard Sha, 124–46. Cambridge: Cambridge University Press, 2014.

---. "The Study of Affect and Romanticism." *Literature Compass* 6, no. 6 (2009): 1159–66. https://doi.org/10.1111/j.1741-4113.2009.00666.x.

---. *War at a Distance: Romanticism and the Making of Modern Wartime*. Princeton, NJ: Princeton University Press, 2010.

Felski, Rita. *The Limits of Critique*. Chicago: University of Chicago Press, 2015.

Ferguson, Frances. *Language as Counter-Spirit*. New Haven, CT: Yale University Press, 1977.

Festa, Lynn. *Sentimental Figures of Empire in Eighteenth-Century Britain and France*. Baltimore, MD: Johns Hopkins University Press, 2006.

Field, Barron. *Barron Field's Memoirs of Wordsworth*. Edited by Geoffrey Little. Sydney: Sydney University Press, 1975.

Fielding, Henry. *Tom Jones*. New York: Barnes and Noble Classics, 2004.

Finseth, Ian. "Evolution, Cosmopolitanism, and Emerson's Antislavery Politics." *American Literature* 77, no. 4 (December 2005): 729–60.

Fisher, Philip. *Hard Facts: Setting and Form in the American Novel*. Oxford: Oxford University Press, 1985.

---. *Wonder, the Rainbow, and the Aesthetics of Rare Experiences*. Cambridge, MA: Harvard University Press, 1998.

Ford, Jennifer. *Coleridge on Dreaming: Romanticism, Dreams, and the Medical Imagination*. Cambridge: Cambridge University Press, 1998.

Forman-Barzilai, Fonna. *Adam Smith and the Circles of Sympathy: Cosmopolitanism and Moral Theory*. Cambridge: Cambridge University Press, 2010.

Foucault, Michel. *The Care of the Self*. Translated by Robert Hurley. New York: Vintage, 1986.

———. *Technologies of the Self*. Edited by Luther Martin, Huck Gutman, and Patrick Hutton. Amherst: University of Massachusetts Press, 1988.

Fox, Charles James. *Speeches during the French Revolution*. London: J. M. Dent and Sons, 1924.

Francis, James A. *Subversive Virtue: Asceticism and Authority in the Second-Century Pagan World*. University Park: Pennsylvania State University Press, 1995.

François, Anne-Lise. *Open Secrets: The Literature of Uncounted Experience*. Stanford, CA: Stanford University Press, 2008.

Franklin, Caroline. *Byron's Heroines*. Oxford: Clarendon, 1992.

Fry, Paul. *Wordsworth and the Poetry of What We Are*. New Haven, CT: Yale University Press, 2008.

Frye, Northrop. "Towards Defining an Age of Sensibility." *ELH* 23, no. 2 (June 1956): 144–52.

Furst, Lillian. *Romanticism in Perspective*. New York: Humanities Press, 1970.

Galperin, William. *The Historical Austen*. Philadelphia: University of Pennsylvania Press, 2003.

———. *The History of Missed Opportunities: British Romanticism and the Emergence of the Everyday*. Stanford, CA: Stanford University Press, 2017.

Garnsey, Peter. *Ideas of Slavery from Aristotle to Augustine*. Cambridge: Cambridge University Press, 1996.

Garrod, H. W. *Wordsworth: Lectures and Essays*. Oxford: Clarendon, 1923.

Garvey, T. Gregory. "Simular Man: Emerson and Cosmopolitan Identity." In *Emerson for the Twenty-First Century: Global Perspectives on an American Icon*, edited by Barry Tharaud, 513–42. Newark: University of Delaware Press, 2010.

Gataker, Thomas. "Preliminary Discourse." In *The Emperor Marcus Antoninus: His Conversation with Himself*, translated by Jeremy Collier, 1–35. London: Richard Sare, 1708.

Gay, Peter. *The Enlightenment: An Interpretation, the Rise of Modern Paganism*. New York: Alfred A. Knopf, 1967.

Genette, Gérard. "Introduction to the Paratext." *New Literary History* 22, no. 2 (Spring 1991): 261–72.

Gerard, Albert. "The Systolic Rhythm: The Structure of Coleridge's Conversation Poems." *Essays in Criticism* 10, no. 3 (July 1960): 307–19.

Godwin, William. *Collected Novels and Memoirs of William Godwin*. Edited by Mark Philp. 8 vols. London: Pickering and Chatto, 1992.

———. *The Political and Philosophical Writings of William Godwin*. Edited by Mark Philp. 7 vols. London: Pickering and Chatto, 1993.

Goldsmith, Oliver. *Collected Works of Oliver Goldsmith*. Edited by Arthur Friedman. 5 vols. Oxford: Clarendon, 1966.

Goldsmith, Steven. *Blake's Agitation: Criticism and the Emotions*. Baltimore, MD: Johns Hopkins University Press, 2013.

Gonda, Caroline. "*Lodore* and Fanny Derham's Story." *Women's Writing* 6, no. 3 (1999): 329–44.

Goodman, Kevis. *Georgic Modernity and British Romanticism*. Cambridge: Cambridge University Press, 2004.

Graham, Kenneth. *William Godwin Reviewed: A Reception History, 1783–1834*. New York: AMS, 2001.
Graver, Bruce. "Duncan Wu's *Wordsworth's Reading, 1770–1799*: A Supplementary List with Corrections." *Romanticism on the Net*, no. 1 (February 1996). https://doi.org/10.7202/005711ar.
———. "Romanticism." In *A Companion to the Classical Tradition*, edited by Craig W. Kallendorf, 72–86. Malden, MA: Blackwell, 2007.
———. "Wordsworth and the Stoics." In *Romans and Romantics*, edited by Timothy Saunders, Charles Martindale, Ralph Pite, and Mathilde Skoie, 145–60. Oxford: Oxford University Press, 2012.
Graver, Margaret. *Stoicism and Emotion*. Chicago: University of Chicago Press, 2007.
Gray, Erik. *The Poetry of Indifference from the Romantics to the Rubáiyát*. Amherst: University of Massachusetts Press, 2005.
Greenham, David. *Emerson's Transatlantic Romanticism*. Basingstoke, UK: Palgrave Macmillan, 2012.
Gregg, Melissa, and Gregory Seigworth, eds. *The Affect Theory Reader*. Durham, NC: Duke University Press, 2010.
Greiner, Rae. *Sympathetic Realism in Nineteenth-Century British Fiction*. Baltimore, MD: Johns Hopkins University Press, 2012.
Griffin, Robert. *Wordsworth's Pope: A Study in Literary Historiography*. Cambridge: Cambridge University Press, 1995.
Griswold, Charles. *Adam Smith and the Virtues of Enlightenment*. Cambridge: Cambridge University Press, 1999.
Guest, Harriet. "Bluestocking Feminism." In *Reconsidering the Bluestockings*, edited by Nicole Pohl and Betty Schellenberg, 59–80. San Marino, CA: Huntington Library, 2003.
———. *Small Change: Women, Learning, Patriotism, 1750–1810*. Chicago: University of Chicago Press, 2000.
Guiccioli, Teresa. *Lord Byron's Life in Italy*. Translated by Michael Rees. Edited by Peter Cochran. Newark: University of Delaware Press, 2005.
Gurton-Wachter, Lily. *Watchwords: Romanticism and the Poetics of Attention*. Stanford, CA: Stanford University Press, 2016.
Hack, Daniel. *Reaping Something New: African American Transformations of Victorian Literature*. Princeton, NJ: Princeton University Press, 2017.
Hadot, Pierre. *The Inner Citadel: The "Meditations" of Marcus Aurelius*. Translated by Michael Chase. Cambridge, MA: Harvard University Press, 1998.
———. *Philosophy as a Way of Life: Spiritual Exercises from Socrates to Foucault*. Edited by Arnold Davidson. Translated by Michael Chase. Oxford: Blackwell, 1995.
Hanlon, Christopher. *Emerson's Memory Loss: Originality, Communality, and the Late Style*. Oxford: Oxford University Press, 2018.
Harding, Anthony John. *Coleridge and the Idea of Love*. Cambridge: Cambridge University Press, 1974.
Hartman, Geoffrey. *Wordsworth's Poetry 1797–1814*. New Haven, CT: Yale University Press, 1964.
Harvey, Samantha C. *Transatlantic Transcendentalism: Coleridge, Emerson, and Nature*. Edinburgh: University of Edinburgh Press, 2013.

Hawley, Judith. "Carter, Elizabeth." In *Oxford Dictionary of National Biography*, September 23, 2004, last updated May 21, 2009, https://doi.org/10.1093/ref:odnb/4782.

Hayot, Eric. *The Hypothetical Mandarin: Sympathy, Modernity and Chinese Pain*. Oxford: Oxford University Press, 2009.

Hazlitt, William. *Collected Works of William Hazlitt*. Edited by P. P. Howe. 21 vols. London: J. M. Dent and Sons, 1933.

Hegel, G.W.F. *Aesthetics: Lectures on Fine Art*. Translated by T. M. Knox. 2 vols. Oxford: Clarendon, 1975.

———. *The Phenomenology of Mind*. Translated by J. B. Baillie. Mineola, NY: Dover, 2003.

Hickman, Jared. *Black Prometheus: Race and Radicalism in the Age of Atlantic Slavery*. Oxford: Oxford University Press, 2017.

Higginson, Thomas Wentworth. "The Personality of Emerson." *Outlook* 73, no. 4 (May 23, 1903): 221–27.

Hill, Bridget. "A Tale of Two Sisters: The Contrasting Careers and Ambitions of Elizabeth Montagu and Sarah Scott." *Women's History Review* 19, no. 2 (March 2010): 215–29.

Hirschman, Albert. *The Passions and the Interests*. Princeton, NJ: Princeton University Press, 1977.

Hobbes, Thomas. *Leviathan*. Edited by A. P. Martinich and Brian Battiste. Peterborough, ON: Broadview, 2011.

Holmes, Richard. *Coleridge: Early Visions, 1772–1804*. New York: Pantheon Books, 1989.

Horace. *Satires, Epistles, and Ars Poetica*. Translated by H. Rushton Fairclough. Cambridge, MA: Harvard University Press, 1926.

Howe, Anthony. *Byron and the Forms of Thought*. Liverpool: Liverpool University Press, 2013.

Howe, Daniel Walker. *The Unitarian Conscience*. Cambridge, MA: Harvard University Press, 1970.

Hume, David. *Essays Moral and Political*. 2 vols. Edinburgh: A. Kincaid, 1742.

———. *Essays: Moral, Political, and Literary*. Edited by Eugene Miller. Indianapolis: Liberty Fund, 1987.

———. *The Letters of David Hume*. Edited by J.Y.T. Greig. 2 vols. Oxford: Clarendon, 1932.

———. *A Treatise of Human Nature*. Edited by David Fate Norton and Mary J. Norton. Oxford: Oxford University Press, 2000.

Hutcheson, Francis, and James Moor, trans. *The "Meditations" of the Emperor Marcus Aurelius Antoninus*. Edited by James Moore and Michael Silverthorne. Indianapolis: Liberty Fund, 2008.

Jackson, Virginia. *Dickinson's Misery*. Princeton, NJ: Princeton University Press, 2005.

Jackson, Virginia, and Yopie Prins, eds. *The Lyric Theory Reader: A Critical Anthology*. Baltimore, MD: Johns Hopkins University Press, 2014.

Jaffro, Laurent, Christian Maurer, and Alain Petit. "Pathologia, A Theory of the Passions." *History of European Ideas* 39, no. 2 (2013): 221–40.

James, Henry. *Notes and Reviews*. Cambridge, MA: Dunster House Bookshop, 1921.

Jarvis, Simon. *Wordsworth's Philosophic Song*. Cambridge: Cambridge University Press, 2007.

Johnson, Barbara. *A Life with Mary Shelley*. Stanford, CA: Stanford University Press, 2014.
Johnson, Claudia. *Equivocal Beings: Politics, Gender, and Sentimentality in the 1790s*. Chicago: University of Chicago Press, 1995.
Johnson, Samuel. *The Yale Edition of the Works of Samuel Johnson*. Edited by E. L. McAdam Jr., W. J. Bate, J. M. Bullitt, L. F. Powell, A. B. Strauss, A. Sherbo, M. Lascelles, et. al. 23 vols. New Haven, CT: Yale University Press, 1958–2018.
Johnston, Kenneth. *Unusual Suspects: Pitt's Reign of Alarm and the Lost Generation of the 1790s*. Oxford: Oxford University Press, 2013.
———. *Wordsworth and "The Recluse."* New Haven, CT: Yale University Press, 1984.
Jones, Chris. *Radical Sensibility*. London: Routledge, 1993.
Jones, Ewan James. *Coleridge and the Philosophy of Poetic Form*. Cambridge: Cambridge University Press, 2014.
Justman, Stewart. *The Autonomous Male of Adam Smith*. Norman: University of Oklahoma Press, 1993.
Kames, Henry Home. *Essays on the Principles of Morality and Natural Religion*. Edited by Mary Catherine Moran. Indianapolis: Liberty Fund, 2005.
Kant, Immanuel. *Critique of Practical Reason*. Translated and edited by Mary Gregor. Cambridge: Cambridge University Press, 1997.
———. *Lectures on Ethics*. Edited by Peter Heath and J. B. Schneewind. Translated by Peter Heath. In *The Cambridge Edition of the Works of Immanuel Kant*, edited by Paul Guyer and Allen W. Wood. Cambridge: Cambridge University Press, 1997.
———. *Perpetual Peace*. Translated by M. Campbell Smith. London: George Allen and Unwin, 1917.
Kateb, George. *Emerson and Self-Reliance*. Thousand Oaks, CA: Sage, 1995.
Kay, Carol. "Canon, Ideology, and Gender: Mary Wollstonecraft's Critique of Adam Smith." *New Political Science* 7, no. 1 (1996): 63–76.
Keats, John. *Selected Letters*. Edited by Robert Gittings and Jon Mee. Oxford: Oxford University Press, 2002.
Klausen, Jimmy Casas. *Fugitive Rousseau: Slavery, Primitivism and Political Freedom*. New York: Fordham University Press, 2014.
Klein, Lawrence. *Shaftesbury and the Culture of Politeness: Moral Discourse and Cultural Politics in Early Eighteenth-Century England*. Cambridge: Cambridge University Press, 1994.
Kojève, Alexandre. *Introduction to the Reading of Hegel*. Edited by Allan Bloom. Translated by James Nichols Jr. Ithaca, NY: Cornell University Press, 1969.
Koselleck, Reinhart. *Futures Past: On the Semantics of Historical Time*. Translated by Keith Tribe. Cambridge, MA: MIT Press, 1985.
Lake, Crystal B. "Redecorating the Ruin: Women and Antiquarianism in Sarah Scott's *Millenium Hall*." *ELH* 76, no. 3 (Fall 2009): 661–86.
Lamb, Charles. *Essays of Elia*. Iowa City: University of Iowa Press, 2003.
Landor, Walter Savage. *Poems, Dialogues in Verse, and Epigrams*. Edited by Charles G. Crump. London: J. M. Dent, 1892.
———. *Imaginary Conversations*. Edited by Charles G. Crump. 6 vols. London: J. M. Dent, 1891.
Lansdown, Richard. "Byron's Relativism." *Critical Review* 37 (January 1997): 96–118.

Lanser, Susan. "Tory Lesbians: Economies of Intimacy and the Status of Desire." In *Lesbian Dames: Sapphism in the Long Eighteenth Century*, edited by John C. Benyon and Caroline Gonda, 173–89. Farnham, UK: Ashgate, 2010.

Leask, Nigel. *British Romantic Writers and the East*. Cambridge: Cambridge University Press, 1992.

Lee, Wendy. *Failures of Feeling: Insensibility and the Novel*. Stanford, CA: Stanford University Press, 2019.

Locke, Don. *A Fantasy of Reason: The Life and Thought of William Godwin*. London: Routledge and Kegan Paul, 1980.

Lockridge, Laurence. *The Ethics of Romanticism*. Cambridge: Cambridge University Press, 1989.

Long, A. A. *Epictetus: A Stoic and Socratic Guide to Life*. Oxford: Clarendon, 2002.

———. *Stoic Studies*. Berkeley: University of California Press, 1996.

Long, A. A., and D. N. Sedley, eds. *The Hellenistic Philosophers: Translations of the Principal Sources with Philosophical Commentary*. 2 vols. Cambridge: Cambridge University Press, 1987.

Lovejoy, Arthur. "Coleridge and Kant's Two Worlds." *ELH* 7, no. 4 (December 1940): 341–62.

Lynch, Deidre Shauna. *The Economy of Character: Novels, Market Culture, and the Business of Inner Meaning*. Chicago: University of Chicago Press, 1998.

Macaulay, Catherine. *Letters on Education, with Observations on Religious and Metaphysical Subjects*. Cambridge: Cambridge University Press, 2014.

Macaulay, Thomas Babington. *Critical and Historical Essays*. 3 vols. London: Longman, Brown, Green, and Longmans, 1848.

MacCarthy, Fiona. *Byron: Life and Legend*. London: John Murray, 2002.

MacFarquhar, Larissa. *Strangers Drowning: Grappling with Impossible Idealism, Drastic Choices, and the Overpowering Urge to Help*. New York: Penguin, 2015.

Maclear, J. F. *Church and State in the Modern Age: A Documentary History*. Oxford: Oxford University Press, 1995.

MacLeish, Archibald. *Collected Poems, 1917–1982*. Boston, MA: Houghton Mifflin, 1985.

Mandeville, Bernard. *"The Fable of the Bees" and Other Writings*. Edited by E. J. Hundert. Indianapolis: Hackett, 1997.

Manning, Peter J. *Byron and His Fictions*. Detroit, MI: Wayne State University Press, 1978.

Manning, Susan. *Poetics of Character: Transatlantic Encounters, 1700–1900*. Cambridge: Cambridge University Press, 2013.

Marcus Aurelius. *The Meditations*. Translated by G.M.A. Grube. Indianapolis: Hackett, 1983.

Marshall, David. *The Figure of Theater: Shaftesbury, Defoe, Adam Smith, and George Eliot*. New York: Columbia University Press, 1986.

Massumi, Brian. *Parables for the Virtual: Movement, Affect, Sensation*. Durham, NC: Duke University Press, 2002.

Mays, J.C.C. *Coleridge's Experimental Poetics*. New York: Palgrave Macmillan, 2013.

McCarter, Stephanie. *Horace between Freedom and Slavery*. Madison: University of Wisconsin Press, 2015.

McCarthy, William. *Anna Letitia Barbauld: Voice of the Enlightenment*. Baltimore, MD: Johns Hopkins University Press, 2008.

McFarland, Thomas. *Romanticism and the Forms of Ruin*. Princeton, NJ: Princeton University Press, 1981.
McGann, Jerome. *The Beauty of Inflections: Literary Investigations in Historical Method & Theory*. Oxford: Clarendon, 1985.
———. *Byron and Romanticism*. Edited by James Soderholm. Cambridge: Cambridge University Press, 2002.
———. *Don Juan in Context*. Chicago: University of Chicago Press, 1976.
———. *Towards a Literature of Knowledge*. Chicago: University of Chicago Press, 1989.
McInnes, Andrew. *Wollstonecraft's Ghost: The Fate of the Female Philosopher in the Romantic Period*. Abingdon, UK: Routledge, 2017.
McKeon, Michael. *The Secret History of Domesticity: Public, Private, and the Division of Knowledge*. Baltimore, MD: Johns Hopkins University Press, 2005.
McKillop, Alan. "Local Attachment and Cosmopolitanism: The Eighteenth-Century Pattern." In *From Sensibility to Romanticism*, edited by Frederick W. Hilles and Harold Bloom, 191–218. Oxford: Oxford University Press, 1965.
Medwin, Thomas. *Journal of the Conversations of Lord Byron*. London: Henry Colburn, 1824.
Mee, Jon. *Conversable Worlds: Literature, Contention, and Community, 1762 to 1830*. Oxford: Oxford University Press, 2011.
———. *Romanticism, Enthusiasm, and Regulation: Poetics and the Policing of Culture in the Romantic Period*. Oxford: Oxford University Press, 2003.
Mellor, Anne. *Mary Shelley: Her Life, Her Fiction, Her Monsters*. New York: Routledge, 1988.
Michael, Timothy. *British Romanticism and the Critique of Political Reason*. Baltimore, MD: Johns Hopkins University Press, 2016.
Mill, John Stuart. *Three Essays on Religion*. Edited by Louis J. Matz. Peterborough, ON: Broadview, 2009.
Miller, Perry. "From Edwards to Emerson." *New England Quarterly* 13, no. 4 (December 1940): 589–617.
Millingen, J. G. *Recollections of Republican France, from 1790 to 1801*. London: Henry Colburn, 1848.
Mitchell, John. *Biographies of Eminent Soldiers of the Last Four Centuries*. Edited by Leonhard Schmitz. Edinburgh: William Blackwood and Sons, 1865.
Mole, Tom. *Byron's Romantic Celebrity: Industrial Culture and the Hermeneutic of Intimacy*. Basingstoke, UK: Palgrave Macmillan, 2007.
Molesky, Mark. *This Gulf of Fire: The Destruction of Lisbon, or Apocalypse in the Age of Science and Reason*. New York: Alfred Knopf, 2015.
Montagu, Elizabeth. *The Letters of Mrs Elizabeth Montagu*. Edited by Matthew Montagu. 4 vols. Cambridge: Cambridge University Press, 2015.
Mooallem, Jon. "Megafire." *New York Times Magazine*, August 4, 2019, 28–41, 50–51, 53.
Moses, Omri. *Out of Character: Modernism, Vitalism, Psychic Life*. Stanford, CA: Stanford University Press, 2014.
Moyn, Samuel. *The Last Utopia: Human Rights in History*. Cambridge, MA: Harvard University Press, 2010.
Myerson, Joel, ed. *Emerson and Thoreau: The Contemporary Reviews*. Cambridge: Cambridge University Press, 1992.

Nehamas, Alexander. *The Art of Living: Socratic Reflections from Plato to Foucault.* Berkeley: University of California Press, 1998.

Nersessian, Anahid. *Utopia, Limited: Romanticism and Adjustment.* Cambridge, MA: Harvard University Press, 2015.

Nietzsche, Friedrich. *Beyond Good and Evil: Prelude to a Philosophy of the Future.* Translated by Walter Kaufmann. New York: Vintage, 1989.

——. *Daybreak: Thoughts on the Prejudices of Morality.* Edited by Maudemarie Clark and Brian Leiter. Translated by R. J. Hollingdale. Cambridge: Cambridge University Press, 1997.

Noggle, James. *The Skeptical Sublime: Aesthetic Ideology in Pope and the Tory Satirists.* Oxford: Oxford University Press, 2001.

Nussbaum, Felicity. *Torrid Zones: Maternity, Sexuality, and Empire in Eighteenth-Century English Narratives.* Baltimore, MD: Johns Hopkins University Press, 1995.

Nussbaum, Martha C. *The Cosmopolitan Tradition: A Noble but Flawed Ideal.* Cambridge, MA: Harvard University Press, 2019.

——. "Kant and Stoic Cosmopolitanism." *Journal of Political Philosophy* 5, no. 1 (1997): 1–25.

——. "Poetry and the Passions: Two Stoic Views." In *Passions and Perceptions: Studies in Hellenistic Philosophy of Mind*, edited by Jacques Brunschwig and Martha Nussbaum, 97–149. Cambridge: Cambridge University Press, 1993.

——. *The Therapy of Desire: Theory and Practice in Hellenistic Ethics.* Princeton, NJ: Princeton University Press, 1994.

Nuttall, A. D. "Gulliver among the Horses." *Yearbook of English Studies* 18 (1988): 51–67.

Outram, Dorinda. *The Body and the French Revolution.* New Haven, CT: Yale University Press, 1989.

Packer, Barbara. *Emerson's Fall.* New York: Continuum, 1982.

Pagden, Anthony. *The Enlightenment and Why It Still Matters.* New York: Random House, 2013.

Paknadel, Felix. "Shaftesbury's Illustrations of *Characteristics*." *Journal of the Warburg and Courtauld Institutes* 37 (1974): 290–312.

Paley, Morton. *Coleridge's Later Poetry.* Oxford: Clarendon, 1996.

Palumbo-Liu, David. *The Deliverance of Others: Reading Literature in a Global Age.* Durham, NC: Duke University Press, 2012.

Parker, Harold. *The Cult of Antiquity and the French Revolutionaries.* Chicago: University of Chicago Press, 1937.

The Parliamentary History of England, from the Earliest Period to the Year 1803. Vol. 29. London: T. C. Hansard, 1817.

Parrish, Stephen. *Coleridge's Dejection: The Earliest Manuscripts and the Earliest Printings.* Ithaca, NY: Cornell University Press, 1988.

Pasanek, Brad. *Metaphors of Mind: An Eighteenth-Century Dictionary.* Baltimore, MD: Johns Hopkins University Press, 2015.

Pascoe, Judith. *Romantic Theatricality: Gender, Poetry, Spectatorship.* Ithaca, NY: Cornell University Press, 1997.

Paul, Annie Murphy. "Reading Literature Makes Us Smarter and Nicer." *TIME*, June 3, 2013. https://ideas.time.com/2013/06/03/why-we-should-read-literature/.

Peacock, Thomas Love. *Peacock's Four Ages of Poetry*. Edited by H.F.B. Brett-Smith. Boston, MA: Houghton Mifflin, 1921.
Pennington, Montagu, ed. *A Series of Letters between Mrs. Elizabeth Carter and Miss Catherine Talbot, from the Year 1741 to 1770*. 4 vols. London: F. C. and J. Rivington, 1809.
Pennington, Sarah. *An Unfortunate Mother's Advice to Her Absent Daughters; in a Letter to Miss Pennington*. London: S. Chandler, 1761.
Pfau, Thomas. "A Certain Mediocrity: Adam Smith's Moral Behaviorism." In *Romanticism and the Emotions*, edited by Joel Faflak and Richard Sha, 48–75. Cambridge: Cambridge University Press, 2014.
———. *Minding the Modern: Human Agency, Intellectual Traditions, and Responsible Knowledge*. Notre Dame, IN: Notre Dame University Press, 2013.
———. *Romantic Moods: Paranoia, Trauma, and Melancholy, 1790–1840*. Baltimore, MD: Johns Hopkins University Press, 2005.
Phillipson, Nicholas. *Adam Smith: An Enlightened Life*. New Haven, CT: Yale University Press, 2010.
Pinch, Adela. *Strange Fits of Passion: Epistemologies of Emotion, Hume to Austen*. Stanford, CA: Stanford University Press, 1996.
Plutarch. *Plutarch's "Morals" Translated from the Greek by Several Hands*. Edited by William W. Goodwin. 5 vols. New York: Athenaeum Society, 1878.
Poirier, Richard. *The Renewal of Literature: Emersonian Reflections*. London: Faber and Faber, 1987.
Polwhele, Richard. *The Unsex'd Females: A Poem, Addressed to the Author of the Pursuits of Literature*. London: Cadell and Davies, 1798.
Poovey, Mary. *The Proper Lady and the Woman Writer: Ideology as Style in the Works of Mary Wollstonecraft, Mary Shelley, and Jane Austen*. Chicago: University of Chicago Press, 1984.
Pope, Alexander. *The Poems of Alexander Pope*. Edited by John Butt. London: Routledge, 1963.
Potkay, Adam. *The Passion for Happiness: Samuel Johnson and David Hume*. Ithaca, NY: Cornell University Press, 2000.
———. *The Story of Joy: From the Bible to Late Romanticism*. Cambridge: Cambridge University Press, 2007.
———. *Wordsworth's Ethics*. Baltimore, MD: Johns Hopkins University Press, 2013.
Pratt, Mary Louise. *Imperial Eyes: Travel Writing and Transculturation*. New York: Routledge, 2008.
Price, Richard. *A Discourse on the Love of Our Country, Delivered on Nov. 4, 1789*. London: T. Cadell, 1790.
Ramsey, Neil. *The Military Memoir and Romantic Literary Culture, 1780–1835*. Farnham, UK: Ashgate, 2011.
Reddy, William. *The Navigation of Feeling: A Framework for the History of Emotions*. Cambridge: Cambridge University Press, 2001.
Reed, Mark. *Wordsworth: The Chronology of the Middle Years*. Cambridge, MA: Harvard University Press, 1975.
Richardson, Alan. *British Romanticism and the Science of the Mind*. Cambridge: Cambridge University Press, 2001.

Richardson, Alan. ed. *Verse*. Vol. 4 of *Slavery, Abolition and Emancipation: Writings in the British Romantic Period*, edited by Peter Kitson and Debbie Lee, 8 vols. London: Pickering and Chatto, 1999.

Richardson, Robert D., Jr. *Emerson: The Mind on Fire*. Berkeley: University of California Press, 1995.

Rieff, Philip. *Freud: The Mind of the Moralist*. Chicago: University of Chicago Press, 1979.

Risinger, Jacob. "Coleridge, Politics, and the *Theory of Life*." *SEL: Studies in English Literature, 1500–1900* 55, no. 3 (Summer 2015): 647–67.

———. "*The Excursion* as Dialogic Poem." In *The Oxford Handbook of William Wordsworth*, edited by Richard Gravil and Daniel Robinson, 430–46. Oxford: Oxford University Press, 2015.

Rivers, Isabel. *Reason, Grace, and Sentiment: A Study of the Language of Religion and Ethics in England, 1660–1780*. 2 vols. Cambridge: Cambridge University Press, 1991–2000.

Robbins, Bruce. "Is Literature a Secular Concept? Three Earthquakes." *MLQ: Modern Language Quarterly* 72, no. 3 (September 2011): 293–317.

———. *Perpetual War: Cosmopolitanism from the Viewpoint of Violence*. Durham, NC: Duke University Press, 2012.

Robinson, David. *Emerson and "The Conduct of Life": Pragmatism and Ethical Purpose in the Later Work*. Cambridge: Cambridge University Press, 1993.

Robinson, Henry Crabb. *Diary, Reminiscences, and Correspondence of Henry Crabb Robinson*. Edited by Thomas Sadler. 2 vols. London: Macmillan, 1872.

Robinson, Mary. *A Letter to the Women of England and The Natural Daughter*. Edited by Sharon M. Setzer. Peterborough, ON: Broadview, 2003.

Robson, Catherine. *Heart Beats: Everyday Life and the Memorized Poem*. Princeton, NJ: Princeton University Press, 2012.

Rohrbach, Emily. *Modernity's Mist: British Romanticism and the Poetics of Anticipation*. New York: Fordham University Press, 2016.

Rothschild, Emma. *Economic Sentiments: Adam Smith, Condorcet, and the Enlightenment*. Cambridge, MA: Harvard University Press, 2001.

Rousseau, Jean-Jacques. *The Basic Political Writings*. Translated and edited by Donald Cress. Indianapolis: Hackett, 2011.

———. *Confessions*. Translated by Angela Scholar. Oxford: Oxford University Press, 2000.

Sabertash, Orlando. "The Sliding Scale of Manners." *Fraser's Magazine*, May 1844, 580–97.

Sachs, Jonathan. *The Poetics of Decline in British Romanticism*. Cambridge: Cambridge University Press, 2018.

———. *Romantic Antiquity: Rome in the British Imagination, 1789–1832*. Oxford: Oxford University Press, 2010.

Sacks, Kenneth S. "Stoicism in America." In *The Routledge Handbook of the Stoic Tradition*, edited by John Sellars, 331–45. New York: Routledge, 2016.

Schama, Simon. *Citizens: A Chronicle of the French Revolution*. New York: Alfred A. Knopf, 1989.

Schneewind, J. B. *The Invention of Autonomy: A History of Modern Moral Philosophy*. Cambridge: Cambridge University Press, 1998.

Schofield, Malcom. "Stoic Ethics." In *The Cambridge Companion to the Stoics*, edited by Brad Inwood, 233–56. Cambridge: Cambridge University Press, 2003.
———. *The Stoic Idea of the City*. Cambridge: Cambridge University Press, 1991.
Scott, Sarah. *The History of Cornelia*. Edited by Caroline Franklin. London: Routledge, 1992.
———. *The Letters of Sarah Scott*. Edited by Nicole Pohl. 2 vols. London: Pickering and Chatto, 2014.
———. *Millenium Hall*. Edited by Gary Kelly. Peterborough, ON: Broadview, 2004.
Scott, Walter. "Childe Harold's Pilgrimage, Canto III and Other Poems." *Quarterly Review* 16 (October 1816): 172–208.
———. "Childe Harold's Pilgrimage, Canto IV." *Quarterly Review* 19 (April 1818): 215–32.
Sedgwick, Eve Kosofsky. *Touching Feeling: Affect, Pedagogy, Performativity*. Durham, NC: Duke University Press, 2003.
Sellars, John. *The Art of Living: The Stoics on the Nature and Function of Philosophy*. Aldershot, UK: Ashgate, 2003.
———. *Stoicism*. Berkeley: University of California Press, 2006.
Seneca, Lucius Annaeus. *Hardship and Happiness*. Translated by Elaine Fantham, Harrry M. Hine, James Ker, and Gareth D. Williams. In *The Complete Works of Lucius Annaeus Seneca*, edited by Elizabeth Asmis, Shadi Bartsch, and Martha C. Nussbaum. Chicago: University of Chicago Press, 2014.
———. *Letters on Ethics to Lucilius*. Translated by Margaret Graver and A. A. Long. In *The Complete Works of Lucius Annaeus Seneca*, edited by Elizabeth Asmis, Shadi Bartsch, and Martha C. Nussbaum. Chicago: University of Chicago Press, 2015.
Shaftesbury, Anthony Ashley. *Askêmata*. Edited by Wolfram Benda, Christine Jackson-Holzberg, Patrick Müller, and Friedrich A. Uehlein. Vol. 2, pt. 6 of *Anthony Ashley Cooper, Third Earl of Shaftesbury*, Standard Ed., edited by Benda, Jackson-Holzberg, Müller, and Uehlein. Stuttgart-Bad Cannstatt: Frommann-holzboog, 2011.
———. *Characteristics of Men, Manners, Opinions, Times*. Edited by Lawrence E. Klein. Cambridge: Cambridge University Press, 2000.
———. *The Life, Unpublished Letters, and Philosophical Regimen of Anthony, Earl of Shaftesbury*. Edited by Benjamin Rand. London: Swan Sonnenschein, 1900.
Shelley, Mary. *The Journals of Mary Shelley, 1814–1844*. Edited by Paula R. Feldman and Diana Scott-Kilvert. 2 vols. Oxford: Clarendon, 1987.
———. *The Last Man*. Edited by Morton Paley. Oxford: Oxford University Press, 1994.
———. *The Letters of Mary Wollstonecraft Shelley*. Edited by Betty T. Bennett. 3 vols. Baltimore, MD: Johns Hopkins University Press, 1983.
———. *Lodore*. Edited by Lisa Vargo. Peterborough, ON: Broadview, 1997.
Shelley, Percy. *The Complete Works of Percy Bysshe Shelley*. Edited by Roger Ingpen and Walter Peck. 10 vols. New York: Gordian, 1965.
Sidney, Philip. "The Defence of Poesy." In *The "Defence of Poesy" and Selected Renaissance Literary Criticism*, edited by Gavin Alexander, 3–54. London: Penguin, 2004.
Siegel, Lee. "Should Literature Be Useful?" *New Yorker*, November 6, 2013.
Simpson, David. *Wordsworth, Commodification, and Social Concern: The Poetics of Modernity*. Cambridge: Cambridge University Press, 2009.
Singer, Kate. *Romantic Vacancy: The Poetics of Gender, Affect, and Radical Speculation*. Albany: State University of New York, 2019.

Singer, Peter, Leslie Cannold, and Helga Kushe. "William Godwin and the Defence of Impartialist Ethics." *Utilitas* 7, no. 1 (May 1995): 67–86.
Smith, Adam. *The Correspondence of Adam Smith*. Edited by Ernest Campbell Mossner and Ian Simpson Ross. Oxford: Clarendon, 1987.
———. *Lectures on Rhetoric and Belles Lettres*. Edited by J. C. Bryce. Indianapolis: Liberty Fund, 1985.
———. *Theory of Moral Sentiments*. Edited by D. D. Raphel and A. L. Macfie. Indianapolis: Liberty Fund, 1982.
Smith, Orianne. *Romantic Women Writers, Revolution, and Prophecy: Rebellious Daughters, 1786–1826*. Cambridge: Cambridge University Press, 2013.
Soni, Vivasvan. *Mourning Happiness: Narrative and the Politics of Modernity*. Ithaca, NY: Cornell University Press, 2010.
Sorabji, Richard. *Gandhi and the Stoics: Modern Experiments on Ancient Values*. Chicago: University of Chicago Press, 2012.
Southey, Robert. *The Collected Letters of Robert Southey*. Romantic Circles Electronic Ed. Edited by Lynda Pratt, Tim Fulford, and Ian Packer. Romantic Circles, 2009–17. https://romantic-circles.org/editions/southey_letters.
Spiegelman, Willard. *Majestic Indolence: English Romantic Poetry and the Work of Art*. Oxford: Oxford University Press, 1995.
———. *Wordsworth's Heroes*. Berkeley: University of California Press, 1985.
Spivak, Gayatri. *A Critique of Postcolonial Reason: Toward a History of the Vanishing Present*. Cambridge, MA: Harvard University Press, 1999.
Stabler, Jane. *Byron, Poetics, History*. Cambridge: Cambridge University Press, 2002.
Stack, Frank. *Pope and Horace: Studies in Imitation*. Cambridge: Cambridge University Press, 1985.
Stafford, Fiona. "*Lodore*: A Tale of the Present Time?" In *Mary Shelley's Fictions: From Frankenstein to Falkner*, edited by Michael Eberle-Sinatra, 181–93. Basingstoke, UK: Macmillan, 2000.
Stauffer, Andrew. *Anger, Revolution, and Romanticism*. Cambridge: Cambridge University Press, 2005.
Stephen, Leslie. *Studies of a Biographer*. 4 vols. New York: G. P. Putnam's Sons, 1907.
Stock, Brian. "The Soliloquy: Transformations of an Ancient Philosophical Technique." In *Augustin philosophe et prédicateur: Hommage à Goulven Madaec*, edited by Isabelle Bochet, 315–47. Collection des Études Augustiniennes, Série antiquité 195. Paris: Études Augustiniennes, 2012.
Strange, Steven, and Jack Zupko, eds. *Stoicism: Traditions & Transformations*. Cambridge: Cambridge University Press, 2004.
Striker, Gisela. *Essays on Hellenistic Epistemology and Ethics*. Cambridge: Cambridge University Press, 1996.
Swift, Jonathan. *Gulliver's Travels*. Edited by Albert J. Rivero. New York: Norton, 2002.
———. *The Prose Works of Jonathan Swift*. Edited by Herbert Davis. 14 vols. Oxford: Blackwell, 1939.
Swift, Simon. "Stoicism and Romantic Literature." In *The Routledge Handbook of the Stoic Tradition*, edited by John Sellars, 303–18. London: Routledge, 2016.
Tappan, David. *Sermons on Important Subjects by the Late Rev. David Tappan, D.D.* Boston: W. Hilliard, and Lincoln and Edmands, 1807.

Taylor, Barbara. *Mary Wollstonecraft and the Feminist Imagination*. Cambridge: Cambridge University Press, 2003.
Taylor, Charles. *A Secular Age*. Cambridge, MA: Harvard University Press, 2007.
———. *Sources of the Self: The Making of the Modern Identity*. Cambridge, MA: Harvard University Press, 1989.
Thomson, James. *"Liberty," "The Castle of Indolence," and Other Poems*. Edited by James Sambrook. Oxford: Clarendon, 1986.
Thoreau, Henry David. *Journal*. Edited by by Elizabeth Hall Witherell, William Howarth, Robert Sattelmeyer, Thomas Blanding, Mark R. Patterson, William Rossi, Nancy Craig Simmons, et. al. 8 vols. Princeton, NJ: Princeton University Press, 1981–2002.
Thorslev, Peter. *The Byronic Hero*. Minneapolis: University of Minnesota Press, 1962.
Trilling, Lionel. *The Liberal Imagination: Essays on Literature and Society*. New York: New York Review Books, 2008.
———. *The Opposing Self*. New York: Harcourt, Brace, Jovanovich, 1978.
Trop, Gabriel. *Poetry as a Way of Life: Aesthetics and Askesis in the German Eighteenth Century*. Evanston, IL: Northwestern University Press, 2015.
Tucker, Herbert. *Epic: Britain's Heroic Muse, 1790–1910*. Oxford: Oxford University Press, 2008.
Tuite, Clara. *Lord Byron and Scandalous Celebrity*. Cambridge: Cambridge University Press, 2015.
Van Cromphout, Gustaaf. *Emerson's Ethics*. Columbia: University of Missouri Press, 1999.
Vargo, Lisa. "The Aikins and the Godwins: Notions of Conflict and Stoicism in Anna Barbauld and Mary Shelley." *Romanticism* 11, no. 1 (January 2008): 84–98.
Vernon, Richard. "Mary Wollstonecraft: Stoic, Republican, Feminist." In *Friends, Citizens, Strangers: Essays on Where We Belong*, 58–80. Toronto: University of Toronto Press, 2005.
Vivenza, Gloria. *Adam Smith and the Classics*. Oxford: Oxford University Press, 2001.
Voelz, Johannes. *Transcendental Resistance: The New Americanists and Emerson's Challenge*. Hanover, NH: Dartmouth College Press, 2010.
Voitle, Robert. *The Third Earl of Shaftesbury, 1671–1713*. Baton Rouge: Louisiana State University Press, 1984.
Wallace, Jennifer. "Confined and Exposed: Elizabeth Carter's Classical Translations." *Tulsa Studies in Women's Literature* 22, no. 2 (Autumn 2003): 315–34.
———. *Shelley and Greece: Rethinking Romantic Hellenism*. Basingstoke, UK: Macmillan, 1997.
Wallach, Barbara Price. "Rhetoric and Paradox: Cicero, 'Paradoxa Stoicorum IV.'" *Hermes* 118, no. 2 (1990): 171–83.
Walls, Laura Dassow. "The Cosmopolitical Project of Louisa May Alcott." *ESQ: A Journal of the American Renaissance* 57 (2011): 107–32.
Warren, Andrew. *The Orient and the Young Romantics*. Cambridge: Cambridge University Press, 2014.
Wasserman, Earl. *Shelley: A Critical Reading*. Baltimore, MD: Johns Hopkins University Press, 1971.
Watt, Ian. *The Rise of the Novel*. Berkeley: University of California Press, 1957.
Weinbrot, Howard. *Britannia's Issue: The Rise of British Literature from Dryden to Ossian*. Cambridge: Cambridge University Press, 1993.

Weisbuch, Robert. *Atlantic Double-Cross: American Literature and British Influence in the Age of Emerson*. Chicago: University of Chicago Press, 1986.
Weiss, Deborah. "Sarah Scott's 'Attick School': Moral Philosophy, Ethical Agency, and *Millenium Hall*." *Eighteenth-Century Fiction* 24, no. 3 (Spring 2012): 459–86.
Wenley, R. M. *Stoicism and Its Influence*. New York: Longmans, Green, 1927.
Weston, Rowland. "Politics, Passion, and the 'Puritan Temper': Godwin's Critique of Enlightened Modernity." *Studies in Romanticism* 41, no. 3 (Fall 2002): 445–70.
Whatmore, Richard. *Republicanism and the French Revolution*. Oxford: Oxford University Press, 2000.
Whicher, Stephen. *Freedom and Fate: An Inner Life of Ralph Waldo Emerson*. Philadelphia: University of Pennsylvania Press, 1953.
White, Daniel E. *Early Romanticism and Religious Dissent*. Cambridge: Cambridge University Press, 2006.
Williams, Bernard. *Moral Luck: Philosophical Papers 1973–1980*. Cambridge: Cambridge University Press, 1993.
Williams, Carolyn. "Poetry, Pudding, and Epictetus: The Consistency of Elizabeth Carter." In *Tradition in Transition: Women Writers, Marginal Texts, and the Eighteenth-Century Canon*, edited by Alvaro Ribeiro, SJ, and James Basker. Oxford: Clarendon, 1996.
Wiltshire, John. *Jane Austen and the Body*. Cambridge: Cambridge University Press, 1992.
Woelfel, James. "'The Beautiful Necessity': Emerson and the Stoic Tradition." *American Journal of Theology & Philosophy* 32, no. 2 (May 2011): 122–38.
Wolfson, Susan. *Reading John Keats*. Cambridge: Cambridge University Press, 2015.
Wollstonecraft, Mary. *"A Vindication of the Rights of Woman" and "A Vindication of the Rights of Men."* Edited by Janet Todd. Oxford: Oxford University Press, 1993.
———. *The Works of Mary Wollstonecraft*. Edited by Janet Todd and Marilyn Butler. 7 vols. London: Pickering and Chatto, 1989.
Woloch, Alex. *The One vs. the Many: Minor Characters and the Space of the Protagonist in the Novel*. Princeton, NJ: Princeton University Press, 2003.
Wordsworth, Jonathan. *The Borders of Vision*. Oxford: Clarendon, 1982.
Wordsworth, William. *The Excursion*. Edited by Sally Bushell, James Butler, and Michael Jaye. Ithaca, NY: Cornell University Press, 2007.
———. *The Letters of William and Dorothy Wordsworth*. 2nd ed. Edited by Ernest de Selincourt, Mary Moorman, and Alan G. Hill. 8 vols. Oxford: Clarendon, 1967–93.
———. *Poems, in Two Volumes and Other Poems, 1800–1807*. Edited by Jared Curtis. Ithaca, NY: Cornell University Press, 1983.
———. *The Prose Works of William Wordsworth*. Edited by W.J.B. Owen and Jane Worthington Smyser. 3 vols. Oxford: Clarendon, 1974.
———. *The Thirteen Book Prelude*. Edited by Mark Reed. Ithaca, NY: Cornell University Press, 1991.
Worthington, Jane. *Wordsworth's Reading of Roman Prose*. New Haven, CT: Yale University Press, 1946.
Wright, Gillian. "Women Reading Epictetus." *Women's Writing* 14, no. 2 (August 2007): 321–37.
Wu, Duncan. *Wordsworth's Reading: 1770–1799*. Cambridge: Cambridge University Press, 1993.

———. *Wordsworth's Reading: 1800–1815*. Cambridge: Cambridge University Press, 1995.

Yeats, W. B. *The Poems*. Edited by Daniel Albright. London: J. M. Dent, 1990.

Yousef, Nancy. "'Emotions that Reason Deepens': Second Thoughts about Affect." *Nineteenth-Century Gender Studies* 11, no. 3 (Winter 2015). http://www.ncgsjournal.com/issue113/yousef.html.

———. *Romantic Intimacy*. Stanford, CA: Stanford University Press, 2013.

Yu, Christopher. *Nothing to Admire: The Politics of Poetic Satire from Dryden to Merrill*. Oxford: Oxford University Press, 2003.

Zimmerman, Sarah. *Romanticism, Lyricism, and History*. Albany: State University of New York Press, 1999.

INDEX

Abrams, M. H.: on expressing emotion, 107; out-in-out process in conversation poems, 114; on Romantic lyric, 108–9

Adams, James Eli, ascetic self, 151

Adams, Robert, 4

Addison, Joseph: *Cato*, 3, 4, 206; on Stoicism, 29

Aeschylus, 16, 17

affect: study of, 13–14; theory, 14, 218n59

All the Works of Epictetus (Carter), 170, 172

Amundeville, Adeline, Byron's analysis of, 141–44

The Anatomy of Melancholy (Burton), 8

Anderson, Amanda: contemporary theory and philosophy, 128; critical distance, 85

Aravamudan, Srinivas: on Stoicism, 147; *Tropicopolitans*, 3, 231n74; virtualization, 231n74

Armstrong, Isobel, on women's poetry, 162

Arrian, 190; Zeno and, 182, 193

Arsić, Branka, on Emerson, 196, 235n9

art of living, philosophy, 158, 186, 232n103

Askêmata (Shaftesbury), 32, 38–41, 52, 116

Augustine: on Stoic pride, 98; *The City of God*, 98

Aurelius, Marcus, 64, 186, 196, 197; Coleridge on the Stoics, 104, 114–15; on conversation, 118; Emerson and Arnold on, 234n2; emotions, 97; inner dialogue, 114; *The Meditations*, 32, 35, 84, 102, 114; self-examination, 48; Shaftesbury on, 31–32, 35, 36, 107; on Stoicism, 9

Austen, Jane, *Persuasion*, 160, 162–64

Baker, Samuel, on Smith, 46

Bakewell, Thomas, poetry on Stoicism and bodily pain, 105–6, 227n62

Bakhtin, Mikhail, self-examination, 48

Barbauld, Anna, *Eighteen Hundred and Eleven*, 162; Stoic inquiry, 15

Barrell, John, on disinterestedness, 85

Batho, Edith, on Wordsworth, 60

Baucom, Ian: on Smith, 221n74; on Stoicism as repression, 11

Beattie, James, *Elements of Moral Science*, 24

Beaty, Frederick, satire in *Don Juan*, 158

Beckford, Peter, *Thoughts upon Hunting*, 154–55

Behn, Aphra, Oroonoko's sovereignty, 151

Bell, Charles: fundamental law of our nature, 97; on thought, 105

Bender, John, on Smith, 49–50

Berlant, Lauren, styles of composure, 13

Bevilacqua, Alexander, on Cloots's philosophy, 232n106

Biographia Literaria (Coleridge), 94, 106, 107, 123

Blackwood's Magazine, 108

Blake's *Marriage of Heaven and Hell*, 4

Blessington's *Conversations of Lord Byron*, 130

Blind Man Traces the Circle (Cooke), 229n13

Bloom, Harold: conversation poems, 114; "strong poets," 217n14

Boswell, James, *Life of Johnson*, 140–41, 154

Bowen, Francis, on affections, 198

Boyd, Elizabeth, on Byron, 159

Brooke, Christopher, evolution of Stoicism, 2, 99–100

Brooke, Dorothea, 185

Brown, John, 214

Brucker, Johann Jakob, 95; *Historia Critica Philosophiae*, 100–101

Buchan, William, *Domestic Medicine, or The Family Physician*, 106

Buell, Lawrence, trajectory of Emerson's career, 189

Burke, Edmund, 31, 68, 82, 193–94; Emerson on, 203; on French Stoicism, 66; *Reflections on the Revolution in France*, 66; sensibility, 65–66; sentiment and prejudice, 65; Smith and, 54; on Smith's *Theory of Moral Sentiments*, 55; Wollstonecraft and, 20, 43, 55–57, 196

Burton, Robert, *The Anatomy of Melancholy*, 8

[261]

Butler, Judith, 131
Byron (Eisler), 129
Byron, George Gordon, 19; analysis of Lady Adeline Amundeville, 141–44; *The Corsair*, 129, 132–34; *Don Juan*, 22, 126–27, 129–30, 134–38, 141, 144, 149, 151–53, 158–59; Harrow, 128, 136, 139, 148; interest in Stoicism, 231n74; on legal and moral slavery, 232n101; life as citizen of world, 195; mistress Teresa Guiccioli, 130, 134; playing the Stoic, 129–34; prohibition of admiration, 134–44; scorn of life, 149–52; sense of himself, 229n19; Stoicism at character level, 21–22; on Stoics, 232n100; things to shake a Stoic, 152–59; on Windham, 231n94

Caleb Williams (Godwin), 72–73, 199
Cameron, Sharon, on Emerson, 189, 235n9
Canuel, Mark: on Coleridge, 116; on Godwin, 63
Carlson, Julie: on Godwin, 73, 224n68; on Shelley, 177
Carlyle, Thomas: on Byron, 132; *Sartor Resartus*, 212
Carter, Elizabeth, 164; appearances of things, 221n56; on Stoic philosophy, 30; on stoniness, 71; translation of Epictetus, 169–71, 172, 175, 221n56, 232n103; *The Works of Epictetus*, 214
Cassirer, Ernst, modern world and Stoic philosophy, 20
Cato (Addison), 3, 4
Cato's Tears and the Making of Anglo-American Emotion (Ellison), 15, 29, 146, 167
Cavell, Stanley, *In Quest of the Ordinary*, 89
Chai, Leon, on Emerson, 190
Chandler, James: archaeology of sympathy, 15; Byron's defense of Pope, 138; on Wordsworth poetry, 65
Channing, William Ellery, American Unitarianism of, 198–200
Characteristics of Men, Manners, Opinions, Times (Shaftesbury), 32, 33–38, 41–42, 90, 220n33, 221nn54, 60
Cheeke, Stephen, classical commonplace, 136–37
Childe Harold's Pilgrimage (Scott), 125, 130, 153

China, 52, 197
Christ: Augustine on, 98; exemplifying Stoic training, 99
Christensen, Jerome: citation compulsion, 136; performance of lordship, 132
Christianity, 67; circumvention of will, 97; Coleridge on, 102, 104, 106; cult of Supreme Being, 67; Stoicism and, 99, 100, 102, 106, 170, 174, 197, 200; supplement of all philosophy, 95
Chrysippus, Stoic instructor, 7, 54, 120
Cicero, 128, 147, 181; attainable virtues, 46; *De finibus*, 7, 185; *De Officiis*, 30, 53, 138, 193; *Paradoxa Stoicorum*, 209, 236n64; Roman Stoicism, 61; *Tusculan Disputations*, 16, 22, 76, 118, 139, 185
Citizen of the World (Goldsmith), 81
The City of God (Augustine), 98
Clairmont, Claire, Byron and, 131
Clery, E. J., 162
Cloots, Anacharsis, 232n106; citizen of the world, 159
Cohen-Vrignaud, Gerard, affect theory, 14
Cohn, Elisha, lyrical suspension, 150
Coleridge, Samuel Taylor, 19, 34; *Biographia Literaria*, 94, 106, 107, 123; on Christianity, 99, 102; conversation poems, 37–38, 228n108; "Dejection: An Ode," 26, 91, 92, 94, 97; Emerson and, 7; "Fears in Solitude," 115–18; on Hume, 90–91, 104; *Lectures on the History of Philosophy*, 94, 98, 101, 119, 201; *Lyrical Ballads*, 62; lyric askesis, 106–11, 161; notebooks and writings of, 31, 111–19; objection to Kant, 103; "Ode to Tranquillity," 21, 119–23, 178; "On the Passions," 13, 104; *Opus Maximum*, 92, 103; "The Pains of Sleep," 112–13; philosophy as work in progress, 227n76; Rousseau as Stoic mole, 226n39; son Hartley, 93; *The Statesman's Manual*, 96, 120; Stoicism of, 21, 79, 92–99, 105; Stoic label, 92, 225n9; stoic lecture, 94–99; *Table Talk*, 86; Wordsworth and, 63, 71, 74
Colley, Linda, confronting slavery, 153
Combe, William, *The Tour of Doctor Syntax*, 124, 150
The Conduct of Life (Emerson), 188, 211–13
Confessions (Rousseau), 124–25

Connor, Steven, *Giving Way*, 10
The Convention of Cintra (Wordsworth), 85
Conversations of Lord Byron (Blessington), 130
Cooke, George Willis, on Emerson, 191
Cooke, Michael: *Blind Man Traces the Circle*, 229n13; on Stoicism, 59
Cooper's Hill (Denham), 84
The Corsair (Byron), 129, 132–34
cosmopolitanism, 11, 14, 20–22, 25, 50–54, 81–82, 154, 159, 191–97
Cox, Jeffrey, military entanglements, 11
Crane, Gregg, 191
critical semantics, 7–10
Cudworth, Ralph, 101; *True Intellectual System of the Universe*, 100
Culler, Jonathan, lyric theory, 108, 109
The Curse of Kehama (Southey), 210

Darwin, Erasmus, on the corporeality of thought, 105
David, Jacques-Louis, sketch of Marie Antoinette, 134
De Constantia (Lipsius), 99
Dedalus, Stephen, 31
De finibus (Cicero), 7, 185
Defoe's *Robinson Crusoe*, 153
Denham, John, *Cooper's Hill*, 84
De Officiis (Cicero), 30, 53, 138, 193
De Quincey, Thomas, Stoic philosophy, 21, 30
Diderot's *Encyclopédie*, 100
Dionysius the Turncoat, 17
Discourse on the Origin and Foundations of Inequality Among Men (Rousseau), 148
Domestic Medicine, or The Family Physician (Buchan), 106
Don Juan (Byron), 22, 126–27, 129–30, 134–38, 141, 144, 149, 151–53, 158–59
Douglass, Frederick, *My Bondage and My Freedom*, 154
Du Bois, W.E.B., *The Souls of Black Folk*, 231n90
Duff, David, anti-didacticism, 111
Duncan, Ian, on Smith, 45

earthquake drill, Smith's, 49–54
Eighteen Hundred and Eleven (Barbauld), 162
Eisler, Benita, *Byron*, 129

Elements of Moral Science (Beattie), 24
Eliot, George, *Middlemarch*, 185
Eliot, T. S., on emotion in poetry, 23
Ellison, Julie: *Cato's Tears and the Making of Anglo-American Emotion*, 15; culture of sensibility, 146, 149, 167; on needs of global culture, 167; on Stoic positions, 29, 146
Elmer, Jonathan, Stoic sovereignty, 147
Emerson (Richardson), 189
Emerson, Ralph Waldo, 182; abolitionist discourse, 236n75; "Circles," 195; *The Conduct of Life*, 188, 211–13; cosmopolitanism, 191–97; death of son Waldo, 189, 205–8, 210–11, 236n50; death of wife Ellen, 200, 205; disposition and doctrine, 9; "Experience," 187, 191, 193, 201, 205–11; on Gataker, 101; making sense of, 186–88; *Nature*, 188–89, 191, 200, 202–3, 208; perspective on world, 187–88; "Self-Reliance," 202–5; Stoic cosmopolitanism, 22; Stoicism of, 7, 188–91, 196, 235n9; sympathy, 211–15; Unitarianism of, 191, 197–99
Emerson and Self-Reliance (Kateb), 203
The Emperor Marcus Antoninus (Gataker), 101, 104, 115
Enchiridion (Epictetus), 44, 207
Enfield, William, 95, 100
Enlightenment, 14; advent of, 99; Byron's inversion of cosmopolitanism, 154; Emerson and, 197; evaluation of passion, 122; Godwin and, 63; rationality, 49; Scottish, 46, 131; Smith and, 51; Stoic hypocrisy, 131; Stoicism and, 25, 100; Unitarianism and, 198
Enquiry Concerning Political Justice (Godwin), 5, 20, 21, 48, 62, 63, 69, 85, 92, 125, 199
Epictetus, 62, 128; on appearances of things, 10; Carter translating, 169–71, 172, 175, 214, 221n56, 232n103; on Citadel within ourselves, 115; *Discourses*, 8; emotions, 97; *Enchiridion*, 44, 207; inner dialogue, 114; Landor on, 8; on mechanical passion, 38–39; philosophy of, 26; Roman practitioner, 7; self-examination, 48; Shaftesbury on, 35; Stoicism of, 215; sympathy, 48
Epicureanism, 34, 74, 95, 96, 224n72
Epistles (Horace), 66, 135, 139

Epistulae Senecae et Pauli, authenticity
   of, 99
Epithalamion (Spenser), 75
An Essay on Man (Pope), 61, 135
Essay on Sepulchres (Godwin), 74–75, 78
Essay on the Principles of Human Action
   (Hazlitt), 48
Essays upon Epitaphs (Wordsworth),
   75, 77
The Excursion (Wordsworth), 21, 59–60,
   63, 65, 73–77, 79, 80–81, 83, 85, 87–88,
   199, 205 224n72
expressive individualism, 2

Faflak, Joel, on feeling, 13
Fairclough, Mary, Smith and sympathy, 47
false humanity, sympathizing of whole
   and, 38–40
Favret, Mary: everyday war, 11; military
   violence, 231n86
"Fears in Solitude" (Coleridge), 115–18
Felski, Rita, intellectual persona of critique,
   128–29, 229n15
Fénelon, François, in Godwin's fire case,
   68–69
Ferguson, Frances, Wordsworth's poetics, 59
Festa, Lynn, sensibility, 29
Fielding, Henry, *Tom Jones*, 135
Finseth, Ian, on Emerson, 235n14
Fisher, Philip, on Stoicism, 140
Ford, Jennifer, on Coleridge's dreams, 105
Foucault, Michel: philosophy as art of liv-
   ing, 158; self-culture, 188; self-practice,
   86; work of oneself on oneself, 93
Fox, Charles James, French Stoicism, 67
François, Anne-Lise, *Open Secrets*, 12
Fraser's Magazine, 144
French Revolution, 5–6, 55, 159, 164, 196,
   230n56; moral philosophy, 33, 44;
   revolutionary Stoicism and, 65–66, 74;
   Romantic Stoicism forms after, 214;
   Shelley and, 16, 18; Solitary's radical
   diffusion at outset, 83, 86; Stoicism
   and, 14, 30, 158; Stoicism in aftermath
   of, 71; Stoic phenomenon in fallout of,
   144, 190; Tappan on, 199; Wordsworth
   and, 21
Fry, Paul, Wordsworth's poetry, 71
Frye, Northrop, reptilian Classicism, 60
Fugitive Slave Law, 213

Furst, Lillian, 217n8
Futures Past (Koselleck), 230n56

Galperin, William: account of everyday,
   217n6; on Austen, 164
Garnet, Henry Highland, urging insurrec-
   tion, 154
Garrod, H. W., Wordsworth's decline, 59
Garvey, T. Gregory, 191
Gataker, Thomas, *The Emperor Marcus
   Antoninus*, 101, 104
Genuine Works (Leighton), 121
Gérard, Albert, on Coleridge, 114
Giving Way (Connor), 10
Godwin, William: autobiography of,
   224n43; *Caleb Williams*, 72–73, 199;
   Carlson on Stoicism of, 224n68; *Essay
   on Sepulchres*, 74–75, 78; famous fire
   case, 69; "fire of Vesta," 79; Hazlitt on,
   223n20; Kippis as tutor of, 35; *Political Justice*, 5, 20, 21, 48, 62, 63, 69,
   72, 85, 92, 125, 199; radical philosophy
   of, 60; rational justice, 98; Stoicism of,
   63–65, 66, 68, 70, 73, 76–77, 79, 82–83,
   143–44, 178, 197, 214; turn from Stoicism,
   224n65; Wollstonecraft and, 43, 45, 182,
   196; Wordsworth and, 21, 60; writings
   of, 224n66
Goldsmith, Oliver, *Citizen of the World*, 81
Goldsmith, Steven, on sympathy, 24
Goodman, Kevis, Wanderer analysis, 82
Grannan, Katy, photographs of fire
   aftermath, 1
Graver, Bruce, on Stoicism, 15, 60–61
Great Reform Bill, 185
Greiner, Rae, Smith's cognitive model,
   222n89; sympathy, 45, 53
Guest, Harriet, 171
Guiccioli, Teresa, Byron's mistress, 130, 134
Gulliver's Travels (Swift), 27–28
Gurton-Watcher, Lily, poetics of atten-
   tion, 116–17

Hadot, Pierre, 6, 111; on living philosophical life, 108; Stoic dissimulation, 6; on
   Stoicism, 37, 114; view from above, 84
Harper, George McLean, conversation
   poems, 113
Hartley, David, on corporeality of
   thought, 105

Hartman, Geoffrey, on Wordsworth, 83
Hawkshead Grammar School, 61
Hayot, Eric, China and, 52
Hazlitt, William: Abrams on, 109; on Byron, 129, 137; *Essay on the Principles of Human Action*, 48; on Godwin, 69, 87, 223n20; on French Revolution and reversals, 6; *The Spirit of the Age*, 64
Hegel, G.W.F.: on account of lyric, 109–10; *The Phenomenology of Spirit*, 5, 61; sense of poetry, 227n88
Henley, William Ernest, "Invictus," 232n99
Hickman, Jared, on abolitionists, 153
Hierocles, oikeiosis and, 53, 193–94
Higginson, Thomas Wentworth, Emerson and, 214–15
Hirschman, Albert, on the passions, 32
Historia Critica Philosophiae (Brucker), 100–101
Hobbes, Thomas, 33–34, 71; *Leviathan*, 33, 70
Hogg, James, 190
Horace, 115, 136, 144; *Epistles*, 66, 139; motto, 135; *nil admirari*, 140–43, 230n52; Pope and, 136–39
Hume, David: affections, 44; Godwin reframing sentiment of, 72; seeking medical advice, 89–90; on Stoics, 25–26, 29, 90–91; on sympathy, 13, 35, 49; *Treatise of Human Nature*, 25, 89
Hutcheson, Francis, 102; *The "Meditations" of the Emperor Marcus Aurelius Antoninus*, 101
Hutchinson, Sara, on Coleridge, 120

Imitations of Horace (Pope), 136
inhumanity of the Stoics, 24, 25, 28, 151
Inquiry Concerning Virtue and Merit (Shaftesbury), 34

Jackson, Virginia, lyric theory, 108
James, Henry, 215
Jarvis, Simon, 107; Wordsworth's poetic thinking, 71
Johnson, Barbara, on Mary Shelley, 176
Johnson, Claudia: idyls of female society, 174; gendered dynamics of Stoic rationalism, 15, 28, 57
Johnson, Samuel: on Elizabeth Carter, 175; essay on weather, 28; on *nil admirari*, 140–41; *The Rambler*, 37; *Rasselas*, 206; Stoic virtue, 28–29 "The Vanity of Human Wishes," 4
Johnston, Kenneth, 79
Jones, Chris: radical sensibility, 15; on Shaftesbury, 30, 43
Jones, Ewan, on Coleridge's poetry, 107

Kames, Lord: benevolence, 43; on sympathy, 24
Kant, Immanuel: *Critique of Practical Reason*, 103, 104; moral imperative, 98, 104, 197; moral self-mastery, 219–20n8; *Perpetual Peace*, 214; Spinoza and, 21, 92, 103; on Stoicism, 25, 102–6, 219–20n8
Kateb, George, Emerson and Self-Reliance, 203
Kay, Carol, on Wollstonecraft, 56
Keats, John, Stoic sense of self, 23
Kelly, Gary, on *Millenium Hall*, 168
Kippis, Andrew, as Godwin's tutor, 35
Klein, Lawrence, on Shaftesbury, 37, 220n46
Kojève, Alexandre, slave ideology, 5

Lake, Crystal, *Millenium Hall* and antiquarianism, 233n28
Lamb, Charles: on Godwin, 69, 74; on sympathy, 25; on Coleridge's conversation, 228n106
Landor, Walter Savage: Epictetus and Seneca conversation, 8; *Imaginary Conversations*, 8; *nil admirari*, etc., 137
Lanser, Susan: account of Scott's desire, 233n34; female intimacy, 174
Laon and Cythna (Shelley), 18
The Last Man (Shelley), 48
Leask, Nigel, on imperialist self, 146
Lectures on Rhetoric and Belles Lettres (Smith), 44
Lectures on the History of Philosophy (Coleridge), 94, 98, 101, 119, 201
Lee, Wendy: Austen's affective chainmail, 164; insensibility and contempt, 148
Leighton, Robert, *Genuine Works*, 121
Letters on Education (Macaulay), 30, 55
Letter to the Women of England (Robinson), 161
Leviathan (Hobbes), 33, 70
Life of Johnson (Boswell), 140–41, 154

Lipsius, Justus: *De Constantia*, 99; Stoicism of, 29
Locke, Don, on Godwin's writings, 224n66
Locke, John, relation to Shaftesbury, 34
Lodore (Shelley), 22, 162, 164–65, 177–81, 183, 185; history of Fanny Derham, 179–83
Long, A. A., on critiques of Stoicism, 5; on emotions, 14
Lovejoy, Arthur, on Coleridge, 106
Lynch, Deidre, on character, 134, 148, 230n30
Lyrical Ballads (Wordsworth and Coleridge), 8, 62

Macaulay, Catherine, *Letters on Education*, 30, 55
McFarland, Thomas: on Coleridge's Stoicism, 92; on Wordsworth's Stoicism, 60
MacFarquhar, Larissa, 211
McGann, Jerome: Byron's staged sincerity, 132; social relations, 134; on style of *Don Juan*, 138
Manning, Peter, composite portrait of Byronic hero, 133
Manning, Susan: on character, 131–32; reality of personal identity, 155
Marriage of Heaven and Hell (Blake), 4
Marshall, David, 221n76; internalized discourse, 37; theatrical situation of moral philosophy, 45
Marvell, Andrew, translation of Seneca's *Thyestes*, 177–78
The Mask of Anarchy (Shelley), 133
Massumi, Brian, on affect, 13
Mays, J.C.C., 227n68; on "Dejection: An Ode," 120; notebook poetry, 112
Meditations (Aurelius), 32, 35, 84, 102, 114
The "Meditations" of the Emperor Marcus Aurelius Antoninus (Hutcheson and Moor), 101
Mee, Jon: on conversation, 118; human beings as sympathetic creatures, 24
Middlemarch (Eliot), 185
Mill, John Stuart: on nature, 201; on poetry, 108, 109
Millenium Hall (Scott), 22, 162, 164, 165–69, 172, 174–76, 178–82, 233n38
Miller, Perry, transcendentalism, 188
Mirror and the Lamp (Abrams), 108

Mitchell, John (Major General), 144
Montagu, Elizabeth, 168, 170, 171
Montagu, Lady Barbara, cohabitation of Scott and, 168–69, 233n34
Mooallem, Jon, Paradise fire, 1
Moore, James, *The "Meditations" of the Emperor Marcus Aurelius Antoninus*, 101
Moore, Thomas, 135
Moral Epistles (Seneca), 125, 157
The Moralists (Theocles), 34, 36, 43
More, Hannah, "Slavery," 155
Morning Post (newspaper), 120
Moses, Omri, modernism, 230n30
Murray, John, Byron and, 126, 152, 159
My Bondage and My Freedom (Douglass), 154

Napoleon, 59, 143
Napoleonic Wars, 117, 144, 160
National Assembly, 66
National Convention, 67
natural affection, perils of, 41–43
Nature (Emerson), 188–89, 191, 200, 202–3, 208
Nehamas, Alexander: *Art of Living*, 232n103; independence of philosophical ideas, 9
Nersessian, Anahid, Romanticism and limitation, 13, 167
New York Times Magazine, 1
Nietzsche, Friedrich: on *nil admirari*, 140; objection to Stoicism, 97
Nussbaum, Felicity, 166
Nussbaum, Martha, 195; model of cosmopolitanism, 192; Smith's Stoicism, 29, 49; Stoicism and women, 161

"Ode to Tranquillity" (Coleridge), 21, 119–23, 178
oikeiosis: doctrine of, 50, 52–53, 184, 193–94, 210; Hierocles and, 53, 193–94; Smith's, 222n93
Open Secrets (François), 12
Opus Maximum (Coleridge), 92, 103
Original Stories from Real Life (Wollstonecraft), 55
Outram, Dorinda, classical Stoicism in revolutionary France, 66, 223n36

Pagden, Anthony, on Stoicism and the Enlightenment, 25
Paley, Morton, on the mole in Coleridge's work, 101

Palumbo-Liu, David, on Smith, 49
Paradise, CA, fire, 1
Paradoxa Stoicorum (Cicero), 209, 236n64
Parallel Lives (Plutarch), 124, 190
Parrish, Stephen, on Coleridge, 120
Peacock, Thomas Love: "The Four Ages of Poetry," 19–20; Shelley to, 16
Pennington, Sarah, *An Unfortunate Mother's Advice to Her Absent Daughters*, 30, 172
Perpetual Peace (Kant), 214
Perpetual War (Robbins), 192
Perry, Seamus, on Coleridge, 228n103
Persuasion (Austen), 160, 162–64
Peterloo Massacre, 17
Pfau, Thomas: on affection in Shaftesbury, 41; lyric, 110; *Romantic Moods*, 11; on Smith and the Stoics, 50
The Phenomenology of Spirit (Hegel), 5, 61
Philosophic Pride (Brooke), 2
Pinch, Adela, epistemology of emotion, 15
Pitt, William, "Reign of Alarm," 5
Plato, 102, 178, 181, 183
Plutarch, 90, 208–9; favorite writer of Emerson, 195; *Parallel Lives*, 124, 190
Poetry as a Way of Life (Trop), 110
Poirier, Richard, self-erasure, 209
Political Justice (Godwin). See *Enquiry Concerning Political Justice* (Godwin)
Polwhele, Richard: *The Unsex'd Females*, 171; on Wollstonecraft and unsex'd females, 56
Poovey, Mary, on Shelley, 176, 184
Pope, Alexander, 135; controversy of, 138–39; *An Essay on Man*, 61, 135; *Imitations of Horace*, 136; poet of reason, 139; on Stoicism, 25–26
Potkay, Adam: on *The Excursion*, 80, 82; moral philosophy, 40; on Stoicism, 15, 28, 80
Pratt, Mary Louise, feminotopia, 166
The Prelude (Wordsworth), 6, 61, 63, 64, 70, 72, 79, 84
Price, Richard: citizens of the world, 222n109; in Wollstonecraft, 57
Prometheus Unbound (Shelley), 16–19, 181

Quarterly Review, 125
In Quest of the Ordinary (Cavell), 89

The Rambler (Johnson), 37
Ramsey, Neil, wartime Stoicism, 12
Rasselas (Johnson), 206
Recluse project, Wordsworth, 73–74
Reed, Mark, 78
Reflections on the Revolution in France (Burke), 66
religion, Stoicism and Christianity, 99–102
Republic (Zeno), 18, 161, 176, 195
revolutionary Stoicism, perils of, 65–69
Richardson, Alan, 226n24; on dreams, 105
Richardson, Robert: *Emerson*, 189, 236n50; on Emerson's grief, 207
Rieff, Philip, Stoicism and psychoanalysis, 5
Rise of the Novel (Watt), 217n6
Robbins, Bruce, *Perpetual War*, 192
Robespierre, Maximilien, 5; Cloots and, 159; execution of, 68; Stoicism of, 67, 131; sublime sect of the Stoics, 7, 66–67
Robinson, Henry Crabb: *Diary*, 59; on Wordsworth, 71
Robinson, Mary, *Letter to the Women of England*, 161
Robinson Crusoe (Defoe), 153
Robson, Catherine, on memorized poem, 111
Rohrbach, Emily, 165; on unpredictable futurity, 164
Romantic Antiquity (Sachs), 218n33, 230n56
Romanticism, 125, 218n59; American, 190; British, 24, 189–91, 190, 197, 199; Byron and, 158, 160; Enlightenment, 25; European, 16, 190; Furst on, 217n8; impact of Stoicism on, 3; Pope and, 138; revolution and, 2; Scott and, 162, 167; self-mastery, 219–20n8; Shelley and, 162, 165, 184; Stoic, 3, 10–16, 22, 189, 215; Stoicism and, 5, 7, 15–16, 190, 191, 211, 215, 217n14; Wollstonecraft and, 55, 58; Wordsworth and, 60–61
Romantic Moods (Pfau), 11
Rothschild, Emma, on Smith, 46
Rousseau, Jean-Jacques: Coleridge on, 226n39; *Confessions*, 124–25; *Discourse on the Origin and Foundations of Inequality among Men*, 148; *Emile*, 153; on slavery and primitivism, 232n101
Rufus, Musonius, women and Stoicism, 161

Sabertash, Orlando, on manners, 144–46
Sachs, Jonathan, 125; future temporality, 165; Pope controversy, 138; *Romantic Antiquity*, 218n33, 230n56
sage, ideal of, 8
Saint-Just, Antoine de, 66; Stoicism as alternative to terror, 5
Sandemanianism, 62
Sartor Resartus (Carlyle), 212
Scaevola, 124–25
Schneewind, J. B., 38
Scott, George Lewis, 168
Scott, Sarah, 19; cohabitation with Barbara Montagu, 233n34; *Millenium Hall*, 22, 162, 164, 165–69, 172, 174–76, 178–82, 233n38; Stoicism of, 164; Stoic reformers, 165–69
Scott, Walter, 143; "Childe Harold's Pilgrimage," 125, 130, 153; Stoicism and justice, 125–26
The Seasons (Thomson), 84
Sedgwick, Eve, on affect, 13, 15
Seneca, 62, 128; attainable virtues, 46; ideal of a sage, 8; Landor on, 8; *Moral Epistles*, 125, 157; philosophy of, 26; Roman practitioner, 7; Roman Stoicism, 61; on Stoicism, 9, 114; on tranquility, 120–21; translation of *Thyestes*, 177–78
Sha, Richard, on feeling, 13
Shaftesbury, Anthony Ashley: Askêmata, 38–41, 52, 116; *Characteristics of Men, Manners, Opinions, Times*, 32, 33–38, 41–42, 90, 220n33, 221nn54, 60; on passion, 25, 28; philosophy of, 20; Stoicism and sentiment, 31–33; Stoicism of, 29; on sympathy, 25, 28, 48
Shakespeare, *The Winter's Tale*, 59
Shelley, Mary: errand into the wilderness, 176–79; *The Last Man*, 48; *Lodore*, 22, 162, 164–65, 177–81, 183, 185; stepsister Claire Clairmont, 131; on Wordsworth, 60
Shelley, Percy: *Laon and Cythna*, 18; *The Mask of Anarchy*, 133; Mont Blanc like god of Stoics, 16; poetry and philosophy, 20; *Prometheus Unbound*, 16–19, 181; Smith on, 45; Stoic reading, 9
Sidney, Philip, table talk fashion, 94
Simonides, 77
Simpson, David, on Wordsworth's poetry, 33
Singer, Kate, on affect, 13
Singer, Peter, on Godwin's impartialism, 69
skepticism, 67, 79, 198; Coleridge and, 91–93, 95, 112, 117; epistemological, 45; Scott's *Millenium Hall*, 164; Stoic, 25, 32, 53, 118
slave ideology, 5, 61
Smith, Adam, 184; changing persons and characters, 129; on citizen of world, 50, 81, 194–95; cosmopolitan frame of reference, 202; on distancing, 85; earthquake drill, 49–54; gendered account of conscience, 29; immense system, 201; *Lectures on Rhetoric and Belles Lettres*, 44; moral priority, 194; on passion, 25, 28; philosophy of, 20; self-command, 148; Shaftesbury and, 60; Stoicism and world commerce, 44–49; on sympathy, 25, 28, 47, 48, 52–53; *Theory of Moral Sentiments*, 30, 37, 44, 46, 51, 55, 164, 206, 213, 233n38; virtues of humanity, 77
Smith, Charlotte, 230n43
Smith, James McCune, 154
Smith, Orianne, Mary Shelley and prophecy, 180
Socrates, 48, 96, 159
Sorabji, Richard, 214
Southey, Robert: Channing and, 199; Coleridge to, 140; *The Curse of Kehama*, 210; Republicanism and Stoicism, 92; on revolutionary Stoicism, 65
Spenser, Edmund, *Epithalamion*, 75
Spiegelman, Willard; on "Ode to Tranquility," 121; on Wordsworth's stoicism, 63
Spinoza, Baruch, 21, 92, 100, 103, 197
The Spirit of the Age (Hazlitt), 64
Spivak, Gayatri, 46
Stabler, Jane, on *Don Juan*, 152
The Statesman's Manual (Coleridge), 96, 120
Stauffer, Andrew, Romantic anger, 15
Steele, Richard, on Stoicism, 29
Stephen, Leslie, on Emerson, 186–87
Stock, Brian, soliloquy, 114
Stoicism, 2; as art of living, 232n103; Christianity and, 99, 100, 102, 106, 127, 170, 174, 197, 200; definition of, 3, 4; doctrine of oikeiosis, 50, 52–53, 184, 193–94, 210; domestic life, 171–76; Emerson's, 188–91, 197, 235n9; Epicureanism and, 224n72; evolution of,

2; French, 66–67; God and nature, 96–97; Godwinian, 63, 69, 79, 82; *Nature* and *Self-Reliance*, 200–205; perils of revolutionary, 65–69; possibility of, 2; resistance to, 4–7
Stoicism: Traditions and Transformations (Strange and Zupko), 9
Stoic Romanticism, 3; situating, 10–16
Stoics, citizens of the world, 50, 58, 81, 146, 154, 156, 159, 194–95, 222n109
Strange, Steven, *Stoicism: Traditions and Transformations*, 9
Strange Fits of Passion (Pinch), 230n43
Sun (newspaper), 67–68
Swift, Jonathan, *Gulliver's Travels*, 27–28
Swift, Simon, on Stoicism, 7
sympathy, 24–25; archaeology of, 15; as artificial commiseration, 52; Emerson on, 211–15; Epictetus on, 48; extreme, 52; Greiner on, 45, 53; Hume on, 35, 49; Lamb on, 25; Shaftesbury on, 25, 28, 48; Smith on, 25, 28, 47, 48, 52–53; soft power of, 52

Table Talk (Coleridge), 86
Talbot, Catherine, 30, 170
Tappan, David, 199
Tasso's *Gerusalemme Liberata*, 149
Taylor, Charles: the disengaged self, 202; modern selfhood, 83; on Stoicism, 10; on truth within us, 217n4
Theory of Moral Sentiments (Smith), 30, 37, 44, 46, 51, 55, 164, 206, 213, 233n38
Thomson, James, *The Seasons*, 84
Thoreau, Henry David, 205, 214
Thoughts upon Hunting (Beckford), 154–55
Thyestes (Seneca), translation of, 177–78
Tom Jones (Fielding), 135
Tomkins, Silvan, 117
Tour of Doctor Syntax (Combe), 124, 150
transcendentalism, 188
Treatise of Human Nature (Hume), 25, 89
Trilling, Lionel: on "Dejection: An Ode," 91; on Wordsworth, 61
Trop, Gabriel, 227n90; *Poetry as a Way of Life*, 110

Tropicopolitans (Aravamudan), 3, 231n74
Tusculan Disputations (Cicero), 16, 22, 76, 118, 139, 185

An Unfortunate Mother's Advice to Her Absent Daughters (Pennington), 30, 172
Unitarianism, Emerson's, 191, 197–99
unsex'd females, Polwhele on, 56, 171

Vargo, Lisa, on *Lodore*, 181
A Vindication of the Rights of Men (Wollstonecraft), 57
A Vindication of the Rights of Woman (Wollstonecraft), 55
Voelz, Johannes, 191
Voitle, Robert, on Shaftesbury, 32

Wallace, Jennifer: on Carter, 170; on classical reception, 10
Walls, Laura Dassow, cosmopolitanism, 192
Warren, Andrew, *The Orient and the Young Romantics*, 229n10
Wasserman, Earl, on Shelley, 17
Watt, Ian, *Rise of the Novel*, 217n6
Weinbrot, Howard, on Stoicism's reappearance, 3
Weiss, Deborah, on *Millenium Hall*, 233n38
Wenley, R. M., on Romanticism, 3
White, Daniel, 115, 223n19
Whitehall Evening Post (newspaper), 67
Wilberforce, William, 153
Williams, Bernard, 69
Wiltshire, John, on Austen, 163
Windham, William, abolition, 155
Wollstonecraft, Mary, 2, 161; critique of sensibility, 20; death of, 72, 83; emotions and, 55–58; figure in radicalization, 30; moral sentimentalism, 55–58; *Original Stories from Real Life*, 55; posthumous reputation, 162; revolution in female manners, 167; Stoic inquiry, 15; Stoic vision, 22, 25, 28; *A Vindication of the Rights of Men*, 57; *A Vindication of the Rights of Woman*, 55
Woloch, Alex, on minor characters, 128
Woolf, Virginia, 186

Wordsworth, Jonathan, 64
Wordsworth, William: apathy of, 61; commanding eminence of, 83–88; *The Convention of Cintra*, 85; *Essays upon Epitaphs*, 75, 77; *The Excursion*, 21, 59–60, 63, 65, 73–77, 79, 80–81, 83, 85, 87–88, 224n72; *Guide to the Lakes*, 70; indifference of, 20; "Ode to Duty," 103; *The Prelude*, 6, 61, 63, 64, 70, 72, 79, 84; *Recluse* project, 73–74; resolution, independence and indifference, 69–73; on Stoicism, 15, 223n17; Stoic management of feelings, 11–12
The Works of Epictetus (Carter), 214

Worthington, Jane, on Wordsworth, 61, 80
Wu, Duncan, on Wordsworth, 74, 223n17

Yeats, William Butler, Shelleyan devotion, 16
Yousef, Nancy: on Coleridge, 113; on Shaftesbury, 33
Yu, Christopher, on Horace's maxim, 135

Zeno of Citium, 95, 120, 155, 166, 175, 214–15; Arrian and, 182, 193; doctrines of, 22, 205; founder of Stoic sect, 7, 17, 54, 67; *Republic*, 18, 161, 176, 195
Zimmerman, Sarah, on capacity of lyric, 80
Zupko, Jack, *Stoicism, Traditions and Transformations*, 9

A NOTE ON THE TYPE

THIS BOOK has been composed in Miller, a Scotch Roman typeface designed by Matthew Carter and first released by Font Bureau in 1997. It resembles Monticello, the typeface developed for The Papers of Thomas Jefferson in the 1940s by C. H. Griffith and P. J. Conkwright and reinterpreted in digital form by Carter in 2003.

Pleasant Jefferson ("P. J.") Conkwright (1905–1986) was Typographer at Princeton University Press from 1939 to 1970. He was an acclaimed book designer and AIGA Medalist.

The ornament used throughout this book was designed by Pierre Simon Fournier (1712–1768) and was a favorite of Conkwright's, used in his design of the *Princeton University Library Chronicle*.

GPSR Authorized Representative: Easy Access System Europe - Mustamäe tee 50, 10621 Tallinn, Estonia, gpsr.requests@easproject.com

www.ingramcontent.com/pod-product-compliance
Lightning Source LLC
Chambersburg PA
CBHW021656230426
43668CB00008B/644